MULTICULTURAL EDUCATION SERIES

James A. Banks, *Series Editor*

(continued)

Culturally Responsive Teaching

Theory, Research, and Practice

THIRD EDITION

GENEVA GAY

TEACHERS COLLEGE PRESS

TEACHERS COLLEGE | COLUMBIA UNIVERSITY
NEW YORK AND LONDON

Published by Teachers College Press, 1234 Amsterdam Avenue, New York, NY
10027

Library of Congress Cataloging-in-Publication Data is available at loc.gov

ISBN 978-0-8077-5876-2 (paper)
ISBN 978-0-8077-7670-4 (ebook)

Printed on acid-free paper
Manufactured in the United States of America

In Memoriam
To Vida,

a shining star who illuminated what many others considered impenetrable darkness. Though you're no longer with us, the gifts you gave to the youth you taught, their children, and their children's children are continually cherished. The model you set for other teachers to follow remains undaunted.

Dedication
To students everywhere.

May you be likewise blessed as those who were fortunate to be taught by Vida. Like them, you deserve the very best of our teaching genius and ingenuity.

Contents

Series Foreword

A number of events that have occurred since the publication of the previous edition of this book have made the racial and ethnic climate in the United States and the world more ominous, increased the vulnerability of minoritized racial and ethnic groups, and endangered the attainment of educational equity for victimized groups. These events include the populist revolts that have arisen in response to immigration, terrorism, globalization, and its effects on jobs and markets, and the creation of "alternative facts" by conservative politicians such as Marine Le Pen in France and Donald Trump in the United States. The passage of the Brexit referendum in the United Kingdom to leave the European Union was also a manifestation of a populist revolt (Erlanger, 2017). These revolts, which manifest xenophobia and institutionalized racism, have stimulated the increase of nationalism and social cohesion in nations around the world (Castles, 2017; Osler, 2017). These trends and developments will make the implementation of culturally responsive teaching described in this visionary book challenging. However, this book is both needed and timely.

Explanations for disparities in the academic achievement of low-income, minority, and mainstream students have a long, complex, and contested history in the United States as well as in other nations (Banks, 2004, 2009, 2017). President Lyndon B. Johnson's War on Poverty, initiated by legislation introduced in 1964, focused attention on the nation's poor (Harrington, 1962), including vulnerable students in schools. In the 1960s, the genetic explanation or paradigm was an institutionalized explanation for the academic achievement of students from low-income and minoritized racial and ethnic groups. Progressive social scientists and educators constructed the cultural deprivation paradigm to provide an alternative to the genetic explanation that was embedded and largely uncontested in American institutions, including schools, colleges, and universities (Baratz & Baratz,1970).

The cultural deprivation explanation—which must be understood within its historical, cultural, and political context—was constructed by progressive social scientists such as Benjamin S. Bloom, Allison Davis, and Robert Hess (1965), who were on the faculty of the highly esteemed education department at the University of Chicago. The cultural deprivation explanation views the limited cultural capital in the home and communities of low-income and minority students as the major factor that explains their low academic achievement. It devotes little attention to other factors, such as the political economy of the larger society or the structure or organization of schools. Consequently, the cultural deprivation paradigm, as Ryan (1971) cogently argues, was widely viewed as "blaming the victims" for their dismal educational status and structural exclusion.

The cultural deficit paradigm still casts a long shadow on the American educational landscape (Payne, 2013), is internalized by many teachers, and results in low teacher expectations (Green, 2014) and uninspiring teaching in many inner-city classrooms populated heavily by African American and Latino students. A group of pioneering scholars constructed the cultural difference paradigm in the 1970s and 1980s to critique and provide an alternative to the cultural deficit paradigm. These scholars included Stephen S. Baratz and Joan C. Baratz (1970), Manuel Ramírez and Aflredo Castañeda (1974), Ronald Edmonds (1986), A. Wade Boykin (1986), and Barbara A. Sizemore (2008).

The cultural difference explanation provides a significant antidote to the cultural deficit paradigm and reveals the strengths and resilience of the families, communities, and cultures of students from diverse racial, ethnic, and linguistic groups (Gorski, 2018; Wang & Gordon, 1994). A second generation of cultural difference theorists—concerned about the disparities in academic achievement between mainstream students and students who are marginalized within the schools and the larger society—have done research and constructed theories that have generated teaching implications for the cultural difference theory. These scholars—who include Kathryn H. Au (1993), Gloria Ladson-Billings (1994), Lisa Delpit (1995), Jacqueline Jordan Irvine (2003), Luis Moll (Moll & González, 2004), and Sonia Nieto (2010)—have constructed a theory of culturally responsive teaching (also called culturally relevant pedagogy) that gives hope and guidance to educators who are trying to improve the academic achievement of students from diverse racial, ethnic, cultural, linguistic, and social-class groups. This theory postulates that the discontinuities between the school culture and the home and community cultures of low-income students and students of color are an important factor in their low academic achievement. Consequently, the academic achievement of these students will increase if schools and teachers reflect and draw on their cultural and language strengths.

Django Paris and H. Samy Alim (2017)—who represent a new generation of cultural difference scholars—respectfully build upon and extend the pioneering work of scholars such as Gloria Ladson-Billings (1994) and Geneva Gay. Paris and Alim maintain that culturally responsive pedagogy is necessary but not sufficient and should be extended. They argue that educators also need to *sustain* the cultural characteristics of students from diverse groups in addition to reflecting or responding to them. They call this concept "culturally sustaining pedagogy" (Paris, 2012).

As one of the progenitors of culturally responsive teaching, Geneva Gay's work is widely cited and influential in nations around the world. As this informative, engaging, incisive, and popular book exemplifies, she is also one of its most respected and eloquent voices.

The rich theoretical insights and pedagogical interventions described in this useful and erudite book will help practicing educators deal effectively with the growing ethnic, cultural, and linguistic diversity within the United States and its schools. Although students in the United States are becoming increasingly diverse, most of the nation's teachers are White, female, and monolingual. Race and institutionalized racism are significant factors that influence and mediate the interactions of students and teachers from different ethnic, cultural, language, and social class groups (G. R. Howard, 2016; T. C. Howard, 2010; Leonardo, 2013). The growing income gap between adults (Stiglitz, 2012)—as well as between youth, as described by Putnam (2015) in *Our Kids: The American Dream in Crisis*—is another significant reason why it is important to help teachers understand how race, ethnicity, gender, and class influence classroom interactions and student learning, and to comprehend the ways in which these variables affect student aspirations and academic engagement (Suárez-Orozco, Pimentel, & Martin, 2009).

American classrooms are experiencing the largest influx of immigrant students since the beginning of the 20th century. Approximately 21.5 million new immigrants—documented and undocumented—settled in the United States in the years from 2000 to 2015. Less than 10% came from nations in Europe. Most came from Mexico and nations in South Asia, East Asia, Latin America, the Caribbean, and Central America (Camarota, 2011, 2016). The influence of an increasingly diverse population on U.S. schools, colleges, and universities is and will continue to be enormous.

Schools in the United States are more diverse today than they have been since the early 1900s, when a multitude of immigrants entered the United States from Southern, Central, and Eastern Europe. In 2014, the National Center for Education Statistics estimated that students from ethnic minority groups made up more than 50% of the students in prekindergarten through 12th grade in public schools, an increase from 40% in 2001 (National Center for Education Statistics, 2014). Language and religious diversity are also increasing in the U.S. student population. The 2012 American Community Survey estimated that 21% of Americans aged 5 and above (61.9 million) spoke a language other than English at home (U.S. Census Bureau, 2012). Harvard professor Diana L. Eck (2001) calls the United States the "most religiously diverse nation on earth" (p. 4). Islam is now the fastest-growing religion in the United States, as well as in several European nations such as France, the United Kingdom, and the Netherlands (Banks, 2009; O'Brien, 2016).

The major purpose of the Multicultural Education Series is to provide preservice educators, practicing educators, graduate students, scholars, and policymakers with an interrelated and comprehensive set of books that summarizes and analyzes important research, theory, and practice related to the education of ethnic, racial, cultural, and linguistic groups in the United States and the education of mainstream students about diversity. The dimensions of multicultural education, developed by Banks (2004) and described in the *Handbook of Research on Multicultural Education* and in the *Encyclopedia of Diversity in Education* (Banks, 2012), provide the conceptual framework for the development of the publications in the series. The dimensions are content integration, the knowledge construction process, prejudice reduction, equity pedagogy, and an empowering institutional culture and social structure. The books in the Multicultural Education Series provide research, theoretical, and practical knowledge about the behaviors and learning characteristics of students of color (Conchas & Vigil, 2012; Lee, 2007), language minority students (Gándara & Hopkins, 2010; Valdés, 2001; Valdés, Capitelli, & Alvarez, 2011), low-income students (Cookson, 2013; Gorski, 2018), and other minoritized population groups, such as students who speak different varieties of English (Charity Hudley & Mallinson, 2011) and LGBTQ youth (Mayo, 2014).

Several books in the Multicultural Education Series complement this book because they describe ways to reform schools so they will become more responsive to the learning characteristics of students from diverse racial, ethnic, cultural, and social-class groups. They include *We Can't Teach What We Don't Know: White Teachers, Multiracial Schools* by Gary R. Howard (2016); *Why Race and Culture Matter in Schools: Closing the Achievement Gap in America's Classrooms* by Tyrone C. Howard (2010); *Is Everyone Really Equal? An Introduction to Key Concepts in Social Justice Education* by Özlem Sensoy and Robin DiAngelo (2017); *Transforming Educational Pathways for Chicana/o Students: A Critical Race Feminista Praxis* by Dolores Delgado Bernal and Erique Alemán Jr. (2017); and *Teaching for Equity in Complex Times: Negotiating Standards in a High-Performing Bilingual School* by Jamy Stillman and Lauren Anderson (2017).

Gay has enriched the Third Edition of this book with new and emergent knowledge, insights, and recommendations for practice. She describes a number of recent developments in culturally responsive teaching, including ways in which culturally responsive teaching is "going global conceptually, geographically, demographically, and epistemologically." Culturally responsive teaching is becoming global conceptually because it is being implemented across fields and disciplines, such as leadership, counseling, performance assessment, and personnel recruitment and retention. It is also being implemented in fields other than education and in nations around the world. An important new addition to this Third Edition is the "practice possibilities" that describe how culturally responsive teaching can be implemented. Gay describes these practice possibilities as "different, novel, innovative, and unconventional."

Readers of the Third Edition of this seminal and luminous book will gain a complex understanding of culture and teaching as well as knowledge of how to make schools more effective and joyous places for students from diverse groups. Geneva Gay brings a lifetime of scholarship, teaching, and reflection to this adept and incisive book. She has worked for nearly 4 decades with schools to improve educational equity. She has listened to the failures and victories of thousands of teachers in inservice settings, written a score of articles and book chapters about diversity and teaching, and mentored a cadre of doctoral students in multicultural education. Gay synthesizes the research on culturally responsive pedagogy, provides new insights and nuances on her work and the work of others, shares stories of successful teachers, and describes how teachers can make a difference in the lives of students. The first and second editions of this book were read by hundreds of practicing and future educators. I am confident that this Third Edition will be received as enthusiastically as the two previous editions and that its influence will be boundless.

—James A. Banks

REFERENCES

Au, K. (1993). *Literacy instruction in multicultural settings*. New York, NY: Harcourt Brace Jovanovich.

Banks, J. A. (2004). Multicultural education: Historical development, dimensions, and practice. In J. A. Banks & C. A. M. Banks (Eds.), *Handbook of research on multicultural education* (2nd ed., pp. 3–29). San Francisco, CA: Jossey-Bass.

Banks, J. A. (Ed.). (2009). *The Routledge international companion to multicultural education*. New York, NY and London, UK: Routledge.

Banks, J. A. (2012). Multicultural education: Dimensions of. In J. A. Banks (Ed.), *Encyclopedia of diversity in education* (Vol. 3, pp. 1538–1547). Thousand Oaks, CA: Sage.

Banks, J. A. (Ed.). (2017). *Citizenship education and global migration: Implications for theory, research, and teaching*. Washington, DC: American Educational Research Association.

Baratz, S. S., & Baratz, J. C. (1970). Early childhood intervention: The social science base of institutionalized racism. *Harvard Educational Review, 40*(1), 29–50.

Bloom, B. S., Davis, A., & Hess, R. (1965). *Compensatory education for cultural deprivation*. New York, NY: Holt.

Boykin, A. W. (1986). The triple quandary and the schooling of Afro-American children. In U. Neisser (Ed.), *The school achievement of minority children: New perspectives* (pp. 57–92). Hillside, NJ: Erlbaum.

Camarota, S. A. (2011, October). *A record-setting decade of immigration: 2000 to 2010*. Washington, DC: Center for Immigration Studies. Retrieved from cis.org/2000-2010-record-setting-decade-of-immigration

Camarota, S. A. (2016, June). *New data: Immigration surged in 2014 and 2015*. Washington, DC: Center for Immigration Studies. Retrieved from cis.org/New-Data Immigration-Surged-in-2014-and-2015

Castles, S. (2017). The challenge of international migration in the 21st century. In J. A. Banks (Ed.), *Citizenship education and global migration: Implications for theory, research, and teaching* (pp. 3–21). Washington, DC: American Educational Research Association.

Charity Hudley, A. H., & Mallinson, C. (2011). *Understanding language variation in U.S. schools.* New York, NY: Teachers College Press.

Conchas, G. Q., & Vigil, J. D. (2012). *Streetsmart schoolsmart: Urban poverty and the education of adolescent boys.* New York, NY: Teachers College Press.

Cookson, P. W. Jr. (2013). *Class rules: Exposing inequality in American high schools.* New York, NY: Teachers College Press.

Delgado Bernal, D., & Alemán, E., Jr. (2017). *Transforming educational pathways for Chicana/o students: A critical race feminist praxis.* New York, NY: Teachers College Press.

Delpit, L. (1995). *Other people's children: Cultural conflict in the classroom.* New York, NY: The New Press.

Eck, D. L. (2001). *A new religious America: How a "Christian country" has become the world's most religiously diverse nation.* New York, NY: HarperSanFrancisco.

Edmonds, R. (1986). Characteristics of effective schools. In U. Neisser (Ed.), *The school achievement of minority children: New perspectives* (pp. 93–104). Hillside, NJ: Erlbaum.

Erlanger, S. (2017, March 29). Pillars of the West shaken by "Brexit," but they are not crumbling yet. *The New York Times.* Retrieved from nytimes.com/2017/03/29/world/europe/uk-brexit-article-50-analysis.html

Gándara, P., & Hopkins, M. (Eds.). (2010). *Forbidden language: English language learners and restrictive language policies.* New York, NY: Teachers College Press.

Gorski, P. C. (2018). *Reaching and teaching students in poverty: Strategies for erasing the opportunity gap* (2nd ed.). New York, NY: Teachers College Press.

Green, R. L. (2014). *Expect the most—Provide the best: How high expectations, outstanding instruction, & curricular innovations help all students succeed.* New York, NY: Scholastic.

Harrington, M. (1962). *The other America: Poverty in the United States.* New York, NY: Macmillan.

Howard, G. R. (2016). *We can't teach what we don't know: White teachers, multiracial schools* (3rd ed.). New York, NY: Teachers College Press.

Howard, T. C. (2010). *Why race and culture matter in schools: Closing the achievement gap in America's classrooms.* New York, NY: Teachers College Press.

Irvine, J. J. (2003). *Educating teachers for diversity: Seeing with a cultural eye.* New York, NY: Teachers College Press.

Ladson-Billings, G. (1994). *The dreamkeepers: Successful teachers of African American children.* San Francisco, CA: Jossey-Bass.

Lee, C. D. (2007). *Culture, literacy, and learning: Taking bloom in the midst of the whirlwind.* New York, NY: Teachers College Press.

Leonardo, Z. (2013). *Race frameworks: A multidimensional theory of racism and education.* New York, NY: Teachers College Press.

Mayo, C. (2014). *LGBTQ youth and education: Policies and practices.* New York, NY: Teachers College Press.

Moll, L., & González, N. (2004). Engaging life: A funds-of-knowledge approach to multicultural education. In J. A. Banks & C. A. M. Banks (Eds.), *Handbook of research on multicultural education* (2nd ed., pp. 699–715). San Francisco, CA: Jossey-Bass.

National Center for Education Statistics. (2014). *The condition of education 2014.* Retrieved from nces.ed.gov/pubs2014/2014083.pdf

Nieto, S. (2010). *The light in their eyes: Creating multicultural learning communities* (10th anniversary ed.). New York, NY: Teachers College Press.

O'Brien, P. (2016). *The Muslim question in Europe: Political controversies and public philosophies.* Philadelphia, PA: Temple University Press.

Osler, A. (2017). Citizenship education, inclusion, and belonging in Europe: Rhetoric and reality in England and Norway. In J. A. Banks (Ed.), *Citizenship education and global migration: Implications for theory, research, and teaching* (pp. 133–160). Washington, DC: American Educational Research Association.

Paris, D. (2012). Culturally sustaining pedagogy: A needed change in stance, terminology, and practice. *Educational Researcher, 41*(3), 93–97.

Paris, D., & Alim, H. S. (Eds.). (2017). *Culturally sustaining pedagogies: Teaching and learning for social justice in a changing world.* New York, NY: Teachers College Press.

Payne, R. K. (2013). *A framework for understanding poverty* (5th rev. ed.). Highlands, TX: aha!.

Putnam, R. D. (2015). *Our kids: The American dream in crisis.* New York, NY: Simon & Schuster.

Ramírez, M., & Castañeda, A. (1974). *Cultural democracy, bicognitive development, and education.* New York, NY: Academic Press.

Ryan, W. (1971). *Blaming the victim.* New York, NY: Pantheon.

Sensoy, Ö., & DiAngelo, R. (2017). *Is everyone really equal? An introduction to key concepts in social justice education* (2nd ed.). New York, NY: Teachers College Press.

Sizemore, B. A. (2008). *Walking in circles: The Black struggle for school reform.* Chicago, IL: Third World Press.

Stiglitz, J. E. (2012). *The price of inequality: How today's divided society endangers our future.* New York, NY: Norton.

Stillman, J., & Anderson, L. (2017). *Teaching for equity in complex times: Negotiating standards in a high-performing bilingual school.* New York, NY: Teachers College Press.

Suárez-Orozco, C., Pimentel, A., & Martin, M. (2009). The significance of relationships: Academic engagement and achievement among newcomer immigrant youth. *Teachers College Record, 111*(3), 712–749.

U.S. Census Bureau. (2012). *Selected social characteristics in the United States: 2012 American Community Survey 1-year estimates.* Retrieved from factfinder2.census.gov/faces/tableservices/jsf/pages/productview.xhtml?pid=ACS_12_1YR_DP02&prodType=table

Valdés, G. (2001). *Learning and not learning English: Latino Students in American schools.* New York, NY: Teachers College Press.

Valdés, G., Capitelli, S., & Alvarez, L. (2011). *Latino children learning English: Steps in the journey.* New York, NY: Teachers College Press.

Wang, M. C., & Gordon, E. W. (Eds.). (1994). *Educational resilience in inner-city America: Challenges and prospects.* Hillside, NJ: Erlbaum.

Acknowledgments

I am deeply indebted to all of the professional colleagues, graduate students, personal friends, and family members who shared their observations, experiences, and memories about teaching and learning. These personal stories were incredibly enriching to the information gleaned from published accounts about the educational needs of underachieving, ethnically diverse students. They enliven, personalize, energize, and crystallize what otherwise might have been a purely academic and dispassionate analysis.

A special note of gratitude is due to my friend and colleague, James A. Banks, who extended the invitation and encouragement to write, and then provided expectations and assistance for me to write better. Even when it seemed most unlikely, I was, and continue to be, very appreciative of his scholarly mentoring.

Many thanks also to "Peppers," who helped most by listening to my expressed concerns and implied doubts about being capable of completing the task. You probably have no idea how much it meant to know that you were there, and how talking to you helped me to refocus, persevere, and reaffirm belief in my capabilities.

The school struggles of all my "fictive children" and their right to receive a better education are the motivation behind the ideas, explanations, and recommendations presented herein. I take their academic situations as my personal cause and professional responsibility, and act accordingly.

A heartfelt thanks is extended to my racially, ethnically, socially, linguistically, and immigrant diverse "academic children" for being so generous and gracious in teaching me your cultural diversity because I was willing to learn.

Preface to the First Edition

"Culturally responsive teaching and learning are necessary and worthy pursuits."

Significant changes are needed in how African, Asian, Latino, and Native American students are taught in U.S. schools. Two characteristics of their current achievement patterns highlight this imperative. One is the *consistency of performance patterns* among ethnic groups across different indicators and measures of school achievement. The other is the *variability of achievement* of subsets of individuals within ethnic groups. These characteristics suggest the need for systematic, holistic, comprehensive, and particularistic reform interventions, simultaneously.

Systemic reforms must be undertaken that deal with multiple aspects of achievement (academic, social, psychological, emotional, etc.) within different subject areas (math, science, reading, writing, social studies) across school levels (prekindergarten; elementary, middle, and high schools; college) and through different aspects of the educational enterprise (curriculum, instruction, administration, assessment, financing, etc.). These reforms also need to be diversified according to the social variance of students, attending deliberately and conscientiously to such factors as ethnicity, culture, gender, social class, historical experiences, and linguistic capabilities. Dealing adequately with all these influences on student achievement and their implications for reform is far beyond the capabilities of a single book. Some choice is needed to ensure quality of analysis. The choice for this book is the use of their cultural orientations to teach ethnically diverse students who are not performing well, especially in reading, writing, math, and science.

Merely belaboring the disproportionately poor academic performance of certain students of color, or blaming their families and social class backgrounds, is not very helpful in implementing reforms to reverse achievement trends. Just as in health care, where treating symptoms does not cure diseases, simply pointing out achievement problems does not lead to their resolution. If this were the case, there would be no need for a book like this. The underachievement of some ethnic groups has been spotlighted again and again over several generations, and the situation has not gotten any better. It may even have worsened in recent years. It is also true that some of the disparity in academic achievement across ethnic groups is attributable to racism and cultural hegemony in the educational enterprise. But to declare this is not enough to direct a functional and effective change agenda. More constructive reform strategies must be employed. Culturally responsive pedagogy as characterized in this book meets these needs.

OVERVIEW OF CHAPTERS

Each chapter in this book opens with a premise or principle that conveys one of its major messages. These epigraphs are developed in detail in the subsequent narrative text. In Chapter 1, "Challenges and Perspectives," a particular perspective on the challenges of more effectively teaching underachieving students of color is presented. It sets the tone and establishes the conceptual parameters for the remaining chapters. A storytelling motif is used to frame the critical issues underlying the need to incorporate the cultural orientations and experiences of students from different ethnic and racial backgrounds into teaching strategies. The achievement patterns among ethnic groups in the United States are too persistent to be attributed only to individual limitations. The fault lies as well within the institutional structures, procedures, assumptions, and operational styles of schools, classrooms, and the society at large.

A conceptual proposal for correcting these achievement problems is presented in Chapter 2, "Pedagogical Potential of Cultural Responsiveness." The theoretical parameters of this proposal—achieving power pedagogy through culturally responsive teaching—are constructed from ideas suggested by different scholars, researchers, and practitioners about teaching modes that work best with ethnically diverse students. This characterization of culturally responsive teaching includes explanations of its salient components as well as its potential power for reversing the achievement trends of students of color. Its key anchors are the simultaneous cultivation of the academic success and cultural identity of ethnically diverse students. These general features serve as benchmarks for organizing and assessing the quality of specific teaching ideas, programs, and actions discussed later in other chapters. Consequently, Chapter 2 acts as a *conceptual bridge* between the need for and the doing of culturally responsive teaching, between theory and practice, between achievement problems and solutions.

Chapters 3 through 6 develop in greater detail four critical aspects of culturally responsive teaching introduced in Chapter 2. These are caring, communication, curriculum, and instruction. No priority ranking is intended, nor should any be attached, to the order in which these chapters are presented. Just because a teaching disposition of caring is discussed first does not mean that it is more important than the other aspects of culturally responsive teaching. The sequence in which these components and the related chapters appear is merely a reflection of one "logical patterning" for thinking about and classifying these issues. Other organizing schemas are possible. Nor should the boundaries drawn for the various components of culturally responsive teaching be perceived as mutually exclusive. The divisions are artificial and arbitrary, and they are used to focus attention, facilitate discussion, and make the presentation of information more manageable. In reality, the components of culturally responsive teaching are dynamic, dialectical, and interwoven.

Interactions between students and teachers as well as among students in the classroom frequently are identified as the "actual sites" where learning success or failure is determined. They are prominent among the major attributes of culturally responsive teaching. Conventional wisdom and research studies suggest that teachers play a pivotal role in these interactions. In fact, the tone, structure, and quality of instruction are determined largely by teachers' attitudes and expectations as well as their pedagogical skills. Therefore, some careful attention to how teachers relate to students is central to realizing the purposes of this book. What these relational patterns are and how they affect the achievement of students from various ethnic groups are presented in Chapter 3, "The Power of Culturally Responsive Caring." Since issues other than intellectual ability have profound effects on assumptions about what students can or cannot achieve, explorations of teachers' expectations are not limited to the academic. Personal, social, and ethical dimensions are included as well.

Effective communication is simultaneously a goal, a method, and the essence of quality classroom instruction. Yet communicating with ethnically diverse students is often problematic for many teachers. Numerous misconceptions and confusions surround interactions among communication, culture, and education. A graphic example of these is the recurring controversy over the place of Ebonics (a style of communication used by many African Americans that sometimes is referred to as Black, African American, or nonstandard English) in the educational process. It, more than any other communication issue related to students of color, symbolizes the complexity, challenge, and academic potential of incorporating elements of different cultural communication styles into classroom instruction. Chapter 4, "Culture and Communication in the Classroom," explains the close interaction among culture, communication, teaching, and learning. It builds on Saville-Troike's (1989) conviction that "there is a correlation between the form and content of a language and the beliefs, values, and needs present in the culture of its speakers" (p. 32). Since how one thinks, writes, and speaks reflects culture and affects performance, aligning instruction to the cultural communication styles of different ethnic groups can improve school achievement. To this end, features of communication styles, how they are manifested in instructional situations, and programs and practices that actually demonstrate the positive effects of using cultural communication as a tool for effective teaching are discussed in Chapter 4. These analyses concentrate on discourse features of non-Academic-English languages and dialects instead of their linguistic structures. An explanation, supported with research evidence, is provided for this choice.

Chapter 5 is devoted to culturally diverse curriculum content. It develops the idea that effective teaching and learning for culturally and ethnically different students make high-quality, high-status knowledge accessible to them. A major part of this accessibility is recognizing the worth of the information ethnic groups have contributed to the fund of knowledge students should learn and making it available to them. The current status of cultural diversity in curriculum designs and instructional materials is explored, along with research about practices that produce positive outcomes for students of color. Formal (e.g., textbooks and standards) and informal (e.g., literary and trade books, mass media) curricular content and materials are examined. The analyses are limited to teaching reading, writing, math, and science. These subjects are selected because of their function as "academic cores" in the educational process, the high status typically attached to them, and the prominent role they play in the determination of student achievement. Squire's (1995) explanation about the importance of "literacy skills" to all educational quality supports this choice. He says, "Reading, writing, and language are the bedrock subjects of the curriculum, for they develop the competencies on which virtually all subsequent instruction and learning depend" (p. 71). The analyses of curricular programs and research presented in Chapter 5 are complemented with suggestions for how to further improve the quality of multicultural curriculum content and its effects on student achievement.

Chapter 6 continues to develop the proposition that deliberately incorporating *specific* aspects of the cultural systems of different ethnic groups into instructional processes has positive impacts on student achievement. It emerges from arguments presented by some educational analysts that interferences to the achievement of ethnically diverse students are often more procedural than substantive. Compelling research demonstrates that school achievement improves when protocols and procedures of teaching are synchronized with the mental schemata, participation styles, work habits, thinking styles, and experiential frames of reference of diverse ethnic groups.

The discussions in Chapter 6, "Cultural Congruity in Teaching and Learning," go beyond the frequent tendency to merely catalogue descriptive traits of bipolar learning styles. They probe the interior of these descriptors to determine their qualitative attributes and implications for instruction. The argument is made that a learning style is actually a *construct* that has multiple elements embedded within it, such as motivational, environmental, relational, and sensory stimulation preferences. All of these may impact the learning process differently. Knowing what these are is necessary to making teaching culturally responsive. Thus, the key message of Chapter 6 is that modifying teaching and learning processes at the level of their component parts generates greater academic success than "generalized global pedagogical reforms."

Four major features are common to the discussions across chapters. First, a combination of information from theory, research, scholarship, and practice is brought to bear on the issues examined. Thus, *simultaneous and integrated multiperspective* analyses are emphasized. They include examples from the past and present, and prospects for the future. This is done to demonstrate the continuity and change, the precedents and innovations, and previous solutions and continuing challenges in using their cultural heritages and funds of knowledge to teach students of color more effectively. While much, if not most, educational scholarship includes these aspects, the usual convention is to explore theory, research, and practice separately from one another. The juxtaposition of them in this book seems more reasonable and useful for filling existing conceptual voids and expanding effective instruction for improving the achievement of ethnically diverse students.

Second, *multiethnic* examples and points of reference are woven throughout the discussion of topics, issues, themes, and strategies. Concerted efforts are made to achieve some ethnic balance in these, but the results are not always ideal, or even desirable. The units of analysis in research, theory, and practice often are skewed more toward some ethnic groups than others. For example, more data are available on the need for and experience with culturally responsive teaching as it relates to African Americans than to other groups of color. Consequently, African Americans appear more often as referents or case examples of practices and proposals throughout the book. This disproportionality is countered somewhat by targeting other ethnic groups in suggestions for extending, refining, and enriching current culturally responsive instructional practices.

Third, whenever possible, other factors, such as gender, age, and social class, that influence the validity of research, theory, and practice and their effect on teaching ethnically diverse students are openly discussed. As with ethnicity, many imbalances exist among these variables. For instance, much of the research available about the effects of gender on communication, interactional styles, and classroom performance deals with middle-class, European American females. Most of the information on teaching students of color is derived from studies of individuals from low socioeconomic and urban backgrounds. Asian Americans are underrepresented in all aspects of research, theory, and practice about culturally responsive teaching.

Fourth, individual scenarios and personal stories are interspersed throughout the presentation of theoretical ideas and research findings. These are included in order to recognize autobiography and narrative as legitimate sources of knowledge and research, and of teaching techniques; to create a more comprehensive portrait of and compelling case for the power and potential of culturally responsive teaching; and to demonstrate how it is made manifest in actual behaviors.

"A Personal Case of Culturally Responsive Teaching Praxis" is presented in Chapter 7. It emerges from the premise that the most powerful evidence of teaching effectiveness is the personal story. Operating on this premise, I provide some brief descriptions of my own beliefs about and styles of teaching. These are presented not as prototypes that everyone should emulate, but as a living example of how one individual exemplifies some of the principles and practices of culturally responsive pedagogy. They also show how this approach to teaching can be used with college and university students enrolled in teacher education programs. Together these beliefs and behaviors constitute parts of my own "Culturally Responsive Pedagogical Creed." They challenge and invite other educators to develop their own ideological creeds about cultural diversity in teaching and learning to guide their instructional behaviors.

Stories often end with epilogues. They provide glimpses into future developments of the characters that occur after the culmination of the present situation. An epilogue signifies an ending, but without the total cessation of all action related to the story. Thus, it is simultaneously a closure and a continuation. Such is the case with the epilogue to the story of culturally responsive teaching constructed here. This function is served by Chapter 8. Its content looks backward to earlier analyses and forward to other possibilities for teaching ethnically diverse students. The information presented is both reflective and projective. It summarizes major messages and principles for future practice in culturally responsive teaching extrapolated from discussions presented in the previous chapters. This is why it is entitled "Looking Back and Projecting Forward." *Culturally Responsive Teaching* ends as it begins, continuing the search (1) to make education more successful for students like Aaron and Amy throughout the United States and (2) to stop the vicious cycle of academic failure so that Amy's and Aaron's children will have a very different story to tell about their school experiences.

READING THE TEXT

Improving the school achievement of students of color who currently are not performing well requires comprehensive knowledge, unshakable convictions, and high-level pedagogical skills. The information presented in the chapters of this book is intended to facilitate the development of these and to resist the temptations of some educators to provide superficial analyses, simplistic interpretations, and quick-fix responses to these complex issues.

This book incorporates research, theory, and practice about culturally contextualized or mediated teaching for marginalized African, Asian, Latino, and Native American students. It is based largely on national data sources and local projects that have gained national recognition. Herein lies a major but unavoidable limitation: Local programs and practices that have not gained national visibility are not included. Many of these probably exist and are worthy of inclusion. No doubt their presence would have further enriched the analyses and recommendations made, but they were not accessible to me.

Culturally Responsive Teaching is about *teaching*, and the teaching of concern is that which *centers* classroom instruction in *multiethnic cultural frames of reference.* Consequently, pedagogical paradigms and techniques that may be effective but are not culturally situated for marginalized, underachieving ethnic groups—such as Latinos, Native Americans, and African Americans—are not included in the discussions. Other dimensions of the educational enterprise that affect student achievement, such as funding, institutional-based school reform, the recruitment and assignment of teachers, and administrative leadership, also are not discussed. Their importance in the scheme of total educational improvement is unquestionable. They simply do not fit within the conceptual parameters of this project. Making all aspects of schooling culturally diverse at the same time would be ideal. But this project was not geared to such a massive task.

Furthermore, schools cannot solve society's problems. This is accepted as a given and is not discussed here. In fact, schools could accomplish much more rapid reforms if society changed first. For instance, if society really stopped being racist, it would insist (and enforce the expectation) that all its institutions, including schools, do likewise. Then the problems of concern to, and even the need for, books like this one would cease. The education of too many students of color is too imperiled for us to wait for these grand hopes to happen. We must act now, and incremental changes are better than none at all. *Culturally Responsive Teaching* recognizes the power of teaching while fully realizing that without accompanying changes in all other aspects of schooling and society, the very best of teaching will not be able to accomplish the systemic reforms needed for ethnically diverse students to receive genuine educational equity and achieve excellence.

The story of culturally responsive teaching that unfolds in the chapters of this book, like any other story, has setting, plot, characters, and action. The separate chapters serve all these functions for their specific topics of analysis, while contributing significantly to the construction of the more comprehensive "character profile and narrative development" of culturally responsive teaching. These characterizations reflect the beliefs that (1) test scores, grade point averages, course enrollments, and other indicators of the school achievement of many students of color are the *symptoms, not causes,* of the problems; (2) academic achievement is not the only significant indicator of school success and/or failure; and (3) while school failure is an *experience* of too many ethnically diverse students, it is not the *identity* of any. These ideas represent both an invitation and a mandate to teachers.

The discussions presented in this book are designed to help equip more teachers to meet these expectations and to accomplish higher levels of success for underachieving students of color.

A CREDO FOR PEDAGOGICAL ACTION

Several years ago Marva Collins (1992), the founder of the Westside Preparatory School in Chicago, created a metaphorical image of educational excellence that captures its spirit and meaning as intended in this book. Using poetic form, Collins gives excellence a personal voice and allows it to speak for itself. Part of this characterization is quoted here because of its inspirational and invigorating quality. Speaking in the first person, "Excellence" says:

> I bear the flame that enlightens the world. I fire the imagination. I give might to dreams and wings to the aspirations of men.
>
> I create all that is good, stalwart, and long-lasting. I build for the future by making my every effort superior today . . .
>
> I am the parent of progress, the creator of creativity, the designer of opportunity, and molder of human destiny . . .
>
> I wear the wisdom and contributions of all ages. I dispel yesterday's myths and find today's facts. I am ageless and timeless . . .
>
> I banish mediocrity and discourage being average . . .
>
> I stir ambition, forge ideals, and create keys that open the door to worlds never dreamed . . .
>
> I am the source of creation, the outlet of inspiration, the dream of aspiration.
> (pp. 218–219)

This credo should inspire all teachers committed to improving the school performance of underachieving students of color. It can serve as the anchor and torchlight for their pedagogical practices. The values, expectations, commitments, and actions it conveys are certainly congruent with the intentions of *Culturally Responsive Teaching*.

Preface to the Third Edition

The book continues to use insights gleaned from research, theory, and practice to make a strong case for why culture and diversity should be central conceptual and methodological themes in educating students in U.S. schools, especially those who are marginalized in mainstream society and victimized by low educational achievement. It also includes some of the important changes that have occurred over the last decade, which have had profound effects on how culture and diversity should be understood and operationalized in instructional practices. As in the first and second editions, these issues are analyzed primarily within teaching contexts, but with a full realization that complete educational reform is needed and demands more than changes in classroom teaching to make the kind of improvements required to ensure total equity and excellence for underachieving students of color.

The issues and concerns that prompted the initial conception of this book still prevail. Admittedly, some changes have occurred since the first and second editions were released, but, unfortunately, these were neither fundamental nor profound. Students of color from ethnic, racial, cultural, and socioeconomic backgrounds different from the dominant Eurocentric, middle-class group still are not receiving proportional, equitable, high-quality educational opportunities and performance outcomes. U.S. society continues to be plagued by resource inequities and human indignities toward diverse populations and communities. Racism, homophobia, classism, and other forms of inequity and oppression are still rampant (in recalcitrant persistence, apparent frequency, and diversified domains and forms). Attending to ethnic, racial, and cultural differences in schools and society too often involves little more than some cosmetic tinkering, rather than any substantive and significant changes. The traditional status quo and historical centers of power and privilege have not been significantly transformed. Consequently, the prior established organizational structures and content emphases of *Culturally Responsive Teaching: Theory, Research, and Practice* are still relevant, and remain largely intact in this Third Edition.

Although some "growth" in the field of educating to and through cultural, ethnic, racial, and social diversity has occurred since the second edition of this book was released in 2010, these are more ideological and theoretical than pragmatic. They are addressed in this edition, but they are more extensions of previously established patterns and trends in multiculturally based teaching and learning than they are profound shifts or radical changes. Therefore, the overall structure of the book remains the same, with updates and extensions inserted throughout where appropriate. Four of these "growth trends" and related "extensions" are particularly apropos.

First, the idea of, need for, and practice possibilities of culturally responsiveness are "going global," conceptually, geographically, demographically, and epistemologically. Conceptually, cultural responsiveness is no longer limited to pedagogy in a literal sense. Instead, virtually all aspects of the educational enterprise are being targeted, including leadership, counseling, classroom management, performance assessment, policy, research, and personnel recruitment and retention. These boundary extensions are laudable, but all of them cannot be adequately addressed in a single volume. Consequently, the focus of this edition continues to be on teaching. Another "globalization" feature of cultural responsiveness is its crossing of professional boundaries; it is no longer limited to education. Rather, many other professional domains have joined the cause, recognizing that being culturally responsive in designing and delivering products and services to their respective clientele improve their effectiveness (and in some cases, their profit margins). These include medical and health care, social work, religion, psychological services, politics, the arts, and business. For example, in a statement released in 2015, Fairview Capital, the largest minority- and women-owned private equity management firm in the United States, noted that there are proven advantages of a diverse workforce, including higher financial returns, better talent development, better decisionmaking and innovation, and greater employee satisfaction. Moreover, diversity at the leadership level of business

> breaks down insular biases, making the organization more likely to act inclusively, foster a communicative culture, and create an environment where workers are free to voice unorthodox views and suggest creative solutions. (Fairview Capital, 2015)

The literal globalization of cultural responsiveness is evident in the fact that countries throughout the world are recognizing the merits of including ethnic and cultural diversity in their educational systems (Banks, 2009; Moll & Combs, 2015; Sutton, 2005). Some of these countries may seem unlikely on the surface, but these impressions are probably due more to faulty assumptions of reality than to truth. For example, China, long considered to be a culturally and ethnically homogeneous country, is now recognizing and promoting its ethnic and cultural diversity. In effect, some countries in every region of the world (Africa, the Americas, Asia, Europe, the Middle East, the South Pacific) are engaged, to some degree, with culturally responsiveness, whether from domestic or international perspectives, or both. Obvious motiving forces for these engagements are the increasing interdependence and interactions of countries worldwide and the multidirectional mobility of populations. These growth trends also add some new challenges and opportunities for how culturally responsive education is understood and implemented nationally

A second trend that reinforces the need for the continuous endorsement (along with some modifications) of culturally responsive teaching involves educational demographics and achievement patterns. School achievement gaps based on economic, racial, cultural, and ethnic diversity are too persistent and extensive to merit elaboration here. Suffice it to say that the gaps require continuing the search for solutions, some of which may be found in culturally responsive teaching. The logic of it, along with research evidence (both of which are presented in this volume), support this claim. A crucial aspect of this discouraging reality, one that is often missing in educational discourse, is the fact that achievement disparities may increase as the percentage of students of color in U.S. schools grows. Even if the performance ratios by ethnic groups remain steady, the magnitude of the negative consequences will be devastating. More and more students in U.S. schools are recent arrivals to the country, or are children of immigrants. Trying to learn across cultural divides often leads to academic failure and perpetual cultural and social marginalization. In order to change the course of achievement events and prevent further crises, some radical changes are needed in how teaching and learning are conducted. Culturally responsive teaching continues to be a possibility worthy of pursuit.

These student demographics add another noteworthy dimension to the "globalization" of culturally responsive teaching. High percentages of ethnically and racially diverse students have diasporic connections to places, people, and experiences that are more genuinely worldwide than previous generations. They also may be less likely to forsake their ancestral heritages and identities in order to accommodate and assimilate totally into mainstream U.S. culture and language. Instead, they may be more inclined to be bi- and multicultural and -linguistic, or to cultivate cultural and linguistic hybridity. These life choices will affect learning in schools, cultural competence, citizenship practices, and other areas of achievement that fall within the purview of culturally responsive teaching, and thus demand some reconceptualizations. Some of these challenges are raised in this Third Edition.

A third "need for" culturally responsive teaching that persists as of the writing of this volume has to do with the inherent nature of the educational process and the rights of diverse students. Both teaching and learning are naturally cultural, and difference is inherent to the human condition. Given that U.S. schools are increasingly ethnically, racially, and economically diverse, culturally responsive teaching is mandatory, or, as some analysts declare, it is "good teaching" in the service of the humanity and rights of diverse students. In other words, since education is intended to serve and reflect the students for whom it is constructed, then it, like U.S. schools and society, should be ethnically, racially, and culturally diverse. This diversity is a fundamental feature of the culturally responsive teaching advocated in this volume.

The priority given to improving the academic achievement of ethnically, racially, culturally, and socially diverse students (e.g., students of color) in earlier editions of this book is reaffirmed in this one. However, not exclusively so, because academic performance does not operate in isolation. Rather, it is connected to other aspects of functionality, such as personal attributes, cultural orientations, political conditions, social class, economic background, and psycho-emotional dispositions. Furthermore, while improved academic performance is imperative, school achievement must be even more inclusive. It also includes cultural competence of self and others, the combating of racism and other forms of oppression, moral and ethical development, and sociopolitical transformation. All of these are part of the characterization of culturally responsive teaching presented in this volume.

A fourth emerging development in the field of culturally responsive teaching that has enriching potential is the *disaggregation of conceptualization through intra- and inter-minority group scholarly engagements*. This takes two primary forms. One is that claims and recommendations made about educating composite categories of ethnic and minority groups (e.g., Asian Americans, African Americans, Latino Americans, Native Americans and Native Alaskans) are increasingly being targeted to the specific groups (i.e., *intra-minority*) that fall within these categories. Thus, increasing attention is given to the Japanese, Korean, Chinese, Vietnamese, and/or Hmong instead of the more general "Asian Americans." These "specific minorities" are telling their own stories, from their own vantage points and in their own ways, and insisting that "outsider others" who write about, research, and teach their children and communities do so in culturally respectful and responsive ways with respect to their particular group. An emerging *inter-group* development involves theorists and researchers of one minority group studying another ethnic minority group (for example, Chinese Americans researching and advocating educational equity for Mexican Americans; a scholar of Greek immigrant heritage conducting research with Somali refugee teenage girls to determine culturally appropriate educational interventions for them). These *inter-minority and intra-minority group studies* should generate more accuracy, authenticity, and nuanced portrayals of ethnic, racial, social, and cultural diversity, which, in turn, should lead to more effective teaching and learning for diverse students of color. Some results of these efforts appear throughout this book

A new feature of this edition is an attempt to explicitly respond to recurrent concerns expressed by many educators about how to actually *do* culturally responsive teaching. Some "practice possibilities" are offered, but they are not the customary kind of suggested teaching strategies frequently seen in books for professional educators. Consistent with thinking that genuine equitable and effective educational opportunities for ethnically, racially, and culturally diverse students need to be different from prevailing pedagogical practices, these suggestions are indeed different, novel, innovative, and unconventional. Aligning with the overall focus of the book on theory, research, and practice related to cultural responsiveness, these action possibilities follow suit. They also are influenced by the need for instructional resources and techniques to be relevant to the students for whom they are intended. Consequently, preference is given to social capital and popular culture content and resources gleaned primarily from the Internet and websites. Both of these are of utmost importance in the lives of this generation of learners and should have high value and utility as shared points of reference between students and their teachers. Another assumption is that more conventional content information and instructional suggestions can be derived from the substantive details presented within the chapters, so the end-of-chapter practice possibilities are complements and extensions of these, rather than replications.

These action ideas are more categorical than specific for two reasons. First, culturally responsive teachers need to be continually learning as they are teaching. Second, cultural responsiveness makes a strong case for contextual appropriateness in determining actual teaching and learning experiences. It is impossible to imagine or respond to all of the conceivable contextual factors affecting the instructional efforts of the wide readership of this book. A more reasonable option is to suggest some general action strategies and related resources for acquiring additional assistance in actualizing culturally responsive teaching.

Practice possibilities are suggested for six of the eight chapters presented. In Chapter 1, which deals with beliefs and ideological foundations, the practice possibilities include sample belief statements made by other individuals, and the names and policies of some professional organizations that advocate for equity, diversity, and social justice in education. Hopefully, from these classrooms teachers will find affinity, affirmation, allegiance, and clarity for their own beliefs and ideologies. Chapters 3, 4, 5, and 6 deal with dimensions of culturally responsive teaching (caring, communication, curriculum, and instruction) that are most susceptible to dilemmas about how to convert ideas to actions. Each one also ends with a set of "practice possibilities" to help teachers make these conversions, or stimulate their own imagination and creativity. Chapter 2 presents some "personality attributes" of culturally responsive teaching extrapolated from its ideological foundations and general purposes. The practice possibilities included are samples of policy statements. There are no practice ideas for Chapters 7 and 8. In Chapter 7 I profile some of my own efforts in culturally responsive teaching. As such, is it a composite case example of practice possibilities. Chapter 8 exemplifies a culturally responsive teaching (and teaching in general) strategy that is commonly endorsed by researchers, theorists, and practitioners. This is critical reflection about experiences to discern lessons learned, and messages and strategies for future pursuit. The focus of the reflections in Chapter 8 is the characterizations of culturally responsive teaching presented in the preceding chapters.

This book is illustrative, not exhaustive. It is also incomplete. The profiles of some key components of culturally responsive teaching presented are my own constructions and undoubtedly they reflect who I am and my perspectives, even though many different individuals and groups contribute to their substance. These presentations are incomplete because I do not speak for or to all conceivable perspectives, advocates, and issues that anchor culturally responsive education, and the field is still evolving. In crafting the profiles presented I have been deliberate about trying to exemplify the salient values, beliefs, and attributes of culturally responsiveness in education. For example, I have been *multiethnic* in references and citations; I have included *multiple perspectives* through examples and explanations; I have been *multisensory* by providing opportunities for readers to develop their knowledge, thinking, beliefs, actions, and reflections about culturally responsive premises and practices; and I have provided *general principles and parameters* for culturally responsive teaching without dictating specific actions transcendent across all educational settings and circumstances. Some readers may think I have done too much, while others may feel I have not done enough. For both reactors I encourage them to use this book as a resource for their own pedagogical empowerment. For the former, choose what affirms your current actions (or level of efficacy) in equity and social justice education for ethnically, racially, and culturally diverse students and communities, and identify directions for your further development. For readers who feel I have not done enough, I invite you to become an ally and complement this book's contributions by adding your own perspectives, experiences, analyses, explanations, and insights. There certainly is still much need and room for continuous growth and development in the field of culturally responsive education.

CHAPTER 1

Challenges and Perspectives

"You can't teach what and who you don't know."

Too many students of color have not been achieving in school as well as they should (and can) for far too long. The consequences of these disproportionally high levels of low achievement are long-term and wide-reaching, personal and civic, individual and collective. They are too devastating to be tolerable. We must insist that this disempowerment stop now and set into motion change strategies to ensure that it does. To realize this transformation, classroom teachers and other educators need to understand that achievement, or lack thereof, is an experience or an accomplishment. It is not the totality of a student's personal identity or the essence of his or her human worth. Virtually every student can do something well. Even if students' capabilities are not directly translatable to classroom learning, they still can be used by teachers as points of reference and motivational devices to evoke student interest and involvement in academic affairs. Teachers must learn to how to recognize, honor, and incorporate the personal abilities of students into their teaching strategies. If this is done, then school achievement will improve. A. Wade Boykin (2002) calls these emphases developing the talent potential of underachieving students of color, and placing them at promise, instead of at risk.

INTRODUCTION

This book offers some suggestions for reversing the underachievement of students of color. They are embodied in the proposal for implementing *culturally responsive teaching*. Research, theory, and practice attest to their potential effectiveness. However, culturally responsive teaching alone cannot solve all the problems of improving the education of marginalized students of color. Other aspects of the educational enterprise (such as funding, administration, and policymaking) also must be reformed, and major changes must be made to eliminate the social, political, and economic inequities rampant in society at large (Anyon, 1997; Kozol, 1991; Nieto, 1999). While the need for comprehensive educational and societal changes is readily

1

recognized, analysis of them is beyond the parameters of this project. It focuses, instead, on teaching in K–12 classrooms.

This chapter sets the tone for the remainder of the book, which builds on the notion of creating a story of culturally responsive teaching. The reason for using a storymaking motif is to suggest that culturally responsive teaching has many different shapes, forms, and effects. A "story" perspective allows the integration of more types of information and styles of presentation than are customary in more conventional styles of scholarly writing and research. This demonstrates how research, theory, and practice are woven together to develop major ideas; establishes the fact that school achievement involves more than academics; attempts to convey a feeling for the personhood of the students of concern in the analyses; and explains why culturally responsive teaching is a dynamic process. To accomplish these goals, the chapter is divided into four sections. The first section explains the importance of storymaking as a technique of educational analysis, research, and reform. The second section includes a "symbolic story" of the achievement problems encountered by many students of color. It is followed in the third section by a discussion of some national achievement trends among students of color. The fourth section of the chapter introduces some assertions made about how student achievement can be improved. These are developed in greater detail in subsequent chapters.

THE NEED FOR AND NATURE OF STORY

Dyson and Genishi (1994) believe that "we all have a basic need for story." They define *story* as a process of "organizing our experiences into tales of important happenings" (p. 2). Stories, according to Denman (1991), are "lenses through which we view and review all of human experience. . . . They have a power to reach deep inside us and command our ardent attention. Through stories we see ourselves. . . . Our personal experience . . . takes on a cloak of significance . . . we see what it is to be alive, to be human" (p. 4). Bruner (1996) adds that narratives, or stories, are the means through which people make sense of their encounters, their experiences, their *human affairs*. He explains further:

> We frame the accounts of our cultural origins and our most cherished beliefs in story form, and it is not just the "content" of these stories that grip us, but their narrative artifice. Our immediate experience, what happened yesterday or the day before, is framed in the same storied way. Even more striking, we represent our lives (to ourselves as well as to others) in the form of narrative. (p. 40)

Stories also are powerful means for people to establish bridges across other factors that separate them (such as race, culture, gender, and social

class), penetrate barriers to understanding, and create feelings of kindredness (Goldblatt, 2007; Witherell & Nodding, 1991). In other words, stories
educate us about ourselves and others; they capture our attention on a very
personal level, and entice us to see, know, desire, imagine, construct, and
become more than what we currently are (Fowler, 2006; Harvey, 1994).

Narratives and stories encompass both the modes of thought and texts
of discourse that give shape to the realities they convey. Their style and
content give form to one another, "just as thought becomes inextricable
from the language that expresses it and eventually shapes it" (Bruner, 1996,
p. 132). Furthermore, the whats and whys of narratives are never chance
occurrences or mere happenstance. They have deliberate intentionality,
"voice," positionality, and contestability. Bruner (1996) believes that stories
are motivated by certain values, beliefs, desires, and theories; that they seek
to reveal intentional states behind actions, or reasons, not causes; that they
are rarely taken as "unsponsored texts"; and that "those worth telling and
worth construing are typically born in trouble" (p. 142).

Stories also "shape, rather than simply reflect, human conduct . . . because they embody compelling motives, strong feelings, vague aspirations,
clear intentions, or well-defined goals" (Rosaldo, 1989, p. 129). They serve
many different functions. They can entertain, educate, inform, evoke memories, showcase ethnic and cultural characteristics, and illuminate abstractions. Stories are means for individuals to project and present themselves,
declare what is important and valuable, give structure to perceptions, make
general facts more meaningful to specific personal lives, connect the self
with others, proclaim the self as a cultural being, develop a healthy sense
of self, forge new meanings and relationships, or build community. Stories
give life to characters, concepts, and ideas through word pictures and verbal
rhythms, which, in turn, convey new experiences and possibilities (Bruner,
1996; Delpit & Dowdy, 2002; Denman, 1991; Franklin & Dowdy, 2005;
N. King, 1993).

In reflecting on incorporating storymaking and storytelling in her own
teaching experience, N. King (1993) declares that these techniques "help
make the abstract more concrete, diverse facts more understandable, and
arouse interest in learning as students become engrossed, not only in the story itself, but in the cultural or social context in which it is told" (p. 2). The
telling of one story is the genesis of yet other stories. The images, rhythms,
and experiences it evokes "reverberate in the memories of audience members, who reconstruct the story with the stuff of their own thoughts and
feelings. In such ways, individual lives are woven together through the stuff
of stories" (Dyson & Genishi, 1994, p. 5). These attributes certainly fit the
character and functions of the "story" of culturally responsive pedagogy
presented in this book. They also are powerfully illustrated in *Becoming
Multicultural Educators* (Gay, 2003a) and *Building Racial and Cultural
Competence in the Classroom* (Teel & Obidah 2008) for giving meaning

to the challenges of preparing teachers to work better with ethnically diverse students. The authors in both volumes provide autobiographical narratives about their personal and professional journeys toward becoming more proficient in engagement with ethnic, racial, and cultural diversity for themselves and the students they teach. The content and techniques of their storytelling are models and motivation for others to emulate.

Even though "story" is usually associated with people telling about themselves and/or events in which they have been involved, the explanations of educational ideas, paradigms, and proposals constitute "story" as well. Educators need to organize their conceptions and experiences in working with students of color into meaningful "tales of important happenings," as much as individuals need to do so with their personal encounters. Without being so ordered, successful efforts cannot be easily shared or replicated. And educating some students of color is in dire need of much more success than currently exists. This is why I want to create a "story" of power pedagogy in the form of culturally responsive teaching.

In constructing this story, I weave together the images, ideas, meanings, and experiences produced by other researchers, scholars, and practitioners with my own interpretations to create even richer meanings and broader possibilities. The results are intended to be more effective ways of improving the educational achievement of students of color. Thus, *Culturally Responsive Teaching: Theory, Research, and Practice* is presented as a *story for academic success*. In some instances it is already happening, but in most it is still an envisioned possibility yet to be realized.

A PERSONAL STORY AND SYMBOL OF A TREND

Any good story has a setting and context, and develops around some topic, issue, event, theme, or situation of felt importance to the storyteller. Sometimes this is accomplished by using smaller events or experiences to launch larger ones. This is how the creation of the story of culturally responsive teaching begins—that is, with a mini-story as an entrée into the bigger story. This mini-story acts as a preview, a prelude to what is developed in greater detail later on. It is simultaneously metaphorical and literal, symbolic and representative, personal and collective, real and imagined, factual and fictional. It gives name to the motivation for and message of this book, and it places them within somewhat of a personal context. It acts as a point of reference and identifies the constituent issues and individuals for whom culturally responsive pedagogy is advocacy and agency.

This beginning story might be entitled "Simultaneously Winning and Losing." While its situations are about real-life individuals and events, the characters' names are pseudonyms. The story begins:

As learners, siblings Aaron and Amy are a study in contradiction. Outside of school they exhibit some of the attributes typically associated with giftedness, but in school they are, at best, average students. They are caring, conscientious, and courteous teens who are sought out by peers as friends. They are insatiably curious about people, events, and experiences that they encounter in their social lives. They interact easily, confidently, and effectively with a wide range of people, diversified by age, position, gender, ethnicity, race, and education. They are as comfortable with deans of colleges of education as they are with age mates and their little toddler nephew.

Amy and Aaron know how to ask engaging, thoughtful, probing questions so that they can gain information about things they do not understand and simultaneously be actively engaged participants in conversations. Not knowing something is not perceived by them as a negative reflection on their egos, intelligence, or self-worth. They consider inquiry and questioning as natural means of knowing, and they use them prolifically in their social settings. They are very adept at making contributions to interactions with others that are appropriate to the context and purpose. Amy and Aaron love to learn and are interested in exploring a wide variety of topics and issues. They are not reluctant to try out new experiences and think about different things, but this is done with thoughtful care, not impulsiveness or irresponsibility. They probe diligently with others to extend their knowledge, but with respect and honor. They "process" their experiences and knowledge, are good listeners, and know how to help others build conversations. They routinely reflect on, analyze, evaluate, and classify knowledge and experiences into arrangements other than those in which they initially were received. Amy and Aaron love to tell stories about their encounters and to share their experiences and knowledge with others. Consequently, they are verbally articulate and very skilled in their interpersonal and social relations.

Aaron and Amy also are good problem-solvers and critical thinkers. They know well how to assess their strengths and weaknesses and to determine what needs to be done to deal effectively with problematic situations. They are honest and above board about their responsibilities and the fallacies of their behaviors; they do not shirk obligations or make disavowing excuses for irresponsibilities. They are resourceful and self-initiating in finding answers and solutions to problems. A case in point happened when they were several years younger. A frightening experience with a severe thunderstorm left them very much afraid of thunder and lightning. After some time living with this fear, they decided to find a way to manage it. So they began to watch the weather channel on TV and taught themselves how to read weather maps in newspapers. This way they could determine in advance what the weather was going to be like, and emotionally and mentally prepare themselves for it. Thus, instead of letting this fear overwhelm them, they took control of it and taught themselves to grow beyond it.

With all of these attributes and skills, one would expect Amy and Aaron to be high achievers in school. Unfortunately, this was not the case. They struggled academically from the time they began school as kindergartners. They complained about their subjects being dull and boring; about not being able to understand what the teachers were talking about; about teachers who were impatient with students asking them questions; about teachers who didn't seem to care or be genuinely concerned about students; about all the tests they had to take, with no one explaining *why* the answers they gave to the questions weren't correct; and about not having time to get everything done that school and classes required. These were agonizing and disconcerting concerns for them. Yet Aaron and Amy were able to separate their achievement problems from their personal quality. While they talked candidly about failing a test or not performing adequately on a class task, they were never heard saying, "I am a failure." They also continued to view school as a place where they went to learn. This was evident in their conversations about happenings in school. More often than not, events they recounted had something to do in some way with learning. Although they had a wide and diverse circle of friends at school, socializing and connecting with them was not their primary point of reference in talking about going to school and the events that occurred in the course of the school day.

Despite their academic struggles, Amy and Aaron never expressed disdain for education or schooling. They never complained about or considered not going to school. On occasion they even found a few teachers, lessons, tasks, and readings exciting and intellectually stimulating. One of their teachers who wove lots of information about African Americans into U.S. history, and had the students do critical analyses and alternative interpretations of historical events, is remembered fondly and held in high esteem. His teaching style is considered by them to be "the way all teachers should teach." Reading *The Cay* (T. Taylor, 1969), *Let the Circle Be Unbroken* (M. Taylor, 1981), *Roll of Thunder, Hear My Cry* (M. Taylor, 1984), and *The Autobiography of Malcolm X* (Malcolm X & Haley, 1966) and viewing *Roots* (Haley, 1976) were particularly memorable and intellectually successfully events for them that generated much excitement and exuberant sharing of insights and reactions with family and friends at home. Reports written and tests taken on these learning tasks received high grades and positive accolades from their teachers.

As they approached the end of their senior year, Aaron and Amy waited, with trepidation yet cautious hopefulness, for the results of their latest attempts on their school district's proficiency tests. Math and writing were the particular nemeses for one, and math and science for the other. They had taken these tests several times before, unsuccessfully. If they did not pass them, what would they do? Would they try yet again to pass? How many more times would they go through this agony before becoming so discouraged and demoralized that they refused to persist any longer in trying to pass these tests? Most certainly, if they did not pass the proficiency tests, they would not be allowed to graduate, even though they had completed all the required courses with passing grades. If they did not graduate, the chances of them pursuing any postsecondary educational opportunities were virtually nil.

What was happening to Amy and Aaron inside school? Why were these youths intelligently curious and capable out of school, but not in? Was this seeming contradiction in their academic capabilities because they were African American and poor urban residents? What was repeatedly not passing a set of tests doing to their internal sense of self, although outwardly they still seemed to be very confident and positive about who they were? If teachers knew how, or cared, to *consistently* incorporate African American content and styles of learning into their classroom instruction and preparation for testing, would Aaron's and Amy's academic story be different?

ACHIEVEMENT CHALLENGES

Amy and Aaron began their testing saga in 8th grade. They passed some of the required tests in subsequent years, but not math, science, or writing. They took some form of proficiency tests for 5 consecutive years. Late in their senior year Aaron and Amy received the good news that they finally had passed the last required tests and would graduate with their class. The announcement was more of a psychological relief for them than a symbol of academic achievement. Comments made by Aaron attest to the heavy weight that the threat of failure carried for them. After the final test results were positive, he revealed a carefully veiled and deep worry. He wondered, "What would have happened to me if I hadn't graduated? Would I have ever gotten a decent job? Would any respectable girls have dated me? What would people in my community have thought of me? I would have been so embarrassed." These are serious concerns for teenagers and probably are suffered by many other students as well.

Unfortunately, Aaron and Amy's situation is not an idiosyncratic or isolated one. There are hundreds of thousands of students like them in schools throughout the United States. According to a 2017 report by Catherine Gewertz in *Education Week*, 12 states required students to pass competency tests in order to graduate from high school. This is down from 24 in 2008. However, all 50 states use standardized testing for other reasons, such as diagnosis of student needs and placement, improvement of instruction, program evaluation, and school performance reporting (*Digest of Education Statistics*, 2008). Added to these figures are local school districts that are instituting various forms of required standardized tests of essential learnings, performance proficiencies, and graduation requirements. The numbers are growing by leaps and bounds annually as politicians and policymakers demand "data-based" evidence that students are reaching established performance standards.

Students struggling to pass proficiency tests and other presumed "high standards of academic excellence" throughout the United States are not only African American, but Native American, Latino American, Asian American, and European American; male and female; poor and middle-class; urban and rural dwellers; English-dominant speakers and others who have limited proficiency in English; native-born citizens and immigrants. Many are in worse shape than Aaron and Amy, who, at least, continued to go to school, found some moments of value and intellectual stimulation in their classes, and did not internalize their academic difficulties as negative statements about their value as human beings. They know well the meaning of an inspirational motto advertised recently by a small business enterprise that says, "Failure is an experience, not any individual." Unfortunately, this is not true for many students who are unsuccessful in school. They and their teachers connect their academic difficulties to their personal worth, and the individuals are deemed failures.

ASSERTIONS ABOUT IMPROVING STUDENT ACHIEVEMENT

Six major premises or assertions undergird the discussions in this book. They give shape to the text and tone of the analyses presented and the strategies proposed for improving the performance of underachieving students of color. Since echoes of them reverberate throughout the development of the narrative text of all the chapters, it seems best to make them explicit up front.

Culture Counts

The first premise is that culture is at the heart of all we do in the name of education, whether that is curriculum, instruction, administration, or performance assessment. As used here, *culture* refers to a dynamic system of social values, cognitive codes, behavioral standards, worldviews, and beliefs used to give order and meaning to our own lives as well as the lives of others (Delgado-Gaitan & Trueba, 1991). Even without our being consciously aware of it, culture strongly influences how we think, believe, communicate, and behave, and these, in turn, affect how we teach and learn. Because teaching and learning are always mediated or shaped by cultural influences, they can never be culturally neutral (Ginsberg, 2015; Kuykendall, 2004; Ortiz, 2013). As Pai, Adler, and Shadiow (2006) explain, "There is no escaping the fact that education is a sociocultural process. Hence, a critical examination of the role of culture in human life is indispensable to the understanding and control of educative processes" (p. 6). George and Louise Spindler (1994) extend and further clarify these arguments. In so doing, they make a compelling case for teachers to understand how their own and their students' cultures affect the educational process. They explain:

> Teachers carry into the classroom their personal cultural background. They perceive students, all of whom are cultural agents, with inevitable prejudice and preconception. Students likewise come to school with personal cultural backgrounds that influence their perceptions of teachers, other students, and the school itself. Together students and teachers construct, mostly without being conscious of doing it, an environment of meanings enacted in individual and group behaviors, of conflict and accommodation, rejection and acceptance, alienation and withdrawal. (p. xii)

Boykin (1994) provides another perspective on the interaction between culture and education that helps to frame the analyses presented in the various chapters of this book. He, too, believes that "there has always been a profound and inescapable cultural fabric of the schooling process in America" (p. 244). This "cultural fabric," primarily of European and middle-class origins, is so deeply ingrained in the structures, ethos, programs, and etiquette of schools that it is considered simply the "normal" and "right" thing to do. Because of this, formal education

> is about learning how to read, write, and think . . . in certain prescribed ways consistent with certain beliefs, prescribed vantage points, value-laden conditions and value-laden formats. These prescribed ways of educating, these certain vantage points, conditions, proper practices and inherent values are the materials and texture of a profound cultural socialization process that forms the very fabric of the medium through which schooling is done. (pp. 245–246)

The connection between culture and education suggested by Pai and associates, Boykin, and the Spindlers is made even more explicit by Flippo, Hetzel, Gribouski, and Armstrong (1997). They declare that "the relationship between literacy and culture is bidirectional. Not only will cultural diversity mediate the acquisition and expression of literacy, but literacy education will also influence and mold an individual's cultural identity" (p. 645). Erickson (2010) offers another view of the importance, inevitability, and challenge of culture in education. He explains:

> In a sense, everything in education relates to culture—to its acquisition, its transmission, and its invention. Culture is in us and all around us, just as the air we breathe. In its scope and distribution it is personal, familial, communal, institutional, societal, and global. Yet culture as a notion is often difficult to grasp. As we learn and use culture in daily life, it becomes habitual. Our habits become for the most part transparent to us. Thus, culture shifts inside and

outside our reflective awareness. We do not think much about the structure and characteristics of culture as we use it, just as we do not think reflectively about any familiar tool in the midst of its use. (p. 35)

These observations underscore the importance of placing culture at the center of the analysis of techniques for improving the performance of under-achieving students of color, or of explicitly acknowledging that it is already there, and broadening the "center" of educational practices to make it culturally pluralistic rather than homogeneous. This shift of emphasis in teaching is imperative because, as Eisenhart and Cutts-Dougherty (1991) suggest, "access to knowledge . . . is socially situated and culturally constructed." This means that "social barriers or cultural norms define and limit the types and the amount of information that is supposed to be exchanged within and between social groups" (p. 28).

Culture, like any other social or biological organism, is multidimensional and continually changing. It must be so to remain vital and functional for those who create it and for those it serves. Wurdeman-Thurston and Kaomea (2015) acknowledge that although cultures are complex, dynamic, and fluid, some of their aspects persist across many generations. As manifested in expressive behaviors, culture is influenced by a wide variety of factors, including time, setting, age, economics, and social circumstances. This expressive variability does not nullify the existence of some core cultural features and focal values in different ethnic groups. Instead, members of ethnic groups, whether consciously or not, share some core cultural characteristics. Shade, Kelly, and Oberg (1997) refer to these as the *modal personality*, which means cultural characteristics most likely to be found in a sample of an ethnic population. Designating core or modal characteristics does not imply that they will be identically manifested by all group members. Nor will these characteristics be negated if some group members do not exhibit any of them as described. How individual members of ethnic groups express their shared features varies widely for many different reasons. Some of the causes of this variance, and the relationships among them as conceived and applied throughout this book, are depicted visually in Figure 1.1.

The information in this figure suggests that *culture is dynamic, complex, interactive, and changing, yet a stabilizing force in human life*. As Adichie (2009) explains, in dealing with culture it is dangerous to assume, seek, or attempt to present a monolithic or single story for an ethnic group or individual. "Ethnicity and culture," as shown at the bottom of Figure 1.1, are the *foundational anchors* of all other behaviors. They operate expressively on continua of being and intensity, ranging from high to low, as symbolized by the double-headed arrow. How core characteristics of ethnic groups' cultures are manifested in *expressive behaviors* (e.g., thinking, talking, writing, etc.) is influenced by different *mitigating variables* such as

Figure 1.1. Cultural Dynamics

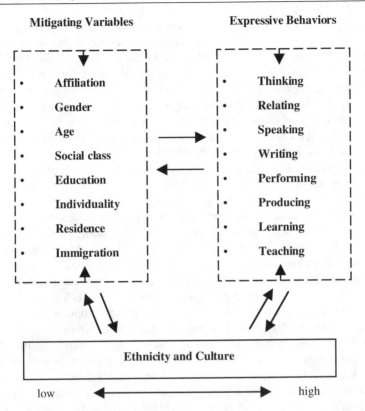

gender, education, social class, and degrees of affiliation. The variables identified in the model are representative of *types* of influences rather than being all-inclusive. The two-directional arrows between ethnicity and culture, the mitigating variables, and the expressive behaviors suggest that the relationships among all of these are dialectic and dynamic.

The mitigating variables also interact with and influence one another, as do the various kinds of expressive behaviors. These relationships are indicated by the bidirectional arrows in each block. However, the influences are not always in the same directions or of equal degrees of intensity. For instance, high levels of education do not necessarily correlate positively with high degrees of ethnic affiliation and learning-style characteristics. High degrees of ethnic affiliation do correlate with high cultural identity and ownership. Chronological maturity does not guarantee heightened ethnic affiliation or cultural identity. Although males and females express their cultural heritage in somewhat different ways, this is due more to their engendered socialization than to their being more or less culturally affiliated because of their gender.

The discussions of cultural influences on teaching and learning presented in this book focus on core characteristics, as manifested on a range of clarity, specificity, purity, and authenticity that is closer to the "high" end of the continuum. The imagined individuals exhibiting these cultural characteristics are *highly ethnically affiliated with a strong cultural identity.* But they may not be able to cognitively articulate their culture and ethnicity to others, or to themselves. The descriptions included here are not intended to capture every conceivable manifestation of culture for every single individual and circumstance for all individuals within different ethnic groups. Furthermore, cultural features are *composite constructions* of group behaviors that occur over time and in many different situations. They are not pure descriptors of specific individuals within groups or behaviors at a particular point in time. Instead, *descriptions of culture are approximations of reality— templates, if you will—through which actual behaviors of individuals can be filtered in search of alternative explanations and deeper meanings.* In this sense the cultural descriptions included in this book are intended to serve purposes similar to those served by any other conceptual schemas in education, such as characterizations of good teaching, being at risk, giftedness, and gender-related behaviors. Few, if any, individuals will manifest the characteristics, as described, in every place and at all times.

Nor are the cultures of schools and different ethnic groups always completely synchronized. These discontinuities can interfere with students' academic achievement, in part because how some ethnically and culturally diverse individuals customarily engage in intellectual processing, self-presentation, and task performance is different from the processes used in school. Demonstrating knowledge and skills may be constrained as much by structural and procedural inconsistencies (Au, 1980; Cazden, John, & Hymes, 1985; Holliday, 1985; Spindler, 1987; Spring, 1995) as by lack of intellectual ability. Therefore, teachers need to understand different cultural intersections and incompatibilities, minimize the tensions, and bridge the gaps among different cultural systems. Congruency between how the educational process is ordered and delivered, and the cultural frames of reference of diverse students, will improve school achievement for students of color.

Conventional Reform Is Inadequate

The second guiding assumption of this book is that *conventional* paradigms and proposals for improving the achievement of students of color are doomed to failure. This is due largely to their being deeply enmeshed in a deficit orientation—that is, concentrating on what ethnically, racially, and culturally different students don't have and can't do—and their claims of cultural neutrality. These positions are evident in current thinking about "at-risk" students and highly structured, scripted instructional programs that emphasize only the technical and academic dimensions of learning. There are some high-profile innovations of this kind that appear to be having some significant positive impacts on the achievement of students of color, such as Reading Recovery, Reading First, and Open Court (PreK to 12: Results Matter, n.d.; U.S. Department of Education, 2007). But their effects may not stand the test of time or be as comprehensive as they claim to be. They may inadvertently cause students to compromise their ethnic and cultural identity to attain academic achievement—a situation that is problematic, to say the least.

These programs attempt to deal with academic performance by divorcing it from other factors that affect achievement, such as culture, ethnicity, and personal experience. The Advancement Via Individual Determination (AVID) project, which began in 1980 in the San Diego County public schools, has proven the fallacy of this for Latino and African American students from urban areas. The directors and teachers of AVID found that achievement was much higher when academic interventions were reinforced by an infrastructure of social supports. These included personal caring, mutual aid and assistance, use of cultural anchors and mediators in instruction, and creating a sense of community among students and teachers (Mehan, Hubbard, Villanueva, & Lintz, 1996; Swanson, Mehan, & Hubbard, 1995). Fortunately, some ingenious teachers such as Lawrence Tan are continuing these efforts within the context of highly structured, mandated curricular designs and materials for helping students reach achievement standards. They are finding ways to include other important competencies, such as social justice and cross-cultural knowledge, in programs like Reading First and Open Court (L. Tan, 2002–2003).

Intention Without Action Is Insufficient

A third assumption is that many educators have good intentions about not being academically unjust and discriminatory toward ethnically and racially different students. Others understand and even endorse the importance of being *aware* of cultural differences in classroom interactions. However important they are, good intentions and awareness are not enough to bring about the changes needed in educational programs and procedures to prevent academic inequities among diverse students. Goodwill must be accompanied by pedagogical knowledge and skills as well as the courage to dismantle the status quo. Many years ago Carter G. Woodson (1933/1969) made some provocative observations about the limitations of good intentions without skill proficiency, evident in attempts to educate African Americans shortly after the end of the Civil War. The missionary workers who went South to enlighten the freedmen were earnest and admirable in their endeavors but were largely ineffective because they

> had more enthusiasm than knowledge. They did not understand the task before them. This undertaking, too, was more of an effort toward social uplift than actual education. Their aim was to transform the Negroes, not to develop them. The freedmen who were to be enlightened were given little thought, for the best friends of the race, ill-taught themselves, followed the traditional curricula of the times which did not take the Negro into consideration except to condemn or pity him. (p. 17)

Even though these observations were prompted by situations a century and a half ago and Woodson's comments were first made more than 75 years ago, they are not mere historical events and memories. Nor is it reasonable, unfortunately, to dismiss them as obsolete. The fact that they are still applicable today indicates that the issue of providing appropriate education for African Americans and other ethnic groups of color is long-standing, persistent, and increasingly urgent.

The worst kinds of condemnation of groups of color no longer exist in very overt ways, but residuals of the missionary zeal in dealing with social issues affecting them continue. They take the form of benign oversight, in which students of color often are ignored and left alone as long as they are not challenging teachers or disrupting classroom procedures. Another frequent contemporary manifestation of the "enlightenment intentions" described by Woodson is declarations that awareness of and appreciation for cultural differences are sufficient for dealing with the challenges of providing effective education for ethnic groups of color. Defenders of these positions seem to be unaware of the complexity of the issues; awareness or appreciation without action will not change the educational enterprise. Mastery of knowledge and skills related to working with culturally diverse students in pedagogical situations is imperative for this task.

Another "good intentions" position often taken is that "race, culture, and ethnicity are as important as social class. The educational issue of utmost concern is the individual and his or her academic outcomes." The race, culture, ethnicity, individuality, and intellectuality of students are not discrete attributes that can be neatly assigned to separate categories, some to be ignored while others are tended to. Instead, they are inseparably interrelated; all must be carefully understood, and the insights gleaned from this understanding should be the driving force for the redesign of education for cultural diversity. In the spirit of Woodson's message, this comprehensive understanding is a more appropriate basis for developing the intellectual capabilities of students of color than is the attempt to get them to abandon their ethnic identities and cultural foundations.

Strength and Vitality of Cultural Diversity

A fourth major assertion underlying the discussions in this book is that cultural diversity is a strength—a persistent, vitalizing force in our personal and civic lives. However, its full potential may not be realized. It is, then, a useful resource for improving educational effectiveness for all students. Just as the evocation of their European American, middle-class heritage contributes to the achievement of White students, using the cultures and experiences of Native Americans, Asian and Pacific Islander Americans, Latino Americans, and African Americans facilitates their school success.

Several researchers and practitioners have provided evidence to support the verity of these claims. For example, McCarty, Wallace, Lynch, and Benally (1991) and McCarty (2002) found that the image of Navajo children as silent and passive students was totally destroyed by teaching that connected school learning with cultural backgrounds and lived experiences. When their social experiences were incorporated into curriculum and instruction, and their cultural and linguistic resources were used to solve academic problems, the Navajo students became physically energized, intellectually engaged, and verbally fluent in the classroom. Boggs, Watson-Gegeo, and McMillen (1985), Tharp and Gallimore (1988), and Au (1993) report similar results from using culturally familiar content and styles of teaching for the academic achievement of Native Hawaiian students. Krater, Zeni, and Cason (1994), Boykin (2002), and C. Lee (1993, 2007) have done likewise for African Americans; Escalante and Dirmann (1990) and Sheets (1995a) for Latinos; Philips (1983) for students on the Warm Springs Reservation and Greenbaum (1985) for Cherokees in elementary school; and Wigginton (1985, 1991) for poor, rural European Americans living in Appalachian communities. Practices such as these, and the effects they have on student achievement, give name, substance, and validity to the title and intentions of this book. They support the transformative effects of sociocultural contextual factors on the academic achievement of students of color. In other words, "matching the contextual conditions for learning to the cultural experiences of the learner increases task engagement and hence increases task performance" (B. Allen & Butler, 1996, p. 317).

Learning experiences and achievement outcomes for ethnically and culturally diverse students should include more than cognitive performances in academic subjects and standardized test scores. Moral, social, cultural, personal, and political developments are also important. All of these are essential to the healthy and complete functioning of human beings and societies. If education is, as it should be, devoted to teaching the whole child, then this comprehensive focus should be evident throughout curriculum, instruction, and assessment. John Gardner (1984) makes this point powerfully and persuasively. He tells us that excellence in education is a process of perpetual self-discovery, perpetual reshaping to realize one's best self, to be the person one could be. It includes not only the intellect but the emotions, character, and personality . . . not only surface but deeper layers of thought and action . . . adaptability, creativeness, and vitality . . . [and] ethical and spiritual growth. (p. 124)

Fostering this comprehensive scale of development for culturally diverse students in U.S. schools should take place within a framework of ethical values and multiple cultural perspectives because "every age, in every significant situation, in every conceivable way" (J. Gardner, 1984, p. 125) has to re-create itself. These important nonacademic learnings typically are not included on standardized test scores. If tests are the only measures used to determine student performance, some critical areas of achievement will be systematically and repeatedly overlooked. Therefore, just as students should be seen as multidimensional and contextually diverse, so should techniques routinely used to assess their performance in schools.

Jeffrey Kane, the executive editor of *Holistic Education Review*, offers another perspective of quality education that resonates with the assumptions and intentions of this book. It is about "knowing and being" (1994), and it speaks to the moral dimensions of education. It is presented here because education in general and specific reform actions to eliminate the educational injustices perpetuated toward students of color are both moral as well as pedagogical challenges. As Kane (1994) explains:

Knowing and being are intimately entwined. Knowledge is embedded in and created by a constellation of human intelligences, and such intelligences exist within a universe of inner experience, of the experience of being. Every fact, every skill a child acquires, however small and seemingly discreet, addresses our sense of meaning, purpose, and identity. . . . Whether we develop the capacity to wonder, to explore the depth of our own being, to rise to the challenge to speak the words "I am" or whether we resign ourselves to questions of technique and method to problems . . . may well depend upon the equality of the experiences we provide for children in the course of their education. (p. 4)

Competence or Incompetence Is Never Universal or All-Inclusive

Prevailing tendencies in educational practice operate on the assumptions that student capabilities as shown in any one area of performance will be the same in all areas. Even though ideological claims are made to the contrary, too often these are not reflected in practice. Consequently, students who are gifted and talented in science are assumed to be similarly capable in math, social studies, language arts, and fine arts. Conversely, low achievement in reading, for example, will parallel poor performance in writing, civic education, science, and mathematics. Another example of this assumption of the universality of competence is the interaction between economics, ethnicity, and educational achievement. The tendency is for educators to act as if *all* children of poverty and of color are at risk of school failure. While there is supportive evidence that there are high positive correlations among these factors, nevertheless there are notable *and regular* exceptions. Yet, profiles of academically successful poor students of color (beyond the exceptional few, or in unusual occurrences) are conspicuously absent in regular educational discourse. These assumptions are also imposed on students who are not native English speakers. Frequently their limited English skills are associated with low intellectual abilities, thereby assuming that limited ability in one area usually extends to other areas of educational abilities.

In fact, competence is always contextual and evolving. However challenging and difficult some (or even most) school learning may be for some students, there is always something that they can do well. These competencies may not be recognized and valued as such by educators, and they may not be viable in school settings, but that does not mean that they are nonexistent. They may be social, cultural, personal, or political, rather than academic, and not necessarily applicable across all times and circumstances, but they do exist and are functional. Conversely, competencies that generate the highest academic performance are not applicable at all times and in every situation. Students who do very well academically may struggle with social skills and self-esteem. Others who are social outcasts and academic failures in school are youth leaders, mentors, and activists in their cultural communities. Culturally responsive teaching recognizes and further develops this natural diversity and fluidity of competence among diverse student populations. Some theoretical developments associated with these emphases are referred to as funds of knowledge (Gonzalez, Moll, & Amanti, 2005; Moll, Amanti, Neff, & Gonzales, 1992), or as asset or strength-based teaching (Lopez, 2017) or talent development (Boykin, 2002).

Test Scores and Grades Are Symptoms, Not Causes, of Achievement Problems

The final key premise underlying the discussions in the forthcoming chapters is that scores on standardized tests and grades students receive on classroom learning tasks do not explain why they are not performing at acceptable levels. These are the symptoms of, not the causes of or remedies for, the problems. Unless teachers understand what is interfering with students' performance, they cannot intervene appropriately to remove the obstacles to high achievement. Simply blaming students, their socioeconomic background, a lack of interest in and of motivation for learning, and poor parental participation in the educational process is not very helpful. The question of "why" continues to be unanswered. Some other reasons may explain why disproportionally high percentages of African Americans,

Latinos, Native Americans, and some Asian American groups are not doing well in school. Among these are intragroup variability, differential skills and abilities, stress and anxiety provoked by racial prejudices and stereotypes, discontinuities between the cultures of the school and the homes of ethnically diverse students, and a lack of confirming support from educational programs and institutions (Fuligni, 2007; Steele, 1997, 2010). They offer insights that can generate more hopeful possibilities for reversing current achievement patterns.

The search for reasons why different students are performing as they are should begin with a much more careful disaggregation of achievement data. Describing performance in "averages" across ethnic groups and for "composite skills" can disguise more than illuminate. So can leaving the impression that students tested in a particular grade one year are the same ones tested in the same grade the next year. For example, reports that 8-, 13-, and 17-year-old African American students have the lowest reading scores of any ethnic group on National Assessment of Educational Progress measures and various states' proficiency tests leave out a lot of critical information. They do not specify how performance is distributed by gender, social class, residential location, immigrant status, and linguistic background of the students; nor do they specify the various skills (e.g., vocabulary, comprehension, inference, decoding, etc.) that constitute reading. These reports blatantly ignore the *within-group variability* that exists among African Americans. Yet this variance must be understood, and the insights gained should influence the design and implementation of instructional reforms to facilitate better school achievement for these students.

No ethnic group is culturally or intellectually monolithic. For instance, African Americans include people who are descendants of Africans enslaved in the United States, others whose origins are in the Caribbean, and recent immigrants from various African nations. Some are fluent speakers of academic English, some are dialect speakers, and others speak English as a second language. Some African Americans are academically gifted, some are average students, and some are failing in school. This kind of variability exists in all ethnic groups in the United States, and it affects the achievement of students in different ways. What these differences are must be more clearly defined if teachers are to further encourage those students who are already performing well and remediate those who are not. Thus, effective teaching and learning for diverse students are contingent upon the thorough disaggregation of achievement data by student demographics and types of academic skills.

Research on the education of immigrants to the United States provides graphic illustrations of why immigration should be understood as one of the reasons for the achievement patterns of some ethnic groups. Vernez and Abrahamese (1996) found that immigrants were less likely to attend high school (87%) than U.S.-born students (93%). Latino immigrants, especially those from Mexico, accounted for almost all of this difference. In 1990 only one in four Mexican immigrant youths between the ages of 15 and 17 was enrolled in school; Latino immigrants performed lower than other immigrant groups, but higher than their U.S.-born counterparts. McDonnell and Hill (1993) and Fass (1989) reported that the highest-performing Asian immigrant students are Japanese, Chinese, Filipinos, Koreans, and Asian Indians. Southeast Asians, such as Vietnamese, Cambodians, Hmongs, and Thais, do not perform as well.

Other researchers (First & Carrera, 1988; Igoa, 1995; Lee & Bean, 2010; Lee & Zhou, 2015; Olneck, 2004) suggest that many immigrant families and their children are caught in a sociocultural paradox. They come to the United States to escape poverty and persecution, and to improve the general quality of their lives. In doing so, they often suffer deep affective losses of supportive networks and familial connections. The formal schooling of many of these children prior to immigration was sporadic and fragmented. After arriving in the United States, some immigrant families experience frequent changes in residence, which interfere with the children's educational continuity. They have to adjust to a new culture, language, style of living, and educational system. This geographic, cultural, and psychoemotional uprootedness can cause stress, anxiety, feelings of vulnerability, loneliness, isolation, and insecurity. All these conditions can have negative effects on school achievement.

Both immigrant and native-born students of color also may encounter prejudices, stereotyping, and racism that have negative impacts on their self-esteem, mental health, and academic achievement. The work of several researchers attests to these effects on African, Asian, and Native American students. Plummer and Slane (1996) and C. Jones and Shorter-Gooden (2003) found racism to be highly stress-provoking for African Americans, requiring them to engage in coping behaviors quite different from those of European Americans. Both studies concluded that individuals do not have to personally experience racist attitudes and actions directed at their ethnic groups to be victimized because "race, in and of itself, is a potential source of stress" (p. 314).

Steele (1997, 2010), Steele and Aronson (1995), and Aronson (2004) have examined how societal stereotypes about ethnic and gender groups can affect the intellectual functioning and identity development of individual members. They call this effect a "stereotype threat." It is defined as "the event of a negative stereotype about a group to which one belongs becoming self-relevant, usually as a plausible interpretation for something one is doing, for an experience one is having, or for a situation one is in, that has relevance to one's self-definition" (Steele, 1997, p. 616). Steele and Aronson (1995) propose that stereotype threat is most salient for those students who care most about performing well. Allegations about their ethnic group's intellectual inability create additional self-threat, which interferes with achievement by reducing the range of intellectual cues students are able to use, diverting attention onto task-irrelevant worries, creating self-consciousness and undue caution, and causing them to disengage from academic efforts. Similar results also are reported by Landrine and Klonoff (1996), Gougis (1986), and Perry, Steele, and Hilliard (2003).

The racial discrimination against Navajo students recorded by Deyhle (1995) was a serious threat to their achievement. It took many different forms, ranging from explicit acts of racism to more subtle paternalism, to distortion of cultural values, to belittling the students' intellectual capability. The youth who attended school off the Navajo Reservation talked about the psychoemotional pressure, embarrassment, and anger caused by repeatedly being picked on, ridiculed, and subjected to overt declarations of dislike for and demeaning assumptions about Navajos; teachers' being uncomfortable with or afraid of them; and being offered low-level, nonacademic instruction, presumably because Navajo students do better in basic classes and with hands-on instruction. Their cultural beliefs and practices were often mocked or dismissed as insignificant. Some Navajo students retaliated by stereotyping European American students and teachers in kind, while others tried harder to dispel the stereotype and avoid the limelight. Still others overtly resisted classroom rules or removed themselves from the situation entirely—by dropping out of school or, more accurately, being "pushed out."

Kiang and Kaplan (1994) reported similar examples and effects of racial stress and anxiety on Vietnamese students at a Boston high school. The students told about encountering racial conflicts daily that included being rendered irrelevant and invisible; being ridiculed for speaking Vietnamese; being called derogatory names and subjected to racist slurs; witnessing and experiencing harassment on a regular basis; feeling threatened and angry; and being teased and insulted (Kiang & Kaplan, 1994). These experiences may be carryovers from what is happening in society at large. Min (1995) provides some evidence that anti-Asian prejudices and "hate crimes" are on the rise, due to the increase of Asian Americans in the U.S. population being considered an economic threat by some other groups. The FBI annual reports on racial hate crimes show continuing high incidences of racial hate crimes against African Americans, and significant increases against Latino citizens and immigrants, and Muslims as well ("New FBI Hate Crimes," 2008). It is not difficult to imagine the profound negative consequences these kinds of experiences have for academic, social, and personal achievement, or the emotional and intellectual benefits that could result from the removal of prejudicial conditions from schools and society. Despite these odds, most ethnic minorities create community and engage in productive lives. Graphic examples of this are the Vietnamese community in New Orleans, as described by Zhou and Bankston (1999), and the Hmong and Cambodian refugees in four U.S. cities studied by Hein (2006).

Other factors that help to explain the achievement patterns of ethnically different students and locate opportunities for reform are offered by Fordham (1993, 1996) and Goto (1997). They posit that some students with high academic potential deliberately sabotage or camouflage their intellectual abilities to avoid being alienated from their ethnic friends who are not as adept in school. Fordham explains that the intellectually capable African American females in her study sometimes engaged in "intentional silence," wherein they rarely spoke in class, answered questions but only tersely and without elaboration, and generally avoided bringing attention to themselves. Goto found that Chinese American students did the same kinds of things. To escape being ridiculed by peers or spotlighted by teachers, the students worked hard to give the impression that they were just "normal." They sought a classroom identity that would grant them "comfortable anonymity."

"Double dealing," or being at once highly ethnically affiliated and academically achieving, can take a terrible toll on students when the two agendas are not complementary, as is frequently the case in conventional schools. Negotiating both ways of being can be stress-provoking and emotionally exhausting; it can even cause some students to drop out of the academic loop entirely. Others may sacrifice their friendship networks and ethnic connections for school success. Neither of these choices is desirable for the students involved, nor does either offer the best conditions for maximum achievement of any kind. Students should be able to achieve academically, ethnically, culturally, and socially simultaneously, without any of these abilities interfering with the others.

CONCLUSION

Much intellectual ability and many other kinds of intelligences are lying untapped in ethnically diverse students. If these are recognized and used in the instructional process, school achievement will improve radically. Culturally responsive teaching is a means for unleashing the higher learning potentials of ethnically diverse students by simultaneously cultivating their academic and psychosocial abilities.

The highest-quality educational programs and practices can never be accomplished if some ethnic groups and their contributions to the development of U.S. history, life, and culture are ignored or demeaned. All schools and teachers, regardless of the ethnic and racial makeup of their local student populations, must be actively involved in promoting equity and excellence, and all students must be benefactors of these efforts. Education that is minimally adequate has to teach students the knowledge, values, and skills they need to function effectively as citizens of the pluralistic U.S. society. These are requirements, not voluntary choices, for all students.

Despite an increasingly diverse population, most people in the United States live in communities with others more alike than different from themselves. Students from these communities arrive at school knowing little of significance about people who are different. Yet their lives are intertwined with these "unknown others" and will become even more so in the future. If we are to avoid intergroup strife and if individuals are to live the highest-quality lives possible, we simply must teach students how to relate better to people from different ethnic, racial, cultural, language, and gender backgrounds. These *relational competencies* must encompass knowing, valuing, doing, caring, and sharing power, resources, and responsibilities. Hence, developing sociocivic skills for effective membership in multicultural communities is as important a goal of culturally responsive pedagogy as improving the academic achievement and personal development of students of color.

Both research and lived experience verify the imperative need for and positive effects of multiple diversities to the many different aspects of human life. These include but extend beyond teaching and learning, and racial minority students. Diversity is inherent to humanity. Therefore, enhancing our humanness and embracing multiple diversities are interconnected. This lived reality is affirmed by research, such as that conducted by Phillips (2014). Although her study was located in the corporate world, the conclusions derived from the findings are applicable elsewhere. Phillips conceded that dealing with diversity is difficult, yet necessary. Being around people who are different from us makes us more creative, more diligent, and harder-working. In other words, socially diverse groups are more innovative than homogenous ones. This is a strong and instructive message for teachers in multiracial, multiethnic, multilingual, and multicultural classrooms and schools.

To maximize their human potential culturally, diverse students must be "in community" with self and others. As they evoke various diversities in crafting their connections and relationships, they will become smarter and more fully human, as did the participants in Phillips's study. Her conclusions are worth repeating here to motivate educators to hasten the implementation of culturally responsive teaching:.

> If you want to build teams and organizations capable of innovating, you need diversity. Diversity enhances creativity. It encourages the search for novel information and perspectives, leading to better decisionmaking and problem solving. Diversity can improve the bottom line of companies and lead to unfettered discoveries and breakthrough innovations. Even simply being exposed to diversity can change the way you think. . . . When people are brought together to solve problems in groups, they bring different information, opinions, and perspectives. This makes obvious sense when we talk about diversity of disciplinary backgrounds. . . . The same logic applies to social diversity. People who are different from one another in race, gender, and other dimensions bring unique information and experiences to bear on the task at hand. (Phillips, 2014, pp. 3–4)

She adds that these observations are "not just wishful thinking"; rather they derive from "decades of research from organizational scientists, psychologists, sociologists, economists, and demographers" (p. 4). Although Phillips is speaking specifically about diversity in corporate organizations, she could easily be describing student learning, or school and classroom membership. Since culturally responsive teaching is grounded in multiple diversities, it is fundamental to accomplishing both.

PRACTICE POSSIBILITIES

Some controversy and uncertainty surround teacher beliefs, but there is general agreement that they are important, interact with behavior in some ways, and are often implicit and unconscious. They are often considered as guides to action (Fives & Gill, 2015). This perception implies, then, that beliefs are antecedent to or precede behavior. Much research, scholarship, and practice indicate that teachers' beliefs about ethnic, racial, social, and cultural diversity and its "place" in education are often ambivalent or problematic (Gay, 2015). Such orientations are not very conducive to diligent and unequivocal support of culturally responsive teaching. Therefore, an important beginning for implementing culturally responsive teaching is for teachers to develop consciousness and clarity about their beliefs associated with ethnically, racially, culturally, socially, linguistically, and residentially diverse students, communities, heritages, and education. The list of quotes and proverbs shown below are belief statements that can be used to stimulate teachers' consciousness and crystallization of their own beliefs, to provide some options for adoption, and to act as prompts for critical analyses with students as a culturally responsive learning activity.

Notable Quotes and Proverbs That Can Inspire
Culturally Responsive Educational Ideology, Research, and Practice

- "To those accustomed to privilege, equality feels like oppression." —Anonymous
- "Equal rights for others does not mean fewer rights for you."—George Orwell
- "Rather than accepting the things you cannot change, change the things you cannot accept."—Angela Davis
- "We all should know that diversity makes for a rich tapestry, and we must understand that all the threads of the tapestry are equal in value no matter what their color."—Maya Angelou
- "Respect existence or expect resistance."
- "No one is free when others are oppressed."
- "Never look down on someone unless you are helping them up."

- "In diversity there is beauty and there is strength."—Maya Angelou
- "Equality is not in regarding different things similarly; equality is in regarding different things differently."—Tom Robbins
- "Equality is the soul of liberty; there is, in fact, no liberty without it." —Frances Wright
- "The ultimate measure of a man [woman] is not where he [she] stands in moments of comfort and convenience, but where he [she] stands at times of challenge and controversy."—Martin Luther King, Jr.
- "Injustice anywhere is a threat to justice everywhere."
- "The moral arc of the universe bends at the elbow of justice." —Martin Luther King, Jr.
- "Power concedes nothing without a demand. It never did and it never will."—Frederick Douglass
- "People without knowledge of their past history, origin, and culture are like trees without roots."—Marcus Garvey
- "The best view comes from the hardest climbs."
- "There is very little difference in people, but that little difference makes a big difference."—W. Clement Stone
- "Beloved community is formed not by the eradication of difference but by its affirmation, by each of us claiming the identities and cultural legacies that shape who we are and how we live in the world."—bell hooks
- "There's no beauty without difference and diversity."—Rasheed Ogunlaru

Organizations That Advocate for Cultural Diversity, Equity, and Social Justice

Teachers need support on multiple levels for implementing culturally responsive teaching. Two of these levels are ideological and practical. These organizations can be helpful resources in both areas.

A Better Chance (ABC). A resource for identifying, recruiting, and developing leaders among young people of color in the United States.

The American Friends Service Committee (AFSC). A Quaker organization committed to social justice, peace, and humanitarian service. Its work is based on belief in the worth of every person, and faith in the power of love to overcome violence and injustice.

American Indian Higher Education Consortium (AIHEC). A community of tribally and federally chartered institutions working to strengthen tribal nations and make a lasting difference in the lives of American Indians and Alaska Natives.

The American Textbook Council. Dedicated to conducting textbook analyses, reviews, and evaluations; ensuring the integrity of humanities curricula, history standards, and textbook accuracy; and educating the nation about multiculturalism.

Anti-Defamation League. Fights anti-Semitism and broad-based threats to democracy, including cyberhate, bullying, bias in schools and in the criminal justice system, terrorism, hate crimes, coercion of religious minorities, and contempt for anyone who is different.

Asian American Psychological Association (AAPA). Promotes the mental health and education of Asian Americans, and is in the forefront of the multicultural psychology movement.

Association of Black Culture Centers (ABCC). Committed to supporting centers as places to celebrate, promote, and critically examine the ways of life of ethnic groups, ABCC collaborates with centers across the country to develop programming and ideas to educate all people on the history and culture of African Americans, Latinos, Asian Americans, and Native Americans.

Association of Black Women in Higher Education (ABWHE). Promotes the intellectual growth and educational development of Black women in higher education; strives to eliminate racism, sexism, classism, and other social barriers that hinder Black women from achieving their potential; and documents the personal and professional achievements of Black women and men.

The Association of Women's Rights in Development (AWRD). An international, feminist, membership organization committed to achieving gender equality, sustainable development, and women's human rights.

The Children's Defense Fund (CDF). Its mission is to ensure that every child has a Healthy Start, a Head Start, a Fair Start, a Safe Start, and a Moral Start in life. Particular attention is given to the needs of poor and minority children and those with disabilities, and to preventive investment before they get sick or into trouble, drop out of school, or suffer family breakdown.

Chinese American Educational Research & Development Association (CAERDA). Promotes excellence in education for all students, particularly among Chinese and Chinese Americans, and provides opportunities for scholarly discourse and research related to these issues.

The Committee for Hispanic Families and Children (CHFC). Develops and implements programs that meet the needs of low-income Hispanic families and children in such critical areas as youth development, child care, HIV/AIDS prevention and education, immigrant services, public policy, and advocacy.

Equity Alliance. Promotes research and school reform efforts for equity, access, inclusion, and quality outcomes for all students; values diversity; and supports the civil rights of students.

Girls Incorporated. A national nonprofit youth organization dedicated to inspiring all girls to be strong, smart, and bold, particularly those in high-risk, underserved areas.

Japanese American Citizens League (JACL). Addresses issues of discrimination against people of Japanese ancestry residing in the United States. It is the largest and one of the oldest Asian American organizations in the United States.

Korean American Coalition (KAC). A nonprofit service, education, and advocacy organization that facilitates Korean American participation in civic, legislative, and community affairs

National Alliance of Black School Educators (NABSE). Dedicated to improving the educational experiences and accomplishments of African American youth through the development and use of instructional and motivational methods that increase levels of inspiration, attendance, and achievement.

National Association for Multicultural Education (NAME). Impacts policies, programs, and practices that advance social, political, economic, and educational equity, justice, and excellence for ethnically, racially, and culturally diverse students and communities.

National Black Child Development Institute (NBCD). Develops and delivers culturally relevant resources and services that respond to the unique strengths and needs of Black children around issues of early childhood education, health, child welfare, literacy, and family engagement.

National Coalition of 100 Black Women (NCBW). Develops leaders who help rebuild their communities, fosters principles of equal rights and opportunities, promotes awareness of Black culture, and develops effective leadership and participation in civic affairs.

National Congress of American Indians (NCAI). The oldest, largest, and most representative American Indian and Alaska Native organization in the country; advocates on behalf of tribal governments and their citizens.

National Council of Jewish Women (NCJW). Promotes social change through championing the needs of women, children, and families— while taking a progressive stance on such issues as child welfare, women's rights, and reproductive freedom.

National Council of La Raza (NCLR) (Name changed to **UnidosUS** in July 2017). The largest U.S. national constituency-based Latino American organization, established to reduce poverty and discrimination, and to improve life opportunities for Latino Americans.

National Indian Child Care Association (NICCA). A representative American Indian and Alaska Native organization serving the 266 Tribal communities across the United States; provides children,

families, and communities with high-quality child care services all
across Indian Country.

National Organization for Women (NOW). The largest organization
of feminist activists in the United States, its goal is to take action to
achieve equality for all women.

Native Peoples **Magazine.** The only Native American-oriented magazine
sold nationwide in the United States; considered the periodical voice of
record of the collective Native American community.

Rethinking Schools. Promotes the reform of elementary and secondary
education, with a strong emphasis on racial equity and social justice,
especially in urban schools; tries to balance classroom practice and
educational theory in publications written by and for teachers,
parents, and students.

Teaching Tolerance. A project of the Southern Poverty Law Center; is
dedicated to reducing prejudice, improving intergroup relations, and
promoting equality, inclusiveness, and equitable learning environments
in the classroom.

Women Empowering Women for Indian Nations (WEWIN). Provides
Native women with knowledge, support, and resources necessary to
achieve success in their personal and professional lives, and to engage
in professional renewal, inspiring others, and networking.

CHAPTER 2

Pedagogical Potential of Cultural Responsiveness

"Personal narratives and cultural stories are vital teaching content and methodology."

Teaching is a contextual, situational, and personal process, a complex and never-ending journey. William Ayers (2001) describes three key phases of this journey:

> A first step is becoming the student to your students, uncovering the fellow creatures who must be partners to the enterprise. Another is creating an environment for learning, a nurturing and challenging space in which to travel. And finally, the teacher must begin work on the intricate, many-tiered bridges that will fill up the space, connecting all the dreams, hopes, skills, experiences, and knowledge students bring to class with deeper and wider ways of knowing. (p. 122)

As such, teaching is most effective when ecological factors, such as prior experiences, community settings, cultural backgrounds, and ethnic identities of teachers and students, are included in its implementation. This basic fact often is ignored in teaching some Native, Latino, African, and Asian American students, especially if they are poor. Instead, they are taught from the middle-class, Eurocentric frameworks that shape school practices. This attitude of "cultural blindness" stems from several sources.

One of these is the notion that education has nothing to do with cultures and heritages. It is about teaching intellectual, vocational, and civic skills. Students, especially underachieving ones, need to learn knowledge and skills that they can apply in life, and how to meet high standards of academic excellence, rather than wasting time on fanciful notions about cultural diversity. Second, too few teachers have adequate knowledge about how conventional teaching practices reflect European American cultural values. Nor are they sufficiently informed about the cultures of different ethnic groups. Third, most teachers want to do the best for all their students, and they mistakenly believe that to treat students differently because of their cultural orientations is racial discrimination. Fourth, there is a belief that good teaching is transcendent; it is identical for all students, settings, and circumstances. Fifth, there is the claim that education is an effective doorway of assimilation into mainstream society for people from diverse cultural heritages, ethnic groups, social classes, and points of origin. These students need to forget about being different and learn to adapt to U.S. society. The best way to facilitate this process is for all students to have the same experiences in schools.

INTRODUCTION

This chapter calls these assumptions into question. It begins by exposing the fallacy of cultural neutrality and the homogeneity syndrome in teaching and learning for Native, African, Latino, and Asian American students who are not performing very well on traditional measures of school achievement. It also debunks the notion that school success for students of color can be generated from negative perceptions of their life experiences, cultural backgrounds, and intellectual capabilities. Instead, instructional reforms are needed that are grounded in positive beliefs about the cultural heritages and academic potentialities of these students. A pedagogical paradigm that has these characteristics is presented. The conceptual explication of this paradigm includes a brief historical background, descriptive characteristics, two case examples of its theoretical principles exemplified in practice, and some suggestions for how teachers can begin their pedagogical transformation toward greater cultural responsiveness in working with students of color.

FROM CAN'T TO CAN

Many educators still believe that good teaching transcends place, people, time, and context. They contend that it has nothing to do with the class, race, gender, ethnicity, or culture of students and teachers. This attitude is manifested in the expression, "Good teachers anywhere are good teachers everywhere." Individuals who subscribe to this belief fail to realize that their standards of "goodness" in teaching and learning are culturally determined and are not the same for all ethnic groups. The structures, assumptions, substance, and operations of conventional educational enterprises are European American cultural icons (Pai et al., 2006). A case in point is the protocols of attentiveness and the emphasis placed on them in classrooms. Students are expected to pay close attention to teachers for prolonged, largely uninterrupted periods of time. Specific signs and signals have evolved that are associated with appropriate attending behaviors. These include nonverbal communication cues, such as gaze, eye contact, and body posture. When

they are not exhibited by learners at times, intervals, and durations designated by teachers, the students are judged to be uninvolved, distracted, having short attention spans, and/or engaging in off-task behaviors. All these
are "read" as obstructive to effective teaching and learning.

Many students are admonished by teachers to "Look at me when I'm
talking to you." Direct eye contact as a signal of attentiveness may be perceived as staring, a cultural taboo that causes resentment among some
Apache students (Spring, 1995), or disrespect for authority and challenge
by some Latino, Asian, and African Americans (McCarthy, Lee, Itakura, &
Muir, 2006). Other discontinuities in behavioral norms and expectations
are not isolated incidents or rare occurrences in culturally pluralistic classrooms. They happen often and on many different fronts, simply because
teachers fail to recognize, understand, or appreciate the pervasive influence
of culture on their own and their students' attitudes, values, and behaviors.

Decontextualizing teaching and learning from the ethnicities, cultures,
and experiences of students minimizes the chances that their achievement
potential will ever be fully realized. Pai and associates (2006) agree with
this assertion and make the point even more emphatically, explaining that

> how we teach, what we teach, how we relate to children and each other, what
> our goals are—these are rooted in the norms of our culture. Our society's pre-
> dominant worldview and cultural norms are so deeply ingrained in how we
> educate children that we very seldom think about the possibility that there may
> be other different but equally legitimate and effective approaches to teaching
> and learning. In a society with as much sociocultural and racial diversity as the
> United States, the lack of this wonderment about alternative ways often results
> in unequal education and social injustice. (p. 233)

Another common and paradoxical manifestation of the notion that
good teaching is devoid of cultural tenets is the frequent declaration that
"respecting the individual differences of students is really what counts in
effective teaching, not race, ethnicity, culture, or gender." Simultaneously,
too many teachers plead ignorance of Latino, African, Native, and Asian
Americans, and immigrant groups. It is inconceivable how educators can
recognize and nurture the individuality of students if they do not know
them. Ignorance of people different from us often breeds negative attitudes,
anxiety, fears, and the seductive temptation to turn them into images of
ourselves. The individuality of students is deeply entwined with their ethnic
identity and cultural socialization. Teachers need to understand very thoroughly both the relationships and the distinctions between these to avoid
compromising the very thing they are most concerned about—that is, students' individuality. Inability to make distinctions among ethnicity, culture,
and individuality increases the risk that teachers will impose their notions
on ethnically different students, insult their cultural heritages, or ignore

them entirely in the instructional process. Teachers don't seem to realize that the declaration, "It's treating students as individuals that counts," is a cultural value, or that culture, ethnicity, and individuality are not mutually exclusive. In reality, ethnicity and culture are significant filters through which one's individuality is made manifest.

To help prospective teachers enrolled in a multicultural teaching class begin to grapple with these distinctions and interrelationships, my teaching assistant and I asked them to complete a three-part project. In the first part they were to do a free-write on what race, culture, and ethnicity meant to them personally. Many divergent perspectives and much ambiguity were evident in these short essays on ethnicity and culture, but not race. Therefore, in the second phase of the activity the students were to construct a "dialogic mirror image" poem about their ethnicity, culture, and individuality. They were to ask a significant person in their lives to comment on these three dimensions of their being, and use the results to create a dialogue, in poetic form, between the significant other and themselves. After sharing the poems in small groups, the students as a whole class compiled a list of eight consensual points important for describing these three dimensions of a person's being. These points then were used as guidelines for individual students to create poster collages representing their ethnicity, culture, and individuality. The project culminated with a gallery walk of the posters displayed around the classroom, and the "artists" answering questions about their creations.

The second troubling feature of conventional educational ethos and practices with respect to improving the achievement of ethnically, racially, and culturally diverse students is the "deficit syndrome." Far too many educators attribute school failure to what students of color don't have and can't do. Some of the specific reasons given for why Navajo students do poorly in school are representative of this kind of thinking. In a school district in which 48% of the students are Navajo, and one of every four Navajos leaves before graduation, the causes of school failure identified by the administrators were all "deficits." Among them were lack of self-esteem; inadequate homes and prior preparation; poor parenting skills and low parental participation in the schooling process; lack of language development; poor academic interests, aspirations, and motivation; few opportunities for cultural enrichment; high truancy and absentee rates; and health problems, such as fetal alcohol syndrome (Deyhle, 1995). Except for fetal alcohol syndrome, similar "deficits" have been attributed to underachieving Latinos, African Americans, and some groups of Asian Americans.

Trying to teach from this "blaming the victim" and deficit mindset sounds more like a basis for "correcting or curing" than educating. Success does not emerge out of failure, weakness does not generate strength, and courage does not stem from cowardice. Instead, success begets success. Mastery of tasks at one level encourages individuals to accomplish tasks of even greater complexity (Boykin, 2002; Kim, Roehler, & Pearson, 2009;

Ormrod, 1995). High-level learning is a very high-risk venture. To pursue it with conviction, and eventual competence, requires students to have some degree of academic mastery, as well as personal confidence and courage. In other words, learning derives from a basis of strength and capability, not weakness and failure. Ormrod (1995) refers to this as having self-efficacy, meaning that "students feel more confident that they can succeed at a task . . . when they have succeeded at that task or similar ones in the past" (p. 151). Conversely, "when students meet with *consistent* failure in performing a particular task, they will have little confidence in their ability to succeed . . . in the future," and "each new failure confirms what they already 'know' about the task—they can't do it" (p. 152, emphasis in original). This "learned helplessness" and "cumulative failure" are devastating to many different kinds of achievement possibilities—academic, school attendance, personal well-being, dropout prevention, and avoidance of discipline problems.

Therefore, a very different pedagogical paradigm is needed to improve the performance of underachieving students from various ethnic groups—one that teaches *to and through* their personal and cultural strengths, their intellectual capabilities, and their prior accomplishments. Culturally responsive teaching is this kind of paradigm. It is at once a routine and a radical proposal. It is routine because it does for Native American, Latino, Asian American, African American, and low-income students what traditional instructional ideologies and actions do for middle-class European Americans. That is, it filters curriculum content and teaching strategies through their cultural frames of reference to make the content more personally meaningful and easier to master. It is radical because it makes explicit the previously implicit role of culture in teaching and learning, and it insists that educational institutions accept the legitimacy and viability of ethnic-group cultures in improving learning outcomes.

These are rather commonsensical and obvious directions to take, particularly in view of research evidence and classroom practices that demonstrate that *socioculturally centered teaching* does enhance student achievement. This is especially true when achievement measures are not restricted solely to academic indicators and standardized test scores. Most of this research and practice have focused on African Americans (e.g., Chapman, 1994; Erickson, 1987; M. Foster, 1991, 1994, 1995, 1997; Hollins, 1996; Irvine, 1990; Ladson-Billings, 1992, 1995a, 1995b, 1995c, 2009; C. Lee, 1993; C. Lee & Slaughter-Defoe, 1995) and Native Hawaiians (Au, 1993; Au & Kawakami, 1994; Boggs et al., 1985; Cazden et al., 1985; Tharp & Gallimore, 1988).

The close interactions among ethnic identity, cultural background, and student achievement (i.e., between culture and cognition) are becoming increasingly apparent. So is the transformative potential of teaching grounded in multicultural contributions, experiences, and orientations. It is these interactions, and related data, that give source and focus, power and direction to the proposal made here for a paradigmatic shift in the pedagogy used with non-middle-class, non-European American students in U.S. schools. This is a call for the widespread implementation of *culturally responsive teaching*.

If educators continue to be ignorant of, ignore, impugn, and silence the cultural orientations, values, and performance styles of ethnically different students, they will persist in imposing cultural hegemony, personal denigration, educational inequity, and academic underachievement upon them. Accepting the validity of these students' cultural socialization and prior experiences will help to reverse achievement trends. It is incumbent upon teachers, administrators, and evaluators to *deliberately create cultural continuity* in educating ethnically diverse students. To the extent that all this entails is done systematically and effectively, dilemmas like those described by Fordham and Ogbu (1986) and Fordham (1996) may decrease significantly. Academically capable African American students (or any other ethnic group of color) will feel less compelled to sabotage or camouflage their academic achievement to avoid compromising their cultural and ethnic integrity or relationships with peers from ethnic groups who are not as successful. Nor will children like Amy and Aaron (described in Chapter 1) continue to have such painful experiences and memories of school.

IDEOLOGICAL BEGINNINGS

The ideas on which culturally responsive teaching are based have been a major part of education for and about cultural diversity from its inception. Their persistence is not surprising, since multicultural education originated in the early 1970s out of concerns for the racial and ethnic inequities that were apparent in learning opportunities and outcomes, and that continue to prevail. Abrahams and Troike (1972) argued that if racial minority students are to be taught effectively, teachers "must learn wherein their cultural differences lie and . . . capitalize upon them as a resource, rather than . . . disregarding the differences . . . [and] thereby denigrating . . . the students" (p. 5). Educators also need to analyze their own cultural attitudes, assumptions, mechanisms, rules, and regulations that have made it difficult for them to teach these children successfully. This is imperative because there is "no other way of educating . . . [racial-minority] students than to provide them with a sense of dignity in the selves they bring with them into school, and to build on this by demonstrating the social and linguistic and cultural alternatives around them" (p. 6).

Chun-Hoon (1973) suggested that teaching cultural diversity in schools offers intellectual and psychological benefits for both mainstream society and Asian Americans. It helps to circumvent dangers to open, democratic communities by not homogenizing diverse peoples, and it assists Asian Americans in transcending the psychological colonization promoted by the mass media, which make them virtually invisible and totally silenced. Without these kinds of educational interventions, individuals of color and society at large are shortchanged, because "intellectual freedom can exist only in the context of psychic space, while psychic space can be created only between distinct and contrasting points of view" (Chun-Hoon, 1973, p. 139). Both "intellectual freedom" and "psychic space" are necessary to facilitate maximum academic and other forms of school achievement. Teaching students of color from their own cultural perspectives is one way to make this happen.

The strong convictions expressed by Abrahams and Troike and by Chun-Hoon about the potentials of using diverse cultural referents in teaching also permeate the thinking of educators who were instrumental in shaping the multicultural education movement. Early comments from several of them illustrate the similarity of these messages. Arciniega argued in 1975 that "educational processes are needed which enable *all* students to become positive contributors to a culturally dynamic society consistent with cultural origins" (p. 165, emphasis in original), to understand one another's cultures, and to attain higher levels of academic achievement. One of the most powerful benefits to be derived from a culturally pluralistic educational paradigm is "the creative ability to approach problem-solving activities with a built-in repertoire of bicultural perspectives. This is what is involved when we talk about eliminating incongruities between the cultural lifestyles of ethnic minority students and current schools" (p. 167). Carlson (1976) advised educators to stop trying to avoid the realities of ethnic differences and the roles they play in U.S. education. He reasoned that "since it is a fact that ethnic differences exist in important dimensions . . . it must be acknowledged that they exist and that they affect learning and academic outcomes" (p. 28).

Forbes (1973) developed this theme further as it relates to teaching Native American students. He outlined an educational agenda centered in the focal values of Native American cultures and comprehensive components of learning. Forbes suggested that cultural values, and the sociocultural, religio-philosophical, and political behavioral styles resulting from them, should be the foundation of all curricular and instructional decisions. Native American students should be taught knowledge and skills for the continued survival and development of their tribal groups or nations; personality characteristics valued by particular Native American societies; means of functioning harmoniously with nature and with other people; and ways to achieve the highest levels of mastery possible in different spheres of life. All these skills were to be developed within the context of reciprocal relationships, mutual sharing, showing hospitality toward others, self-realization, and spiritual and character development of individuals and groups. Forbes also expressed some ideas about the importance of community-building and "success" for Native American students, which later became core elements of culturally responsive teaching in general. He advised:

> The individual should develop a profound conception of the unity of life, from the fact of his belonging to a community of related people in which he owes his existence and definition of being, to the total web of natural life, to which he and his people also owe their existence. . . . The individual should develop a realization that "success" in life stems from being able to contribute to the well-being of one's people and all life. This means that the individual seeks to perfect behavior and skills which will add "beauty" to the world. To create "beauty" in actions, words, and objects is the overall objective of human beings in the world. (Forbes, 1973, p. 205)

Banks admonished teachers of racial minority students to stop conducting business as usual, or using traditional instructional conventions. Instead, they should "respect the cultural and linguistic characteristics of minority youths, and change the curriculum so that it will reflect their learning and cultural styles and greatly enhance their achievement." Moreover, "minority students should not be taught contempt for their cultures. Teachers should use elements of their cultures to help them attain the skills which they need to live alternative life styles" (J. Banks, 1974, pp. 165–166). Cuban (1972) warned educators to avoid looking for simple, one-dimensional solutions to complex challenges in educating students of color. The mere inclusion of ethnic content into school curricula would not resolve these dilemmas. Some radical changes were needed in the instructional process as well. While ethnic content has the potential to stimulate intellectual curiosity and make meaningful contact with ethnically diverse students, it should be combined with instructional strategies that emphasize inquiry, critique, and analysis, rather than the traditional preferences for rote memory and regurgitation of factual information.

Aragon (1973) shifted the focus of reform needs to teacher preparation. He argued that the reason ethnic minorities were not doing well in school was more a function of teacher limitations than student inabilities. Teachers, rather than students, were "culturally deprived" because they did not understand or value the cultural heritages of minority groups. Educational reform needed to begin by changing teacher attitudes about non-mainstream cultures and ethnic groups, and then developing skills for incorporating cultural diversity into classroom instruction. These changes would lead to improvement in student achievement.

As early as 1975, Gay identified some specific ways to develop multicultural curriculum content and some important dimensions of achievement other than basic skills and academic subjects. Her conceptions of achievement encompassed ethnic identity development, citizenship skills for pluralistic societies, knowledge of ethnic and cultural diversity, and cross-cultural interactional competence as well as academic success. She suggested that content about cultural diversity has both intrinsic and instrumental value for classroom instruction. The instrumental value includes improving interest in and motivation for learning for diverse students, relevance of school learning, and establishing linkages among school, home, and community. Specifically, Gay (1975) suggested:

> Ethnic materials should be used to teach such fundamental skills as reading, writing, calculating, and reasoning. Students can learn reading skills using materials written by and about Blacks, Mexican Americans, Italian Americans, and Jewish Americans as well as they can from reading "Dick and Jane." Ethnic literature . . . can be used to teach plot, climax, metaphor, grammatical structure, and symbolism as well as anything written by Anglo Americans. . . . ethnic literacy, reflective self-analysis, decision making, and social activism . . . are as essential for living in a culturally and ethnically pluralistic society as are knowing how to read and having a salable skill. . . . Ethnic content serves the purpose of bringing academic tasks from the realm of the alien and the abstract into the experiential frames of reference of ethnically different youth. (pp. 179–181)

QUALITATIVE ATTRIBUTES

Although called by many different names, including *culturally relevant, sensitive, centered, congruent, reflective, mediated, contextualized, synchronized*, and *responsive*, the ideas about why it is important to make classroom instruction more consistent with the cultural orientations of ethnically diverse students, and how this can be done, are virtually identical. Hereafter, they are referred to by my term of preference, *culturally responsive pedagogy*. It represents a compilation of ideas and explanations from a wide variety of scholars. Throughout this discussion, labels other than "culturally responsive" appear only when the scholars quoted directly use different terminology. The following eight descriptors comprise a "character profile" of culturally responsive teaching—that is, its distinguishing traits or qualities.

Culturally Responsive Teaching Is Validating

Culturally responsive teaching can be defined as using the cultural knowledge, prior experiences, frames of reference, and performance styles of ethnically diverse students to make learning encounters more relevant to and effective for them. It teaches *to and through* the strengths of these students. Culturally responsive teaching is the behavioral expressions of knowledge, beliefs, and values that recognize the importance of racial and cultural diversity in learning. It is contingent on a set of racial and cultural competencies amply summarized by Teel and Obidah (2008). They include seeing cultural differences as assets; creating caring learning communities where culturally different individuals and heritages are valued; using cultural knowledge of ethnically diverse cultures, families, and communities to guide curriculum development, classroom climates, instructional strategies, and relationships with students; challenging racial and cultural stereotypes, prejudices, racism, and other forms of intolerance, injustice, and oppression; being change agents for social justice and academic equity; mediating power imbalances in classrooms based on race, culture, ethnicity, and class; and accepting cultural responsiveness as essential to educational effectiveness in all areas of learning for students from all ethnic groups. Culturally responsive teaching *is validating and affirming* because

- It acknowledges the legitimacy of the cultural heritages of different ethnic groups, both as legacies that affect students' dispositions, attitudes, and approaches to learning and as worthy content to be taught in the formal curriculum.
- It builds bridges of meaningfulness between home and school experiences as well as between academic abstractions and lived sociocultural realities.
- It uses a wide variety of instructional strategies that are connected to different learning styles.
- It teaches students to know and praise their own and one another's cultural heritages.
- It incorporates multicultural information, resources, and materials in all the subjects and skills routinely taught in schools.

Thus, the study of different literary genres is replete with samples and examples from a wide variety of ethnic authors. The study of math concepts and operations (such as calculations, pattern, proportionality, statistics) in everyday life can engage students in explorations of the crafts, economics, architecture, employment patterns, population distributions, and consumer habits of different ethnic groups. Opportunities provided for students to practice and demonstrate mastery of information, concepts, and skills in language arts, social studies, and science can include a wide range of sensory stimuli (visual, tactile, auditory), and individual and group, competitive and cooperative, active participatory and sedentary activities in order to tap into the learning styles of different students. These approaches to teaching are based on the assumption that positive self-concepts, knowledge of and pride in one's own ethnic identity, and improved academic achievement are interactional. Furthermore, the cultural affiliation and understanding, knowledge, and skills needed to challenge existing social orders and power structures are desirable goals to be taught in schools.

Culturally Responsive Teaching Is Comprehensive and Inclusive

In a four-volume *Encyclopedia of Diversity in Education*, Banks (2012) and the contributing authors provide an extensive range and variety of topics, issues, groups, and perspectives that fall within the purview of educating for and about ethnic, racial, cultural, social, linguistic, and national diversity. Ladson-Billings (1992) explains that culturally responsive teachers develop intellectual, social, emotional, and political learning by using cultural resources to teach knowledge, skills, values, and attitudes. In other words, they teach the whole child. Hollins (1996) adds that education designed specifically for students of color incorporates "culturally mediated cognition, culturally appropriate social situations for learning, and culturally valued knowledge in curriculum content" (p. 13). Along with improving academic achievement, these approaches to teaching are committed to helping students of color maintain identity and connections with their ethnic groups and communities; develop a sense of community, camaraderie, and shared responsibility; and acquire an ethic of success. Expectations and skills are not taught as separate entities but are woven together into an integrated whole that permeates all curriculum content and the entire modus operandi of the classroom. Students are held accountable for one another's learning as well as their own. They are expected to internalize the value that learning is a communal, reciprocal, interdependent affair, and manifest it habitually in their expressive behaviors. These expectations and related behaviors are delivered to students in different but complementary ways, and at various levels of the educational enterprise. They involve teachers, counselors, administrators, and support staff; the classroom, the school, and the district; formal (policies, programs, and instructional practices) and informal (extracurricular activities, school image, community relations) dimensions of schooling; and teaching to and through cultural diversity across the entire school curriculum.

Ladson-Billings (2009) observed these values being exemplified in actual instruction in the elementary classrooms she studied. She saw expectations expressed, skills taught, interpersonal relations exhibited, and an overall esprit de corps operating where students were part of a collective effort designed to promote academic and cultural excellence. They functioned like members of an extended family, assisting, supporting, and encouraging one another. The entire class was expected to rise or fall together, and it was in the best interest of everyone to ensure that each individual member of the group was successful. By building an academic community of learners, the teachers responded to the sense of belonging that youths need, honored their human dignity, and promoted their individual self-concepts. Students engaged in caring relationships, shared resources, and worked closely together and with the teacher to attain common learning outcomes. Educational excellence included academic success as well as cultural competence, critical social consciousness, political activism, and responsible community membership. A strong belief in the right of students to be part of a mutually supportive group of high achievers permeated all these learning processes and outcomes (M. Foster, 1995, 1997; Irvine & Foster, 1996; Ladson-Billings, 1995a, 1995b; Lipman, 1995). Other dimensions of the inclusive nature of culturally responsive teaching include (1) addressing students across the entire educational spectrum, from preschool to graduate studies; (2) targeting both minority and majority students, but for different reasons and in different ways; and (3) developing cultural border-crossing skills for navigating different living and learning contexts for native and immigrant students.

Culturally Responsive Teaching Is Multidimensional

Multidimensional culturally responsive teaching encompasses curriculum content, learning context, classroom climate, student–teacher relationships, instructional techniques, classroom management, and performance assessments. For example, language arts, music, art, and social studies teachers may collaborate in teaching the concept of protest. It can be examined from the perspective of their respective disciplines, such as how protest against racial discrimination is expressed by different ethnic groups in poetry, song lyrics, paintings, and political actions. The students and teachers may decide to simulate time periods when social protest was very prominent, analyzing and role-playing various ethnic individuals. Within these simulations, coalition meetings can be held in which individuals from different ethnic groups express their positions on the issues of contention in various genres (e.g., rhetoric, sit-ins, songs, political slogans, visual and performing arts). Part of the challenge is for students to understand the major points made in these different forms of expression and to see whether any consensus and collaborative action can be achieved across ethnic groups. Students also can help teachers decide how their performance will be evaluated, whether by written tests, peer feedback, observations, ability to extrapolate information about ethnic protest presented in one expressive form and transfer it to another, or some combination of these.

To do this kind of teaching well requires tapping into a wide range of cultural knowledge, experiences, contributions, and perspectives. Emotions, beliefs, values, ethos, opinions, and feelings are scrutinized along with factual information and physical behaviors to make curriculum and instruction more reflective of and responsive to ethnic diversity. However, every conceivable aspect of an ethnic group's culture is not replicated in the classroom. Nor are the cultures included in the curriculum used only with students from that ethnic group. Culturally responsive pedagogy focuses on those elements of cultural socialization that most directly affect learning. It helps students clarify their ethnic values while correcting factual errors about cultural heritages. In the process of accomplishing these goals, students are held accountable for knowing, thinking, questioning, analyzing, feeling, reflecting, sharing, and acting.

Culturally Responsive Teaching Is Empowering

Because culturally responsive teaching is empowering, it enables students to be better human beings and more successful learners (Rajagopal, 2011). Empowerment translates into academic competence, personal confidence, courage, and the will to act. In other words, students have to believe they can succeed in learning tasks and be willing to pursue success relentlessly until mastery is obtained. Teachers must show students that they expect them to succeed and commit themselves to making success happen. These can be high-risk endeavors. Culturally responsive teachers are aware of the risks involved in learning and the need for students to have successes along the way to mastery. They plan accordingly and create infrastructures to support the efforts of students so that they will persevere toward high levels of academic achievement (Tomlinson & Javius, 2012). This is done by bolstering students' morale, providing resources and personal assistance, developing an ethos of achievement, and celebrating individual and collective accomplishments. However, empowerment also has some other dimensions, in addition to academic ones, that fall within the purview of culturally responsive teaching. These include cultural, social, civic, and moral development dimensions. This broader view of teaching to empower culturally diverse students is somewhat analogous to Ginsberg's (2015) notions of enhancing meaning and engendering competence. They encompass learning experiences that address the human desire to be effective at what is valued, and that benefit students as whole human beings, not just with regard to their academic achievement.

The Advancement Via Individual Determination (AVID) project is an excellent example of how this empowering process operates in practice (Mehan et al., 1996; Swanson et al., 1995). Low-achieving Latino and African American students are encouraged to enroll in Advanced Placement classes. The accompanying instructional interventions are reinforced by what Mehan and associates (1996) call a system of "social scaffolding." These are social and personal supports that buffer students as they are being taught high-level academic skills and how to take ownership of their own learning. They include students'

- explaining their problem-solving techniques to one another in small groups,
- displaying insignia (e.g., emblems, signs, pins, badges, logos) that identify them as AVID participants,
- spending time together in a space specifically designated for AVID,

- learning the "cultural capital" of school success (test-taking strategies, self-presentation techniques to fit teaching styles, study skills, note-taking, time management), and
- being mentored in academic and social skills by other students who have successfully completed the program.

Shor (1992) elucidates further on the nature and effect of empowering education. Although his explanations do not derive explicitly from concerns about improving the school achievement of marginalized students of color, they are nonetheless apropos. He characterizes empowering education as

> a critical-democratic pedagogy for self and social change. It is a student-centered program for multicultural democracy in school and society. It approaches individual growth as an active, cooperative, and social process, because the self and society create each other. . . . The goals of this pedagogy are to relate personal growth to public life, to develop strong skills, academic knowledge, habits of inquiry, and critical curiosity about society, power, inequality, and change. . . . The learning process is negotiated, requiring leadership by the teacher, and mutual teacher–student authority. In addition, . . . the empowering class does not teach students to seek self-centered gain while ignoring public welfare. (pp. 15–16)

Implicit in these conceptions of education for empowerment are ideological mandates as well as parameters for the substantive content to be taught, the instructional processes to be used, and the behavioral outcomes expected of students. Within them students are the primary source and center, subjects and outcomes, consumers and producers of knowledge. Classroom instruction embodies and unfolds within a context of what Shor (1992) calls "an agenda of values" that emphasize participatory, problem-posing, situated, multicultural, dialogic, desocializing, democratic, inquiring, interdisciplinary, and activist learning.

Culturally Responsive Teaching Is Transformative

Culturally responsive teaching defies conventions of traditional educational practices with respect to ethnic students of color. This is done in several ways. It is very explicit about respecting the cultures and experiences of African American, Native American, Latino, and Asian American students, and it uses these as worthwhile resources for teaching and learning. It recognizes the existing strengths and accomplishments of these students and then enhances them further in the instructional process. For instance, the verbal creativity that is apparent among some African Americans in informal social interactions is recognized as a storytelling gift and used to teach them writing skills. This can be done by having the students verbalize their writing assignments, recording and transcribing them, and then teaching technical writing skills using the transcriptions of their own verbalized thoughts. The tendency of many Japanese, Chinese, and Filipino students to study together in small groups can be formalized in the classroom, providing more opportunities for them and other students to participate in cooperative learning.

Culturally responsive teaching makes academic success a nonnegotiable mandate for all students and an accessible goal. It promotes the idea, and develops skills for practicing it, that students are obligated to be productive members of and render service to their respective ethnic communities as well as to the national society. It does not pit academic success and cultural affiliation against each other. Rather, academic success and cultural consciousness are developed simultaneously. Students are taught to be proud of their ethnic identities and cultural backgrounds instead of being apologetic or ashamed of them. Culturally responsive teaching also circumvents the tendency toward learned helplessness for some students of color in traditional public schools, where their achievement levels decrease the longer they remain in school (Holliday, 1985).

The features and functions of culturally responsive pedagogy meet the mandates of high-quality education for ethnically diverse students proposed by J. Banks (1991). He contends that if education is to empower marginalized groups, it must be transformative. Being transformative involves helping "students to develop the knowledge, skills, and values needed to become social critics who can make reflective decisions and implement their decisions in effective personal, social, political, and economic action" (p. 131). Students must learn to analyze the effects of inequities on different ethnic individuals and groups, have zero tolerance for these, and become change agents committed to promoting greater equality, justice, and power balances among ethnic groups. They practice these ethics and skills in different community contexts—classrooms, schools, playgrounds, neighborhoods, and society at large. Therefore, the transformative agenda of culturally responsive teaching is double-focused. One direction deals with confronting and transcending the cultural hegemony nested in much of the curriculum content and classroom instruction of traditional education. The other develops social consciousness, intellectual critique, and political and personal efficacy in students so that they can combat prejudices, racism, and other forms of oppression and exploitation.

Culturally Responsive Teaching Is Emancipatory

Culturally responsive pedagogy is *liberating* (Asante, 1991/1992; Au, 1993; Erickson, 1987; Gordon, 1993; Lipman, 1995; Pewewardy, 1994; Philips, 1983) in that it releases the intellect of students of color from the constraining manacles of mainstream canons of knowledge and ways of knowing. Central to this kind of teaching is making authentic knowledge about different ethnic groups accessible to students. The validation, information, and pride it generates are both psychologically and intellectually liberating. This freedom allows students to focus more closely and concentrate more thoroughly on academic learning tasks. The results are improved achievement of many kinds. Among them are more clear and insightful thinking; more caring, concerned, and humane interpersonal skills; better understanding of interconnections among individual, local, national, ethnic, global, and human identities; and acceptance of knowledge as something to be continuously shared, critiqued, revised, and renewed (Chapman, 1994; M. Foster, 1995; Hollins, 1996; Hollins, King, & Hayman, 1994; Ladson-Billings, 1992, 1995a, 1995b, 2009; C. Lee, 1993; C. Lee & Slaughter-Defoe, 1995).

Crichlow, Goodwin, Shakes, and Swartz (1990) provide another explanation for why education grounded in multiculturalism is emancipatory for teaching and learning. According to them, it

> utilizes an inclusive and representational framework of knowledge in which students and teachers have the capacity to produce ventilated narratives. . . . By collectively representing diverse cultures and groups as producers of knowledge, it facilitates a liberative student/teacher relationship that "opens up" the written text and oral discourse to analysis and reconstruction. (p. 103)

In other words, culturally responsive pedagogy lifts the veil of presumed absolute authority from conceptions of scholarly truth typically taught in schools. It helps students realize that no single version of "truth" is total and permanent. Nor should it be allowed to exist uncontested. Students are taught how to apply new knowledge generated by various ethnic scholars to their analyses of social histories, issues, problems, and experiences. These learning engagements encourage and enable students to find their own voices, to contextualize issues in multiple cultural perspectives, to engage in more ways of knowing and thinking, and to become more active participants in shaping their own learning (Crichlow et al., 1990; J. King & Wilson, 1990; Ladson-Billings & Henry, 1990). These revelations about knowledge and their attendant skills constitute the heart of the intellectual and cultural liberation facilitated by culturally responsive teaching. They are analogous to Freire's (1980) notions that critical consciousness and cultural emancipation are the gateways to each other. To them can be added that the freedom to be ethnically expressive removes the psychological stress associated with and psychic energy deployed in "covering up" or "containing" one's cultural inclinations. This reclaimed psychoemotional energy can be rechanneled into learning tasks, thereby improving intellectual attentiveness and academic achievement.

Cooperation, community, and connectedness are also central features of culturally responsive teaching. Students are expected to work together and are held accountable for one another's success. Mutual aid, interdependence, and reciprocity as criteria for guiding behavior replace the individualism and competitiveness that are so much a part of conventional classrooms. The goal is for all students to be winners, rather than some winning and others losing, and for students to assume responsibility for helping one another achieve to the best of their ability. In her studies of effective African American teachers, M. Foster (1989, 1994, 1995) found that these values and behaviors were demonstrated in their classrooms. The teachers were personally affiliated with and connected to the African American cultural community. They taught the students values, knowledge, and skills for participating in the larger society as well as their own cultural communities. They also drew on community patterns and norms to structure and operate their classrooms, and they incorporated the students' cultural and communication styles into instructional practices.

Culturally Responsive Teaching Is Humanistic

As such, it is ultimately concerned with the human welfare, dignity, and respect of the various individuals and groups who comprise the United States and the world. While its primary constituency is individuals and groups whose humanity has been, and often still is, denigrated by mainstream peoples, policies, and practices, others are considered benefactors as well. This means that culturally responsive teaching has value for majority and minority students, for both similar and different reasons, and that these benefits are direct and indirect, individually and collectively. A benefit for all students across ethnic, racial, and social groups is acquiring deeper and more accurate knowledge about the cultures, lives, experiences, and accomplishments of diverse peoples in U.S. society and humankind. This knowledge is needed to correct factual distortions and errors, some of which have perpetuated impressions that ethnic and racial minority groups have been on the sidelines of the construction and development of the United States when, in fact, they have been (and continue to be) active participants in and significant contributors to every phase. These contributions have not been limited to the United States.

Culturally responsive teaching helps students acquire knowledge of self and others, and the attendant values that come with having a better and more accurate understanding of who diverse people are and how they came of be as individuals, groups, and nations. It thus develops the idea that interdependence is an inherent attribute of humanity; when people know, respect, and relate to each other, all groups and individuals are better off. Culturally diverse people also need to be culturally responsive to each other. This involves: being open, receptive, and respectful to the viewpoints, thoughts, experiences, and perceptions of self and others, including a willingness to critique them; learning from and relating to members of one's own and other cultures, races, ethnicities, and social classes; exploring and honoring the differences of self and others; recognizing that people view the world and life through different lenses; and actively promoting equality and social justice (Goodman, 2013; Williams, 2017)

Culturally Responsive Teaching Is Normative and Ethical

A part of the 2011 policy statement of the American Evaluation Association (AEA) on the need for cultural competence in education evaluation captures the essence of culturally responsiveness as normative and ethical. Its message is applicable to other aspects of the educational enterprise as well. The statement said, in part,

> Evaluations cannot be culture free. Those who engage in evaluation do so from perspectives that reflect their values, their ways of viewing the world, and their culture. Culture shapes the ways in which evaluation questions are conceptualized, which in turn influence what data are collected, how the data will be collected and analyzed, and how data are interpreted. (AEA, 2011)

Undoubtedly, some features and forms of culture are always embedded in teaching and learning. This presence and its influence are not exceptional, unusual, or abnormal—given that countries create schools to assist their preservation and perpetuation by teaching youth the nations' cultural heritages, values, and behavioral expectations. Yet an apparent contradiction is commonly associated with this reality in the conception and conduct of U.S. mainstream education. One part is the denial that programs and practices routinely implemented in schools reflect *anybody's* culture; the other part is the failure of these procedures to reflect *everybody's* culture. Culturally responsive teaching corrects this misconception and exclusion by making explicit how and why mainstream educational policies and practices are shaped by and reflective of the Eurocentric culture, perspectives, and experiences of the powerful, privileged, and demographically dominant ethnic group. In other words, what is commonly thought of as cultureless mainstream U.S. schooling is, in reality, *Eurocentric culturally responsive education.*

Educational discourse about equity and social justice recommends extending similar rights and opportunities to students from other ethnic groups, especially those discriminated against, oppressed, and marginalized (that is, minority groups of color). They deserve parallel rights and opportunities like those received by majority group students. Since culture and education are inseparably linked, and different ethnic groups have different cultures, it is both the normal and the right thing to do to incorporate cultural diversity into educative processes intended for ethnically, racially, and socially diverse students. In effect, then, the recommendation is for *ethnically diverse (or minority groups') culturally responsive education*. Ideologically, this is not an unusual or exceptional proposal; rather it is simply the right, necessary, and honorable thing to do given the customary or regular purposes, designs, functions, and deliveries of education in U.S. schools

CULTURALLY RESPONSIVE TEACHING PERSONIFIED

Two stories are presented here to illustrate how the attributes of culturally responsive teaching operate in practice. Neither alone is a complete portrait. Each provides a capsule view of one or a few dimensions of this style of teaching. Together, they come closer to creating a complete picture. It is helpful to consider them both separately and together in visualizing the move of culturally responsive teaching from theory to practice. Doing so is consistent with a major feature of the paradigm itself—that is, the importance of dealing simultaneously with general issues and particular cases in teaching African American, Latino American, Asian American, and Native American underachieving students. The stories deal with critiquing and symboling.

Critiquing

The setting is a teacher education class. The students are studying the philosophical foundations of culturally responsive pedagogy. The principle under analysis is "K–12 education is a free, public, and equal access enterprise for all students in the United States." Students are expected to engage in critical, analytical, reflective, and transformative thinking about the issues, ideas, and assertions they encounter. The instructor invites them to "think about" what this principle means within the context of ethnic and cultural diversity. The students respond to this invitation as follows:

> *Student 1*: What does "educational freedom" really mean for Native American students? If freedom means the right to learn without undue obstructions, how much freedom did they have when early missionary educators took them away from their families and communities, and forced them to "look" like European Americans, accept their religion, and ascribe to their values? Where is the freedom in this? And what about today? How unrestricted are the opportunities for Native Americans to learn, practice, and celebrate their cultural heritages in modern schools?
>
> *Student 2*: I'm concerned about Filipinos and other immigrant or first-generation, U.S.-born students who may not be fluent in English. What does freedom to learn and the right to equal educational opportunities mean for them? Where is the equality when teachers

in schools don't speak Tagalog, Thai, Cambodian, Spanish, or some other languages, and these students have to try to function in a language system that is alien to them? Do they have opportunities for educational mastery comparable to children who are competent in the language of instruction? People may say, as they often do, that "these children are now in the United States and they must learn to speak English." I'm not opposed to this, but I am still left wondering, What about the possibility of loss of language? How might this loss affect students' cultural affiliation and sense of identity? How does having to learn in an unfamiliar language affect achievement level? What is the connection between "freedom to learn" and "equalizing opportunities"? Where do bi- or multilingualism and cultural diversity fit into the equal opportunity equation?

Student 3: It seems to me that public education as the "great equalizer" really meant Anglicizing all students from non-European origins. I think schools have done much more to homogenize culturally diverse students than to make the educational experience a true amalgamation of contributions from all the different ethnic groups and cultures that make up the United States. If this had happened years ago, there would be no grounds for current appeals for ethnic studies, women's studies, multicultural education, and bilingualism to be included in school programs.

Student 4: I don't think there is much equality in never seeing your own ethnic group's contributions represented in textbooks, or having them depicted in biased and stereotypical ways. Imagine what African American students must have felt being told over and over that they are descendants of slaves, chattel, unintelligent buffoons, who were treated almost like animals. Or Native Americans being portrayed as uncivilized heathens and murdering savages. Or, for that matter, the ego inflation potential of the notion of "manifest destiny" for European Americans. These seem to me far, far removed from educational freedom and equality. They sound more like "psychological and cultural imperialism." Can students from diverse ethnic backgrounds perform to the best of their intellectual ability under these conditions? I think not.

Student 5: The whole idea is a hustle, a myth. Education has never been free and equal in this country. Children who have the least have always had to make the greatest sacrifices, pay the highest prices, and get the lowest benefits. Look at the desegregation experiment. Who were on those buses going where? Look at the condition of city schools compared with suburban ones. Where are the best teachers assigned? The best buildings and materials? The best programs? Where is the most money for education being spent? If true equality had existed from the beginning, we would not have the kind of achievement disparities we currently have.

Student 6: I think we need to take a closer look at who came up with these ideas, and what did *they* mean by them. Their conceptions probably were quite different from ours. If we knew this, we would be better able to make better sense of them conceptually, and decide whether to continue to accept them on blind faith or to revise them so that they are more appropriate for today's realities. I guess I am proposing here that we do what one of my other professors means by "positionality analyses."

Student 7: (*Laughing in response to the comments made by Student 6*) Girl, *we* know who *they* be. *They* most definitely ain't *us*. If *we* had made glib statements like that, *you* wouldn't be wondering what *we* meant, 'cause *we* would have told you explicitly and up front what was what.

Several other students: Uh-huh (*and other signs of endorsement of Student 7's comments*).

Instructor: This is good. You are questioning, critiquing, deconstructing, evoking a variety of points of reference, seeking out specific cultural grounding of applicability of general pedagogical ideas. Continue to "think about."

Symboling

The kindergarten class Lois teaches comprises immigrant and first-generation U.S. students from many countries, as well as a mixture of different native ethnic groups. Consequently, there is a lot of ethnic, racial, cultural, and linguistic diversity present. Looking into her classroom provides a glimpse of how culturally responsive teaching can be accomplished through the use of visual imagery and symbols. The school year has been in session for a little more than 4 months. Lois has established some clear routines with her students for embracing and celebrating one another's cultural diversity. As we take a quick tour of this classroom, we witness the following:

Attached to the entrance door is a huge welcome sign brightly decorated with the children's own art. The sign reads "Welcome to Our Academic Home." This message is accompanied by a group photograph of the members of the class and "welcome" in different languages (Spanish, Japanese, German, French, various U.S. dialects, etc.). Stepping inside the room, one is bombarded with an incredibly rich and wide range of ethnically and culturally diverse images. Maps of the world and the United States are prominently displayed on the front wall, under the heading "We Come from Many Places." Strings connect different parts of the world to the United States. They represent the countries of origin of the families and/or ethnic groups of the students in the class. A display in another corner of the room is labeled "Our Many Different Faces." It includes a montage of close-up facial photographs of the members of the class. These are surrounded by pictures of adults from different ethnic groups in ceremonial dress for various rites of passage (e.g., marriage, adulthood, baptism) and occupations (clergy, doctors, construction workers, dancers).

The room's "Reading Center" is a prototype of multicultural children's literature—a culturally responsive librarian's dream! Many different ethnic groups, topics, and literary types are included. Books, poems, comics, song lyrics, posters, magazines, and newspapers beckon the students to discover and read about the histories, families, myths, folktales, travels, troubles, triumphs, experiences, and daily lives of a wide variety of Asian, African, European, Middle Eastern, Latino, Native American, and Pacific Islander groups and individuals. Audio- and videotapes, DVDs, and CDs are liberally sprinkled among these items, including music, books on tape, storytelling, and television programs. Others look like student productions. In the midst of all these media materials, a video camera and a tape recorder stand in readiness for use. Another curious item captures the attention. It is a pile of tattered, well-used photo albums. These resources invite students to explore the past, to reflect on the present, to imagine the future.

The extent and quality of this collection of materials prompt the question, "Lois, how did you come by all of this?" She credits parents for the accomplishment. At the beginning of the academic year, she gets the parents of the students to make a contractual agreement to donate two books or other forms of media to the class collection. One of these books is to be about their own ethnic group and the other about some other group, and the books should be ones that they either use with their children at home or would like their children to learn about in school. The families are given credit for their contributions by having each item stamped "Donated by _____." When the collection becomes too large to be easily accommodated in the classroom, or the students "outgrow it," some of the items are donated to the school library or community agencies. This is a class project, with the students deciding which items they will keep and which they will give away. Only one stipulation is attached to the gifts. The recipients must agree to acknowledge the donors with the credit line "Donated by the Kindergarten Class of Room _____ at _____ Elementary School."

Lois is a strong believer in "representative ethnic imagery." She is very conscientious about ensuring that the visual depictions of ethnic groups and individuals in her classroom are accurate, authentic, and pluralistic. She explains that she wants students to readily recognize who the ethnic visuals represent rather than having to wonder what they are supposed to be. She also wants the students to be exposed to a wide variety of images within and among groups to avoid ethnic stereotyping. To assist the students with this identification, all of the pictures of ethnic individuals displayed throughout the classroom include personal and ethnic identities. These read, "My name is

_____; I am _____ [ethnic group]." Lois justifies this protocol by saying simply, "Students need to know that it's OK to recognize other people's ethnicity and to expect others to acknowledge theirs. Ethnicity is an important feature of our personal identities."

Two other permanent culturally pluralistic displays exist in this stimulating, intellectually invigorating, and culturally diverse classroom. One is entitled "We Can Do Many Things." Here are images, samples, and symbols of the contributions and accomplishments of different ethnic groups, such as crafts, arts, science, technology, medicine, and music. They include children and adults of different ages, famous and common folks, profound achievements and regular, daily occurrences. For example, there is one photograph of three students who have been especially helpful to classmates from other ethnic groups and another of six great-grandparents who are 75 years of age or older. The master tape representing different ethnic groups' contributions to music includes excerpts from operas, jazz, rap, spirituals, movie soundtracks, country, pop, and children's songs. The names of other individuals are accompanied by miniature samples of their contributions. There is the athlete with a little basketball, but it's refreshing to see that she is a member of the 1996 U.S. Olympic team, and Venus and Serena are there with their little tennis rackets. Some kernels of corn appear next to Native Americans, and a little make-believe heart operation kit is connected to African Americans.

The other permanent display is a multicultural alphabet streamer. Different ethnic groups and contributions are associated with each of the letters in the alphabet. For example, "Jamaican" and "Japanese American," as well as "jazz," appear under the letter *J*, and "lasso" and "Latino" appear under *L*.

The tour of this classroom also offers a glimpse into how Lois incorporates the ethnically diverse symbols into her formal instruction. Small groups of students are working on different skills. As Lois circulates among them, activities in the reading and math groups are riveting. It is Carlos's turn to select the book to be read for storytime. He chooses one about a Japanese American family. Lois asks him to tell the group why he made this choice. Carlos explains that he had seen Yukiko (a classmate) at McDonald's over the weekend, and he wanted to do something nice for her by reading "her" book. He also said he saw some other people like those in the book, and he wanted to know more about them because they don't look like people where he lives.

Before Lois begins to read the story, she tells the students a little about this ethnic group, like the proper name, its country of origin, some symbol of its culture (they eat a lot of different kinds of noodles), and where large numbers of its members live in the United States. She asks if anyone can find Japan and California on the maps. She helps the group locate these places. As the students return to their places and settle down for the story, we hear Lois asking, "If we wanted to go to the places where there are a lot of Japanese Americans, how would we get there? Who would like to go?" Several hands pop up quickly at the thought of such an imagined journey. Incidentally (maybe not!), the book Carlos chose to read is about a little boy taking his first airplane ride with his parents to go visit his grandparents, who live far away. Once this "context setting" is completed, Lois proceeds through a dialogic reading of the book. She pauses frequently to probe the students' understanding of associated meaning prompted by the narrative text, to examine their feelings, and to predict upcoming developments in the story.

In math, the students are practicing bilingual counting. They already know how to count in English and to associate the number with the appropriate word. On this occasion, they are learning to count to 10 in Spanish. Under Lois's supervision, the students go through an oral exercise using the Spanish words for the numbers. One student points to the words as the others say them aloud. After some giggling and gentle consternation about their pronunciation, Lois compliments the students' efforts, while sympathizing with their concerns and reminding them that people who are learning a language do not sound like those who are native speakers. Tamika reminds everyone that Rosita speaks Spanish at home and announces, with conviction, "I bet she can say those words real good." Lois asks Rosita if she would like to give it a try. After a little encouragement from other members of the group, she agrees. Lois tells the group that Rosita is now the teacher and the other students are to practice saying the words as she does. After this is done, the students are asked to sit quietly, listen, and observe another native Spanish speaker counting. This is presented in the form of a videotape, using a motif similar to *Sesame Street*.

Symbols are powerful conveyers of meaning, as Lois's classroom attests. Her students are inundated with positive images of and interactions with ethnic and cultural diversity. They learn about and celebrate their own and one another's identities and abilities, while simultaneously being invited to extend the boundaries of their knowledge and skills. All of this occurs in a warm, supportive, affirming, and illuminating classroom climate, in which the use of culturally diverse referents in teaching and learning is habitual. This type of instruction is very conducive to high levels of many different kinds of achievement for students from all ethnic groups.

ROLES AND RESPONSIBILITIES OF TEACHERS

Implicit in these mandates, attributes, and personifications of culturally responsive pedagogy are some key roles and responsibilities for teachers. Diamond and Moore (1995) have organized them into three major categories: *cultural organizers, cultural mediators,* and *orchestrators of social contexts for learning*. Gentemann and Whitehead (1983) combined these tasks into the single role of *cultural broker*. As *cultural organizers*, teachers must understand how culture operates in daily classroom dynamics, create learning atmospheres that radiate cultural and ethnic diversity, and facilitate high academic achievement for all students. Opportunities must be provided for students from different ethnic backgrounds to have free personal and cultural expression so that their voices and experiences can be incorporated into teaching and learning processes on a regular basis. These accommodations require the use of various culturally centered ways of knowing, thinking, speaking, feeling, and behaving.

As *cultural mediators*, teachers provide opportunities for students to engage in critical dialogue about conflicts among cultures and to analyze inconsistencies between mainstream cultural ideals/realities and those of different cultural systems. They help students clarify their ethnic identities, honor other cultures, develop positive cross-ethnic and cross-cultural relationships, and avoid perpetuating prejudices, stereotypes, and racism. The goal is to create communities of culturally diverse learners who celebrate and affirm one another and work collaboratively for their mutual success, where empowerment replaces powerlessness and oppression.

As *orchestrators of social contexts* for learning, teachers must recognize the important influence culture has on learning and make teaching processes compatible with the sociocultural contexts and frames of reference of ethnically diverse students. They also help students translate their cultural competencies into school learning resources. Spring's (1995) definition of a cultural frame of reference can be helpful in achieving these teaching–learning synchronizations. He defines it as "those elements that cause a cultural group to interpret the world . . . in a particular manner" (p. 5), or the filter through which impressions of, experiences with, and knowledge of the outside world are ordered and made meaningful.

CONCLUSION

To recapitulate, culturally responsive pedagogy simultaneously develops, along with academic achievement, social consciousness and critique, cultural affirmation, competence, and exchange; community-building and personal connections; individual self-worth and abilities; and an ethic of caring. It uses ways of knowing, understanding, and representing various ethnic and cultural groups in teaching academic subjects, processes, and skills. It cultivates cooperation, collaboration, reciprocity, and mutual responsibility for learning among students and between students and teachers. It incorporates high-status, accurate cultural knowledge about different ethnic groups into all subjects and skills taught.

Culturally responsive teachers have unequivocal faith in the human dignity and intellectual capabilities of their students. They view learning as having intellectual, academic, personal, social, ethical, and political dimensions, all of which are developed in concert with one another. They scaffold instruction and build bridges between the cultural experiences of ethnically diverse students and the curriculum content of academic subjects to facilitate higher levels of learning. These teachers use a variety of approaches to all aspects of the educational process, including curriculum, instruction, and assessment, embedded in multicultural contexts. They consider critical and reciprocal dialogue and participatory engagement as central to the acquisition and demonstration of learning. Academic success is a nonnegotiable goal for everyone and the responsibility of all participants in the teaching–learning process. In their interpersonal relationships with students, culturally responsive teachers are warm, supportive, personable, enthusiastic, understanding, and flexible (Shade, Kelly, & Oberg, 1997), yet rigorous in demanding high-quality academic performance from both themselves and their students.

Thus, culturally responsive pedagogy validates, facilitates, liberates, and empowers ethnically diverse students by simultaneously cultivating their cultural integrity, individual abilities, and academic success. It is anchored on four foundational pillars of practice—teacher attitudes and expectations, cultural communication in the classroom, culturally diverse content in the curriculum, and culturally congruent instructional strategies.

If the potential of culturally responsive pedagogy is to be realized, then widespread instructional reform is needed, as well as major changes in the professional development, accountability, and assessment of teaching personnel. It requires teachers who have (1) thorough *knowledge* about the cultural values, learning styles, historical legacies, contributions, and achievements of different ethnic groups; (2) the *courage* to stop blaming the victims of school failure and to admit that something is seriously wrong with existing educational systems; (3) the *will* to confront prevailing educational canons and convictions, and to rethink traditional assumptions of cultural universality and/or neutrality in teaching and learning; (4) the *skills* to act productively in translating knowledge and sensitivity about cultural diversity into pedagogical practices; and (5) the *tenacity* to relentlessly pursue comprehensive and high-level performance for children who currently are underachieving in schools. Hopefully, then, schooling experiences like those of Amy and Aaron, described in Chapter 1, will be historical memories, not everyday occurrences, and their children will have more successful stories to tell about their learning encounters and academic achievement.

PRACTICE POSSIBILITIES

Educators need to be explicit and transparent about the ethics and ideologies that anchor their culturally responsive practices. These can be presented as policy statements—declarations of commitment to desirable and intended courses of action. They indicate general behavioral expectations and directions that mirror values and beliefs. Thus, policy statements about culturally responsive teaching and learning can be considered as the first phase in converting ideological claims and beliefs into behaviors. Novice culturally responsive teachers may be uncertain as to how to craft a policy statement for related teaching and learning. Excerpts from six different policy statements about diversity and equity in education are presented below as starters to help teachers develop their own policies of envisioned expectations, classroom dynamics, and behavioral outcomes. To make this exercise more meaningful, the readers may consider their beliefs about cultural, ethnic, and racial diversity and education that they began to clarify after engaging with Chapter 1, and make them the focus of their policy statements.

Excerpts from Sample Policy Statements on Cultural Diversity and Equity in Education

"Culturally competent teaching is increasingly necessary if educators are to connect with their students. And to connect, educators need to acquire new teaching strategies that match students' ways of understanding and interacting with the world. These approaches will help increase student performance as measured by grades and tests, enhance student access to more rigorous curriculum, and advance student attainment to high school completion and beyond. Culturally competent teaching, in other words, will play a major role in closing the achievement gaps that exist among race, gender, language, and social class groups. . . . As we learn about the cultures that students bring to school . . . and how to connect these experiences and cultures to what educators teach, we must also reflect on the culture that permeates schools and how it advantages or disadvantages certain students." (National Educational Association; nea.org)

"We all want children to grow up in a world free from bias and discrimination, to reach for their dreams and feel that whatever they want to accomplish in life is possible. We want them to feel loved and included and never to experience the pain of rejection or exclusion. But the reality is that we do live in a world in which racism and other forms of bias continue to affect us. Discrimination hurts and leaves scars that can last a lifetime, affecting goals, ambitions, life choices, and feelings of self-worth. . . . How can we best prepare children to meet the challenges and reap the benefits of the increasingly diverse world they will inherit? We can raise children to celebrate and value diversity and to be proud of themselves and their family traditions. We can teach children to respect and value people regardless of the color of their skin, their physical abilities, or the language they speak." (Association for Supervision and Curriculum Development; Rajagopal, 2011, p. 3).

"Teachers in a multicultural society need to hold an attitude of respect for cultural differences, know the cultural resources their students bring to class, and be skilled at tapping students' cultural resources in the teaching-learning process. While these attributes have always been needed, organizing schools to provide culturally responsive teaching may be a powerful tool in advancing the goals of No Child Left Behind [and its successor, Every Student Succeeds Act—ESSA]. By reducing alienation of minority students and improving their motivation to learn, students and teachers work more effectively together to improve achievement. . . . Cultural understandings (political, historical, literary, technological, financial, medical, legal, and others) . . . [should not be] transmitted accidentally, but by design." (ERIC Clearinghouse on Rural Education and Small Schools; ericdigests.org/2005-1/teaching.htm).

"Multicultural education values cultural pluralism; . . . rejects the view that schools should seek to melt away cultural differences; . . . affirms that schools should [promote] the cultural enrichment of all children and youth through . . . the preservation and extension of cultural alternatives; . . . recognizes cultural diversity as a fact of life in American society; and affirms that . . . it is a valuable resource that should be preserved and extended.

To endorse cultural pluralism is to endorse the principle that there is no one model American. . . . It is to see [differences among the nation's citizens] as a positive force in the continuing development of a society which professes a wholesome respect for the intrinsic worth of every individual. Cultural pluralism is more than a temporary accommodation to placate racial and ethnic minorities. It is a concept that aims toward a heightened sense of being and of wholeness of the entire society based on the unique strength of each of its parts." (American Association of Colleges of Teacher Education, 1973)

"PTAs [Parent/Teacher Associations] everywhere must understand and embrace the uniqueness of all individuals, appreciating that each contributes a diversity of views, experiences, cultural heritage/ traditions, skills/abilities, values and preferences. When PTAs respect differences yet acknowledge shared commonalities uniting their communities, and then develop meaningful priorities based upon their knowledge, they genuinely represent their communities [and] gain strength and effectiveness. . . . The recognition of diversity within organizations is valuing differences and similarities in people through actions and accountability. These differences and similarities include age, ethnicity, language and culture, economic status, educational background, gender, geographic location, marital status, mental ability, national origin, organizational position and tenure, parental status, physical ability, political philosophy, race, religion, sexual orientation, and work experience." (National PTA; pta.org/members/content.cfm?ItemNumber=4483)

"We believe that the responsibility for student success is broadly shared by District staff, administrators, instructors, communities and families. We are focused on closing the opportunity gap and creating learning communities that provide support and academic enrichment programs for all students. Additionally, we believe that it is the right of every student to have an equitable educational experience within the Seattle Public School District.

The concept of educational equity goes beyond formal equality—where all students are treated the same—to fostering a barrier-free environment where all students, regardless of their race, class or other personal characteristics such as creed, color, religion, ancestry, national origin, age, economic status, gender, sexual orientation including gender expression or identity, pregnancy status, marital status, physical appearance, the presence of any sensory, mental or physical disability, or the use of a trained dog guide or service animal by a person with a disability, have the opportunity to benefit equally. This means differentiating resource allocation, within budgetary limitations, to meet the needs of students who need more supports and opportunities to succeed academically. A student whose history and heritage are appreciated and celebrated will learn better and be more successful than if that student is forced to overcome a cultural barrier." (Seattle Public Schools; seattleschools.org/cms/One.aspx?portalId=627&pageId=15155).

CHAPTER 3

The Power of Culturally Responsive Caring

"Caring teachers expect (highly), relate (genuinely), and facilitate (relentlessly)."

She routinely begins her classes with declarations to the effect that "I believe in collaborative teaching and successful learning for all students. This course is designed to ensure these. We are going to work hard; we are going to have fun doing it; and we are going to do it together. I am very good at what I do, and since you are going to be working in partnership with me, you are going to be good, too. In fact, as my students, you have no choice but to be good." These declarations are at once a promise and a mandate, an ethic and an action. They set in motion an esprit de corps, an ambiance, an instructional style, a set of expectations that are directed toward high-level student achievement. The message intended for students is, "I have faith in your ability to learn, I care about the quality of your learning, and I commit myself to making sure that you will learn."

INTRODUCTION

These declarations set the tone and contours for the discussions of caring presented in this chapter. They also meet criteria proposed by Webb, Wilson, Corbett, and Mordecai (1993), Gilligan (1982), and Obidah, Jackson-Minot, Monroe, and Williams (2004) that caring is a value, an ethic, and a moral imperative that moves "self-determination into social responsibility and uses knowledge and strategic thinking to decide how to act in the best interests of others. Caring binds individuals to their society, to their communities, and to each other" (Webb et al., pp. 33–34). The interest of concern here is improved achievement, and the "community" is underachieving students of color and their teachers.

Caring is one of those things that most educators agree is important in working effectively with students, but they are hard-pressed to characterize it in actual practice, or to put a functional face on it that goes beyond feelings of empathy and emotional attachment. Feelings are important, and as Garza, Alejandro, Blythe, and Fite (2014, p. 1) explain, "Educators cannot disregard the significance of the affective domain in developing successful academic students." But culturally responsive caring as an essential part of the educational process is much more. It focuses on caring *for* instead of *about* the personal well-being and academic success of ethnically diverse students, with a clear understanding that the two are interrelated. While *caring about* conveys feelings of concern for one's state of being, *caring for* is active engagement in doing something to positively affect it. Thus, it encompasses a combination of concern, compassion, commitment, responsibility, and action. Eaker-Rich and Van Galen (1996) support shifting the focus of caring in culturally diverse educational environments and interactions from "about" to "for." For them "caring about" is attitude, while "caring for" is practice or action; "caring about" is emotionality without intentionality or purposeful action, whereas "caring for" is deliberate and purposeful action plus emotionality. The intended outcomes of "caring for" are improved competence, agency, autonomy, efficacy, and empowerment in both the role functions (student) and quality of being (person) of ethnically, racially, and culturally diverse students in school settings and elsewhere.

Mayeroff (1971) explained many years ago that caring for others requires being able to understand them and their worlds from insider perspectives; being able to understand what they are striving to be, and what they require to grow. A caring person is emotionally invested in the cared for, as well as *acts* in their best interest. Murdock and Miller (2003) suggested that beyond interpersonal and emotional support and respect, caring includes behaviors that demonstrate commitment to making student learning happen. Tarlow (1996) elaborated further by including within this commitment specific actions such as teachers being (1) present and prepared to assist students—that is, being accessible, approachable, welcoming, and dependable; (2) cognizant of and attending to students' moods and emotions; (3) promoting and facilitating student success by supporting, modeling, empowering, and fostering self-confidence and self-reliance; and (4) using any and all means or methods necessary to facilitate student learning

By *seeing, respecting,* and *assisting* diverse students from their own vantage points, teachers can better help them grow academically, culturally, and psycho-emotionally. They do not impose their desires on students (or expect them to be imitations of themselves), or assume the absence of capability and responsibility. Rather, caring teachers "explicitly reject deficit-based thinking and embrace the belief that students from culturally diverse backgrounds are [or can be] capable learners" (Bartell 2011, p. 60). They seek to know what these strengths or assets are, and to act relevantly and responsively to facilitate students' further growth and development. Thus, the essence of "caring for" is assisting others to be better in who and what they currently are. To genuinely and effectively care, in culturally responsive ways, for marginalized students of color, it is imperative for teachers to *know* before they can and should *do*. As Owens and Ennis (2007, p. 402) explained,

> Caring teachers assume responsibility for initiating action in their relationships with students based on the best judgment and anticipation of what students need . . . accumulate information about individual students in order to recognize, interpret, and attend to behavioral changes . . . constantly reassess needs, make decisions, and institute new ways and means of caring . . . [and] devote serious attention to thinking about, negotiating, and carrying out actions in the best interest of their students.

This kind of caring is one of the major pillars of culturally responsive teaching for ethnically diverse students. It is manifested in the form of teacher attitudes, expectations, and behaviors about students' human value, intellectual capability, and performance responsibilities. Teachers demonstrate caring for children as *students* and as *people*. This is expressed in concern for their psychoemotional well-being and academic success, personal morality and social actions, obligations and celebrations, communality and individuality, and unique cultural connections and universal human bonds. In other words, teachers who really care for students honor their humanity, hold them in high esteem, expect high performance from them, and use strategies to fulfill their expectations. They also model academic, social, personal, and moral behaviors and values for students to emulate. Students, in kind, feel obligated to be worthy of being so honored. They rise to the occasion by producing high levels of performance of many different kinds—academic, social, moral, and cultural.

Conventional wisdom, personal experience, theoretical assertions, research findings, and best practices attest to the positive effects of genuine teacher caring on student achievement (Bartell, 2011; Eaker-Rich & Van Galen, 1996; Garza, Alejandro, Blythe, & Fite, 2014). They suggest that the heart of the educational process is the interactions that occur between teachers and students. These interactions are major determinants of the quality of education children receive (U.S. Civil Rights Commission, 1973). Unfortunately, all teachers do not have positive attitudes toward, expectations of, and interactions with students of color. Racial biases, ethnic stereotyping, cultural ethnocentrism, and personal rejections cause teachers who don't care to devalue, demean, and even fear some African American, Latino American, Native American, and Asian American students in their classrooms. These devaluations are accompanied by low or negative expectations about their intellectual abilities, which have deleterious effects on student achievement (Good & Brophy, 2003; Harry, 1992; Oakes, 1985; Papageorge & Gershenson, 2016).

While most teachers are not blatant racists, many probably are cultural hegemonists. They expect all students to behave according to the school's cultural standards of normality. When students of color fail to comply, the teachers find them unlovable, problematic, and difficult to honor or embrace without equivocation. Rather than build on what the students have in order to make their learning easier and better, the teachers want to correct and compensate for their "cultural deprivations." Culturally responsive teaching should first confront existing instructional presumptions and practices before it proceeds with the more regenerative aspects of reform. It should simultaneously deconstruct and transform, critique and create, correct and direct, reflect and project. Therefore, four key topics related to pedagogical caring are examined in this chapter. They are (1) characterizing caring; (2) predominant teacher attitudes and expectations toward ethnically and culturally different students; (3) effects of teacher expectations on instructional behaviors and students' achievement; and (4) becoming more culturally competent in classroom caring. Ideas and insights gleaned from research, theory, and practice are woven together throughout these discussions. These are further augmented by personal experiences of teachers who cared and students who were cared for.

OVERVIEW OF CARING CHARACTERISTICS

Caring interpersonal relationships are characterized by patience, persistence, facilitation, validation, and empowerment for the participants. Uncaring ones are distinguished by impatience, intolerance, dictations, and control. The power of these kinds of relationships in instructional effectiveness is expressed in a variety of ways by educators, but invariably the message is the same. Teachers who genuinely care for students generate higher levels of all kinds of success than those who do not. They have high performance expectations and will settle for nothing less than high achievement. Failure is simply unacceptable to them, so they work tenaciously to see that success for students happens.

Several scholars make distinctions between two kinds of caring, calling one *aesthetic* and the other *authentic*, and emphasizing the latter. Valenzuela (1999) associates *authentic caring* with the Mexican American cultural concept of *educación,* which views sustained, trusting, respectful, and reciprocal relationships between students and teachers as cornerstones of all learning. Siddle-Walker and Snarey (2004) add morality and social justice dimensions to caring in their proposals for effectively teaching African American students. They extend the meaning of caring beyond personal humaneness and instructional judiciousness to embrace rightness, fairness, and equality. They suggest that in educating students of color,

> teachers who seek to be caring, but refuse to care in a culturally appropriate way are still unfair. Likewise, teachers who seek to do justice, without attention

to caring for the individual, are still hurtful. Overall . . . fairness and carefulness are each empty without the other. (pp. 144–145)

Ayers (2004) and Thompson (2004) create powerful profiles of caring teachers that focus more on the quality of personal being and relationship with students than on the proficiency of instructional methodology. Ayers's profile includes teachers making explicit the vital linkages between personal fulfillment and social and moral responsibility, between self and students, between being and doing; viewing their roles as opening doors, minds, and possibilities for students; combining consciousness with conduct; constantly seeking ways to know their students, for themselves and their students to be in better personal and pedagogical relationship; and building bridges between the known and the unknown. Caring teachers also place students at the center of the learning orbit and turn their personal interests and strengths into opportunities for academic success. They are persistent in their instructional efforts; they do not give up on students, or diminish or belittle their possibilities, even when it appears that everyone else does. At the "being" level these teachers

> seek an authentic meeting of subject . . . that acknowledges the humanity, intentions, agendas, maps, dreams, desires, hopes, fears, loves, and pains of each—and in that meeting they try to model what they themselves value. They work to make explicit . . . their own values, priorities, and stories, because they know that these things will impact teaching practices. (pp. 10–11)

The "doing" dimension of caring, according to Ayers (2004), involves

> assum[ing] a deep capacity in students, an intelligence (often obscure, sometimes buried), as well as a wide range of hopes, dreams, and aspirations; . . . acknowledg[ing] . . . obstacles to understand and overcome, deficiencies to repair, injustices to correct. With this as a base the teacher creates an environment . . . that has multiple entry points for learning and multiple pathways to success. (p. 11)

Thompson (2004) suggests that teachers who demonstrate culturally responsive caring

> *see* the world that the children see, and . . . help them develop thoughtful responses both to cultural difference and to racism. . . . It is a responsibility owed to White students as well [as students of color]. We cannot prepare children to make a better world if we cannot see *this* world for what it is. . . . To truly *see* White, Black, and Brown relations in a raced and racist society—both as they are and as they might be—we must care enough to abandon our willed ignorance and political blindness. (p. 37, emphasis in original)

The world we must care enough to see and help students transform is both inside and outside schools and classrooms. An essential part of this seeing and caring is teachers and students not trying to be color-blind, but routinely employing what Thompson (2004) calls "colortalk." Thus, caring-based education has academic, civic, social, personal, cultural, political, moral, and transformative learning goals and behavioral dimensions.

Together the ideas of these scholars (and many others), along with practitioners at Central Park East School in New York (Bensman, 2000) and El Puente Academy for Peace and Justice (De Jesus, 2003), two highly successful institutions for ethnically, racially, socially, and culturally diverse students, create a *functional profile of culturally responsive caring-in-action*. It includes teachers

- providing spaces and relationships where ethnically diverse students feel recognized, respected, valued, seen, and heard;
- fostering warmth, intimacy, unity, continuity, safety, and security;
- knowing culturally diverse students thoroughly, personally and academically;
- cultivating a sense of kindredness and reciprocal responsibility among culturally diverse students;
- responding to the needs of diverse students for friendship, self-esteem, autonomy, self-knowledge, social competence, personal identity, intellectual growth, and academic achievement;
- being academic, social, and personal confidantes, advocates, resources, and facilitators for culturally diverse students;
- acquiring knowledge of and accepting responsibility for culturally diverse students that go beyond the school day and its organizational parameters;
- helping students of color develop a critical consciousness of who they are, their values and beliefs, and what they are capable of becoming;
- enabling ethnically and culturally diverse students to be open and flexible in expressing their thoughts, feelings, and emotions, as well as being receptive to new ideas and information;
- building confidence, courage, courtesy, compassion, and competence among students from different ethnicities and cultural communities;
- being academically demanding but personally supportive and encouraging;
- allowing for the active assertion of student interest and curiosity;
- creating habits of inquiry, a sense of criticalness, and a moral edit among students to care for self and others;
- treating everyone with equal *human* worth;
- acknowledging social, cultural, ethnic, racial, linguistic, and individual differences among students without pejorative judgments;

- promoting cultural, communal, and political integrity and solidarity among different ethnic and cultural groups;
- dealing directly and bluntly with the vicissitudes of racism, and the unequal distribution of power and privilege among diverse groups;
- preparing students to understand and deal realistically with social realities (what is), along with possibilities for transformation (what can be);
- teaching ethnic, racial, and cultural knowledge, identity, and pride;
- providing intellectually challenging and personally relevant learning experiences for socially, ethnically, racially, and culturally diverse students.

These elements of caring require confronting some long-held educational conventions and assumptions. Teachers can no longer be dispassionate and distant in their relationships with students, or attempt to avoid controversial topics and harsh social realities. Nor can they focus on students' limitations instead of their strengths and potentialities. They can no longer find solace in beliefs that their teaching responsibilities are limited to academic skills and textbook content. These are important, but genuine caring involves much more. Teachers must be *involved* in students' lives; accept that teaching and learning are holistic enterprises; and teach knowledge and skills students need to negotiate in the society that currently exists, and to construct a better one for the future. They must always place students in learning environments and relationships that radiate unequivocal belief in their promise and possibility. They cannot wait until students are teenagers in middle and high school, or young adults in college, before beginning this pursuit. Justice-based and authentic caring must be an integral part of all students' entire educational careers, starting when they begin their formal learning journeys in kindergarten classrooms, and continuing thereafter.

ATTRIBUTES OF CARING IN DETAIL

Four of the attributes of caring summarized above are discussed in more detail here to show how they operate in practice. These elaborations are presented for two reasons. One is to demonstrate how caring is nuanced when placed within the context of culturally responsive teaching. The other reason is to further clarify the idea that caring as an approach to teaching is more action-driven than emotionally centered. Emotions (such as concern and compassion) are important anchors and catalysts in culturally responsive teaching, but they lack the behavioral embodiments that are fundamental to facilitating student learning. Thus, all attributes of caring must be translated into actions for them to be of much value in improving the achievement of culturally diverse students. Loving children should not become a proxy for teaching them. Focusing on the action dimensions of caring will prevent this from happening.

Caring Is Attending to Person and Performance

Research by Mercado (1993), Walker-Dalhouse and Dalhouse (2006), and Case and Hemmings (2005) illustrates how beliefs about students shape the instructional behaviors of teachers. These beliefs are formed early in a teacher's career (even before and during preservice initiation) and are extremely difficult to change. Mercado is convinced that the academic accomplishments of the middle school Latino students with whom she and her colleagues worked resulted as much from the ethic of caring the instructional team demonstrated as from promoting literacy and academic learning. A common theme that emerged from interviews with African American students about their experiences in segregated schools was the interpersonal caring of the teachers and administrators. They remembered these schools as "homes away from home," places where they were nourished, supported, protected, encouraged, and held accountable on personal, academic, and civic levels. The students recalled their teachers having faith and conviction in the students' abilities; being demanding, yet supportive and encouraging; and insisting that students have high aspirations to be the best that they could be. The teachers and administrators did not limit their interactions with students to merely teaching subject matter. They demonstrated concerns for the students' emotional, physical, economic, and interpersonal conditions as well. In so doing, they created a *consistently* caring climate that made students more willing to participate in learning tasks and accomplish higher levels of achievement (F. Jones, 1981; Siddle-Walker, 1993; Sowell, 1976). Consequently, "the psychological and tangible attention revealed in the interpersonal relationships . . . contributed strongly to [the students'] academic and life success" (Siddle-Walker, 1993, p. 75).

Results of research in more contemporary classroom settings (M. Foster, 1994, 1995, 1997; Howard, 1998; Ladson-Billings, 2009) indicate that effective teachers of African American students demonstrate the same kind of beliefs, attitudes, and behaviors. M. Foster (1995) found that these teachers "concern themselves with the complete development of children" (p. 576) and model multidimensional caring in their personal behaviors and instructional practices. They are explicit about teaching and modeling personal values that they view as foundations of learning and living. These include patience, persistence, and responsibility to self and others. They also foster the development of student interests, aspirations, self-confidence, and leadership skills. Their instructional practices incorporate skills for self-determination in a society that perpetuates institutional racism while proclaiming equality for all (M. Foster, 1995). In other words, culturally responsive caring teachers cultivate efficacy and agency in ethnically diverse students.

Caring Is Action-Provoking

As these descriptions indicate, there is much more to interpersonal caring than teachers merely exhibiting feelings of kindness, gentleness, and benevolence toward students, or expressing some generalized sentiments of concern or love. Caring is grounded in attitudes but must exemplify actions. In fact, attitudes without concomitant competence-producing actions constitute a form of academic neglect. When teachers fail to demand accountability for high-level performance from ethnically diverse students under the guise that "I don't want to put them on the spot in case they don't know how to do the academic tasks," they really are abdicating their pedagogical responsibilities. This is not real caring. A most effective way to be uncaring and unconcerned is to tolerate and/or facilitate academic apathy, disengagement, and failure. To avoid doing this, teachers must thoroughly understand their own and their students' perspectives and experiences (Noddings, 1992, 1996). Learning is contingent on their cultural inclusion and confirmation in the educational process. The attitude that drives this kind of caring "accepts, embraces, and leads upward. It questions, it responds, it sympathizes, it challenges, it delights" (1996, p. 29). Thus, caring in education has dimensions of emotion, intellect, faith, ethics, action, and accountability.

These attributes are further refined by Tarlow's (1996) study of caring in families, schools, and voluntary agencies. She describes caring as an ongoing, action-driven process of "supportive, affective, and instrumental interchanges embedded in reciprocal relationships" (p. 81). A caring person is sensitive to, emotionally invested in, and attentive to the needs and interests of others. Caring has elements of both reciprocity and community because the "caring process . . . confronts the person cared for, calling out to him or her to reciprocate . . . [and is] an acknowledgment of and respect for the meaning of the group" (pp. 80–81).

Ladson-Billings (2009) found evidence of caring similar to that described by Tarlow, in her study of successful teachers of African American students in an urban elementary school. When she asked the students in one of the classes what they liked about it, they responded, "the teacher." In elaborating on this choice, they explained that she listened to and respected them, encouraged them to express their opinions, and was friendly toward them both in and out of class. The African American students in Hanley's (1998) study of knowledge construction through dramatic preparation and performance spoke with similar convictions. They unanimously and enthusiastically declared that good teachers are respectful of them, care about them, provide choices, and are tenacious in their efforts to make the information taught more understandable for them. Conversely, poor teachers are those who don't listen, don't care, are too hurried and harried to persist in facilitating learning, and are unconcerned about the general well-being of students. These are very revealing comments. Many students feel a need to have a personal connection with teachers. It is symbolized by the practice among Asian-ancestry college students (especially recent immigrants) of referring to professors to whom they closely relate as their "academic mothers and fathers." This relationship happens when teachers acknowledge their presence, honor their intellect, respect them as human beings, and make them feel like they are important. In other words, they empower students by legitimizing their "voice" and visibility.

Caring Prompts Effort and Achievement

Personal anecdotes of individuals in many walks of life, reflecting on their school days, provide variations on the same theme of the importance of teacher caring to student achievement as reported by Ladson-Billings, Foster, Hanley, and other researchers. Long after leaving school, they remember fondly, and in graphic detail, those teachers who cared, and painfully those who did not. They may not recall the content these teachers taught, but their human impact is indelibly imprinted in their minds. Forty years after high school, Johnnie is still fond of telling how much he feared, but respected, his 11th-grade social studies teacher because "she was hard on you, and you couldn't run no game on her. She knew everybody, and she didn't make you feel stupid even if you didn't know the answers. That's why I made sure I got her homework done even when I wouldn't do it for anybody else." This teacher and Johnnie had the same last name, and she would often tell him, "People with our name always do the best they possibly can." This connection further motivated him to exert greater efforts on learning tasks than he otherwise might have. His cousin Betty, who attended the same school at the same time as Johnnie, has very different memories of another teacher. Many years later, this teacher's name still provokes negative responses from her, such as, "That dog. I hated him. He was evil, and didn't care nothing about nobody. You couldn't talk to him. He thought he was bad, and acted like he was a king or something. All he wanted to do was flunk everybody."

These stories add other important dimensions to caring—or the lack thereof—as a necessary feature of effective teaching for students of color. In addition to respecting the cultural backgrounds, ethnic identity, and humanity of students, teachers who care hold them accountable for high-quality academic, social, and personal performance, and ensure that this happens. They are demanding but facilitative, supportive and accessible, both personally and professionally. And they do not have to be of the same ethnic groups as students to do this well. Some of the teachers in Ladson-Billings's study were European Americans. So were Johnnie's and Betty's teachers, while they are African Americans. St. John (1971) described these kinds of teachers as "child-oriented" and "interpersonally competent." This orientation was expressed in the instructional interactions as kindliness, adaptability, and optimism. These teachers also had little faith in test scores as good indicators of student ability; they used other indicators of success. They produced greater gains in reading improvement, attendance, and classroom conduct for African American students than teachers who were more task-oriented.

Kleinfeld (1973, 1974, 1975) found similar characteristics among the effective teachers of rural Athabascan Eskimo and Native American students she studied. They created classroom climates of emotional warmth; consistently and clearly demanded high-quality academic performance; spent time establishing positive interpersonal relationships between themselves and students, and among students; extended their relationships with and caring for students beyond the classroom; and communicated with students through nonverbal cues, such as smiles, gentle touch, teasing, and establishing a "kinesthetic feeling of closeness" (1975, p. 322). Academic demands were complemented with emotional support and facilitative instruction; a coaching and cajoling rather than a dictatorial style of teaching was used; and reciprocal responsibility for learning was developed. This emotionally warm, personally caring, and interpersonally supportive instructional style had a substantial positive effect on the intellectual performance of students, as indicated by increases in verbal participation in classroom discourse and improved levels of cognitive understanding. Kleinfeld attributes the success of the teachers in her studies to two major factors: (1) congruency between their styles of teaching and the cultural socialization and interactional styles of rural Eskimo and Indian students, and (2) the instructional style of the teachers, not their ethnic-group membership. She, along with later researchers (Bondy & Ross, 2008; Ware, 2006), calls these kinds of teachers "warm demanders."

Vida Hall's success with African American students in an urban high school further validates Kleinfeld's conclusions and illuminates the power of caring in teaching. Vida was one of those "warm demanders," as confirmed by former students and her own personal reflections. She achieved levels of performance with students other teachers thought were almost unteachable, long before multicultural education or culturally responsive teaching was initiated. A high school social studies teacher, she taught students in the full spectrum of "A," "R," and "L" (advanced, regular, and low-achieving) classes. She was notorious for "taking no stuff" and for being "hard but fair." Vida insisted that students in her classes perform to the best of their abilities and consistently conveyed to them that they were capable of doing much more than they imagined. She refused to accept unfounded excuses for incomplete or undone work. "I can't do" was taboo in her classes.

When this explanation was offered by students, Vida responded with gentle but firm insistence, "Of course you can. Now, tell me what I need to do to help you out. Do I need to review the instructions or go over the content again? Do you and I need to spend some time one-on-one together? Do you need to work with another student in class? Or do I need to let the coach know that you are spending so much time with athletics that it's interfering with you completing your social studies assignments?" These were not threats or intimidations; rather, Vida was proposing different avenues to take to remove obstacles to student achievement. And she stood in readiness to aggressively pursue any or all of them to ensure that her students were successful. When they succeeded she applauded them, while simultaneously cajoling them to reach for even higher levels of achievement.

Concern for and commitment to helping students be the best they could did not end at the threshold of Vida Hall's classroom door. She held similar high expectations for their social behavior and personal decorum outside the classroom. Many times she diffused potentially confrontational situations among her students in the hallways and cafeteria by stepping up to them and saying, "Aren't you in my _____-period class? Using fisticuffs to solve problems is beneath your dignity. You are better than that." Nor was she above setting some boundaries for her students about how young men and women were expected to "carry themselves." A frequent comment of hers, upon observing behaviors in students she considered socially unacceptable, was, "Young men [or women] don't behave that way." In more than 40 years of teaching, she recalled few occasions when students became belligerent and hostile in the face of these chastisements.

Both Vida and her former students attribute this incredible record to the fact that the students knew what she expected of them and that she was "in their corner." As their teacher, she deserved to be honored as she honored them. They worked hard to meet her expectations. The result was reciprocal and complementary achievement for the students and the teacher. The achievements were of many different kinds. Some of her greatest successes did not get the best grades in class, or the highest scores on standardized tests, but they shone brightly in other ways—by demonstrating good manners, being respectful, having high positive self-concepts, persisting in their academic efforts, and even improving their school attendance.

Caring Is Multidimensional Responsiveness

Obviously, then, caring is a multidimensional process. Its essence, according to Berman (1994), is *responsiveness*, which is contingent on understanding people in context. Speaking more specifically about teaching, Bowers and Flinders (1990) suggest that being responsive is understanding cultural influences on the behaviors and mental ecology of the classroom, and using this knowledge to guide actions. Hence, for teachers to do culturally responsive teaching, they must be competent in cultural diversity and committed to its inclusion in the educational process. Sullivan (1974) made this observation over 40 years ago when he proposed that it is not enough for teachers merely to like ethnically different students. Instead, "the challenge is to effectively teach them within a cultural context" (p. 56). To do this well, they must have *commitment, competence, confidence,* and *content* about *cultural pluralism.* These five Cs (as Sullivan called them) are as applicable today as they were then.

Within the context of culturally responsive teaching, these various aspects of caring, when acted upon, place teachers in an ethical, emotional, and academic partnership with ethnically diverse students. This partnership is anchored in respect, honor, integrity, resource-sharing, and a deep belief in the possibility of transcendence, that is, an unequivocal belief that marginalized students not only can but *will* improve their school achievement under the tutelage of competent and committed teachers who *act* to ensure that this happens. Marva Collins (1992) developed a "creed of caring" that helped to guide her interactions with students at the Westside Preparatory School in Chicago, which she founded. Called "Into My Heart," it is a personification of the ethics and power of caring. Part of it is quoted to illustrate how general principles of caring are manifested in Collins's personal creed of behavior with students. It may inspire readers to give expression to their own commitment to caring for culturally diverse students. Collins says, in part:

> I discourage being average. I believe all of my students can learn if I do not teach them too thoroughly that they cannot . . .
>
> I will teach them to think for themselves . . .
>
> I will teach them to have the fortitude to build their own bridges . . . to be courageous enough not to run from everything that is difficult, but to face unflinchingly the problems of life and see them . . . as challenges of living.
>
> I shall encourage them to never rest on their past laurels . . . to [know] that excellence is a non-ending process, and that they will never arrive in the land of the done.
>
> I [believe] . . . my students will become like stars that will light the world with excellence, with self-determination, with pride. (pp. 260–262)

EXPECTATION TRENDS AND EFFECTS

Because expectations and beliefs, along with their concomitant behaviors, are critical components of caring in classroom instruction, teachers need to know what they are and how they affect teaching and learning. They also need to understand that expectations are manifestations of beliefs or assumptions. As such, expectations and caring are closely interconnected. In fact, negative beliefs about students of color that generate low expectations for their personal and academic performance constitute *uncaring,* since caring for these students means believing in and facilitating the maximal development of their potentials. Some of the recurrent trends in teacher expectations are summarized here, but a thorough analysis of them is beyond the scope of this book. Hopefully the information provided will entice (and guide) prospective and practicing teachers to carefully study their own and others' expectations, and make changes where necessary to achieve more congruity with the criteria for culturally responsive caring for ethnically diverse students discussed earlier.

By virtue of being unilaterally in charge of classrooms, teachers control and monopolize academic interactions. They decide who will participate in what, when, where, and how (Goodlad, 1984; Kohn, 1999; Kozol, 2007). These decisions, and their consequences, are direct reflections of teacher attitudes and expectations, and whether they care for students. As Page (1987) explains, teachers' "perceptions are potent and assume a life of their own: they furnish a rationale for curriculum decisions and thereby provide the conditions for their own re-creation" (p. 77). Students who are perceived positively are advantaged in instructional interactions. Those who are viewed negatively or skeptically are disadvantaged, often to the extent of total exclusion from participation in substantive academic interactions. These observations are affirmed by the Education Commission of the States in its 2012 review of research on the interactions between teacher beliefs and expectations and student academic performance:

> The expectations a teacher sets for an individual student can significantly affect the student's performance. Teacher expectations can, for example, be based on student characteristics such as race, ethnicity, and family income level, or indicators of past performance. These expectations can cause teachers to differentiate their behavior towards individual students, such that [they] set lower expectations for some students, provide briefer (or no) feedback on student errors—and less positive feedback after correct answers—and grant students less time to answer questions. All of these teacher behaviors, when repeated day in, day out, over the course of a year or multiple school years, can negatively impact student performance and ultimately perpetuate the achievement gaps that plague the American education system. (Education Commission of the States, 2012)

Influences on Expectations

Disparities in classroom interactional opportunities are affected by many different variables, most of which have little to do with the intellectual abilities of students. Of utmost importance among them are racial identity, gender, ethnicity, social class, and home language. Even physical appearance can affect teacher expectations of students. In their meta-analysis of pertinent research, Ritts, Patterson, and Tubbs (1992) found that physically attractive students received higher grades, higher scores on standardized tests, and more academic assistance; they also were considered to be more friendly, attentive, popular, and outgoing, as well as better behaved. The effects were greater on social than academic skills assessments. However, distinctions among these domains of schooling are not clearly demarcated, and effects in one can easily influence the other.

Culture also influences student and teacher expectations, as well as how they engage in classroom interactions (Boggs et al., 1985; Boykin, 1994; Pai et al., 2006; Philips, 1983; Shinn, 1972). Social etiquette and rules of decorum about appropriate interactions with teachers and other students can hinder participation for some students and expedite it for others. Consider the following three examples of impediments. Immigrant students from traditional cultures with a rather rigid hierarchical social structure enter U.S. classrooms. They have been socialized to be passive and deferential in interactions with teachers and to treat teachers with respect at all times. U.S. education promotes a more fluid relationship, with students encouraged to engage actively with teachers. The immigrant students may appear to be overly quiet, accommodating, and reluctant to engage freely in instructional interactions, despite repeated invitations and enticements. In reality, these expectations may be very disconcerting and baffling to students new to the United States. They also may be overwhelmed by the gregarious style of other students. After their efforts to pull them into the interactions continue to fail, teachers stop trying and leave these students alone. Their learning opportunities and achievement potential are thus minimized because of a mismatch in cultural expectations about student–teacher relationships and interactional styles.

Another compelling example of cultural intrusion on quality interactions between students and teachers involves African Americans. The energy and exuberance with which highly culturally affiliated African Americans invest their interactions (what Boykin, 1986, calls "verve") is troublesome to many teachers. They may view this behavior as impulsive, overemotional, and out of control. Consequently, much of their classroom interaction with these students is of a disciplinary and controlling manner, directed toward getting them to "settle down" and "spend more time on task." The students often are reprimanded for undesirable behaviors more than they are instructed on academic learning. High-level achievement is seriously constrained under these conditions. These kinds of assumptions are counterproductive to teachers genuinely caring for ethnically, racially, and culturally diverse students.

The third example is a personal one, more positive, and more conducive to caring teaching. Its cultural nuances are subtle, but the achievement results are somewhat more explicit. The situation occurred while I was an undergraduate. The instructor of one of my classes had the reputation of being a "grill king." He would select a student to probe and keep him or her on the "hot seat" for the entire duration of the class, except for an occasional diversion here and there to allow others to make brief comments about something the targeted student had said. He told us repeatedly that he wanted us to think about what we were learning rather than merely regurgitating textbook information. His teaching style lived up to this expectation, for he probed, cajoled, and, with rapid-fire questions, challenged us to critique, analyze, interpret, explain, reflect, and extend. Today we probably would say he was a liberator, transformative, or constructivist teacher because he was committed to freeing our minds from the restraints of rote memory and helping us become articulate critical thinkers. At the time, I was too consumed with dread at the prospect of my time in the hot seat to think about this. I agonized for the greater portion of the semester about what would happen when I was called on. Would I be able to think? What did thinking mean? Would I be able to say anything? Would I sound and look stupid?

This was the first time I could recall any teacher demanding that I think and refusing to let me abdicate this responsibility. I needed to be prepared, so I tried to practice thinking beforehand. But I was trying so hard to get myself to think that I couldn't think about anything but thinking. I was traumatized as much by how the professor went about probing and prompting students as by the prospect of this thing called thinking. If two or three other students could have joined me in the spotlight, they would have deflected some of the attention away from me and made everything easier to bear. But that was not to be. This professor believed firmly in students being "lone riders" through the thinking journey. Finally, my time came. I don't know what I said, but evidently I did *think*. I met the professor's expectations. The conversation flowed rather smoothly, and he complimented me on being so well prepared and clear in my explanations. I was in a state of shock that I had pulled it off—I actually had *thought* about something. This was a teacher who genuinely cared about his students' learning; he insisted that we think; he held us accountable for demonstrating critical thinking; and he was diligent in his facilitation of this skill development.

Holliday (1981, 1985) used a "transactional, theoretical perspective" to explain how disjunctures in the frames of reference of schools and the home cultures of ethnically different students can generate negative teacher expectations, which in turn can compromise academic achievement. She contends that social competence is a prerequisite for academic opportunities; that is, students must be able to comply with the procedural or managerial rules and regulations that surround the educational process before they are granted permission to participate in its substantive dimensions. An example of this is denying students an opportunity to read or participate in storytime because they did not raise their hands or wait for permission from the teacher before speaking out. In this situation, the speaking out is a management issue, while reading is an academic opportunity. The punishment does not fit the crime.

Over time, negative teacher attitudes and low expectations can produce "learned helplessness" among African American students (Holliday, 1981, 1985). If told too often for too long that their contributions and competencies are not worthy, students will stop being intellectually engaged in classroom interactions. Philips (1983) found similar results for Native Americans at the Warms Spring Reservation in Oregon. Many of the achievement problems of the students in her study derived from the interactional and procedural protocols of teaching rather than the substantive content of what was taught. How teachers talked to students interfered more with their academic engagement than did the topics being discussed. Biklen and Pollard (1993), Klein (1982), the AAUW Report (1995), and Grossman and Grossman (1994) found that teacher expectations are affected also by the gender of students, leading to disparities in the quality of learning opportunities provided to males and females. Gender interactions, then, are other crucial "sites" where academic achievement is either facilitated or obfuscated.

Good and Brophy (2003) have compiled one of the most comprehensive summaries of research on teacher expectations and related classroom behaviors, and the effects of these on student achievement. In an earlier edition of this review, these authors noted that "many students in most classrooms are not reaching their potential because their teachers do not expect much from them and are satisfied with poor or mediocre performance when they could obtain something better" (1978, p. 70). Goodlad's (1984) national study of schooling, and Oakes's (1985, 1986a, 1986b) analyses of the effects of tracking on learning opportunities, substantiate these findings and provide additional explanations.

An important ingredient for achievement that is missing in most of the classrooms Goodlad observed was the kind of engagement in learning activities demanded by Vida Hall's, Marva Collins's, and my undergraduate college professor's ethos of caring described earlier in this chapter. Goodlad (1984) characterized the classes as being void of intellectual energy and excitement, lacking "exuberance, joy, laughter, abrasiveness, praise and corrective support of individual student performance, punitive teacher behavior, or high interpersonal tension" (p. 112). Students' interactions with one another and with teachers were characterized by "neutrality . . . considerable passivity . . . and emotional flatness" (p. 113). If the teachers had cared deeply for their students, they would have been more conscientious about making their teaching exciting, stimulating, and captivating, realizing that motivation and engagement have positive effects on the persistence of learning efforts and the quality of learning outcomes (Ginsberg, 2015).

Another problem in effectively teaching students of color is the discrepancy in the quality of instruction that occurs in high- and low-curriculum tracks, as revealed by Oakes. This is particularly troubling because of the overrepresentation of Latino Americans, African Americans, and Native Americans in low-track curriculum options and low-status classes. These "emotionally flat" and "intellectually dull" classrooms result from instructional strategies that emphasize teacher dominance, didactic and large-group teaching, a narrow range of learning activities, workbook assignments, and very little interactive dialogue (Good & Brophy, 2003; Goodlad, 1984; Kohn, 1999; Kozol, 1991). They violate elements of caring that focus on helping culturally diverse students develop personal and academic competence, agency, autonomy, and empowerment.

Persistent Trends in Expectations

Four other specific trends in teacher expectations have emerged from research and practice that support and explicate these general conclusions. They offer some important insights for caring for ethnically diverse students in ways that improve their school achievement. First, *teacher expectations significantly influence the quality of learning opportunities provided to students*. Values do not necessarily translate to behavior, but beliefs and expectations do. Many teachers profess to believe that all students can learn, but they do not expect some of them to do so (Good & Brophy, 2003). Therefore, they allow students to sit in their classes daily without insisting on and assisting their engagement in the instructional process. This behavior is justified with statements to the effect that "you can't teach these students because they are not motivated to learn."

Teachers may believe in gender and ethnic equity yet do nothing to promote it in their classroom instruction. This lack of action is justified on the basis of not having enough time and the issues not being appropriate to the subjects they teach. They may bemoan the inadequacies of textbooks' information on the contributions of women and ethnic groups, but continue to use them without providing any compensating material. Some teachers are adamant about the individual differences of students, while simultaneously declaring intentions to treat all of them the same and disavowing the importance of ethnicity, culture, and gender in pedagogical decisionmaking.

If teachers *expect* students to be high or low achievers, they will act in ways that cause this to happen. Good and Brophy (2003) refer to this as the "self-fulfilling prophecy effect." This concept was popularized by Rosenthal and Jacobson in their 1968 landmark study (*Pygmalion in the Classroom*) of teacher expectations on the learning opportunities and outcomes of students. It means that teachers' assumptions about students' intellect and behavior affect how they treat the students in instructional interactions. Over time, these treatments strongly influence the extent of student learning.

The mere existence of a generalized expectation does not lead to the self-fulfilling prophecy, nor is it something that happens incidentally or instantaneously. It requires *focused beliefs* and *deliberate and systematic action* over a period of time. According to Good and Brophy (2003), six steps are involved in the creation of a self-fulfilling prophecy: (1) the teacher expects specific achievement from specific students; (2) the teacher behaves toward students according to these expectations; (3) the teacher's behaviors convey to the students what is expected of them and are consistent over time; (4) students internalize teachers' expectations, and these affect their self-concepts, achievement motivations, levels of aspiration, classroom conduct, and interactions with teachers; (5) over time students' behavior becomes more and more attuned to what the teacher expects, unless they engage in deliberate resistance and change strategies; and (6) ultimately, students' academic achievement and other outcome measures are affected.

A second trend indicates that *teacher expectations about students are affected by factors that have no basis in fact and may persist even in the face of contrary evidence.* And teachers are "more likely to be affected by information leading to negative expectations than information leading to positive expectations" (Good & Brophy, 1994, p. 95). This is true even when the information derives from prejudices or stereotypes. Thus, some students are more susceptible to negative teacher expectations than others because of biases associated with the ethnic groups to which they belong, and it is very unlikely that teachers will care for them in constructive ways.

Two of my friends tell a gripping story about a situation involving their teenage son that illustrates this point. Randy is African American, a high school senior well over 6 feet tall. He routinely meets four of his male friends (also African Americans) in the schoolyard at the end of the day to visit and socialize as they wait to be picked up by their parents. One day, while waiting for him to end his visit, Randy's father watched a teacher approach the group. He threatened the young men with disciplinary action and police intervention if they didn't disperse immediately. The students were baffled by these reactions since they were simply visiting, not doing anything wrong. In fact, all were good students and had no disciplinary records, and some were on the school's basketball team. What prompted this teacher's reactions? Randy's parents were convinced the motivation was negative attitudes toward and expectations about African American young men. The father speculated, "In his mind, that teacher saw potential gang members and a bunch of Black troublemakers. He didn't bother to see that these guys were team members and were exhibiting good behavior. They weren't even being loud or rambunctious."

Assumptions about connections among the intellectual capability, ethnicity, gender, and classroom adjustment of students attest to the tenacity of teacher expectations, even in the face of contrary evidence. This third trend was partially demonstrated by Rosenthal and Jacobson (1968) in their study, *Pygmalion in the Classroom.* They told teachers some students had higher IQs than others when, in reality, there were no differences. The teachers expected the students with the supposed higher IQs to perform better in reading, and they did. In situations where teachers expect boys and girls to perform equally well, they do, even though there are real ability differences between them. Palardy (1969) found this to be the case with reading achievement. Some teachers expect the schoolwork of students who speak African

American and working-class dialects to be of lower quality than that of students who speak mainstream Standard English, and they tend to assess their performance accordingly (Bowie & Bond, 1994; Grossman & Grossman, 1994). Many teachers assume that Japanese, Chinese, and Korean American youth will always be studious, high-achieving, and obedient students. They are surprised to find that some individuals from these groups have serious learning difficulties (S. Lee, 2009; Osajama, 1991; Wong, 1980, 1995). Conversely, many teachers expect Latino and African Americans to be low achievers and disciplinary problems. When they demonstrate high performance, teachers who expected otherwise are awed or suspicious, or declare them to be "overachievers." Some African American professionals lament being complimented with "you speak so well" or "you are so articulate" in circumstances in which coherent speech is a normal occurrence, not deserving of special note. Their response, in thought if not deed, is, "Why is my competence surprising? What did you expect?" Unfortunately, many of these and other negative expectations about students of color and poverty still exist in education today.

Traditionally, teachers have different expectations of and interactions with male and female students. Race, ethnicity, social class, and culture have profound influences on these attitudes and behaviors. When the unit of analysis is exclusively females, European Americans tend to have better-quality personal and pedagogical interactions with teachers than do Latinas, Native Americans, African Americans, and Asian Americans (Grossman & Grossman, 1994; Masland, 1994; Streitmatter, 1994). Research patterns in the past indicated that males had more interactions with teachers regardless of type—academic or social, intellectual or managerial, positive or negative, verbal or nonverbal, student- or teacher-initiated. As Streitmatter (1994) explained, males dominated classrooms "both in the positive sense as learners, as well as in a negative sense as behavioral problems" (p. 128). The magnitude of this ratio varied somewhat by the nature of the communication. It tended to be greatest in disciplinary encounters and smallest in instructional interactions. European American males also initiated more contacts with teachers; received more encouragement, feedback, and praise; were cued, prompted, and probed more; were rewarded more for academic accomplishments; were asked more complex, abstract, and open-ended questions; and were taught how to become independent thinkers and problem-solvers. By comparison, European American females initiated less; received less academic encouragement, praise, prompts, rewards, and expectations for success; had less total interactional time with teachers; were asked more questions that required descriptive and concrete answers; and were rewarded more for social than for academic accomplishments (AAUW, 1995; Good & Brophy, 2003; Sadker & Sadker, 1982; E. Scott & McCollum, 1993).

There are some recent indications that gender disparities in learning opportunities are dissipating somewhat, at least for European American females. Some accounts suggest that the gains are so significant that European American males are now the ones suffering from gender inequities. Still other researchers and scholars say these conclusions are overly optimistic; that traditional gender patterns of learning opportunities and outcomes are persistent in complex analyses; and that inequities are more qualitative than quantitative, and include more variables than grades and test scores. These deeper patterns of inequity become apparent when gender trends in achievement are examined in relation to race, ethnicity, social class, power, and privilege. For example, they indicate that both male and female students of color (including high-achieving Asian Americans) continue to receive less varied, supportive, and intellectually challenging learning opportunities than European Americans.

Females from other ethnic groups are severely underresearched. Were it not for literary publications in which various females of color are the protagonists, they would be almost totally invisible in educational scholarship and discourse. A recent book edited by Larke, Webb-Hasan, and Young (2017) begins to fill this void. Their contributing authors offer different perspectives on both the problems and possibilities of African American girls of different ages in U. S. society and schools. The insights that can be gleaned from these analyses and narratives are very valuable for educators creating ways to be more culturally responsive in caring for these students.

Therefore, in designing interventions to counteract persistent patterns of gender-based teacher attitudes, beliefs, and expectations, gender equity cannot be considered in isolation from race, ethnicity, class, and culture (Ginsberg, Shapiro, & Brown, 2004; Lopez, 2003; Sadker, Sadker, & Zittleman, 2009; Skelton, Francis, & Smulyan, 2006). A wide variety of strategies are available for being gender-responsive in classroom interactions and relationships. They usually include teachers learning how to *see* gender inequities in classroom dynamics; being critically reflective of their own gender-related instructional behaviors; understanding the intersections among gender, race, class, ethnicity, and culture; and being deliberate about engaging in transformative gender-equity actions (Sadker et al., 2009). Bravo (2007) proposes a specific five-step action strategy called DREAM that illustrates these emphases. In involves *D*aring to imagine a world of justice, equity, and caring across genders, ethnicities, and cultures; *R*eaching out to others of a like mind for support and camaraderie; *E*ducating oneself on theory, research, and practice about equity issues; *A*cting on many levels to make a difference; and *M*ultiplying initiatives and efforts by joining groups and organizations engaged in similar pursuits. This could easily be a paradigm for practice on other issues essential to culturally responsive teaching as well as gender equity.

Often classroom discipline also correlates strongly with student ethnicity, gender, and intellectuality, and is a problematic location for demonstrating caring. The challenge is how teachers can demonstrate caring for diverse students in the midst of disciplining them. For instance, some teachers expect students of color and males to create more classroom management problems than European Americans and females, and for reverse correlations to exist between discipline and achievement (McFadden, Marsh, Price, & Hwang, 1992; Mickelson, 1990). Low achievers are expected to create more disciplinary problems than high achievers. English language learners may be perceived as more intellectually challenging students because of their limited English abilities. Sheets (1995b) found that high school teachers sometimes behaved in ways that instigated disciplinary problems for African Americans and, to a lesser degree, Latinos. This was done by not allowing students to explain potentially problematic situations, giving them harsher punishments, and punishing them for some infractions that were ignored when committed by European and Asian Americans. Denying students the opportunity to defend themselves or tell their versions of conflictual situations is a violation of their basic human rights, and highly inconsistent with the ethics of caring.

The achievement effects of these expectations and behaviors are exponential. As teachers' expectations and caring for higher achievers increase, so does student performance, while the performance of low achievers becomes even worse when teachers have low expectations and are uncaring. This cycle is particularly dangerous for low achievers because it can "confirm or deepen the students' sense of hopelessness and cause them to fail even where they could have succeeded under different circumstances" (Good & Brophy, 1994, p. 114). It explains what Holliday (1985) means by "learned helplessness," and it accounts for the cumulative failure that some students experience in schools.

Finally, *teachers' expectations and sense of professional efficacy are interrelated*. Teaching efficacy stems from the beliefs teachers hold about their abilities to positively affect the academic achievement of particular students. It influences teachers' choices of activities, the efforts they exhibit, and their persistence in the face of obstacles and challenging situations (Ashton & Webb, 1986; Miller, 1991; Pang & Sablan, 1995). Teachers who have low performance expectations for students do not feel very efficacious about their own competencies with those students. But they attribute student failure to lack of intellectual ability and poor home environments rather than to the quality of their teaching. They also spend little time helping low-achieving students and may even ignore them entirely. These behaviors are justified on the basis that the students are unteachable anyway. Ashton and Webb (1986) explain further that teachers with a low sense of efficacy avoid learning activities they feel incapable of facilitating and are consumed with thoughts about their own inadequacies or limitations. These preoccupations create stress, divert attention from instructional to personal issues, and further reduce teaching effectiveness.

Conversely, teachers with strong self-confidence and feelings of efficacy in their teaching abilities have high achievement expectations for students. Furthermore, their teaching behaviors reflect these expectations. They use a greater variety and range of teaching strategies; hold themselves and their teaching accountable for the achievement of difficult learners; are more persistent in their efforts to facilitate learning; and spend more time in planning for instruction and professional development activities to improve their teaching quality than low-efficacy teachers (Miller, 1991). Teachers with a strong sense of efficacy also "choose challenging activities and are motivated to try harder when obstacles confront them. They become engrossed in the teaching situation itself, are not easily diverted, and experience pride in their accomplishments when the work is done" (Ashton & Webb, 1986, p. 3).

A significant number of the pre- and inservice teachers in the Pang and Sablan (1995) study felt they could not effectively teach or influence African American students in their classrooms. These attitudes were supported by beliefs that poor discipline in the home and lack of interest in academic success are the main reasons for the achievement gaps that exist between African and European American students. Ashton and Webb's (1986) research revealed positive correlations between teachers' sense of efficacy and the mathematics and communications, but not reading, skills of low-achieving students. They attributed these results to teachers' feeling more efficacious about teaching some subjects than others, thereby affirming their contention that teacher attitudes about efficacy are situation-specific. The "situations" to which attitudes are directly connected include subjects or skills to be taught, as well as the ethnic identity and ability level of students. These troubling results led Pang and Sablan (1995) to posit that "teacher efficacy is an important construct in student achievement, and teacher educators need to seriously examine what teachers believe about their ability to teach children from various underrepresented groups" (p. 16).

These studies suggest that some part of the failure to learn that unsuccessful teachers attribute to students results from their own low levels of efficacy (Ashton & Webb, 1986) and caring. This is as much of a deterrent to effective teaching as students who consider themselves incapable of learning, whether that perception is based in fact or the distorted impositions of others. Thus, changing teachers' attitudes, beliefs, expectations, and feelings of efficacy—their capacity to care—is as imperative to the design and implementation of culturally responsive teaching as is increasing their knowledge about and commitment to cultural diversity and mastery of related pedagogical skills.

Teacher expectations affect students' academic self-efficacy and performance as well. Students may internalize how they think teachers view them, and act accordingly. These effects can be positive or negative, facilitative or debilitative. If students think their teachers consider them to be capable students and worthy human beings, most of them will see themselves similarly, and act accordingly (Garcia & Chun, 2016; Harlin, Sirota, & Bailey, 2009. The converse is true, too. Negative teacher perceptions, attitudes, and expectations can generate parallel student dispositions about themselves and their peers. These reciprocal effects bring to mind Claude Steele's (1997, 2010) explanations of stereotype threat, and attest to the important role teachers play in students' lives, especially those who are most vulnerable in schools and society. They also underscore the need for teachers to be deliberate, forthright, and persistent about caring constructively and positively for underserved and marginalized minority students.

ACTUALIZING CULTURALLY RESPONSIVE CARING

In working with students of color, more teachers need to exhibit culturally responsive caring and to be "tough" and "take no stuff," like the individuals introduced earlier in this chapter; that is, "tough" and intractable in the sense of having high performance expectations and diligence in facilitating their achievement. This style of teaching is anchored in caring, commitment, cultural competence, and an understanding that school performance takes place within a complex sociocultural ecology and is filtered through cultural screens both students and teachers bring to the classroom. Caring (in the form of teacher expectations and their attendant instructional behaviors) is too pivotal in shaping the educational experiences and outcomes of ethnically different students to be taken for granted or left to chance. Nor should it be assumed that constructive caring for and pedagogical responsiveness to cultural diversity will emerge naturally from the professional ethics or personal altruism of teachers. Instead, it must be deliberately cultivated. Culturally responsive caring is launched through teachers acquiring more knowledge about ethnic and cultural diversity, becoming more conscious of themselves as cultural beings and cultural actors in the process of teaching, and engaging in courageous conversations about issues fundamental to social justice in society and educational equity for ethnically diverse students.

Acquiring a Knowledge Base

Teachers need to begin the process of becoming more caring and culturally competent by acquiring a *knowledge base about ethnic and cultural diversity in education*. This can be derived from the rich bodies of social science, educational, and literary scholarship on ethnic groups' histories, heritages, cultures, and contributions. A publication by G. Smith (1998), *Common Sense About Uncommon Knowledge*, may expedite the identification of this knowledge base even more. He has culled from the scholarship 13 wide-ranging components of multicultural education that he considers essential for inclusion in teacher education. Among these are ideological foundations, learning styles, sociocultural contexts of human growth and development, essentials of culture, experiential knowledge, and principles of culturally responsive curriculum design and classroom instruction. Another valuable resource in reconceptualizing and transforming the professional preparation of teachers for culturally responsible pedagogy is *Preparing Teachers for Cultural Diversity*, edited by J. King, Hollins, and Hayman (1997). The contributing authors to this book place cultural diversity in historical perspective; identify critical dimensions of cultural diversity for teacher education; and suggest a variety of culturally sensitive pre- and in-service teaching processes and strategies. The anthology *Building Racial and Cultural Competence in the Classroom*, compiled by Teel and Obidah (2008), includes personal stories of 12 researchers, scholars, and practitioners about their culturally responsive teaching. These stories offer other powerful, enriching, and encouraging lessons for moving key ideas about cultural diversity in teaching from theoretical principles to actual practices in different learning settings.

Personal and Professional Self-Awareness

The recommendations of G. Smith (1998) and King and colleagues (1997) include a wide range of content and pedagogical knowledge that teachers need in order to become competent and caring culturally responsive instructors for ethnically diverse students. However, this knowledge alone is not sufficient. It should be complemented with careful *self-analyses* of what teachers believe about the relationship among culture, ethnicity, and intellectual ability; the expectations they hold for students from different ethnic groups; and how their beliefs and expectations are manifested in instructional behaviors. These examinations are necessary and viable if Good and Brophy's (2003) contention is correct that most teachers are unaware, in any systematic way, of what they do while in the act of teaching. One cannot start to solve a problem until it is identified and understood. If teachers do not know how their own cultural blinders can obstruct educational opportunities for students of color, they cannot locate feasible places, directions, and strategies for changing them. Therefore, a critical element of culturally responsive teaching is *cultural self-awareness* and *consciousness-raising* for teachers.

Spindler and Spindler (1993, 1994) and Bennett (1995) offer models that are useful in facilitating the development of this awareness. They are techniques for teachers to use in studying their own classroom behaviors as they are occurring. The Spindler and Spindler model is called "cultural therapy." It is a process for bringing individuals' own cultural identities to a level of cognitive consciousness; deconstructing one's cultural embeddedness (Bowers & Flinders, 1991; Schram, 1994) in perceptions; analyzing why the cultural behaviors of others are perceived as objectionable, irritating, or shocking; and making explicit unequal power relationships and interactions in classrooms. Its purpose is to empower teachers through self-knowledge, the creation of a systematic basis for self-renewal, and the development of greater appreciation for the fallibility of presumed cultural universality.

Cultural therapy combines personal awareness with professional analysis, and cultural knowledge with instructional action. It includes explicating culturally patterned assumptions, values, and roots that drive expectations, communications, and behaviors; identifying culturally determined mechanisms for the expression, defense, and protection of "the enduring self"; recognizing cultural conflicts in the classroom between diverse students and teachers; and understanding the various kinds of *instrumental competencies* and *situational self-efficacy* required for school success for students, such as social etiquette, study skills, interactional rules, bureaucratic protocols, and high-level achievement in high-status subjects and skills.

Cultural therapy is beneficial to the implementation of culturally responsive teaching because it helps teachers to "see" more clearly the imprints of culture in their own and their students' behaviors—or to understand that "behavior is largely a matter of communicating in culturally prescribed ways" (Bowers & Flinders 1990, p. xi) and that people internalize patterns of thinking and behaving prescribed by their own cultural socialization. Cultural therapy also makes teachers more receptive to the notion that they may misread some of the behaviors of their culturally different students and, as a result, mistreat or disempower them, personally and pedagogically (Spindler & Spindler, 1994). For example, they come to realize that students who do not rise eagerly to expectations of individual competition in academic tasks are not necessarily unmotivated and uninterested in learning. They simply may be culturally cued to demonstrate motivation and academic competition in other ways, such as in cooperative group arrangements. These "cracks" in the sense of certainty about their own cultural claims and mechanisms, or what Bowers and Flinders (1990) call "taken-for-granted" assumptions of reality, are windows of opportunity for acknowledging the presence and legitimacy of cultural frames of reference in the classroom other than those of the teacher. Therefore, the purpose of cultural therapy is to alleviate the suffering caused when one's cultural biases are implicitly or explicitly forced upon others.

Bennett's (1995) model emerged from the Teacher as Decision Maker Program at Indiana University, which emphasizes decisionmaking and reflective practice in preservice teacher preparation. Both of these emphases are prominent in caring, culturally responsive teaching. Referred to as the "Teacher Perspective Framework," it is designed to develop skills in pedagogical self-awareness, self-analysis, and self-reflection. Preservice teachers are asked first to declare their personal perspectives on teaching philosophies by selecting from among seven conceptual options, and then to study their instructional actions to determine whether assumed and actual behaviors are congruent. Self-recorded observations of teaching behaviors are accompanied by periodic self-reflections and interviews to further heighten awareness and understanding of teaching modes. If incongruencies are apparent, the teachers are challenged to explain and resolve them. This resolution may require making another conceptual choice or adapting behaviors to fit better with ideals. Although the Teaching Perspective Framework was not designed specifically for analyzing the perspectives of teachers on the cultural behaviors of self and others, it can be adapted for this purpose.

In their self-study as Chicanos teaching a cultural diversity course to mostly preservice teachers of color, Prado-Olmos, Rios, and Castañeda (2007) made some observations that illustrate the importance of self-awareness and critical consciousness to culturally responsive caring for both teachers and students. These included strong relationships and connectedness; high levels of trust and respect; personal and professional experiential sharing; acquiring cultural knowledge of and renewal for self and others; engaging in questioning, critiquing, and reflecting; collaborative effort and accountability; and being "in community" with students personally, culturally, and academically.

Dialoguing About Cultural Diversity

In addition to engaging in self-reflections about their expectations and interactions with cultural diversity in classrooms, teachers need to discuss them with others. These dialogues should be informative and analytical, and they should involve individuals who are in positions of authority and/ or expertise to help teachers make better sense of their behaviors and improve them. Ideally, they will include professional peers and supervisors, as well as students, and participants in the dialogues will be multiethnic. The discussions should be inquiring and collaborative in nature, with the participants working together to share perceptions and expose their deep thinking on the topics under consideration. In this instance, the focus of analysis will be teacher expectations for and interactional styles with students from different ethnic groups and how these affect performance. The purpose of these dialogues is not merely to engage in cathartic "emotional massaging" or "psychological bashing," but for the participants to learn how to talk openly and deeply about cultural differences and racial inequities, acquire a heightened level of cultural sensitivity and critical consciousness, reevaluate cultural assumptions underlying behavior, and identify themes, ideas, and issues that have generative potential for pedagogical renewal. Intergroup dialogues can be used to facilitate these discussions. Singleton and Linton (2005) call these discussions "courageous conversations on race." They are designed to get educators to clarify and articulate their thinking about the role of race and racism in teaching and learning, and to commit themselves to an active antiracist educational agenda. This commitment involves *passion* in supporting significant changes in educational policies, programs, and procedures to achieve academic equity and social justice; *practice*, or actions to be taken to educate ethnically and racially diverse students to their highest potential; and *persistence* in staying focused on anti-racism regardless of what other issues of concern may be on the educational landscape.

Schoem, Frankel, Zuniga, and Lewis (1993) describe how dialogues were developed and used in the Program on Intergroup Relations and Conflict at the University of Michigan. The intent was to help college students learn about different ethnic groups' cultures and experiences, deconstruct racial myths and stereotypes, and combat racism. The technique involves several different progressional stages of learning. Zuniga and Nagda (1993) identify these as (1) creating a learning atmosphere conducive to cross-racial discussions and the constructive confrontation of misinformation and conflict; (2) examining ethnic group membership and cultural identity; (3) critically analyzing impressions and stereotypes people from different ethnic and racial groups have about one another; (4) exploring connections among attitudes, feelings, values, and behaviors; and (5) building alliances, coming to closure, and engaging in action for social change.

These kinds of examinations and dialogues can be both intimidating and empowering. They should be led by individuals skilled in conducting group discussions about ethnic and racial issues. One of the major challenges for the facilitator is getting the participants talking in constructive and mutually supportive ways. Many participants may want to find safety in silence and may resist sharing genuine beliefs and feelings for fear that they will be accused of being racists. Group leaders may overcome this hurdle by creating some "personal distance" for the members to begin to actively engage with the issues. Educational and commercial films and videos that depict issues of ethnic and cultural diversity in education can provide this stimulus and opportunity. There are many excellent examples on the market. Among them are *The Color of Fear* (Mun Wah, 1994), *Rosewood* (Peters & Barone, 1997), *Eye of the Storm* (1970) and its sequel, *A Class Divided* (1986), *Stand and Deliver* (Menendez, 1988), *Something Strong Within* (Nakamura, 1994), *Ethnic Notions* (Biggs, 1987), *Eyes on the Prize* (Hampton, 1987), *Ruby Bridges* (Palcy, 1998), *Skin Deep* (Reed, 1995), *Race the Sun* (Kanganis, 1996), *Valuing Diversity* (1987), *The Wedding* (C. Burnett, 1998), and *Smoke Signals* (Estes & Rosenfelt, 1998).

Written stories and scenarios, as well as films and videos, can be very provocative prompts to initiate and focus intergroup dialogues among teachers on ethnic diversity. They are available in various genres, including fiction and nonfiction, essays and novels, poetry and prose, autobiographical and biographical documents. Illustrative of these are *The Joy Luck Club* (A. Tan, 1989), *A Man's Life* (Wilkins, 1982), *Let the Circle Be Unbroken* (M. Taylor, 1981), "Incident" (Cullen, 1970), *Father Song: Testimonies of African-American Sons and Daughters* (Wade-Gayles, 1997), *Tearing the Silence: On Being German in America* (Hegi, 1997), *I Am Joaquin* (Gonzales, 1972), and *Fitting In* (Bernardo, 1996).

Teachers also can use video recordings of their own classroom behaviors to develop awareness and understanding of how they interact with ethnically different students. After recording segments of instruction, they can view the tapes critically and analytically to discern differences in their expectations and behaviors by the gender and ethnicity of students. These analyses should be both quantitative and qualitative. In the first category, teachers simply might count the number of times they have any kind of verbal and nonverbal contact with students from different ethnic and gender groups during the course of a lesson. These contacts could include how many questions asked of whom; praise, prompts, or guidance given; and discipline imposed. The qualitative assessments will require deeper analyses and may be more challenging and disconcerting.

In conducting these analyses, teachers might consider working with a colleague, supervisor, or external consultant who is more informed about cultural influences on classroom behaviors. The focus of attention should be on discrepancies in the *quality* of interactions teachers have with different students by ethnicity and gender. These might include what kinds of questions are asked of boys and girls, of Latino, African, Native, Asian, and European Americans; who is praised and who is criticized; to what extent experiences and perspectives of different ethnic groups are woven into instruction; which students are encouraged to think deeper and extend, clarify, or refine their verbal contributions; which students are ignored by the teacher; and what subtle ways teachers use to signal students that they are, or are not, expected to be masterful, high-level achievers. Once these interactional patterns are discerned and clearly understood, teachers can begin to design strategies for changing them, beginning with strategies to abort the negative and accelerate the positive. The next step will be to learn how to modify instructional interactions so that they are responsive to some of the cultural orientations of students from different ethnic groups. Some strategies for doing this can be gleaned from the information presented in Chapters 4–7.

CONCLUSION

Out of these processes of self-awareness and self-renewal, reflection and introspection, deconstruction and reconstruction, should emerge teachers with expectations and interactions, knowledge and skills, values and ethics that exhibit the power of caring—individuals like those introduced earlier in this chapter. They will be more inclined toward and effective in implementing culturally responsive teaching because they will know that this is an unavoidable moral mandate for educating ethnically different students.

And they will join the ranks of other teachers who are already moving forward on this agenda with conviction and effectiveness, such as those M. Foster (1997) writes about in *Black Teachers on Teaching* and exemplified by Mable Bette Moss, who says:

> My students know that they have to learn something every day, even if it's just a little bit. . . . They also know that if they don't know something or didn't learn something it's not their fault. . . . When the children tell me they can't do something, . . . I will say, "I know you can't do it now, but we'll work together and soon you will be able to do it on your own." . . . I want them to just keep persevering until they can. I have a lot of patience. (quoted in M. Foster, 1997, pp. 172–173)

Genuinely caring teachers are "warm demanding" academic taskmasters. All students are held accountable for high academic efforts and performance. It is not uncommon to hear these teachers making declarations to students to the effect that "there is no excuse for not trying to learn," "you will never know what you can do unless you try," and "'I can't do' is unacceptable in my classroom." Their performance expectations are complemented with uncompromising faith in their students and relentless efforts in helping them meet high academic demands. The results are often phenomenal. Students who others feel can reach only minimal levels of academic and social achievement produce stellar performance for caring, culturally sensitive teachers. The success of these teachers demonstrates that the idea of caring as essential to instructional effectiveness is not merely a truism; it is a fact. When combined with pedagogical competence, caring becomes a powerful ideological and praxis pillar of culturally responsive teaching.

PRACTICE POSSIBILITIES

Caring, like other aspects of culturally responsive teaching, is learned, and like learning in general, it requires guided practice. Teachers should not expect their initial efforts at caring for ethnically, racially, socially, and linguistically diverse students to be ideal. Instead, they will have to practice learning how to do culturally responsive caring before they can do it routinely, and with ease, fluidity, and maximum effectiveness. The following suggestions for how teachers can enhance their caring capabilities with students of color and members of other marginalized groups complement those offered within the chapter, and they should be helpful in these pursuits:

- Be critically cognizant of your attitudes, beliefs, and expectations about different ethnic, racial, and cultural groups, cultures, experiences, and issues, and track how they are manifested in instructional practices and relational behaviors (e.g., in professional and personal habits of being).

- Be an unequivocal advocate and ally for ethnically and racially diverse students. These students appreciate knowing that teachers are trustworthy, that they "got their back," and will come to their aid and assistance when in need and in situations within and beyond the classroom.
- Model desirable and expected culturally diverse values, attitudes, and behaviors. Show students what these ideas look like in action. Don't ask students to do something that you, as the teacher, are not willing to do yourself. This increases your credibility with students.
- Learn to see, hear, and listen to diverse students, especially when they "speak" without words. Much can be learned by simply being present with and paying close attention to students. Furthermore, students are astute enough to know when this does or does not happen.
- Demand reciprocity. Hold yourself and students accountable for declared components of caring relationships.
- Create and engage in active and functional partnerships with students in developing skills for culturally diverse learning and living.
- Develop classroom communities of practice in which teachers assist students in mastering academic knowledge and skills, cross-cultural learning, and relational expectations.
- Demand high-quality performance, and exercise reciprocal accountability for its accomplishment. That is, teachers should be multicultural learners, and culturally diverse learners should be teachers in developing one another's skill sets.
- Admit occurrences of fallibility, error, ignorance, and accomplishment in cultural diversity endeavors, and specify contingent pursuits of corrections and/or celebrations.
- Do not hold the academic achievement of ethnically and racially diverse students hostage to the compromising of or sacrificing of their cultural identities and heritages.
- Teach students the normalcy and necessity of crossing cultural borders in multicultural societies and the world (both in and out of school), and demonstrate skills for how this can be done. Reveal your own success and challenges in doing so.
- Be a culture, behavior, and knowledge broker. This involves interpreting, translating, and illustrating some of the learning and living challenges demanded of culturally diverse people and communities in and beyond schools. These translations may be prerequisites for their mastery of knowledge and skills. In other words, if students do not understand requests imposed on them, it is impossible for them to deliver appropriate behaviors.

- Never ask students to eliminate a way of thinking, behaving, and communicating without providing alternative replacement options. Simply saying, "Don't do or say . . ." is not a very effective strategy for students to develop different repertoires of abilities, habits of being, and self-regulatory skills. A goal of genuine care-based teaching is student self-autonomy and responsibility, rather than always being controlled and directed by teachers, parents, and others.
- Ask students to give personal feedback on how classroom climate and teaching styles affect their learning efforts, engagement, and outcomes. Use this information to modify or embellish the classroom climate and instructional strategies. Give public credit for the sources of the reforms.
- Be transparent and explicit in explaining what facilitates and interferes with what you expect to accomplish in teaching, and how you and your students will proceed. Students need to know what you expect specifically rather than generally. That is, establish parameters for various events and situations as they occur. After a range of these has been taught, students can be held accountable for self-regulation.
- Create and use a regular protocol, ritual, or routine for how your teaching dynamics unfold, and teach it to students. This way students know in advance the habitual pattern, process, and rhythm of teaching, and may be able to regulate and manage their engagement more effectively. One such protocol is KWL (what do you Know?, what do you Want to know?, and what did you Learn?). Another is KTFDR (Know, Think, Feel, Do, and Reflect as habitual phases of a teaching exchange).
- Diversify instructions and interactions. Caring teachers honor differences of and among students. They respond, in multiple ways, to the fact that students have different experiences, preferences, and capabilities, and that novelty, variety, and innovation stimulate interest and attention, which, in turn, improves academic engagement and performance outcomes.
- Working with students, create a montage of pictorial images, symbols, and sayings that symbolize the diverse heritages of students in your classroom, Use your own imagination and creativity instead of stock images. These can be made into posters that are displayed prominently in the classroom and elsewhere in the school, or printed as insignia on notepaper that is used regularly in correspondence with students and parents.

CHAPTER 4

Culture and Communication in the Classroom

"Language is incredibly powerful and diverse; it identifies and humanizes, and gives cultures, ideas, and thoughts the capacity to speak."

A semiotic relationship exists among communication, culture, teaching, and learning, and it has profound implications for implementing culturally responsive teaching. This is so because "what we talk about; how we talk about it; what we see, attend to, or ignore; how we think; and what we think about are influenced by our culture . . . [and] help to shape, define, and perpetuate our culture" (Porter & Samovar, 1991, p. 21). Making essentially the same argument, Bruner (1996) states that "learning and thinking are always situated in a cultural setting and always dependent upon the utilization of cultural resources" (p. 4). Culture provides the tools to pursue the search for meaning and to convey our understanding to others and thereby has strong shaping influences on the communication styles prominent among different ethnic groups and their children. For example, because Asian American cultures tend to encourage docility, respect for authority, and restraint in expressing strong feelings and thoughts directly, many students from these backgrounds are reluctant to participate in open classroom discourse, question or criticize disciplinary experts and scholars, and join teachers as partners in decisionmaking processes (Pai et al., 2006). Consequently, communication cannot exist without culture, culture cannot be known without communication, and teaching and learning are more effective for ethnically diverse students when classroom communication is culturally responsive.

INTRODUCTION

The discussions in this chapter explicate some of the critical features and pedagogical potentials of the culture–communication semiotics for different ethnic groups of color. The ideas and examples presented are composites of group members who strongly identify and affiliate with their ethnic group's cultural traditions. They are not intended to be descriptors of specific individuals within ethnic groups, or their behaviors in all circumstances. If, how, and when these cultural characteristics are expressed in actual behavior, and by whom, are influenced by many different factors, some of which were discussed in Chapter 1. Therefore, the ethnic interactional and communication styles described in this chapter should be seen as *general and traditional referents of group dynamics across many wide-ranging contexts, times, and circumstances* rather than static attributes of particular individuals.

Students of color who are most traditional in their communication styles and other aspects of culture and ethnicity are likely to encounter more obstacles to school achievement than those who think, behave, and express themselves in ways that approximate school and mainstream cultural norms. In making this point about African Americans, Dandy (1991) proposes that the language many of them speak "is all too often degraded or simply dismissed by individuals both inside and outside the racial group as being uneducated, illiterate, undignified or simply nonstandard" (p. 2). Other groups of color are "at least given credit for having a legitimate language heritage, even if they are denied full access to American life" (p. 2).

Many of the decisions educators make regarding the potential and *realized* achievement of students of color are dependent on communication abilities (their own and the students'). If students are not very proficient in school communication, and teachers do not understand or accept their cultural communication styles, then their academic performance may be misdiagnosed or trapped in communicative mismatches. Students may know much more than they are able to communicate, or they may be communicating much more than their teachers are able to discern. As Boggs (1985) explains, "The attitudes and behavior patterns that have the most important effect upon children . . . [are] those involved in communication" (p. 301). This communication is multidimensional and multipurposed, including verbal and nonverbal, direct and tacit, literal and symbolic, formal and informal, grammatical and discourse components.

The discussions of culture and communication in classrooms in this chapter are organized into six sections. The first outlines some key assertions about culture and communication in teaching and learning in general. These help to anchor communication within culturally responsive teaching. Several myths about linguistic diversity are presented in the second section. They identify some obstacles that can interfere with understanding, accepting, and using different cultural communication styles as teaching resources. In the third section of the chapter, two recurrent controversies about culturally different communication in classrooms are presented. These are debates over Ebonics and bilingualism. Some major characteristics of the communication *modes* of African, Native, Latino, Asian, and European Americans are summarized in the fourth section. Some effects of teaching academic English as a complement to cultural communication styles are presented in the fifth section of the chapter. The sixth section is devoted to gender variations in communication styles. The primary focus of attention throughout these discussions is discourse dynamics; that is, who participates in communicative interactions and under what conditions, how these participation patterns are affected by cultural socialization, and how they affect teaching and learning in classrooms.

RELATIONSHIP AMONG CULTURE, COMMUNICATION, AND EDUCATION

Too many teachers operate on the assumption that there is only one acceptable way of communicating across all circumstances, audiences, and contexts. In reality, this is not the case. Even within the same linguistic system (e.g., English, Spanish, or Mandarin), speakers talk differently as the contexts of their speech change. Turney and Sitler (2012) attribute this lack of consciousness to the instinctive nature of talking. They consider talking as "something we do without stopping to question how we are doing it. . . . We may consider what to say when speaking, but rarely do we consider how to say it" (n.p.). This tendency can be very problematic for communicating responsively with diverse students since *how* they talk is influenced by their cultural socialization, probably to a greater extent than *what* they talk about. The topical content of cross-cultural communication in classrooms can be the same, but how it is delivered and the ways of engaging with it can differ significantly based on the cultural orientations of the speakers. While culture is not the only variable affecting how teachers and students "do" communication, it is still a very important one.

Teachers also need to recognize and respond to the fact that even when people speak the same language, cultural differences can affect how they communicate (Kim & Park, 2015; Turney & Siter, 2012). A case in point would be the varieties of Spanish-heritage cultures and communities whose ancestry is located in Mexico, Spain, Puerto Rico, and Chile. Another involves people from the many heritage communities that are native speakers of English, such as Jamaicans, Appalachians, New Englanders, and Canadians. Other factors that can cause speakers of the same language to communicate differently are level of acculturation into mainstream society, immigration experiences, age or generation, socioeconomic status, level of education, gender, and racial identity. These dynamics add to the complexity and the necessity of richly nuanced communicative diversity in culturally responsive teaching.

In analyzing the routine tasks teachers perform, B. Smith (1971) declares that "teaching is, above all, a linguistic activity" and "language is at the very heart of teaching" (p. 24). Whether making assignments, giving directions, explaining events, interpreting words and expressions, proving propositions, justifying decisions and actions, making promises, dispersing praise and criticism, or assessing capability, teachers must use language. And the quality of the performance of these tasks is a direct reflection of how well they can communicate with their students. Smith admonishes educators for not being more conscientious in recognizing the importance of language diversity in the performance and effectiveness of their duties. He says, "It could be that when we have analyzed the language of teaching and investigated the effects of its various formulations, the art of teaching will show marked advancement" (p. 24). Dandy (1991) likewise places great faith in the power of communication in the classroom, declaring that "teachers have the power to shape the future, if they communicate with their students, but those who cannot communicate are powerless" (p. 10). These effects of communication skills are especially significant to improving the performance of underachieving ethnically different students.

Porter and Samovar's (1991; Samovar, Porter, McDaniel, & Roy, 2017) study of the nature of culture and communication, the tenacious reciprocity that exists between the two, and the importance of these to intercultural interactions provides valuable information for culturally responsive teaching. They describe communication as "an intricate matrix of interacting social acts that occur in a complex social environment that reflects the way people live and how they come to interact with and get along in their world. This social environment is culture, and if we are to truly understand communication, we must also understand culture" (p. 10). Communication is dynamic, interactive, irreversible, and invariably contextual. As such, it is a continuous, ever-changing performance that takes place between people who are trying to influence one another; its effects are irretrievable once it has occurred, despite efforts to modify or counteract them. Communication also is governed by the rules of the social and physical contexts in which it occurs (Porter & Samovar, 1991; Samovar et al., 2017). Culture is the rule-governing system that defines the forms, functions, and content of communication. It is largely responsible for the construction of our "individual repertoires of communicative behaviors and meanings" (Porter & Samovar, 1991, p. 10). Therefore, understanding connections between culture and communication is critical to improving intercultural interactions. This is so because "as cultures differ from one another, the communication practices and behaviors of individuals reared in those cultures will also be different," and "the degree of influence culture has on intercultural communication is a function of the dissimilarity between the cultures" (p. 12).

Communication entails much more than the content and structure of written and spoken language, and it serves purposes greater than the transmission of information. It is also about creating relationships, cohesion, and community among different people (Lakoff, 2004). Communication takes many different forms beyond the more common written and spoken ones. Prominent among them that are highly susceptible to cultural diversity are images and symbols, especially so in the current visual media–dominated U.S. society and world. The presentations and portrayals of contemporary hip-hop and spoken-word music performers, professional athletes, and visible markers of certain ethnic groups such as Muslim women's traditional dress are graphic examples. These images and symbols are powerful communication devices that "speak loudly" and send strong messages, even if they are not always completely accurate. Ethnic and racial absences from mass media and other parts of society are also compelling forms of social and cultural communication, as are disproportional and distorted portrayals. All of these need to be understood and included by teachers in developing their culturally responsive communication competencies for students and communities of color.

Sociocultural context and nuances, discourse logic and dynamics, delivery styles, social functions, role expectations, norms of interaction, and nonverbal features are as important (if not more so) as vocabulary, grammar, lexicon, pronunciation, and other linguistic structural dimensions of communication (C. Lee, 2007; Smitherman, 1986, 2000). This is so because the "form of exchange between child and adult and the conditions in which it occurs will affect not only what is said, but how involved the child will become" (Boggs, 1985, p. 301). Communication is the quintessential way in which humans make meaningful connections with one another, whether as caring, sharing, loving, teaching, or learning. Montagu and Matson (1979, p. vii) suggest that it is "the ground of [human] meeting and the foundation of [human] community."

Communication is also an indispensable factor in acquiring and demonstrating knowledge. This is the central idea of the Sapir–Whorf hypothesis about the relationship among language, thought, and behavior. It says that, far from being simply a means for reporting experience, language is a way of defining experience, thinking, and knowing. In this sense, language is the semantic system of meanings and modes of conveyance that people habitually use to code, analyze, categorize, and interpret experience (Carroll, 1956; Hoijer, 1991; Mandelbaum, 1968). In characterizing this relationship, Sapir (1968) explains that "language is a guide to 'social reality' . . . [and] a symbolic guide to culture. . . . It powerfully conditions all of our thinking about social problems and processes" (p. 162). People do not live alone in an "objectified world" or negotiate social realities without the use of language. Nor is language simply a "mechanical" instrumental tool for transmitting information. Instead, human beings are "very much at the mercy of the particular language which has become the medium of expression for their society" (p. 162). The languages used in different cultural systems strongly influence how people think, know, feel, and do. They are the mechanisms that give external meaning to internal being.

Whorf (1952, 1956; Carroll, 1956), a student of Sapir, makes a similar argument that is represented by the "principle of linguistic relativity." It contends that the structures of various languages reflect different cultural patterns and values, and, in turn, affect how people understand and respond to social phenomena. In developing these ideas further, Whorf (1952) explains that "a language is not merely a reproducing instrument for voicing ideas but rather is itself the shaper of ideas, the program and guide for the individual's mental activity, for his analysis of impressions, for his synthesis of his mental stock in trade" (p. 5). Vygotsky (1962) also recognizes the reciprocal relationship among language, culture, and thought. He declares, as "indisputable fact," that "thought development is determined by language . . . and the sociocultural experience of the child" (p. 51).

Moreover, the development of logic is affected by a person's socialized speech, and intellectual growth is contingent on the mastery of social means of thought, or language. According to Byers and Byers (1985), "The organization of the processes of human communication in any culture is the template for the organization of knowledge or information in that culture" (p. 28). These arguments are applied specifically to different ethnic groups by theorists, researchers, and school practitioners from a wide variety of disciplinary perspectives, including social and developmental psychology, sociolinguistics, ethnography, and multiculturalism. For example, Ascher (1992) applied this reasoning to language influences on how mathematical relationships are viewed in general. Giamati and Weiland (1997) connected it to Navajo students' learning of mathematics, concluding that the performance difficulties they encounter are "a result of cultural influences on perceptions rather than a lack of ability" (p. 27). This happens because of the reciprocal interactions among language, culture, and perceptions. Consistently, when these scholars refer to "language" or "communication," they are talking more about discourse dynamics than structural forms of speaking and writing.

Thus, languages and communication styles are systems of cultural notations and the means through which thoughts and ideas are expressively embodied. Embedded within them are cultural values and ways of knowing that strongly influence how students engage with learning tasks and demonstrate mastery of them. The absence of shared communicative frames of reference, procedural protocols, rules of etiquette, and discourse systems makes it difficult for culturally diverse students and teachers to genuinely understand one another and for students to fully convey their intellectual abilities. Teachers who do not know or value these realities will not be able to fully access, facilitate, and assess most of what these students know and can do.

A recurring language diversity concern among Pre-K–12 educators is what to do about students who are not proficient in Standard or "Academic" English. Should they be required to abandon the communication systems they have learned though their cultural socialization and living outside of school? Should they be taught in only their indigenous or cultural languages?

Or should schooling accommodate the home languages of different ethnic groups while facilitating the development of mainstream Standard English? In other words, should schools teach culturally diverse students to be bilingual and bidialectic? These questions are not new, but they have very different meanings and consequences for speakers of nonmainstream, socially unacceptable dialects (particularly African Americans), and students whose first language is not English (i.e., English language learners, or ELLs) as their numbers increase among school populations. They take various forms based on time, context, and constituency, but the overarching dilemma is largely the same. That is, "What is the role of languages and communication styles other than Academic English in classrooms instruction?"

In reviewing research on these issues, Carol Lee (2007) explains that "language has always been a source of contention in the United States," and that "schools have long been the cauldron in which to wash away language that marks race, ethnicity, and working class status deemed by the powerful to be wanting" (p. 80)—to declare them deficient, nonstandard, obstructive, dyfunctional, even nonexistent. These attitudes and actions are not morally or pedagogically desirable, especially in the face of claims made about providing the highest-quality education possible for all students, and knowing that diverse children come to school already deeply entrenched in diverse social, cultural, and linguistic heritages. They have profound negative effects on the identity and learning of students from disenfranchised groups (Delpit, 1995; C. Lee, 2000; Lomawaima & McCarty, 2006; Ramirez, Wiley, de Klerk, Lee, & Wright, 2005). As Ramirez and associates (2005) argue:

> No society, as linguistically and culturally diverse as [the United States], which sincerely claims to advocate educational equity and equal opportunity . . . would condone the ascription of these labels to some of its children, unless it were tacitly disingenuous in its affirmation of these principles. (p. xi)

The relationship among language, culture, and learning is too complex to be reduced to an English Only or Academic Dialect Only legal mandate, not to mention that such a policy is inherently contradictory to principles of culturally responsive teaching. Any "one-way" or "one-size-fits-all" mentality or methodology is unacceptable as a criterion of educational quality and equality for diverse students. Regardless of whether the issue is dialects or languages, competency in more than one communication system is a strength, a resource, and a necessity to be cultivated for students living in pluralistic societies. Many scholars (including Delpit, 1995; Lomawaima & McCarty, 2006; Rickford & Rickford, 2000; Smitherman, 1986, 2000, 2006) have commented on the wealth of communicative knowledge and skills that culturally diverse students bring to the classroom and that can be useful instructional resources. In accrediting the oral facility of African

Americans, Delpit (1995) notes that "the verbal adroitness, the cogent and quick wit, the brilliant use of metaphorical language, the facility in rhythm and rhyme" (p. 57) evident in the communication habits of preachers, speakers, singers, and everyday people within the African American cultural community, to whom many African American children are regularly exposed, should be used to facilitate school learning for them. Other scholars (such as Baugh, 1999; C. Lee, 2007; Rickford, Sweetland, & Rickford, 2004; Smitherman, 1986, 2000, 2006; Wheeler & Swords, 2006) agree with these assessments and recommendations particularly as they relate to speakers of a language variety (e.g., dialect) that so often is stigmatized in mainstream political, social, and educational venues.

MYTHS ABOUT LANGUAGE DIVERSITY

Some common myths continue to get in the way of teachers and school leaders seeing the complexity and necessity of language diversity in educating culturally different students (Ball & Muhammad, 2003; Delpit, 1995; C. Lee, 2007; Smitherman, 2000; Smitherman & Villanueva, 2003). One implied myth is that a single form of "Standard English" exists and is always used in the formal and official functions of mainstream U.S. institutions and interactions. It is evident in the English Only debates where no mention is made of multiple forms or dialects of the language. Yet *applied* English has many different variations, and the school version is only one of them. Nor is there a simple form of Dine, Ebonics, Japanese, Spanish, Tagalog, Mandarin, or any other language, for that matter. As Smitherman (2000, p. 145) explains:

> There is not simply one form of standard English, but varieties of standard English—formal, informal, and colloquial. Similarly, there are varieties of Black English conducive to communicating in various social situations; Black church language, proverbs, and street raps are examples. (p. 145)

Ball and Muhammad (2003) suggest that it is better to determine if a particular variety of a language is appropriate for given situations, purposes, and audiences, instead of saying it is right or wrong. The results will show that "a [communication] style that may be generally perceived as nonstandard can be just as appropriate as one that is considered to be standard depending on the demands of the particular communicative situation" (p. 78). Anyway, mastery of only one language (English or otherwise) or a single variant of it (such as Standard or Academic English) fails to equip students with the linguistic skills the real world demands (Canagarajah, 2003).

It is helpful to demystify English as being without internal variability of form and function, and to recognize that students need to be taught multiple versions for them to acquire and demonstrate culturally relevant communicative competence. The idea here is that the more communicative abilities one has, the more capable he or she is of functioning in various relationships and interactions, especially as these cross cultural, social, ethnic, educational, and political boundaries. Canagarajah (2003) captures these needs well in the following advice:

> Rather than judging [linguistic] divergence as error, we should orientate to it as an exploration of choices and possibilities. Rather than teaching rules in a normative way, we should teach *strategies*—creative ways to negotiate the norms operating in diverse contexts. Rather than developing mastery in a "target language," we should strive for competence in a repertoire of codes and discourses. Rather than simply joining a speech community, we should teach students to shuttle between communities. Not satisfied with teaching students to be context-sensitive, we should teach them to be context-transforming. (p. xiii, emphasis in original)

Another mistaken notion is that speaking a nonmainstream dialect or another language interferes with or impedes mastery of English (written and oral) and academic skills such as reading, writing, math, and science. Research (J. Crawford, 2000; Cummins, 1989; E. Garcia, 1999; F. Tong, Lara-Alecio, Irby, Mathes, & Kwok, 2008) does not support this contention; rather, it indicates that ELLs who are most proficient in their first language learn English faster and better. The reverse claim is never made—that is, speaking English prevents one from learning another language. This is not to deny that children who have limited skills in Academic English do not have more difficulty with school learning. But the dilemma is not as much about the potential to learn or any inherent limitations of their native languages as about the practice of teaching. It also may have to do more with teachers' negative attitudes toward language diversity; misunderstandings of how language, culture, teaching, and learning are connected; English language learning being a proxy for a more comprehensive cultural resocialization of marginalized students of color; and the tendency of many teachers to confuse teaching academic skills (such as reading) with teaching new dialects and linguistic forms.

A third common misconception surrounding linguistic diversity is that language teaching and learning are primarily about *form and structure*, when, in fact, *use* is more important. Delpit (1995) defines language use as "the socially and cognitively based linguistic determinations speakers make about style, register, vocabulary, and so forth, when they attempt to interact with or achieve particular goals within their environments" (p. 49). Furthermore, the linguistic codes and communicative styles ethnically diverse students bring to the classroom are "intimately connected to loved ones, community, and personal identity. To suggest that [they are] 'wrong,' or even worse, ignorant, is to suggest that something is wrong with the student and his or her family" (p. 55). This recognition does not preclude the need for students to be taught Standard or Academic English, not as a replacement for their home, first, or indigenous languages, but as a complement to them. Smitherman (2006) makes the point compellingly that teaching Standard Academic English to diverse students

> has never been an issue, despite the moaning, groaning, and gnashing of teeth from language purists and conservatives. . . . I know of no one, not even the most radical-minded linguist or educator (not even the Kid herself!) who has ever argued that American youth, regardless of race/ethnicity, do not need to know the Language of Wider Communication in the U.S. (aka "Standard English"). (p. 142)

These ideas also suggest that being culturally responsive to linguistic diversity involves more than understanding and teaching the structural features of English to ELL students, or understanding these features of their first languages. Knowing the social context factors that affect English language acquisition and use is of equal, if not more, importance. Among these factors are the types of schools students attend, the kinds of opportunities they receive to practice English in the formal and informal operations of schools, and the amount of time spent using English in their social interactions outside of school. Carhill, Suárez-Orozco, and Páez (2008) add that oral English proficiency is a precursor to improved academic achievement for ELL adolescents in secondary schools. The instructional implications of these findings are clear—along with the more typical approaches of teaching written and structural English language components, (1) teachers need to identify the peer, school, and community informal networks, resources, and relationships that help students advance their oral English proficiency, and use them to facilitate their engagement with the subject-matter content and academic language skills taught in schools; and (2) students need to have *authentic opportunities to practice oral English discourse skills* in a wide variety of circumstances and contexts (both within and outside of schools).

Yet another myth that interferes with accepting the validity and viability of language diversity in teaching and learning is the fear that somehow the prominence of English will be jeopardized. Wiley (2005) points out that this fear is unfounded, because there is indisputable evidence that English is "the language of the land," even without wholesale legal mandates, since 98% of all people in the United States speak some form of it at some level. Given the "high status accorded to [English] around the world, there is no rational basis to support the fear that it is in any danger of losing its dominance" (Wiley, 2005, p. 6). Instead, the rate of linguistic assimilation is increasing as newcomers to the United States learn English much more rapidly than previous generations (J. Crawford, 1997b). According to J. Crawford (2000), this argument is a facade for a deeply ingrained disrespect for diversity, a White privilege ploy, and an expression of cultural hegemony of mainstream society.

Brisk (2006) agrees with Crawford but states the case even more forcefully. In her assessment, "much of the debate on bilingual education is wasteful, ironic, hypocritical, xenophobic, and regressive" (p. 199). It is *wasteful* because it promotes preferred models of teaching instead of more general sound educational practices. It is *ironic* because rather than decreasing, English language use actually is increasing in the United States and the world. It is *hypocritical* because many of those who oppose using languages other than English in instruction also endorse foreign language requirements for high school graduation and college admission. It is *xenophobic* because it reflects negative attitudes and prejudices toward ethnic groups of color and recent immigrants from non-Western countries. It is *repressive* because progressive ideology (and many other countries) consider proficiency in two or more languages a sign of high-quality, advanced education. In a 1992 resolution, the National Council of Teachers of English (NCTE) made essentially the same arguments, and added "unfair, dangerous, and unconstitutional" to the problems with English Only ideologies.

Culturally responsive teaching does not contest the need for a common national language or, as Smitherman (2000, 2003) calls it, a "language of wider communication." Rather, the contention is, why can't multiple variations of Standard English and other languages coexist, and be recognized as strength-based complementary tools for teaching culturally diverse students, as well as necessary competencies for living fully and effectively in pluralistic societies? C. Jones and Shorter-Gooden (2003) make this point persuasively in noting:

> Ideally, everyone, no matter what gender or race or background, will become multilingual, developing mastery in more than one language while feeling free to switch between them according to their own predilections rather than out of shame or obligation. . . . When we hear differences in accent, . . . dialect or slang, rather than automatically if subconsciously judging the speaker, we can expand our personal styles instead, borrowing idioms, inflections, and expressions that suit the context we're in, our mood, our sense of self. There is a wonderful beauty to language, to regionalisms, vernacular and patois, and embracing language in whatever form can enrich all of our lives. (p. 120)

CULTURAL COMMUNICATION CONTROVERSIES

Tensions surrounding *linguistic diversity* are displayed most prominently in debates over African American Language (AAL), or Ebonics, and English Only or bilingualism for speakers of other languages in official public discourse (such as government and education). Periodic controversies occur about the place and function of Ebonics in school programs and practices. Across the generations mainstream society has been ambivalent, and sometimes explicitly contradictory, toward African American language—at times borrowing, imitating, and appropriating parts of it, while simultaneously disdaining and invalidating other parts (Alim & Baugh, 2007; Baugh, 1999, 2000; Lee, 2007; Perry & Delpit, 1998; Ramirez et al., 2005; Rickford & Rickford, 2000; Smitherman, 1986, 1998c, 2000, 2006).

A historical irony is embedded in this recurring controversy. At the beginning of enslavement and during the Atlantic crossing, Africans were punished viciously for speaking their indigenous languages; after arrival in the United States they were denied opportunities to formally learn English. And the communication system they constructed in subsequent generations often is looked upon with disdain by mainstream society (instead of being applauded for the ingenuity involved in its creation) (Alim & Baugh, 2007; C. Jones & Shorter-Gooden, 2003; C. Lee, 2007; Rickford & Rickford, 2000; Smitherman, 1986, 1996, 2000, 2006). Now many individuals speak passionately about the rights of African Americans, Latino Americans, Asian Americans, and Native Americans to be empowered, made visible, and have voice. But what better way to make a person or a people voiceless, invisible, and powerless than to invalidate their self-selected or cultural communicative means of speaking their thoughts, their ideas, themselves?

A debate over Ebonics in schools occurred in 1996–1997 in the Oakland, California, public schools. It was prompted by a resolution of the district's Board of Education to recognize Ebonics as a legitimate and viable communication system, and to use it for teaching African American students the Standard Academic English (SAE) of mainstream schooling, power, politics, and commerce (Perry & Delpit, 1998; Ramirez et al., 2005; Rickford, 2005). The essence of the Resolution and related Policy Statement was an appeal for African American students to be recognized and taught as bilingual to improve their academic achievement. These documents also suggested that the initiative should be funded from sources similar to those used to support bilingual education programs for speakers of other languages, such as Spanish.

The controversy that resulted pitted supporters against critics, European Americans against African Americans, scholars against practitioners, age against youth, the popular media against the academic community, and sometimes each of these against itself (for detailed discussion of the Ebonics debate, see Baugh, 2000; *Journal of Black Psychology*, 1997; Perry & Delpit, 1998; Ramirez et al., 2005; Rickford & Rickford, 2000). It did not help matters that some high-profile African Americans, such as Jesse Jackson and Maya Angelou, made scathing attacks on the idea of using Ebonics in schools. Yet both of them (and other orators, literary authors, performers, scholars, and everyday people) frequently use features of Ebonics along with

Standard English in their own professional work (Boyd, 1997; Delpit, 1995; C. Lee, 2000, 2007; Rickford & Rickford, 2000; Smitherman, 2000). In explaining the value of this bilingual ability, Carol Lee (2007) notes that

> academic writing can be done in African American English or other so-called nonstandard varieties. Geneva Smitherman, the noted linguist, . . . routinely includes elements of African American English in her academic writing in the form of aphorisms, titles, and personal commentary. . . . I, too, routinely try to include African American proverbs, sayings, and vocabulary. . . . I think doing so makes an important statement about who I am and what I value. (p. 86)

An example of this occurs in Smitherman's (2005) analysis of the Ebonics debate. She attributes some of the fervor to "a serious lack of knowledge about the scientific approach of language analysis, . . . a galling ignorance of what Ebonics is . . . and who speaks it, . . . [and] an appalling rejection of the language of everyday Black people" (p. 49), which she explains in SAE and the disciplinary language of sociolinguistics. Smitherman then employs a version of Ebonics to describe the personal effects of these linguistic limitations on individual African Americans. She says, "See, when you lambast the home language that kids bring to school, you ain just dissin dem, you talkin bout they mommas! Check out the concept of 'Mother Tongue'"(p. 49). Anyone who knows Ebonics parlance readily recognizes how problematic and potentially volatile it is for one to dis (talk negatively about) another's mother.

Why shouldn't students have similar rights and capabilities to embed their cultures and identities in their school language in deliberate and skillful ways? Can't this be done without jeopardizing facility in the primary languages or Academic English? Carol Lee (2007) and Geneva Smitherman (2003, 2005) explain that when they and others use AAL within the contexts of written and spoken academic discourse, they are not suggesting that Academic English is not necessary, or that the native languages of ethnic groups should be used exclusively. Rather, both are necessary; they do not have to be mutually exclusive or nullifying. They can enrich each other. To be skillful in both is to have high levels of bilingualism and biculturalism. These are goals to which all students should aspire, and schools (as well as society) should admire and facilitate. Youth from all ethnic backgrounds should be encouraged and helped to master them instead of being blamed and punished for speaking a variety of language forms and communication systems. Rickford and Rickford (2000) reinforce this idea with the observation that educators treating African American language (which they call Spoken Soul)

> like a disease is no way to add Standard English to their repertoire. On the contrary, building on Spoken Soul, through contrast and comparison, is likely to

> meet with less resistance from students who are hostile to "acting white." It is
> also likely to generate greater interest and motivation, and as experiments have
> shown, . . . to yield greater success, more quickly. (p. 238)

The most contentious contemporary controversy over English Only
began in 1981 with a proposal for a constitutional English Language
Amendment. Although the proposal failed to pass, it initiated a heated debate and a series of local and state mandates about a mandatory national
language for everyone, or rights to linguistic diversity for individuals whose
first languages are not English. Since then 24 states and numerous towns
and cities have adopted some form of English Only or "Official English"
legislation. Four other states (Illinois, Massachusetts, Nebraska, Virginia)
already had policies in place before 1980. Of the remaining states 15 have
debated making English the official language. Four (New Mexico, Oregon,
Rhode Island, Washington) have enacted English Plus Resolutions. These
are alternatives to the English Only ideology that promote English *and* other
languages (J. Crawford 1997a, 1997b, 2003; Schildkraut, 2005). In 1978
Hawaii passed a constitutional amendment recognizing English and Native
Hawaiian as official languages, thereby declaring the state bilingual.

Despite all the attention given to the debate over whether English should
be *the* official language of the United States in the past 2 decades or so, and
related restrictive policies (such as the high-profile Propositions 63 and 227
in California, Proposition 203 in Arizona, and the national No Child Left
Behind Act), these are not new phenomena. The issue had been raised before, and debated as vigorously as Ebonics. J. Crawford (2000), Bankston
and Zhou (1995), and Schildkraut (2005) indicate that throughout U.S. history English language policies have varied according to ethnic group, times,
demography, and politics. They have "ranged from repression to restriction
to tolerance to accommodation, depending on forces that have little to do
with language" per se (Crawford 2000, p. 5). Historically, there has been
a strong correlation between immigration trends and restrictive language
policies. As the rate of immigration increases, tolerance for language diversity decreases, and there is a resurgence of English Only policies. It is little
wonder, then, that the most recent rages about English Only coincided with
the tremendous increase in immigration from Latino (especially Mexico and
South America) and Asian countries.

Proponents of English Only claimed that their concerns are driven by
altruistic desires to help these immigrants assimilate into mainstream society, learn better, and become more economically mobile more easily and
quickly. Schildkraut (2005) questions the merits of these claims. Instead,
she attributes the concern for making English the official language to a
perceived threat to the country's national identity by its supporters and to
their own sense of self. Crawford (2000) is more graphic in his assessment
of the underlying motivations. He agrees that language conflicts usually

involve struggles over cultural, religious, ethnic, and national identities. However,

> they represent more than contending philosophies of assimilation and plural-
> ism, disagreements about the rights and responsibilities of citizens, or debates
> over the true meaning of Americanism. Ultimately, language policies are . . .
> struggles for social and economic supremacy. . . . In the American experience,
> English-only campaigns can be classed in two categories: as proxies for inter-
> group competition and as mechanisms of social control . . . as means of privi-
> leging certain groups over others and as a tool for maintaining the hegemony
> of ruling elites. (p. 5)

Gutiérrez (2005) adds that English Only instructional practices are actually detrimental to achievement instead of facilitating it. They "exacerbate
the inequitable learning conditions of an already vulnerable student population by dramatically reducing and complicating opportunities to learn."
Such practices define students only on the basis of their language status
"rather than their diverse backgrounds, language skills, interests, and learning needs" (p. 297).

Advocates and opponents, and language policies and practices, change
as societal conditions, educational priorities, and political leadership shift.
Several recent examples are illustrative of these trends. First, little vocal
controversy is currently occurring over Ebonics even though the issues un-
dergirding it have not been resolved. African American students have not
ceased speaking the language, and the educational achievement of disproportionate percentages of their children is still compromised. But other priorities have appeared, such as the controversy over the educational rights of
immigrant youth from nations and heritages U.S. society is unaccustomed to
(e.g., Muslim heritage speakers of Arabic) and those who are undocumented. Second, the voters in California changed their minds about promoting
English-only in education and other public service enterprises (as conveyed
through the passage of Proposition 227 in 1998) by passing Proposition 58
in November 2016. This policy repealed the earlier one and allows non-
English languages in public education. Third, rather than concentrating on
the most expeditious way for English language learners to become competent
in English, the debate has shifted more toward TWI (Two-Way Immersion
in language learning), or dual-language learning for both nonnative and
native speakers of English. An aspect of the language/communications that
has not changed much is the tendency for bilingual discourse to concentrate
primarily on Spanish speakers (with the possible exception of Mandarin),
while other language speakers are largely ignored beyond local boundaries. Yet diverse native language communities in U.S. schools are increasing
as student populations become more diversified, which, in turn, affects the
quality of their in-school communication and performance. For example,

African, Asian, Pacific Islander, and Middle Eastern immigrant student populations who use their indigenous languages as primary means of communication are increasing significantly in some parts of the United States.

English Plus (J. Crawford, 1997a)—that is, using and teaching other languages along with Academic English in schools—is a viable alternative to English Only for educating ethnically and culturally diverse students. It has precedents that are worthy of resurrection, reaffirmation, and contemporary implementation. It is labeled differently depending on proponents and represented constituencies. Among these are dual-language learning, bilingualism, bidialectism, code-shifting or code-switching, linguistic hybridity, and translanguaging (Collins, 2014; Fortune, 2014). Two important precedents for these emphases are the 1974 "Students' Rights to Their Own Language Resolution" and the 1988 National Language Policy, both produced by the Conference on College Composition and Communication (CCCC). The Students' Rights resolution stated, in part:

> We affirm the students' rights to their own patterns and varieties of language—the dialects of their nurture or whatever dialect in which they find their own identity and style. . . . The claim that any dialect is unacceptable amounts to an attempt of one social group to exert its dominance over another. Such a claim leads to false advice for speakers and writers, and immoral advice for humans. A nation proud of its diverse heritage and its cultural and racial variety will preserve its heritage of dialects. (Smitherman, 2003, p. 17)

The three provisions of the National Language Policy endorsed all students acquiring oral and literate competence in English; the legitimacy and maintenance of the native languages and dialects of diverse students; and teaching languages other than English so that students learn a second language (Smitherman, 2003). The CCCC language policy statement also recognized the United States as a multilingual society, and suggested that none of its residents should be denied their civil liberties (including the right to education) because of linguistic differences.

Another noteworthy document legitimizing an ethnic minority group's language in schools is the Native American Language Act (NALA). It was passed in 1990 and authorized for funding 2 years later. It approved the freedom of Native American groups to practice and promote their own languages, and the right to use Native American languages as the medium of instruction in all Native schools funded by the federal government. These provisions were expected to have positive effects on language survival, academic success, knowledge of culture and history, and community and ethnic pride (Lomawaima & McCarty, 2006).

The proposals and sentiments of the CCCC and the NALA are highly consistent with principles of culturally responsive teaching. Among these are building on the knowledge and skills that students already have; focusing on cultural strengths rather than weaknesses; developing skills for both cultural maintenance and cultural border-crossing; and using a multiplicity of orientations and methodologies in helping diverse students develop repertoires of knowledge and skills for wide varieties of situations, contexts, and relationships. They resonate with democratic ideals as well, such as *e pluribus unum*, human dignity, freedom, equality, and justice. No one argues against the importance of learning English. The question in contention is its exclusivity.

The amazing human capacity to multitask and to learn many things simultaneously is an endorsement for linguistic diversity. Ethnically and racially diverse students are not given the credit they deserve when assumptions are made that they cannot be competent in more than one language at a time. Translanguaging challenges these assumptions. It means blending linguistic and discourse features or performance modes of different languages into a single coherent communication system. It is based on the premise that whether they are considered bilingual or not, all people are, in fact, multilingual, with rich internal repertoires of linguistic diversity (Garcia & Wei, 2014; MacSwan, 2017). These should be considered as assets to be respected and used to achieve educational success for culturally diverse students. Translanguaging also emphasizes the use of multiple languages to make schools more welcoming environments for multilingual students (Christian, 2011; MacSwan, 2017). These are reasonable expectations that are highly compatible with experiential reality (in the normal course of living, people routinely use multiple forms of communication, and variations within any given language) and culturally responsive teaching.

Another compelling argument of all in favor of bilingualism, bidialectism, biculturalism, and translanguaging is the interconnections among culture, language, identity, and learning. Educators simply cannot, as A. Wade Boykin proposes (2002), *develop the talent potential* of students from disenfranchised and marginalized ethnic groups and place them *at promise* for educational success without acknowledging their language and cultural diversity as fundamental to their current being and their possibilities for future becoming. Wheeler and Swords (2006) reinforce this idea in their comment that "only when we recognize the robust resource that our students offer can we begin to build bridges between cultures that may allow students to add Standard English to their repertoire" (p. 25).

Gloria Anzaldua (2004), a Latina feminist, makes an even more powerful and personal statement about the connection between language and identity. Her message is an important reminder to teachers and other educators not to be capricious or prejudicial in their attitudes and actions toward the languages of ethnically diverse students. She says:

> If you want to really hurt me, talk badly about my language. Ethnic identity is twin skin to linguistic identity—I am my language. Until I can take pride in my

language, I cannot take pride in myself. Until I can accept as legitimate Chicano Texas Spanish, Tex-Mex, and all other languages I speak, I cannot accept the legitimacy of myself. Until I am free to write bilingually and to switch codes without having always to translate, while I still have to speak English or Spanish when I would rather speak Spanglish, and as long as I have to accommodate the English speakers rather than having them accommodate me, my tongue will be illegitimate. (p. 271)

EFFECTS OF "ENGLISH PLUS" INSTRUCTION ON STUDENT ACHIEVEMENT

Do research and practice support the theoretical and conventional wisdom claims that using culturally diverse languages and communication styles improves the school achievement of students of color? Are the results convincing enough to warrant their use in teaching academic core and high-status knowledge and skills in literacy, math, science, social studies, critical thinking, and civic engagement? Is culturally responsive communication within the context of classroom instruction a viable means of closing a critical part of the achievement gaps? A growing body of research evidence is producing affirmative answers to these questions for languages other than English, and for dialects within English. A few examples of specific studies are included here to illustrate how these general results are being substantiated for particular ethnic groups. They create powerful messages about and methods for including culturally responsive communication in instructional practice.

Bilingual Effects

Both collective research studies and ones dealing with specific ethnic groups demonstrate that proficiency in heritage or indigenous languages correlates positively with higher academic English performance, especially when the former is used as a vehicle to facilitate the latter (Brisk, 2006; Collier, 1992; Garcia-Vasquez, Vasquez, & Lopez, 1997; Nguyen, Shin, & Krashen, 2001; Rickford, 2005; Slavin & Cheung, 2003). In an extensive review of research on proficiency correspondence between heritage languages (primarily Spanish) and English as a second language, edited by August and Shanahan (2006), some significant findings emerged. Although the results were not always positive, conclusive, or unequivocal, they were generally supportive of using bilingualism in teaching diverse students. Among the noteworthy results reported are:

- Certain aspects of second language literacy development, such as word recognition, vocabulary, comprehension, reading strategies, spelling, and writing, are related to performance on similar constructs in the first language.

- Certain types of grammatical errors in oral and written communication can be understood in terms of differences between the structures of first and second languages.
- Well-developed literacy skills in first or heritage languages facilitate second language literacy development.
- Some cross-language influences affect some aspects of second language learning more than others, and operate during some but not all phases of learning.
- The degree of typological similarity between first and second languages (such as Spanish and English) makes it easier for students to develop bilingual competence.
- Bridging home–school differences in interactional patterns and communication styles improves the engagement, motivation, and classroom participation of linguistically diverse students.
- Culturally relevant reading materials, especially those written in languages familiar to the students, facilitate comprehension and mastery.
- Students perform better when they read and learn in the language they know best, or what Geneva Smitherman (2000) calls their "language of nurture."
- Complex, comprehensive, and embedded instruction (such as teaching phonemic awareness, decoding, oral reading, comprehension, vocabulary, writing, and oral speech simultaneously) is more effective for second language mastery than compartmentalized and decontextualized learning.

Based on a review of 17 studies conducted in the 1980s of elementary Spanish bilingual programs in operation for 4 years or more, Collier (1992) added another general achievement trend. The measure of achievement was student performance on standardized tests of reading and mathematics in English. The more instructional support given to language-minority students in their first language, combined with balanced support in English, the greater was their academic achievement. This rate of achievement increased across the years for both math and reading as long as the students remained in bilingual programs (Grades K–6), as opposed to early exits (transferring to English Only instruction after 2 or 3 years). Genesee and associates (2006) reported similar results in their review of 200 studies and articles on the effects of bilingual education on student achievement in math and reading in both Spanish and English.

These general effects of bilingual instruction can be credited to the strong interactive relationship that exists among language, culture, and learning, rather than language alone. Montecel and Cortez (2002) found this to be the case in their analysis of 10 successful bilingual education programs (eight elementary and two high school). These were two-way bilingual programs that used Spanish, English, Russian, Navajo, and English in teaching reading, writing, math, science, and social studies. All of the schools involved in the study also were committed to maintaining the students' primary languages and cultures while teaching them English. They affirmed and validated racial and cultural differences, and cultivated learning climates characterized by caring, belonging, and friendliness. The majority of the participating students improved their achievement across the school year in which the study was conducted (1997–98) more than the comparison group, which did not receive any bilingual instruction. These findings affirm the importance of relevant cultural filters and contextual frames (including language) in teaching linguistically and culturally diverse students. This is particularly imperative when the learning challenges involve unfamiliar content, skills, and processes. Thus, multiple communication systems (or bi- and multilingualism) should be a natural part of high-quality education for ethnically diverse students, and a central feature of culturally responsive teaching for both recent immigrants and long-term residents or citizens of color in the United States.

Research on bilingual teaching for specific ethnic groups reveals similar results and recommendations. For example, Olson (n.d.) used data from the High School and Beyond study to examine the impact of early bilingual interventions on Mexican American high school sophomores. The results showed that teaching reading and writing in Spanish produced improved achievement, but not for math and science. Another important finding was that the addition of ancestral and cultural history to bilingual programs enhanced their effectiveness. The results of these studies suggest that language teaching for diverse students should not be decontextualized or separated from other important components of cultural diversity and learning, such as school and classroom climate, student–teacher relationships, caring, and culturally relevant curriculum content.

A very successful, although short-lived, initiative in the 1990s for Cambodian students was the Khmer Bilingual Program (Wright, 2003, 2006). It was located in an elementary school in California where 90% of the students were English language learners. The two dominant language groups were Khmer (50%) and Spanish (40%). The Khmer Bilingual Program used a transitional design model, but was very aggressive in creating culturally relevant materials and instructional strategies. All language arts for the Cambodian students in Grades K–2 were taught in Khmer, and they transitioned to English by the end of 3rd grade. The students also received at least 30 minutes of instruction in English each day. Language-specific curricular materials for the program were scarce, so the teachers created their own. They translated textbooks and other resources used in the English Only classes for reading, language arts, and social studies in

Grades K–3. Wright (2003) described the learning climates in the class-rooms as "extremely positive" and "rich in both Khmer and English print" (p. 236). For example,

> the walls were adorned with a plethora of teacher-made posters and charts. The Khmer alphabet was displayed prominently along with the English alphabet along the top of the chalkboard. Colorful calendars displayed the days of the week and the months of the year in both languages. In each classroom, a section on a wall was devoted to student writing, with space for each student to display their [sic] latest stories written in Khmer. Student work in other content areas covered the walls, and student artwork hung from the ceilings and lights. (p. 236)

The learning activities and benefits of the Khmer language arts instruction were as rich as the resources. Students engaged in a wide variety of literacy activities, including small-group guided reading and spelling with the teacher; individual writing in journals; working in different learning centers around the room; extracting information from charts and posters on display; reading quietly in the book center; and creating their own books in the writing center. The students involved in the program made comparable or better progress on oral English proficiency tests compared with those in English Only programs. The majority of the students were reading in Khmer at grade level by the end of 2nd grade, and at or above grade level in English by the end of 3rd grade. Other positive results of the program included students being very proud of their heritage language and culture, and parents being able to play more active and competent roles in their children's education. As one teacher in the program explained:

> When students learn Khmer there are many things their parents can help them with from school. When students learn English, their parents are usually unable to help them. Thus, students . . . see their parents with more respect. The students pride themselves in their knowledge of Khmer language and culture. And when they make progress in English, they really see the value of their Khmer language ability. (Wright, 2003, p. 237)

Unfortunately, the Khmer language arts program became a casualty (along with many others) of the 1998 Proposition 227 in California that eliminated bilingual education.

Similar rich teaching resources, varied learning activities, achievement benefits, and threatened continuation characterized the bilingual language arts programs at the Navajo Rock Point and Rough Rock Demonstration Schools. The Rough Rock English–Navajo Language Arts Program (RRENLAP) was designed to develop bilingual proficiency in grades K–6 in the content areas. Students were taught reading and mathematics first in

Navajo and then in English, while Navajo only was used to teach science and social studies. The secondary literacy program at Rock Point focused on student-centered research of local customs and traditions. During the first 3 years all teaching was done in Navajo, then it switched to Navajo and English. Both programs produced impressive academic, social, cultural, and psychoemotional results over the years of their existence, although the performance levels were still below the national averages. The students who initially were taught literacy skills in Navajo over 3 to 5 years made the greatest gains on local and national measures of achievement. They also outperformed their peers who were taught in English Only (Duval, 2005; Lomawaima & McCarty, 2006; McCarty, 2002). Despite these positive outcomes, the continuing existence of RRNELAP and other bilingual heritage language and English Plus initiatives is seriously threatened by the English Only policies passed by states and the federal government (Duval, 2005; Wright, 2006).

Most of the research studies and instructional programs on bilingual education focus on elementary school programs and Spanish speakers. A study conducted by Bankston and Zhou (1995) departs from this trend by examining the effects of literacy in their native language on the academic achievement of Vietnamese high school students. It involved 387 participants in Grades 9–12 in two high schools in New Orleans. Data were collected from students' self-reports of their Vietnamese reading and writing abilities, grades achieved in English, and aspirations and intentions about going to college. The results indicated that (1) the deliberate cultivation of ethnicity has positive effects on students' self-esteem, school persistence, and academic achievement; (2) acquisition of skills in a first language leads to cognitive development that can transfer to other areas of learning; (3) the use of a first language in teaching gives students access to social resources and supports of their ethnic community that they otherwise may not have; and (4) maintaining non-English languages is a valuable goal of academic achievement in and of itself.

Findings specific to Mexican American, Cambodian, Vietnamese, and Navajo ELLs are consistent with research results on bilingual education in general and across an even wider range of ethnic groups. Meta-analyses conducted by Willig (1985), Greene (1998), and Rolstad, Mahoney, and Glass (2005) concluded that bilingual education for ELLs has positive effects on all major academic areas, including reading and math standardized test scores measured in English. Another significant finding indicates that bilingual education is more effective than English Only approaches for improving the academic achievement of ELLs in English and in their heritage languages (Rolstad et al., 2005). Bilingual education (especially TWI and translanguaging) effects extend beyond academic subjects to include intellectual processing skills, along with psychological and emotional benefits. Specifically, some of these are improved executive function, perspective-taking, empathy, cross-cultural interactions, attendance, feelings of belonging, and attachment to schools, along with fewer behavioral problems (Christian, 2011; Collier & Thomas, 2014; Collins, 2014; Fortune, 2014; Garcia & Wei, 2014). The Bilingualism Matters Center at the University of Edinburgh adds that children exposed to different languages become more aware of different cultures, other people, and other points of view; are better than monolinguals at multitasking and focusing attention; and are often more precocious readers (bilingualism-matters.ppls. ed.ac.uk). Another worthy benefit noted by Fortune is that "becoming bilingual leads to new ways of conceptualizing yourself and others. It expands your worldview, so that you not only know more, you know differently." (2014, n.p.).

In view of these findings, Rolstad and associates (2005) suggest that to ban or greatly restrict the use of heritage languages for instructional purposes, or to emphasize rapid transition to English Only, is ill-advised and cannot be justified. Instead, "a national policy unencumbered by politics and ideology, should at least permit, and at best encourage, the development and implementation of bilingual approaches in all U.S. schools serving ELLs" (p. 590). Collins (2014) adds that even if schools do not have the personnel, fiscal resources, and policy regulations to provide formal bilingual education, it is still beneficial to foster a multilingual ecology that welcomes and supports the use of home languages, and to provide opportunities for students to discuss and collaborate with peers in these languages. The benefits of diverse language skills and perceptions of them as assets, cultural capital, and valuable funds of knowledge make them necessary components of and complements to culturally responsive teaching.

Ebonics Effects

Increasingly, research studies and classroom practices are exploring the benefits of using Ebonics in teaching African American students, examining the similarities and interferences between their cultural communicative styles and those of Standard Academic English, and explicitly teaching how and when to shift between the two. These techniques are called *code-switching* and *contrastive analysis* (C. Lee, 2007; Wheeler & Swords, 2006). Some of the results are presented here to demonstrate their feasibility and effectiveness as important features of culturally responsive teaching, and to encourage greater use of them in regular classroom instruction. More detailed explanations for using these instructional devices with dialect and nonnative English speakers are available in the bibliographic summary complied by Rickford, Sweetland, and Rickford (2004), and the research reviews of August and Shanahan (2006).

Project Bidialectism (H. Taylor, 1989) was designed to help African American college students improve their Academic English writing skills.

The intervention extended beyond Standard English syntax to include respect for both Academic English and Ebonics; teaching rule-governing patterns in both languages; understanding the cultural frameworks in which linguistic choices are embedded; teaching explicit contrasts of both languages and cultures; and establishing reciprocal and trustful relationships between students and the teacher. The specific purpose of the contrastive analysis was to "increase the expression of standard English features and decrease interfering black [sic] English features in writing" (H. Taylor, 1989, p. 101). This was done by comparing the grammatical patterns of the Ebonics the students habitually used with those of Standard Academic English. Contrastive analyses were combined with audiolinguistic learning (a teaching method used frequently in second language learning), pattern practice drills, counseling–learning relationship, and *ethnosensitive* (or culturally relevant) curriculum content. In the audiolinguistic technique, learning begins with listening and then progresses through speaking, reading, and writing. It also emphasizes that language appropriateness is determined by use rather than prescription. The practice drills moved the students gradually from recognition to discrimination to reproduction across features of Ebonics and Academic English by having them identify elements of both language varieties in written texts and speech dialogues, translating from one dialect to the other, and editing one another's writing drafts. The counseling-learning orientation developed a dynamic relationship between students and the teacher in which they taught one another, turned the classroom into a community of bilingual practice, and joined together to create contexts for learning that valued and respected both individual and group needs, strengths, resources, and accomplishments. The ethnosensitivity feature of the project attended to affectively and culturally embedded dimensions of language use. The students were assigned to read, observe, discuss, and write about movies, plays, written excerpts from books, essays, and short stories produced by African Americans and European Americans that centered on Black and mainstream U.S. cultures (H. Taylor, 1989).

Project Bidialectism was successful in accomplishing its goals. The total occurrence of African American syntactical features in the writings of the experimental group *decreased* by over 59%, while those of the comparison group *increased* by 8.5%. The most significant changes occurred in fewer uses of third-person singular and hypercorrection. While all students were aware of their dialect and culture, they were not knowledgeable about the grammatical features of Ebonics that interfered with their academic writing before the program. All students involved in the project accepted biculturalism and bilingualism as desirable goals to accomplish (H. Taylor, 1989). An important message of this project is the need for social and cultural factors and contexts to be woven into teaching linguistic diversity.

Fogel and Ehri (2000) provide a powerful example of the positive effects of teaching elementary students the parallels between the syntactical forms of Ebonics and English. They studied 89 Ebonics-speaking 3rd and 4th graders, using a pre- and post-test model, and comparing three different treatments. In one (Treatment E) students merely were introduced to six Standard Academic English and Ebonics grammatical forms. The second treatment group (ES) was exposed to these features and given strategies for how to produce SAE forms. The third group (ESP) received the exposure, strategies, explanation of the linguistic rules, and guided practice, plus feedback, in how to convert from Ebonics syntactic features to SAE ones. The specific skills examined were translation tasks, comprehension, story-writing, and self-efficacy. As expected, the students who received the ESP treatment performed much better than the others in demonstrating SAE translation, writing, and comprehension skills. They also wrote longer and more detailed stories. But, surprisingly, they did not exhibit higher levels of confidence (self-efficacy) in their ability to master Standard English. Fogel and Ehri attributed this unexpected result to the unrealistic and inflated perceptions of the students in the E and ES groups about their Standard English skills; the possibility that these African American students did not realize their writing and speaking styles were not "Standard English"; and the likelihood that once students became "linguistically conscious" of Standard English forms, their performance confidence declined. All of these explanations have serious, although different, implications for teaching students to improve their skills in Academic English.

R. Williams (1997) reviewed three projects from the early 1970s that successfully used Ebonics to improve the achievement of African American students. One translated items on the Boehm Test of Basic Concepts into Ebonics and then administered it to K–2 students. The children scored significantly higher on the Ebonics version. In another project, a translated version of the Peabody Picture Vocabulary Test produced major improvements in the IQ scores of African Americans. The third study dealt with the Bridge reading program. It began instruction by using the students' own language skills and then shifted gradually to Standard English. After 4 months of instruction, the Bridge students showed an increase of 6.2 months in their reading scores on the Iowa Test of Basic Skills.

M. Foster (1989) did an ethnographic analysis of the effects of an African American community college teacher's use of cultural communication styles on the achievement of her students. As the cultural nuances in her instructional discourse increased, so did the students' performance. Improvements occurred in attending behaviors, time-on-task, participation in classroom dialogue, concept mastery, recall of factual information with greater accuracy, and more enthusiasm in and confidence about learning. Similar findings have been reported for young children by Piestrup (1973), Hall, Reder, and Cole (1979), and Howard (1998). These researchers found that using African American communication styles with students in preschool programs and in the elementary and middle school grades improved their reading literacy skills, personal self-concepts, and academic efficacy. The communication features used in teaching included dramatic presentation styles, conversational and active participatory discourse, dialect, gestures and body movements, rapidly paced rhythmic speech, metaphorical imagery, and reading materials about African American culture and experiences written by African Americans. Improvements occurred in students' interest and task engagement, recall of more factual details from stories told, greater word recognition and accuracy of meanings, and higher scores on standardized reading tests.

Even more impressive are the results Carol Lee (1991, 1993, 2007) and Delain, Pearson, and Anderson (1985) obtained from using cultural discourse techniques prominent among African Americans in their contrastive analyses to teach higher-order literary skills to high school and middle school students. Lee used *signifying* as the entrée to teaching high school seniors skills in critical thinking, textual analysis, and literary interpretation. According to Smitherman (1986, 2000), signifying is the verbal art of insult in which speakers use humor, insinuation, and exaggeration to put down and talk about one another. Lee (1993) adds that it is a discourse heuristic for problem-solving that requires analogical reasoning. Metaphor, irony, symbolism, and innuendo are critical tools of signifying. *Sounding* is similar to signifying in content, technique, and effect. Both Lee and Delain and associates hypothesized that using these discourse techniques in classroom instruction would help African American students who were familiar with them to improve their mastery of some literary skills commonly taught in schools.

Carol Lee tested this hypothesis with 109 students, two-thirds of whom had performed in the lowest two quartiles of the local school district- and state-mandated standardized tests of reading achievement. She designed a 6-week experimental intervention that was implemented in four phases. First, the students in the experimental group analyzed samples of signifying dialogues to become consciously aware of their own personal and social communicative competence. Second, two articles written by recognized experts on the meaning and characteristics of signifying were analyzed. Third, students worked in small groups to create their own signifying dialogues. Fourth, the conceptual knowledge acquired about signifying was applied to tasks of literary criticism. The students had to interpret figurative language, ironic verbal constructions, and complex implied relationships in the literary texts of Zora Neale Hurston's *Their Eyes Were Watching God* (1990) and Alice Walker's *The Color Purple* (1985). An inquiry mode of instruction was employed throughout the intervention to conduct close textual analyses of the novels, allow small groups of students to talk about questions related to the readings, and encourage individuals to write about their ideas and opinions related to the questions posed. Students in the control group received no specific instruction beyond what normally occurred in their literature classes.

At the end of the intervention, both groups had made improvements in their literary analysis skills, but those of the experimental group were substantially greater than those of the control group. Of the eight specific literary skills examined, the experimental group made significant improvements in five (key detail, simple implied relationships, application, structural generalizations, complex implied relationships). The control group improved in three of these skills (key detail, simple implied relationships, and structural generalizations). The greatest difference occurred in the ability to infer different types of relationships (stated, simple implied, and complex implied) embedded in literary texts. Students in the experimental group who began the experience at the lowest level of achievement made the greatest gains. Lee attributes this to higher levels of congruency between their prior social knowledge of and skills in signifying, and the metaphors and irony embedded in the literary texts used in the study.

The quality of classroom discourse also differed by treatment groups. Discussions in the experimental classes were more student-initiated, as well as consistently focused on difficult, inferential questions and figurative or metaphorical aspects of the narrative text of the novels being studied; in addition, the students routinely referenced literary texts explaining concepts, principles, and skills. In the control classes, discussions were teacher-dominated, concentrated on students' personal opinions about themes in the texts, and emphasized literal renditions of plots. These students did not engage with the words, images, and ironies in the literary texts, nor were they challenged to analyze their multiple meanings (C. Lee, 1993).

Since these earlier efforts to use a cultural speech genre (signifying, which she later named Cultural Modeling) to teach literary reasoning skills to low-achieving African American high school students, Carol Lee has continued to refine and expand this instructional technique and intervention. More recent versions include elementary students and writing skills. However, the primary purpose remains largely the same as in the earlier projects, that is, to help underachieving African American students learn academic subject matter knowledge, concepts, and skills by making explicit analogies between them and similar ones they use in everyday cultural practices outside of school, through detailed contrastive analyses and recognition of indigenous cultural competence. A Cultural Modeling Narrative Project was implemented with 10- and 11-year-olds to test the specific premise that using familiar African American rhetorical features (i.e., a form of communicative cultural capital) to teach narrative writing skills would improve students' performance. "Cultural data sets" were included in the study as prompts and training tools to develop transfer or conversion skills from African American oral cultural to academic written discourse styles. These were samples of visual art depicting various scenes of African American cultural experiences produced by Annie Lee. Carol Lee and her research team hypothesized that these art scenes were "cultural scripts" familiar to African American students; that the images depicted would evoke concrete memories and feelings of affinity from the students; and that the associated ethnic identity and cultural bonds would prompt more interest in and skills of writing (C. Lee, 2001, 2007, 2009; C. Lee, Rosenfeld, Mendenhall, Rivers, & Tynes, 2004). The results of the intervention supported the hypotheses. The students were more engaged with the learning stimuli and used their funds of knowledge and personal experiences to make meaningful inferences from the cultural data sets. They also incorporated commonly identified African American discourse features, along with other elements of good narrative writing, into the scripts they constructed. However, their command of other basic writing skills, such as spelling, punctuation, and paragraph formation, were unaffected by either the training intervention or its results.

Delain and associates (1985) used sounding as their target of analysis. The participants in their study were 157 7th graders (107 African Americans and 50 European Americans) in two schools. Data were gathered on the students' general verbal ability, figurative language comprehension, skill in sounding, and general ability in Ebonics. Nine measures were used to collect these data. They included the Stanford Diagnostic Reading Test; the Anderson–Freebody vocabulary test; a comprehension test of Standard English double-function words, such as idioms, metaphors, and similes; five different assessments of sounding skills (peer ratings, word completion and translation comprehension measures, a recognition measure, and open-ended "comeback" responses to sounding prompts); and knowledge of double-function items used in only Black English.

The results of the study revealed significant differences between the abilities of the African and European American students on the various experimental tasks. Only general language ability accounted for the White students' figurative language comprehension. The figurative language comprehension of the African American students was influenced by a combination of general verbal ability, sounding, and Ebonics skills. In other words, their general language ability was significantly related to figurative language comprehension, and their Ebonics facility influenced their sounding abilities, which in turn affected their comprehension of figurative language. These findings led Delain and associates (1985) to recommend that since "skills acquired 'in the streets,' so to speak, do transfer to school settings, teachers need to develop a respect for, rather than a bias against, the use of such language" (p. 171). The reasoning behind this recommendation is similar to the idea of *grammatical echos* suggested by Wheeler and Sword (2006). By this they mean that the patterns bilingual learners acquire in their first languages are transferred into their expressions in the second language. This transference can include linguistic features as well as discourse nuances. Therefore, it is possible for an African American to speak Standard English with an Ebonics flavor, as it is for Mexican, Filipino, Japanese, Chinese, or Ethiopian Americans to speak English with an accent. Teachers need to understand these phenomena in order to make better decisions about intervention points and strategies to use in teaching students different language varieties and their appropriate uses.

Even if there were no programmatic and empirical evidence that incorporating the languages and communication styles of different ethnic groups into educational programs and practices produces explicit academic improvements, they still should be routine parts of teaching and learning for all students. Acknowledging and respecting *human* diversity, its multiple variations, and the benefits derived from so doing, such as enhanced human dignity and self-esteem, better interpersonal relationships, and psychoemotional well-being, warrant their inclusion. These sentiments are captured cogently by Abby Figueroa (2004) in a statement about the power derived from her personal habits of speaking "Spanglish" (a mixture of Spanish and English):

> Every time I find myself thinking, speaking, writing and breathing in two languages, . . . I disagree with anyone who thinks that speaking both simultaneously is a disgrace. . . . Not for a second do I believe that my deliberate Spanglish, my twisting and turning through dos idiomas [two languages] is wrong. At the very least it helps me express myself more precisely. A larger vocabulary, dozens more idioms, mas chistes [more jokes], all this and more make my world more colorful. Le da mas sabor a mis pensamientos [It gives more flavor to my thoughts]. (p. 284)

Many speakers of other linguistic varieties and dialects of English, including Ebonics, find strength and validation in their bilingualism comparable to those expressed by Figueroa. When people translate their thoughts, beliefs, values, experiences, and perspectives—themselves—from their first language into a second one, "parts of themselves are sometimes inaccessible or inexpressible" (C. Jones & Shorter-Gooden, 2003, p. 102). This is so because "language is imbued with historical and cultural meaning and serves an important identity function for its speakers" (p. 102). Culturally responsive educators understand these important functions of language and are always alert to Benjamin Alire Saenz's (2004) warning that "to erase a language is to erase a culture" (p. 282). They also remember that educational achievement is more than high scores on reading, writing, math, and science tests. Respect for self and others, civic participation, community membership, moral and ethical behaviors, and multicultural competence are important, too. Teaching to and through linguistic, cultural, ethnic, social, and racial diversity helps to develop these competencies as well as improve academic achievement.

VARIATIONS IN ETHNIC DISCOURSE STYLES

Mention of different ethnic languages and communication styles often evokes images of the vocabulary, grammar, and enunciation of nonnative English and dialect speakers. While these are important, discourse features are even more so as vehicles for making teaching and learning across many different skill areas (not just those specific to linguistic competence) more effective for ethnically diverse students. Geneva Smitherman (2007) reminds us of this caveat, noting that responsiveness to culturally diverse communication in education has never been about "language in some narrow structural sense, but language as discourse, rhetoric, and cultural practice" (p. 153). Some of the most salient features of the discourse styles of different ethnic groups are discussed next.

Participation Structures

In conventional classroom discourse students are expected to assume what Kochman (1985) calls a *passive–receptive* posture. They are told to listen quietly while the teacher talks. Once the teacher finishes, then the students can respond in some prearranged, stylized way—by asking or answering questions; validating or approving what was said; or taking individual, teacher-regulated turns at talking. Individual students gain the right to participate in the conversation by permission of the teacher. The verbal discourse is accompanied by nonverbal attending behaviors and speech-delivery mechanisms that require maintaining eye contact with the speaker and using little or no physical movement. Thus, students are expected to be silent and look at teachers when they are talking and to wait to be acknowledged before they take their turn at talking. Once permission is granted, they should follow established rules of decorum, such as one person speaking at a time, being brief and to the point, and keeping emotional nuances to a minimum (Kochman, 1981; Philips, 1983).

These rules of participation are expressed in other classroom practices as well. Among them are expecting students always to speak in complete sentences that include logical development of thought, precise information, appropriate vocabulary, and careful attention to grammatical features such as appropriate use of vocabulary and noun–verb tense agreement. Student participation in classroom interactions often is elicited by teachers asking questions that are directed to specific individuals and require a narrow range of information-giving, descriptive responses. It is important for individuals to distinguish themselves in the conversations, for student responses to be restricted to only the specific demands of questions asked, and for the role of speaker and listener to be clearly separated.

In contrast to the passive–receptive, linearly ordered, and teacher-dominated character of conventional classroom discourse, some ethnic groups have communication styles that Kochman (1985) describes as *participatory–interactive*. Speakers expect listeners to engage them actively through vocalized, motion, and movement responses *as they are speaking*. Speakers and listeners are action-provoking partners in the construction of the discourse. These communicative styles have been observed among African Americans, Latino Americans, and Native Hawaiians. As is the case with other cultural behaviors, they are likely to be more pronounced among individuals who strongly identify and affiliate with their ethnic groups and cultural heritages. For example, low-income and minimally educated members of ethnic groups are likely to manifest group cultural behaviors more thoroughly than those who are middle-class and educated. They have fewer opportunities to interact with people different from themselves and to be affected by the cultural exchanges and adaptations that result from the intermingling of a wide variety of people from diverse ethnic groups and varied experiential backgrounds.

African Americans "gain the floor" or get participatory entry into conversations through personal assertiveness, the strength of the impulse to be involved, and the persuasive power of the point they wish to make, rather than by waiting for an "authority" to grant permission. They tend to invest their participation with personality power, actions, and emotions. Consequently, African Americans often are described as verbal performers whose speech behaviors are fueled by personal advocacy, passion, fluidity, and creative variety (Abrahams, 1970; Baber, 1987). These communication facilities have been attributed to the oral–aural nature of African American cultural and communal value orientations (Pasteur & Toldson, 1982; Smitherman, 2000). Many teachers view them negatively, as "rude," "inconsiderate," "disruptive," and "speaking out of turn," and they penalize students for them.

Relationship Between Speakers and Listeners

Another feature of the participatory–interactive discourse style among African Americans sometimes is referred to as *call–response* (Asante, 1998; Baber, 1987; Kochman, 1972, 1981, 1985; Smitherman, 1986, 2000). It involves listeners giving encouragement, commentary, compliments, and even criticism to speakers *as they are talking*. The speaker's responsibility is to issue the "calls" (making statements), and the listeners' obligation is to respond in some expressive, and often auditory, way (e.g., smiling, vocalizing, looking about, moving around, "amen-ing") (Dandy, 1991; Smitherman, 1986). When a speaker says something that triggers a response in them (whether positive or negative, affective or cognitive), African American listeners are likely to "talk back." This may involve a vocal or motion response, or both, sent directly to the speaker or shared with neighbors in the audience. Longstreet (1978) and Shade (1994) describe the practice as "breaking in and talking over." This mechanism is used to signal speakers that their purposes have been accomplished or that it is time to change the direction or leadership of the conversation. Either way, there is no need for the speaker to pursue the particular discourse topic or technique any further.

The call–response communication style can be a viable instructional resource for use with African American students if teachers understand its features, dynamics, and codes of delivery. It should not be confused with the rote memory and repetition drills prominent in some current versions of scripted texts and direct instruction. The descriptions offered by Hecht, Jackson, and Ribeau (2003) are helpful guides. They contend that the performance, narrative, and constructive features of African American oral communication serve many cultural functions beyond transmitting information. They extol the unique verbal skills of individuals; showcase assertive ingenuity and creativity; link speaker and audience to each other; reinforce shared identities, norms, and values; reinforce the dialectic of cooperation and competition; and demonstrate facility in code- and style-shifting.

Scholars such as Kochman (1981), Smitherman (1986, 2000b), Rickford and Rickford (2000), Delpit and Doudy (2002), and Delpit (2006) identify several other features that distinguish how African American speakers interact with listeners. They include the prolific use of dramatics, body language, and gesturing; sermonic tone and techniques; cultural references; ethnolinguistic idioms and proverbs; conversational storytelling; and rhetorical devices such as rhythm, rhyme, rate, repetition, improvisation, lyricism, and histocultural contextualization. These are social assets and cultural strengths that can facilitate academic capacity building. Therefore, they are good fits for culturally responsive teaching.

Native Hawaiian students who maintain their traditional cultural practices use a participatory-interactive communicative style similar to the call–response of African Americans. Called "talk-story" or "co-narration," it involves several students working collaboratively, or talking together, to create an idea, tell a story, or complete a learning task (Au, 1980a, 1993; Au & Kawakami, 1985, 1991, 1994; Au & Mason, 1981; Boggs et al., 1985). After observing these behaviors among elementary students, Au (1993) concluded that "what seems important to Hawaiian children in talk story is not individual . . . but group performance in speaking" (p. 114). These communication preferences are consistent with the importance Native Hawaiian culture places on individuals' contributing to the well-being of family and friends instead of working only for their own betterment (Gallimore, Boggs, & Jordan, 1974; Tharp & Gallimore, 1988).

A communicative practice that has some of the same traits of call–response and talk-story has been observed among European American females. Tannen (1990) calls it "cooperative overlapping" and describes it as women "talking along with speakers to show participation and support" (p. 208). It occurs most often in situations where talk is casual and friendly.

This *rapport-talk* is used to create community. It is complemented by other traditional women's ways of communicating, such as the following:

- Being "audience" more often than "speaker" in that they are recipients of information provided by males
- Deemphasizing expertise and the competitiveness it generates
- Focusing on individuals in establishing friendships, networks, intimacy, and relationships more than exhibiting power, accomplishment, or control
- Negotiating closeness in order to give and receive confirmation, support, and consensus
- Avoiding conflict and confrontation (Belenky, Clinchy, Goldberger, & Tarule, 1986; Klein, 1982; Maltz & Borker, 1983; Tannen, 1990)

While these habits of "communal communication and interaction" are normal to the users, they can be problematic to classroom teachers. On first encounter, they may be perceived as "indistinguishable noise and chaos" or unwholesome dependency. Even after the shock of the initial encounter passes, teachers may still consider these ways of communicating socially deviant, not conducive to constructive intellectual engagement, rude, and insulting. They see these habits as obstructing individual initiative and preempting the right of each student to have a fair chance to participate in instructional discourse. These assessments can prompt attempts to rid students of the habits and replace them with the rules of individualistic, passive-receptive, and controlling communication styles that predominate in classrooms. Teachers may not realize that by doing this they could be causing irreversible damage to students' abilities or inclinations to engage fully in the instructional process. Hymes (1985) made this point when he suggested that rejecting ethnically different students' communication styles may be perceived by them as rejection of their personhood. Whether intentional or not, casting these kinds of aspersions on the identity and personal worth of students of color does not bode well for their academic achievement.

Problem-Solving and Task Engagement

A most common practice among teachers is to ask convergent (single-answer) questions and use deductive approaches to solving problems. Emphasis is given to details, to building the whole from parts, to moving from the specific to the general. Discourse tends to be didactic, involving one student with the teacher at a time (Goodlad, 1984). In comparison, students of color who are strongly affiliated with their traditional cultures tend to be more inductive, interactive, and communal in task performance. The preference for inductive problem-solving is expressed as reasoning from the whole to parts, from the general to the specific. The focus is on the "big picture," the pattern, the principle (Boggs et al., 1985; Philips, 1983; Ramírez & Castañeda, 1974; Shade, 1997).

Although these general patterns of task engagement prevail across ethnic groups, variations do exist. Some teachers use inductive modes of teaching, and some students within each ethnic group of color learn deductively. Many Asian American students seem to prefer questions that require specific answers but are proposed to the class as a whole. While many Latino students may be inclined toward learning in group contexts, specific individuals may find these settings distracting and obstructive to their task mastery.

In traditional African American and Latino cultures, problem-solving is highly contextual. One significant feature of this contextuality is creating a "stage" or "setting" prior to the performance of a task. The stage-setting is invariably social in nature. It involves establishing personal connections with others who will participate, as a prelude to addressing the task. In making these connections, individuals are readying themselves for "work" by cultivating a social context. They are, in effect, activating their cultural socialization that an individual functions better within the context of a group. Without the group as an anchor, referent, and catalyst, the individual is set adrift, having to function alone.

These cultural inclinations may be operating when Latino adults begin their task interactions with colleagues by inquiring about the families of the other participants and their own personal well-being, or when African American speakers inform the audience about their present psychoemotional disposition and declare the ideology, values, and assumptions underlying the positions they will be taking in the presentation (i.e., "where they are coming from"). This "preambling" or "stage-setting" is a way for the speakers to prime the audience and themselves for the subsequent performance. Students of color in classrooms may be setting the stage for their engagement with learning tasks (e.g., writing an essay, doing seatwork, taking a test) when they seem to be spending unnecessary time arranging their tests, sharpening pencils, shifting their body postures (stretching, flexing their hands, arms, and legs, etc.), or socializing with peers rather than attending to the assigned task. "Preparation before performance" for these students serves a purpose in learning similar to a theater performer doing yoga exercises before taking the stage. Both are techniques the "actors" use to focus, to get themselves in the mood and mode to perform.

For those Asian Americans who prefer to learn within the context of groups, it is accomplished through a process of *collaborative and negotiated problem-solving*. Regardless of how minor or significant an issue is, they seek out opinions and proposed solutions from all members of the constituted group. Each individual's ideas are presented and critiqued. Their merits are weighed against the ones suggested by every other member of the group. Discussions are animated and expansive so that all parties can participate and understand the various elements of the negotiations. Eventually, a solution is reached that is a compromise of several possibilities. Then more discussions follow to ensure that everyone is in agreement with the solution and understands who is responsible for what aspects of its implementation. These discussions proceed in a context of congeniality and *consensus-building* among the many, not with animosity, domination, and the imposition of the will of a few.

A compelling illustration of the positive effects of this process on student achievement occurred in Treisman's (1985; Fullilove & Treisman, 1990) Mathematics Workshop Program at the University of California, Berkeley. He observed the study habits of Chinese Americans to determine why they performed so well in high-level mathematics classes and to see whether he could use their model with Latinos and African Americans. He found what others have observed more informally—the Chinese American students always studied in groups, and they routinely explained to one another their understanding of the problems and how they arrived at solutions to them. Treisman attributed their high achievement to the time they devoted to studying and to talking through the solution processes with peers. When he simulated this process with African Americans and Latinos, their achievement improved radically. Treisman was convinced that group study made the difference. Given other evidence that compatibility between cultural habits and teaching–learning styles improves student performance, this is probably what occurred. Communal problem-solving and the communicative impulse were evoked, thus producing the desired results.

These are powerful but challenging pedagogical lessons for all educators to learn and emulate in teaching students of color. Collective and situated performance styles require a distribution of resources (timing, collective efforts, procedures, attitudes) that can collide with school norms; for instance, much assessment of student achievement occurs in tightly scheduled arrangements, which do not accommodate stage-setting or collective performance. Students of color have to learn different styles of performing, as well as the substantive content, to demonstrate their achievement. This places them in potential double jeopardy—that is, failing at the level of both procedure and substance. Pedagogical reform must be cognizant of these dual needs and attend simultaneously to the content of learning and the processes for demonstrating mastery. It also must be bidirectional—that is, changing instructional practices to make them more culturally responsive to ethnic and cultural diversity, while teaching students of color how to better negotiate mainstream educational structures.

Organizing Ideas in Discourse

How ideas and thoughts are organized in written and spoken expression can be very problematic to student achievement. Two techniques commonly are identified—*topic-centered* and *topic-associative* or *topic-chaining* techniques. European Americans seem to prefer the first, while Latino Americans, African Americans, Native Americans, and Native Hawaiians (Au, 1993; Champion, 1997, 2003; Gee, 1985; Heath, 1983; Michaels, 1981) are inclined toward the second.

In *topic-centered* discourse speakers focus on one issue at a time; arrange facts and ideas in logical, linear order; and make explicit referential, temporal, and spatial relationships. Speech episodes tend to be short and precise. In this process, cognitive processing moves deductively from discrete parts to a cumulative whole with a discernible closure. Quality is determined by clarity of descriptive details, absence of unnecessary or flowery elaboration, and how well explanations remain focused on the essential features of the issue being analyzed. The structure, content, and delivery of this discourse style closely parallel the expository, descriptive writing and speaking commonly used in schools. A classic example of topic-centered discourse is journalistic writing, which concentrates on giving information about who, what, when, where, why, and how as quickly as possible. Its purpose is to convey information and to keep this separate from other speech functions, such as persuasion, commentary, and critique. Another illustration is the thinking and writing associated with empirical inquiry, or critical problem-solving. Again, there is a hierarchical progression in the communication sequence, beginning with identifying the problem, collecting data, identifying alternative solutions and related consequences, and selecting and defending a solution. There is a clear attempt to separate facts from opinions, information from emotions.

A *topic-associative* style of talking and writing also has been called topic-chaining, performance discourse, and narrative style. It is episodic, anecdotal, thematic, and integrative. More than one issue is addressed at once. Related explanations unfold in overlapping, intersecting loops, with one emerging out of and building on others. Relationships among segments of the discourse are assumed or inferred rather than explicitly established (Cazden, 1988; Champion, 1997, 2003; C. Lee & Slaughter-Defoe, 1995; Michaels, 1981). Thinking and speaking appear to be circular and seamless rather than linear and clearly demarcated. Topic chainers also rely heavily on such paralinguistic devices as tempo, rhythm, intonation, vowel elongation, repetition, and nonverbal gestures. Creativity in delivery is as important to them as quality of content. The speakers are active participants in their own narratives. To those unfamiliar with it, this communication style sounds rambling, disjointed, unfocused, and as if the speaker is unprepared and never ends a thought before going on to something else. For these reasons, Champion (1998, 2003) calls topic-chaining discourse "performative narration." Her research with 6- to 10-year-old African Americans indicated that they used a topic-associative discourse style predominantly but not exclusively. Instead, the children used a repertoire of complex discourse structures (including topic-centered) that were influenced by context, task, social factors, and culture. Undoubtedly, other speakers and their discourse styles are similarly affected.

Goodwin (1990) observed topic-chaining discourse at work in a mixed-age (4- to 14-year-olds) group of African Americans in a Philadelphia neighborhood as they told stories, shared gossip, settled arguments, and negotiated relationships. She noted the ease and finesse with which a child could switch from a contested verbal exchange to an engaging story and dramatically reshape dyadic interactions into multiparty ones. Using a single utterance, the children could evoke a broad history of events, a complex web of identities and relationships that all participants understood, without having elaborate details on any of the separate segments. The talk-story discourse style among Native Hawaiians operates in a similar fashion, which explains why Au (1993) characterizes it as a "joint performance, or the cooperative production of responses by two or more speakers" (p. 113).

Another communicative habit indicative of a topic-chaining or associative discourse style, and particularly evident in writing, is the prolific use of conjunctions and conjunctive phrases. Many African, Asian, and Latino heritage students (both recent immigrants and citizens) frequently begin sentences with words such as "consequently," "therefore," "however," "thus," "moreover," "additionally," "furthermore," and "likewise"—sometimes as often as four of every five or six. It is as if they are literally connecting one sentence to the other, thereby making their thought chains and relationships explicit. In mainstream-culture academic writing, these relationships are implied and signaled by paragraph notations. The assumption and expectation are that all sentences in a paragraph are related to the same topic or idea. This relationship prevails until the beginning of another paragraph and a different set of thoughts is signaled.

Storytelling as Topic-Associative Discourse

African Americans (Delpit, 1995; Kochman, 1981, 1985; Rickford & Rickford, 2000; Smitherman, 1986, 1996, 2000) and Native Hawaiians (Boggs, 1985) have been described as not responding directly to questions asked. Instead, they give narratives, or tell stories. This involves setting up and describing a series of events (and the participants) loosely connected to the questions asked. It is as if ideas and thoughts, like individuals, do not function or find meaning in isolation from context. A host of other actors and events are evoked to assist in constructing the "stage" upon which the individuals eventually interject their own performance (i.e., answer the question). This *narrative-response* style also is signaled by the attention given to "introductions" and preludes in writing. They are extensive enough to prompt such comments from teachers as, "Get to the point" or "Is this relevant?" or "More focus needed" or "Too much extraneous stuff" or "Stick to the topic." The students simply think that these preludes are necessary to setting the stage for the substantive elements of the discourse.

Speaking about the purposes and pervasiveness of storytelling among African Americans, Smitherman (1986, 1996, 2000) surmises that they allow many different things to be accomplished at once. These include relating information, persuading others to support the speaker's point of view, networking, countering opposition, exercising power, and demonstrating one's own verbal aestheticism. She elaborates further on African American speakers' proclivity toward using narrative and storytelling, dramatic performance in reporting events, sociopsychological perspectives on facts, and much contextual framing or stage-setting in presenting information. She also acknowledges that these communication styles can be exasperating to European Americans who are accustomed to more direct and descriptive communication.

It takes African American topic-chaining speakers a while to get to the point—to orchestrate the cast of contributors to the action. The less time they have to develop their story lines, the more difficult it is for them to get to the substantive heart of the matter. Frequently in schools, the time allocated to learning experiences lapses while African Americans are still setting up the backdrop for "the drama"—their expected task performance—and they never get to demonstrate what they know or can do on the proposed academic task.

Posed to an African American student who routinely uses a topic-chaining discourse style, a simple, apparently straightforward question such as, "What did you do during summer vacation?" might prompt a response such as this:

Sometimes, especially on holidays, you know, like July 4, or maybe when a friend was celebrating a birthday, we go to the amusement park. It's a long ways from where I live. And, that is always a big thing, because we have to get together and form car caravans. Jamie and Kelly are the best drivers, but I preferred to ride with Aisha because her dad's van is loaded, and we be just riding along, chilling, and listening to tapes and stuff. Going to the amusement park was a kick 'cause we had to drive a long way, and when we got there people would stare at us like we were weird or something. And we would just stare right back at them. All but Dion. He would start to act crazy, saying things like, "What you lookin' at me for? I ain't no animal in no zoo. I got as much right to be here as you do." You see, Dion gets hyped real quick about this racist thing. And we be telling him, "Man, cool it. Don't start no stuff. We too far from home for that." Then, we just go on into the park and have us a good time. We try to get all the rides before everything closes down for the night. Then, there's the trip home. Everybody be tired but happy. We do this three or four times in the summer. Different people go each time. But, you know something—we always run into some kind of funny stuff, like people expecting us to make trouble. Why is that so? All we doing is out for a good time. Dion, of course, would say it's a racist thing.

The narrator does eventually answer the question, but it is embedded in a lot of other details. In fact, there are stories within stories within stories (e.g., celebration rituals, friendships, drivers, the drive, racism, risk-taking, activities at the amusement park, similarities and differences, continuity and change, etc.). These elaborate details are needed to convey the full meaning of the narrator's answer to the initial question. But to culturally uninitiated listeners or readers (such as many classroom teachers), the account sounds like rambling and unnecessarily convoluted information, or Smitherman's (1986) notion of "belabored verbosity."

Teachers seeking to improve the academic performance of students of color who use topic-associative discourse styles need to incorporate a story-telling motif into their instructional behaviors. This can be done without losing any of the substantive quality of academic discourses. Gee (1989) believes topic-associative talking is inherently more complex, creative, literary, and enriching than topic-centered speech. The assertions are verified by the success of the Kamehameha Early Elementary Program, which produced remarkable improvement in the literacy achievement of Native Hawaiian students by employing their cultural and communication styles in classroom instruction. Boggs (1985) found that the performance of Native Hawaiian students on the reading readiness tests correlated positively with narrative abilities. The children who told longer narratives identified the picture prompts more correctly than those who responded to individually directed questions from adults.

Yet topic-associative discourse is troubling to many conventional teachers. Michaels and Cazden's (1986) research explains why. The European American teachers who participated in their study found this discourse style difficult to understand and placed little value on it. African American teachers gave equal positive value to topic-centered and topic-associative discourse. We should not assume that this will always be the case. Some African American teachers are as troubled by topic-chaining discourse among students as teachers from other ethnic groups. The ethnicity of teachers is not the most compelling factor in culturally responsive teaching for ethnically diverse students. Rather, it is teachers' knowledge base and positive attitudes about cultural diversity, as well as their ability to effectively teach ethnically diverse students, contributions, experiences, and perspectives.

Taking Positions and Presenting Self

In addition to significant differences in the *organization* of thinking, writing, and talking, many ethnically diverse students *relate* differently to the materials, issues, and topics discussed or analyzed. Most of the information available on these patterns deals with African and European Americans. Deyhle and Swisher (1997) concluded their historical review of research conducted on Native Americans with a strong conviction that there are fundamental and significant linkages among culture, communication, and cognition that should help shape classroom instruction for ethnically diverse students. But they do not provide any descriptions of the discourse dynamics of various Native American groups. Fox (1994) examined the thinking, writing, and speaking behaviors of international students from different countries in Africa, Asia, Latin America, and the Middle East studying in U.S. colleges and universities. She found that their cultural traditions valued indirect and holistic communication, wisdom of the past, and the importance of the group. Their cultural socialization profoundly affects how these students interact with professors and classmates, reading materials, problem-solving, and writing assignments. How they write is especially important to their academic performance because, according to Fox (1994), "writing touches the heart of a student's identity, drawing its voice and strength and meaning from the way the student understands the world" (p. xiii).

Kochman (1972, 1981, 1985), Dandy (1991), and Smitherman (1986, 1996, 2000) point out that African Americans (especially those most strongly affiliated with their ethnic identity and cultural heritage) tend to take positions of advocacy and express personal points of view in discussions. Facts, opinions, emotions, and reason are combined in presenting one's case. The worth of a particular line of reasoning is established by challenging the validity of oppositional ideas and by the level of personal ownership of the individuals making the presentations. Declaring one's personal position on issues, and demanding the same of others, is also a way of recognizing "the person" as a valid data source (Kochman, 1981). Publication is not enough to certify the authority of ideas and explanations, or the expertise of the people who author them. They must stand the test of critical scrutiny and the depth of personal endorsement. African Americans are more likely to challenge authority and expertise than are students from other ethnic groups because they

> consider debate to be as much a contest between individuals as a test of opposing ideas. Because it is a contest, attention is also paid to performance, for winning the contest requires that one outperform one's opponents: outthink, outtalk, and outstyle. It means being concerned with art as well as argument. . . . Blacks consider it essential for individuals to have personal positions on issues and assume full responsibility for arguing their validity. Otherwise, they feel that individuals would not care enough about truth or their own ideas to want to struggle for them. And without such struggle, the truth value of ideas cannot be ascertained. (Kochman, 1981, pp. 24–25)

According to Kochman (1981), the discourse dynamics of European Americans are almost the opposite of those of African Americans. He says European Americans relate to issues and materials as reporters, not advocates, and consider the truth or merits of an idea to be intrinsic, especially if the person presenting it has been certified as an authority or expert. How deeply individuals personally care about the idea is irrelevant. Their responsibility is to present the facts as accurately as possible. They believe that emotions interfere with one's capacity to reason and quality of reasoning. Thus, European Americans try to avoid or minimize opposition in dialogue (especially when members of ethnic minority groups are involved) because they assume it will be confrontational and divisive, and lead to intransigence or the further entrenchment of opposing viewpoints. They aim to control impulse and emotions, to be open-minded and flexible, and to engage a multiplicity of ideas. Since no person is privy to all the answers, the best way to cull the variety of possibilities is to ensure congeniality, not confrontation, in conversation. As a result of these beliefs and desires, the European American style of intellectual and discourse engagement "weakens or eliminates those aspects of character or posture that they believe keep people's minds closed and make them otherwise unyielding" (Kochman, 1981, p. 20).

"Playing with and on" Words

African American cultural discourse uses repetition for emphasis and to create a cadence in speech delivery that approximates other aspects of cultural expressiveness such as dramatic flair, powerful imagery, persuasive effect, and polyrhythmic patterns (Baber, 1987; Kochman, 1981; Smitherman, 1986, 2000). Some individuals are very adept at "playing on" and "playing with" words, thereby creating a "polyrhythmic character" to their speaking. It is conveyed through the use of nonparallel structures, juxtaposition of complementary opposites, inclusion of a multiplicity of "voices," manipulation of word meanings, poetic tonality, creative use of word patterns, and an overall playfulness in language usage. Although decontextualized, this statement written by a graduate student illustrates some of these tendencies: "The use of culturally consistent communicative competencies entails teachers being able to recognize the multitude of distinct methods of communication that African American students bring to the classroom." Another example of these discourse habits is the frequent use of verb pairs. Following are some samples selected from the writings of students:

- a number of public issues to be explored and represented . . .
- numerous factors have impacted and influenced . . .
- make an attempt to analyze and interpret . . .
- no model is available to interpret and clarify . . .
- many ways of explaining and understanding . . .

- a framework that will enable and facilitate . . .
- validity was verified and confirmed . . .
- he will describe and give account . . .

Two other examples are helpful in illustrating the dramatic flair and poetic flavor of playing with words that characterize African American cultural discourse. One comes from Smart-Grosvenor (1982), who describes African American cultural communication as "a metaphorical configuration of verbal nouns, exaggerated adjectives, and double descriptives" (p. 138). She adds (and in the process demonstrates that which she explains) that "ours is an exciting, practical, elegant, dramatic, ironic, mysterious, surrealistic, sanctified, outrageous and creative form of verbal expression. It's a treasure trove of vitality, profundity, rhythm—and, yes, style" (p. 138). Smitherman (1972) provides a second example of African American discourse style and aestheticism. She says:

> The power of the word lies in it enabling us to translate vague feelings and fleeting experiences into forms that give unity, coherence, and expression to the inexpressible. The process of composing becomes a mechanism for discovery wherein we may generate illuminating revelations about a particular idea or event. (p. 91)

Ambivalence and Distancing in Communication

Classroom experiences and personal conversations with Asian international and Asian American college students and professional colleagues reveal some recurrent communication features. These individuals tend not to declare either definitive advocacy or adversarial positions in either oral or written discourse. They take moderate stances, seek out compromise positions, and look for ways to accommodate opposites. They are rather hesitant to analyze and critique but will provide factually rich descriptions of issues and events. They also use a great deal of "hedges" and conciliatory markers in conversations; that is, "starts and stops," affiliative words, and apologetic nuances interspersed in speech, such as "I'm not sure," "maybe . . . ," "I don't know, but . . . ," "I may be wrong, but. . . ." These behaviors give the appearance of tentative, unfinished thinking, even though the individuals using them are very intellectually capable and thoroughly prepared academically. And many Asian and Asian American students are virtually silent in classroom discussions.

I have observed Asian and Asian American students frequently interjecting "ritualistic laughter" into conversations with me about their academic performance. This happens in instructional and advising situations in which the students are having difficulty understanding a learning task that is being explained by the teacher. Rather than reveal the full extent of their confusion, or lack of understanding, students will interject laughter into the conversations. It functions to diffuse the intensity of their confusion and give the impression that the problem is not as serious as it really is. Teachers who are unaware of what is going on may interpret these behaviors to mean the students are not taking their feedback or advice seriously. Or they may assume that the students understand the issue so completely that they have reached a point in their intellectual processing where they can relax and break the mental focus (signaled by laughter). When queried about this practice, students invariably say, "It's cultural," and often add an explanation for it that invokes some rule of social etiquette or interpersonal interaction that is taught in their ethnic communities. Interestingly, Japanese, Chinese, Korean, Taiwanese, and Cambodian students offer similar explanations about the motivation behind and meaning of this shared behavior. These students explain that "ritualized laughter" is a means of maintaining harmonious relationships and avoiding challenging the authority or disrespecting the status of the teacher.

These communication behaviors among students of Asian origin are consistent with those reported by Fox (1994). Hers were gleaned from observations, interviews, and working with students from non-Western cultures and countries (Fox refers to them as "world majority students") on their analytical writing skills in basic writing courses at the Center for International Education at the University of Massachusetts. Data were collected over 3 years. Sixteen graduate students from several different disciplines participated in the formal interviews. They represented 12 countries: Korea, Japan, the People's Republic of China, Nepal, Indonesia, Brazil, India, Chile, Sri Lanka, Côte d'Ivoire, Somalia, and Cape Verde. Faculty members who worked closely with these students also were interviewed. Additional information was derived from informal conversations and interactions with other students; analyzing writing samples; the teacher's notes about how she and the students worked through writing difficulties; and students' explanations about what they were trying to say in their writing, why assignments were misunderstood, and connections among language, culture, and writing.

Several common writing habits among these students from different countries emerged that conflict with formal writing styles of academe, known variously as academic argument, analytical or critical writing, and scholarly discourse (Fox, 1994). The characteristics and concerns included:

- Much background information and imprecise commentary
- Exaggeration for effect
- Prolific use of transitional markers, such as "moreover," "nevertheless," and "here again"
- Preference for contemplative instead of action words
- Much meandering around and digressions from the primary topic of discussion

- Emphasis on surrounding context rather than the subject itself
- Being suggestive and trying to convey feelings instead of being direct and concise and providing proof or specific illustrations, as is the expectation of academic writing in the United States
- Tendency to communicate through subtle implications
- Great detail and conversational tonality
- Elaborate and lengthy introductions
- Reticence to speak out, to declare personal positions, and to make one's own ideas prominent in writing

Although these communication tendencies were shared by all the students Fox (1994) studied, how they were expressed in actual behaviors varied widely. Culturally different meanings of "conversational tone" illustrate this point. Fox notes:

> In Spanish or Portuguese . . . speakers and writers may be verbose, rambling, digressive, holistic, full of factual details, full of feeling, sometimes repetitious, sometimes contradictory, without much concern for literal meanings. In many Asian and African languages and cultures, metaphor, euphemism, innuendo, hints, insinuation, and all sorts of subtle nonverbal strategies—even silence— are used both to spare the listeners possible embarrassment or rejection, and to convey meanings that they are expected to grasp. (p. 22)

These descriptions of Asian American and non-Western student discourse are based on observations and conversations with a small number of people, in college classes and professional settings. How widespread they are across other educational settings, ethnic groups, generations of immigrants, and social circumstances is yet to be determined. Much more description and substantiation of these communicative inclinations are needed.

The explanations of Asian students that their discourse styles are cultural are elaborated by S. Chan (1991), Kitano and Daniels (1995), and Nakanishi and Nishida (1995). They point to traditional values and socialization that emphasize collectivism, saving face, maintaining harmony, filial piety, interdependence, modesty in self-presentation, and restraint in taking oppositional points of view. Leung (1998) suggests some ways these values translate to behavior in learning situations, which underscore the observations made by Fox. Students socialized this way are less likely to express individual thoughts, broadcast their individual accomplishments, and challenge or disagree with people in positions of authority, especially in public arenas. These interpretations echo the connections between Asian American culture and communicative styles provided by B. Kim (1978). She suggests that a major function of Asian cultural socialization is to promote social harmony and build community. Consequently, many Asian American students may avoid confrontations as well as the expression of negative feelings or opinions in classroom discourse.

GENDER VARIATIONS IN DISCOURSE STYLES

Most of the detailed information on gender variations in classroom communication involves European Americans. Some inferences can be made about probable gender discourse styles among African, Latino, Native, and Asian Americans from their cultural values and gender socialization, since culture and communication are closely interrelated, but the body of research is rather thin.

Females Communicate Differently from Males

Lakoff (1975, 2004) was among the first to suggest that different lexical, syntactical, pragmatic, and discourse features existed for females and males. She identified nine speech traits prolific among females. L. Crawford (1993) summarizes them as specialized vocabulary for homemaking and caregiving, mild forms of expletives, adjectives that convey emotional reactions but no substantive information, tag comments that are midway between questions and statements, exaggerated expressiveness, superpolite forms, hedges or qualifiers, hypercorrect grammar, and little use of humor.

Other research indicates that European American females use more affiliative, accommodative, and socially bonding language mechanisms, while males are more directive, managing, controlling, task-focused, and action-oriented in their discourse styles. Girls speak more politely and tentatively, use less forceful words, are less confrontational, and are less intrusive when they enter into conversations. By comparison, boys interrupt more; use more commands, threats, and boasts of authority; and give information more often (Austin, Salehi, & Leffler, 1987; M. Crawford, 1995; Grossman & Grossman, 1994; Hoyenga & Hoyenga, 1979; Maccoby, 1988; Simkins-Bullock & Wildman, 1991; Tannen, 1994). Because of these gender patterns, Maccoby (1988) concludes that "speech serves more egoistic functions among boys and more socially binding functions among girls" (p. 758).

These general trends were substantiated by Johnstone (1993) in a study of spontaneous conversational storytelling of men and women among friends. The women's stories tended to be about groups of people (women and men) engaged in supportive relationships and the importance of community-building. The men's stories were more about conquests (physical, social, nature) in which individuals acted alone. Invariably, the characters were nameless men who did little talking but engaged in some kind of physical action. More details were given about places, times, and things than about people. Based on these findings, Johnstone suggests that women are empowered through cooperation, interdependence, collaboration, and community. For men, power comes from individuals "conquering" and acting in opposition to others. These gender differences are transmitted through nuances in communication styles such as tone, rhythm, vocabulary, delivery, body posture, facial expressions, gestures, and proxemics.

Turney and Sitler (2012) substantiated these gender trends in communication from a different disciplinary perspective. Their conclusions are based on observing female and male students in pilot training programs. Although they did not specify the race and ethnicity of their students, the communication descriptions are very similar to other studies that focused on European Americans. Their descriptions of these differences included the following:

> Women's language tends to be more indirect and subtle than men's language. . . . Women tend to tag declarative answers by adding yes/no rising intonations that make statements sound like questions . . . use hyper-polite forms that may involve more word usage , . . [and] include modifiers and query tags, often avoiding definitive statements. Metaphor and superlatives, such as "Nothing is working" characterize women's language, and men mistakenly take these expressions literally since male language is more absolute and female language more abstract. . . . Women use a wider range of pitches than men in all speaking situations, while men tend to keep their voices subdued and monotonous when talking to adults, but use more vocal variation when talking to young children. Despite the ability of both genders to use vocal variation, men are much more selective about when they vary their voices and female language contains greater imagery. Women use intensifiers (e.g., so, such, quite, very, etc.), modifiers, [and] tag questions (e.g., isn't it?). . . . There is a general notion of uncertainty or hesitancy in female speech. Male language is more absolute; female language is more abstract (Turney & Sitler, 2012, n.p.).

There also is the general tendency in gender-based communication to listen to *what* men are saying, their assertions and points being made, but with women the concentration is more on *how* they are talking and where they place emphasis.

However, some speech phenomena called "upspeak," "uptalk," and "vocal fry" are used regularly among both males and females across ethnically, racially, culturally, and socially diverse groups, varieties of English, and in other languages (Lakoff, 2004; Warren, 2016). Among speakers of color they seem to be more prominent among females. Also, females are criticized more than males for using them (Friedman, 2015). Upspeak is using a higher vocal pitch and rising inflections at the end of declarative statements, making them sound like questions, and vocal fry is drawing out or elongating the end of words and sentences in creaky-voiced tones. These speech habits are used in language contexts where questions would not usually be expected. They are sometimes associated with lack of confidence, insecurity, and efforts to avoid conflict or diffuse controversy, especially for females. In fact, they may simply be language and communication modifications that are natural occurrences for different situations, purposes, cultures, and times (Friedman, 2015; Lakoff, 2004; National Public Radio, 2015; Warren, 2016.

Research by Gray-Schlegel and Gray-Schlegel (1995/1996) on the creative writing of 3rd- and 6th-grade students produced results similar to other studies on gender-based communication styles. They examined 170 creative writing samples of 87 students to determine whether differences existed in how control, outcomes, relationships, and violence were used. Clear gender patterns emerged. Both boys and girls placed male characters in active roles more often than females, but this tendency increased with age only for the males. Females were more optimistic about the fate of their characters, while males were inclined to be cynical. Boys usually had their protagonists acting alone, while girls had them acting in conjunction with others. Regardless of age or the gender of the story character, boys included more crime and violence in their narrative than girls. No information was provided on the ethnicity, race, culture, or social class of the students who participated in the study.

Two of the few studies on the communication practices of specifically identified ethnic females were conducted by Houston (2000) and C. Jones and Shorter-Gooden (2003). The participants in both studies were adults. Houston asked 134 undergraduate students and professionals at a women's college in the southeastern United States to identify unique attributes of African American women's talk. Most responses (107) identified celebratory and positive features. They said Black women's talk is imbued with intimacy, deep caring, intuitiveness, candor, pride, strength, inner convictions, intensity, wisdom, assertiveness, strength, fortitude, forthrightness, sincerity, seriousness, and confidence. These results are somewhat at odds with those reported by Jones and Shorter-Gooden. In their study of the African American Women's Voices Project about coping with racism and sexism, they found that the strength-based attributes of the communication of African American females are sometimes compromised when they interact with people outside their own cultural contexts, especially European Americans in privileged and power positions. They called this practice "shifting" and concluded that "shifting one's style of expression and the content of one's message emerged as the predominant way in which Black women accommodate to the social and behavioral codes of White middle-class America" (p. 96). Deciding what to say, when, and how are "at the heart of shifting because . . . it is often the first and most important way that other people . . . size you up, determine where you stand, and decide how to treat and deal with you" (p. 95). These first impressions frequently hinge on whether prejudices and stereotypes will be validated or challenged more than on the relevance, power, and substantive quality of the communication itself.

The "communicative code shifting" Jones and Shorter-Gooden observed entailed changing voice pitch, rhythm of speech, vocabulary, and inflection; constantly censoring conversation; editing dialogue internally; and shifting on multiple levels across forms, content, and contexts. These demands mean that African American women frequently have to make quick decisions about "holding their tongues when they would like to speak up, reining in their emotions when they are quietly outraged, . . . alter[ing] their speech, minding their grammar, [and] purging their conversations of any slang to overcome racist presumptions that they are uneducated and less intelligent" (p. 97). Young Black girls begin developing these communicative devices early in life. The mental gymnastics and cultural border-crossings they demand are intellectually and psychoemotionally challenging. They can be both a blessing and a curse—opportunities for individuals to develop bilingual and bicultural skills, yet be major obstacles to participating in classroom instructional interactions. Undoubtedly, African American males, and members of different ethnic groups of color, have developed other engendered communication styles in response to cultural socialization, multicultural demands, and oppressive conditions. Certainly, English language learners face some of the same challenges as they form thoughts, solve problems, and compose conversation in their first language and then translate them into English before they speak or write. Understanding (and acting on) how racism, race, ethnicity, culture, gender, and communication are conflated falls well within the purview of culturally responsive teaching. Educators must develop and deliver curriculum and instruction in ways that do not "silence" the cultural voices of diverse students, whether they are males or females. As Jones and Shorter-Gooden (2003) remind us, "Voice is the literal expression of one's identity, the echoing of the self. If you can't talk about what you believe in a way that feels natural, you can become alienated from your inner self. You're no longer able to express who you truly are" (p. 98).

Gender Communication Patterns Established Early in Life

Gender-related discourse patterns are established well before 3rd grade, as research by Nicolopoulou, Scales, and Weintraub (1994) revealed. They examined the symbolic imagination of 4-year-olds as expressed in the kinds of stories they told. The girls' stories included more order and social realism. These were conveyed through the use of coherent plots with stable characters, continuous plotlines, and social and familial relationships as the primary topics of and contexts for problem-solving. Their stories emphasized cyclical patterns of everyday domestic life, along with romantic and fairytale images of kings and queens, princesses and princes. They were carefully constructed, centered, and coherent, with elaborate character and theme development, and invariably were directed toward harmonious conflict resolution. Whenever threatening or disruptive situations occurred, the girls were careful to reestablish order before concluding their stories. The boys' stories contained much disorder and a picaresque, surrealistic aesthetic style. These traits were apparent in: the absence of stable, clearly defined characters, relationships, and plots; large, powerful, and frightening characters; violence, disruption, and conflict; and a series of loosely associated dramatic images, actions, and events. The boys were not concerned with resolving conflicts before their stories ended. Instead, their plots were driven by action, novelty, excess, defiance, destruction, and often escalating and startling imagery.

In summarizing differences between how boys and girls construct stories, Nicolopoulou and associates (1994) made some revealing observations that should inform instructional practices. They noted that the stories produced by girls focused on "creating, maintaining, and elaborating structure." In comparison, the stories told by boys emphasized "action and excitement" and involved a restless energy that was often difficult for them to manage (p. 110). Furthermore, the boys and girls dealt with danger, disorder, and conflict very differently. The girls' strategy was *implicit avoidance,* while the boys' technique was *direct confrontation.*

Another fascinating verification of theorized gender differences in communication is provided by Otnes, Kim, and Kim (1994). They analyzed 344 letters written to Santa Claus (165 from boys and 179 from girls). Although the age of the authors was not specified, they were probably 8 years old or younger, since children stop believing in Santa Claus at about this time. The content of the letters was analyzed to determine the use of six kinds of semantic units, or meaning phrases: (1) polite or socially accepted forms of ingratiation, (2) context-oriented references, (3) direct requests, (4) requests accompanied by qualifiers, (5) affectionate appeals, and (6) altruistic requests of gifts for someone other than self. For the most part, results of the study confirmed the hypothesized expectations. Girls wrote longer letters, made more specific references to Christmas, were more polite, used more indirect requests, and included more expressions of affection. By comparison, boys made more direct requests. There were no differences between boys and girls in the number of toys requested or the altruistic appeals made. Findings such as these provide evidence about the extent and persistence of patterns of culturally socialized communicative behaviors.

Early gender patterns of communication may transfer to other kinds of social and educational interactions. They also can entrench disadvantages that will have long-term negative effects on student achievement. Interventions to achieve more comparable communications skills for male and female students should begin early and continue throughout the school years. Efforts also should be undertaken in both research and classroom practices to determine whether or how communicative styles are differentiated by gender in ethnic groups other than European Americans. Undoubtedly some differences do exist, since discourse styles are influenced by cultural socialization, and males and females are socialized differently in various ethnic groups.

Problems with Gendered Communication Styles

The "gendered" style of communication may be more problematic than the gender of the person doing the communicating. If this is so, then a female who is adept at using discourse techniques typically associated with males will not be disadvantaged in mainstream social interactions. Conversely, males who communicate in ways usually ascribed to females will lose their privileged status. Hoyenga and Hoyenga (1979) offer some support for this premise. In their review of research on gender and communication, they report that "feminine communication styles" are associated with less intelligence, passivity, and submissiveness, while "masculine styles" evoke notions of power, authority, confidence, and leadership.

However, M. Crawford (1995) suggests that some of the claims about female–male communication differences need to be reconsidered. For example, indirectness and equivocation in communication are not inherently strategies of female subordination. They can be tools of power as well. Interpretations of speech behaviors may depend more on the setting, the speaker's status and communicative capability, and the speaker's relationship to listeners than on the person's gender per se (Tannen, 1994). Sadker and associates (2009) propose that males may be at greater *emotional risk* than females because of their role socialization. Girls are encouraged to be caring and emotionally expressive, but boys are taught to deny their feelings and to be overly cautious about demonstrating how deeply they care. Thus, male advantages in conventional conceptions of academic discourse may be countered somewhat by the psychoemotional and social advantages that females have in interpersonal relations.

CONCLUSION

Communication is strongly culturally influenced, experientially situated, and functionally strategic. It is a dynamic set of skills and performing arts whose rich nuances and delivery styles are open to many interpretations and instructional possibilities. Ethnic discourse patterns are continually negotiated because people talk in many different ways for many different reasons. Sometimes the purpose of talking and writing is simply to convey information. Talking and writing also are used to persuade and entertain; to demonstrate sharing, caring, and connections; to express contentment and discontentment; to empower and subjugate; to teach and learn; and to convey critical reflections and declare personal preferences. In imagining and implementing culturally responsive pedagogical reform, teachers should not merely make girls talk more like boys, or boys talk more like girls, or all individuals within and across ethnic groups talk like one another. Nor should they assume that all gender differences in communication styles are subsumed by ethnicity or think that all ethnic nuances are obliterated by gender, social class, and education. Instead, we must be mindful that communication styles are multidimensional and multimodal, shaped by many different influences. Although culture is paramount among these, other critical influences include ethnic affiliation, gender, social class, personality, individuality, and experiential context.

The information in this chapter has described some of the patterns, dynamics, and polemics of the discourse styles of different ethnic and gender groups. Since communication is essential to both teaching and learning, it is imperative that it be a central part of instructional reforms designed to improve the school performance of underachieving African, Latino, Native, Asian, and European American students. The more teachers know about the discourse styles of ethnically diverse students, the better they will be able to improve academic achievement. Change efforts should attend especially to discourse dynamics as opposed to linguistic structures. The reforms should be directed toward creating better agreement between the communication patterns of underachieving ethnically diverse students and those considered "normal" in schools.

Knowledge about general communication patterns among ethnic groups is helpful, but it alone is not enough. Teachers need to translate it to their own particular instructional situations. This contextualization might begin with some self-study exercises in which teachers examine their preferred discourse modes and dynamics, and determine how students from different ethnic groups respond to them. They also should learn to recognize the discourse habits of students from different ethnic groups. The purposes of these analyses are to identify: (1) habitual discourse features of ethnically diverse students; (2) conflictual and complementary points among these discourse styles; (3) how, or whether, conflictual points are negotiated by students; and (4) features of the students' discourse patterns that are problematic for the teacher. The results can be used to pinpoint and prioritize specific places to begin interventions for change.

Whether conceived narrowly or broadly, and expressed formally or informally, communication is the quintessential medium of teaching and learning. It also is inextricably linked to culture and cognition. Therefore, if teachers are to better serve the school achievement needs of ethnically diverse students by implementing culturally responsive teaching, they must learn how to communicate differently with them. To the extent that they succeed in doing this, achievement problems could be reduced significantly.

PRACTICE POSSIBILITIES

Communication is always dynamic and complex; it can be even more so cross-culturally. Yet good communication with diverse students is essential to effective culturally responsive teaching. In fact, it is the ultimate test! Because of its dynamic nature, teachers need to continually monitor their own communication habits and learn about those of other ethnic and cultural groups. These suggested strategies may help facilitate these accomplishments:

- Understand the impact of culture on communication and education, and be mindful that communication takes many forms beyond the spoken and written that are prioritized in schools.
- Observe and listen to ethnically diverse individuals and groups (students and others) in a variety of situations and when interacting with different audiences.
- Keep records of unfamiliar words, phrases, and nonverbal nuances exhibited by students from different ethnic groups, and monitor and assess your progress in developing understanding of them.
- Understand the potential problems of communicating cross-culturally in general, and in teaching-learning contexts and with different ethnic groups and individuals specifically.
- Practice active listening to self and to students. The things students talk about with each other in their own contexts are what's important to them. Restate comments and ask frequent questions to ensure clarity of meaning and understanding of observed communication behaviors.
- In teaching diverse students of color, limit the amount of information conveyed at one time, and use simple and direct explanations that are free of cultural encoding.
- Be conscious of cultural codes and cues embedded in regular habits of teaching communications, such as proverbs, parables, colloquialisms, and educational jargon. When these are used, decode, translate, and interpret them for culturally diverse students.
- Teach students the linguistic capital of schooling and different subjects or disciplines taught. Habitual words and phrases used in the routine functioning of these may not be understood by students from different cultural, ethnic, social, and national origin backgrounds.
- During teaching and learning activities, include visualizations to complement verbal and written texts, such as signs, symbols, and images of diverse peoples, cultures, communities, and contributions.
- Approach conversations and interactions with culturally diverse students, parents, and communities with self-reflection and cultural humility.
- View the linguistic and communication facility of different ethnic groups as potential strengths and viable instructional resources.

- Use varied modes of communication in teaching and performance assessment to capitalize on different students' strengths, including written, verbal, visual, tactile, and kinetic modalities.
- Avoid perpetuating ethnic and racial stereotypical, or "typecasting," perceptions of the communication habits of underrepresented students, families, and communities.
- Understand various types of nonverbal communications used by students (and teachers) from different ethnic, racial, cultural, and social groups.
- Identify and cultivate relationships with cultural mediators and interpreters in the classroom, school, and community who can serve as mentors about ethnically diverse cultures and communication.
- Use books, articles, films, music, audio recordings, and a variety of other resources from the Internet that explain and visualize examples of different ethnic groups' cultures and communication.
- Teach students the value of and skills in communicative style or code-shifting.
- Have students tutor the teacher and each other in the communicative cues and codes (both verbal and nonverbal) used by insiders within their cultural groups, and the most recent popular words and phrases used among members of their various social groups.
- Use films and videos of different ethnic groups and individuals communicating in natural contexts (as much as possible) to see various aspects of cultural communication embodied.

Based on some suggestions presented at opencolleges.edu.au/informed/features/culturally-sensitive-educator/; iteslj.org/Articles/Pratt-Johnson-CrossCultural.html; and pinterest.com/pin/357262182923329468

CHAPTER 5

Ethnic and Cultural Diversity in Curriculum Content

"Content about the histories, heritages, contributions, perspectives, and experiences of different ethnic groups and individuals, taught in diverse ways, is essential to culturally responsive teaching."

The fundamental aim of culturally responsive pedagogy is to *empower* ethnically diverse students through academic success, cultural affiliation, and personal efficacy. Knowledge in the form of curriculum content is central to this empowerment. To be effective, this knowledge must be accessible to students and connected to their lives and experiences outside of school. Sleeter and Grant (1991a) explain that knowledge has no intrinsic power. Information and skills that are potentially powerful become so only through interaction with the interests, aspirations, desires, needs, and purposes of students. Almost 90 years earlier Dewey (1902) made essentially the same case in disavowing the notion of an inherent dichotomy between the child and the curriculum, meaning teachers must prioritize one or the other, but not both. He suggested that this is an artificial division detrimental to quality teaching. Curriculum content should be seen as a tool to help students assert and accentuate their present and future powers, capabilities, attitudes, and experiences.

These explanations emphasize the importance of "student relevance and participation" in curriculum decisionmaking. Because of the dialectic relationship between knowledge and the knower, interest and motivation, relevance and mastery, Native Americans, Latino Americans, African Americans, and Asian Americans must be seen as co-originators, co-designers, and co-directors (along with professional educators) of their education. If the "creator, producer, and director" roles of students of color are circumscribed and they are seen as only "consumers," then the levels of their learning also will be restricted. This is too often true of present educational conditions. To reverse these trends, ethnically diverse students and their cultural heritages must be the sources and centers of educational programs. In the words of Dewey (1902), their curriculum must be "psychologized" if it is to be relevant, interesting, and effective to their learning. This does not mean that students should be taught only those things in which they have a personal interest. Nor should they be involved directly in every decision made about curriculum. Rather, culturally relevant curriculum content should be chosen and delivered in ways that are meaningful to the students for whom it is intended. In some instances, this means validating their personal experiences and cultural heritages; in others, it means teaching content entirely new to ethnically and culturally diverse students but in ways that make it easy for them to comprehend.

INTRODUCTION

Discussions in this chapter elaborate this line of thinking as it relates to the importance of multicultural curriculum content in improving the school achievement of marginalized ethnic students. Six key observations provide the conceptual contours and organizational directions for these discussions:

- Curriculum content is crucial to academic performance and is an essential component of culturally responsive pedagogy.
- The most common source of curriculum content used in classrooms is textbooks. Therefore, the quality of textbooks is an important factor in student achievement and culturally responsive teaching.
- Curriculum content that is meaningful to students improves their learning.
- Relevant curriculum content for teaching African American, Latino American, Asian American, and Native American students includes information about the histories, cultures, contributions, experiences, perspectives, and issues of their respective ethnic groups.
- Curriculum content is derived from various sources, many of which exist outside the formal boundaries of schooling.
- There are many different kinds of curricula; they offer different, but important, challenges, opportunities, and entrees for doing culturally responsive teaching.

The chapter is divided into seven sections. The first five examine important sources of curriculum content for culturally responsive teaching. These include textbooks, the Internet, standards, literary and trade books, and mass media. In the sixth section of the chapter some documented effects of ethnic content on student achievement are presented. Some suggestions for improving the quality of multicultural curriculum content are presented in the last section of the chapter. Achievement is conceived broadly to include indicators of performance other than scores on standardized tests and grades. As is the case elsewhere in this book, descriptions, principles, and proposals derived from theory, research, and practice are woven throughout the discussions.

IMPORTANCE OF TEXTBOOKS AS CURRICULUM CONTENT

Research in the 1980s and 1990s revealed that textbooks (in print form, as sources of content to be taught and learned) are the basis of 70% to 95% of all classroom instruction (Apple, 1985; O. Davis, Ponder, Burlbaw, Garza-Lubeck, & Moss, 1986; Tyson-Bernstein & Woodward, 1991; Wade, 1993). Although the rate has lowered somewhat because of the advent of computer-based technologies and multimedia and digital instructional resources, print textbooks continue to be a prominent teaching tool (Crum, 2015; Rosenwald, 2015). As levels of education advance from preschool through college, this influence increases. Another testament to the power of textbooks is the fact that most students consider their authority to be incontestable and the information they present always to be accurate, authentic, and absolute truth (Gordy & Pritchard, 1995; Gullicks, Pearson, Child, & Schwab, 2005). School level has little if any effect on these perceptions. When called upon to defend the validity of their explanations and understandings of issues, students often respond, "Because the book said so."

Conceptions and forms of "textbooks" are changing, especially in pre-K–12 schooling. They no longer appear in print only. Rather, other presentation formats are included, such as digital versions and complementary resources like teachers' guides, audiovisual materials, charts, maps, and student learning activities. As Joseph Farrell (n.d.) points out, increasingly these "leaning materials packets" are replacing basic printed text. Yet whatever form "textbooks" take, teachers and students continue to rely on them as primary teaching and learning tools. Lenkei (2016), and Rosenwald (2015) disagree with Farrell on the "replacement" claim in citing research that "millennials" continue to prefer print sources for pleasure and learning, despite their tendency to consume most other information digitally. Crum (2015) and Baron (2016) add that print books are better than digital resources for quality learning. However, they do not specify the student benefactors by race, ethnicity, class, gender, or culture.

While the prominence of print textbooks in some form is apparent in all subject areas, it is even more so in some than in others (Tyson-Bernstein & Woodward, 1991). Teaching preschool and kindergarten students without textbooks is far more possible than teaching 3rd-, 7th-, or 12th-graders; and art, music, and physical education may be more easily taught without prescribed textbooks than are math, science, or social studies. Textbooks often are thought to be a foolproof means of guaranteeing successful teaching and learning. These practices and associated attitudes are so strongly entrenched in the minds of students that the value of courses without textbooks is sometimes suspect.

Furthermore, most textbooks used in schools are controlled by the dominant group (European Americans) and confirm its status, culture, and contributions. European American subjective experiences and interpretations of

reality are presented as objective truth. These representations are entre
further by the exclusion of certain information about the various racia
norities and social classes in the United States (Sleeter & Grant, 199 ᵕⱼ.
Bryne (2001) describes textbooks as "cultural artifacts" (p. 299) that reflect
the values, norms, and biases of disciplines and societies; convey professionally and politically approved knowledge; and construct images and impressions that become explanations and understandings for students. Farrell
(n.d.) reached similar conclusions in explaining that textbooks are not just
pedagogical instruments. Instead, they are political documents whose content reflects a given vision of a people and their history, heritages, values,
aspirations, and positions in the world. These presentations often lead to
controversies about accuracy and inclusivity, which become disputes about
curriculum content as well, since textbooks basically "carry" the curriculum. Thus, arguments about the treatment of females and racial minorities
in the content and illustrations of textbooks is analogous to their equity in
curriculum content. The largely uncontested authority and pervasiveness of
textbooks are important reasons why understanding how they treat ethnic
and cultural diversity and their effects on student learning are fundamental
to culturally responsive teaching.

ETHNIC AND CULTURAL DIVERSITY IN DIFFERENT TEXTS

Over the years a great deal of research has been done to determine whether
textbooks are dealing adequately with groups of color and cultural diversity
issues. The variables studied include narrative text, visuals, language, student activities and discussion prompts, and overall tone. These have been
filtered through different assessment criteria such as quantitative inclusion,
accuracy of information, placement of diversity features, authenticity, and
significance (AAUW, 1995; O. Davis et al., 1986; Gay, 2003b; Loewen,
1995; Sadker & Sadker, 1982; T. Sanchez, 2007; Tetreault, 1985).

Progress but Some Problems Remain

Blatant ethnic stereotypes, culturally diverse exclusions, and racist depictions have been eliminated from print textbooks (Anyon, 1988; Byrne,
2001; Davis et al., 1986; Deane, 1989; Gordy & Pritchard, 1995; Hogben
& Waterman, 1997; T. Sanchez, 2007; Wade, 1993), but the overall quality
continues to be inadequate. Textbooks still give too little attention to different groups of color interacting with one another and members of their
own ethnic groups; to race, racism, and other forms of oppression; to conflict; and to experiences and interactions that are different from mainstream
norms and standards. Sleeter and Grant (1991b) found these patterns of
treatment of diversity to be the case with 47 textbooks used in Grades 1–8

to teach social studies, mathematics, reading, language arts, and science that they examined. All the books were published between 1980 and 1988. A six-part analysis was applied that included visuals, topics and issues discussed, "people to study," language, portrayals and role functions of characters, and miscellaneous features unique to particular books. Sleeter and Grant were particularly interested in how these books treated different racial groups, gender, social class, and people with disabilities.

Textbooks continue to be flawed with respect to their treatment of ethnic and cultural diversity for several reasons. First, there is an imbalance across ethnic groups of color, with most attention given to African Americans and their experiences. This disparity is consistent across types of instructional materials, subjects, and grade levels. Second, the content included about ethnic issues is rather bland, conservative, conformist, and "safe." It tends to emphasize harmonious relations among racial groups, and is too often a "weapon of deculturalization" (Gullicks et al., 2005) for the heritages and experiences of groups of color. Contentious issues and individuals are avoided, and the unpleasant sides of society and cultural diversity are either sanitized or bypassed entirely. Third, gender and social-class disparities prevail within the representations of ethnic groups, with preference given to males, the middle class, and events and experiences that are closely aligned with mainstream European American values, beliefs, and standards of behavior. Fourth, textbook discussions about ethnic groups and their concerns are not consistent across time, with contemporary issues being overshadowed by historical ones.

A study conducted by Gordy and Pritchard (1995) illustrates how these general trends were demonstrated in a specific sample of textbooks. They analyzed 17 5th-grade social studies textbooks used in Connecticut schools to determine how they represented the perspectives of diverse women and men during slavery and Reconstruction. None of the authors provided thorough critiques of the slave trade, the reduction of Africans to commodities for that trade, or the values and beliefs used to justify slavery. All the texts discussed the living conditions under enslavement, but they excluded the sexual exploitation of female slaves, made no connections between slavery and the present living conditions of African and European Americans, and ignored the role that other ethnic groups, such as Native Americans and Mexicans, played in slavery.

A similar emphasis on description instead of interpretative and critical analysis characterized the treatment of Emancipation and Reconstruction. Because the perspectives of diverse groups were not presented, these textbooks gave partial and incomplete analyses of these critical events in U.S. history and their effects. They continued the long-established tradition of giving mostly European American and male perspectives on sociopolitical issues. Consequently, students using them "will not be given a full understanding of the racial and gender discrimination inherent in the slave system and the consequences of this discrimination on generations of Americans, both African American and White" (Gordy & Pritchard, 1995, p. 213).

Research conducted in the last decade on cultural, ethnic, and racial diversity in print textbooks across subjects and grades reveals results that are largely consistent with earlier findings. Secondary history textbooks continue to be a more frequent target of analysis than those for other subjects and grades. Five examples are presented here to illustrate this scholarship and the reported trends. Giarrizzo (2013) found that secondary school history textbooks often exclude—or present superficial, inaccurate, negative, and stereotypical information about—the lives, values, and experiences of domestic (African, Asian, Latino, and Native American) and global groups of color (especially Muslims and Islam). The American Textbook Council (2003) analyzed the treatment of Islam in seven world history textbooks widely used in grades 7–12. The results were somewhat contradictory. The quality of content about Muslim *people* had improved and expanded, but this was not so for Islam. The texts explained the origins of the Muslim world; intra-group (Sunni and Shi'ite) cultural differences; Islamic art and architecture; science and medicine; and knowledge through the ages. But on significant Islam-related, potentially controversial topics, such as jihad, advocacies of militant Islamists, the roles and rights of women, and the imposition of shari'a law, the textbooks tended to omit, gloss over, or avoid critiquing them. Kahn and Onion (2016) did a gender analysis of 614 trade or popular history books published by 80 companies and included on the 2015 *New York Times* Combined Print & E-Book Nonfiction bestseller list. They found that 75.8% of the total titles had male authors, and that there was a relationship between the gender of authors of biographies and the gender of their subjects. Female authors wrote about girls and women, and males tended to write about boys and men.

Piatek-Jimenez, Madison, and Przybyla-Kuchek (2014) examined equity in three current middle school mathematics textbooks series commonly used in the United States, focusing specifically on gender, race, and ethnicity images, and how these groups were portrayed in activities and careers by analyzing trends found in photographs. They concluded that

> While it is evident that an effort was made for all groups to be represented, the results indicate that groups are not portrayed equally in activities and careers. With respect to gender, males are portrayed as being more mathematical and are shown in more careers than females. Regarding race and ethnicity, Whites are portrayed as being more mathematical and more active and are shown in more careers than minorities. (n.p.)

Of the 26 English language learning books LaBelle (2010) examined, most included some diversity, but unevenly so across ethnic groups. Whites appeared most frequently in both written texts and illustrations, and were depicted as explorative, active, directive, aggressive, and emotional, much more so than minorities. Of the ethnic minority groups in written text, Latinos were presented as active most frequently, while African Americans were more prevalent in illustrations. Also, African Americans were portrayed as the most cooperative of all ethnic groups. Another noteworthy finding of the Labelle study was that textbooks that had significant instances of one ethnic group typically had high occurrences of the others, thus conveying a sense of multi-ethnicity, rather than presenting ethnic groups in isolation from one another.

Even when authors and publishers produce quality content about cultural diversity, it is sometimes not developmentally appropriate for some segments of the student population from the perspective of classroom practitioners. This seems to occur more often in elementary textbooks than in secondary ones. Gwen experienced this situation. She works in a large urban school district (32,000 students) and has taught many different types of students—African and European American, center-city and suburban, middle- and lower-class, academically able and intellectually challenged—in her career. Her district uses a literature approach to teaching reading. The 2nd-grade text is rich in ethnic and cultural diversity. Its content represents a wide variety of literary genres (poetry, short stories, fiction, realistic descriptions, mythology), cultural themes, and ethnic male and female authors and illustrators.

Unfortunately, these strengths are compromised by repeated inappropriateness in the substantive content of the text for second graders. Gwen explains that many of the stories are simply too complex for her 7-year-old, mostly African and European American students. The vocabulary is often too advanced, as are many of the literary techniques (such as simile, metaphor, analogy) used in the narrative text. The topics of the stories are often irrelevant to the experiences and perspectives of the urban students she teaches. Gwen bemoans these dilemmas by observing that "much age-appropriate and good ethnic children's literature already exists that will be interesting to students like mine. Why aren't we allowed to use it to teach reading?" One indeed wonders why not, especially when her school district and others throughout the United States claim to be searching for ways to improve reading achievement by using instructional materials that have high interest appeal and cultural relevance to students.

Analyses of how gender issues are addressed in textbooks, such as those conducted by Powell and Garcia (1985), the American Association of University Women (AAUW, 1995), Gullicks and associates (2005), and others reviewed by Grossman and Grossman (1994), reveal patterns of progress similar to those of ethnic diversity. Blatant gender biases have been eliminated, and females are depicted in less traditional roles and relationships. But males still appear more frequently than females. Men continue to dominate careers, positions, and images of action, power, leadership, and decisionmaking.

Although they are now portrayed in a wider variety of activities, females continue to be overrepresented in supportive and caregiving roles, suggesting that those who behave closer to traditional expectations are preferred.

The extent to which progress has been made in achieving gender equity in instructional materials is a function of subject areas, ethnic groups, and type of resource. The presentation of females in social studies, language arts, and literature print instructional materials comes closer to being egalitarian than in math, science, and computer education. More gender balance exists in supplementary materials—especially those of a literary nature, such as children's picture books—than in required textbooks. As is the case with ethnic group representation in textbooks, there are major imbalances in the treatment of women from different ethnic groups and sociocultural backgrounds. The progress tends to be much better for middle-class and European American females than for those who are poor and from different groups of color. Obviously, then, improvements are still needed in how males and females from different ethnic groups are presented in curriculum content resources routinely used by students.

There is no doubt about the raging fascination with electronic technologies, such as the Internet and digital media. Given this preoccupation, it is likely that high percentages of the time and effort people devote to obtaining information about ethnic, racial, and cultural diversity occur in cyberspace. Consequently, the Internet and other digital resourcing are important "texts" that should be included in the purview of culturally responsive teaching. However valuable computers and other electronic technologies are for learning and connecting across time and space, they are not infallible or sacrosanct, especially within the domains of ethnic, racial, and cultural diversity. Their strengths and weaknesses should be carefully and thoroughly explicated for them to be most beneficial in promoting culturally responsive teaching and learning. Daniels (2012), Nakamura (2002, 2014; Nakamura & Chow-White, 2012), Turkle (2010, 2011, 2015), Levmore and Nussbaum (2010), Graham and Dutton (2014), and Goodwin (2016) provide some compelling reasons why. Generally, they agree that the Internet has some valuable attributes, but it is not without faults. In some ways technology perpetuates problems of inequity representation and relationships for underserved students that are transmitted in other social, cultural, and educational domains within the United States. Goodwin (2016) feels that today's "cyber youth" are missing too much empathy and genuine human touch. To fill these voids, he recommends that educators help these youth balance their high-tech proclivities, lives, and skills by providing more high-touch learning environments. Levmore and Nussbaum (2010) also acknowledge the Internet as a medium for connecting diverse peoples across distant locations, while admitting that it often falls short of fulfilling its intentions, and is plagued by numerous offensive actions, especially toward females and racial minorities

Nakamura begins her critical analyses of electronic technology in teaching and learning with the observation that "those who doubt that racism (and its frequent companion, sexism) is still a serious problem or who believe that it is 'personal' rather than pervasive throughout societal institutions need only look to the Internet for proof that this is not so" (2014, p. 82). Nakamura and Chow-White add, "No matter how 'digital' we become, the continuing problem of social inequality along racial lines persists" (2012, p. 2). Daniels reached a similar conclusion based on her review of research on Internet studies:

> The Internet has not provided an escape route from either race or racism, nor has the study of race or racism proven to be central to the field of Internet studies. Instead, race and racism persist online in ways that are both new and unique to the Internet, alongside vestiges of centuries-old forms that reverberate both offline and on. (2012, p. 2)

Another somewhat elaborated perspective is provided in "Racializing Cyberspaces":

> While "new media" are indeed new in many ways, they too often fall into quite old patterns when dealing with issues of race and ethnicity. Biologists, social scientists and social movements have led us to understand *race* as a socially constructed process, rather than a natural fact, but racial categories, racist structures, and racist representations remain very much alive. New media like the web and video games have the opportunity to challenge old forms of racialization, and in some areas they are doing so. But too often instead they rely upon and reinforce racial and ethnic stereotypes, and leave structural inequality of race unchallenged or reinforced. (culturalpolitics.net/digital_cultures/race)

To substantiate these claims, Nakamura (2014; Nakamura & Chow-White, 2012) focused on gaming in some of her research. She found that racial inequities existed in both the content and dissemination of all genres of games frequently played by youth. Discrimination toward racial minorities and females was prolific in gaming communities. Racial minorities were frequently depicted as criminals and gangsters. Daniels (2012) reviewed race and racism in multiple aspects of Internet studies, including health and science, fandom, blogging, social networking sites, online news and sports, gaming, and identity and community. Across these studies racism was largely ignored in systematic analyses, and the Internet was treated by many as a raceless and color-blind space. When race and racism on the Internet were studied, most of the work was done by researchers of color.

Like some other analysts, Turkle (2010, 2011, 2015) is both complimentary toward and cautious about digital media and technology. She advises not to expect too much from technology in fulfilling needs for human connection. Her advice is especially valuable in imagining possible interfaces between creating community for and among culturally diverse students and cyberspace. There is a common claim that the Internet makes it possible to travel physical distances and existential spaces instantaneously, and brings the world to our fingertips at a moment's notice. This capability should be enticing for teaching students who are isolated or marginalized from mainstream society, and distanced from their ancestral roots. Turkle (2011), who studies the psychology of online connectivity, suggests that these assumptions are overly optimistic because

> These days, insecure in our relationships, and anxious about intimacy we look to technology for ways to be in relationship and protect ourselves from them at the same time. . . . We bend to the inanimate with new solitude. We fear the risks and disappointment of relationships with our fellow humans. We expect more from technology and less from each other. . . . We seem determined to give human qualities to objects and content to treat each other as things. . . .
>
> Technology proposes itself as the architect of our intimacies. These days, it suggests substitutions that put the real on the run. . . . Technology is seductive when what it offers meets our human vulnerabilities. And as it turns out, we are very vulnerable indeed. We are lonely but fearful of intimacy. . . . Digital connections . . . may offer the illusion of companionship without the demands of friendship. Our networked life allows us to hide from each other even as we are tethered to each other. We'd rather text than talk (pp. xiv, 1, 3).

These thoughts challenge some of the capabilities frequently attributed to technological and digitized interactions. They also suggest that teachers need to understand both the capabilities and limitations of the digital world for engaging students of color. If Turkle's analyses are endorsed, some important aspects of understanding cultural diversity, and relating cross-racially and cross-culturally, may be challenged in technologically mediated teaching. They could further marginalize diversity instead of embracing it.

Effects of Absent or Negative Multicultural Textbook Content

Little systematic empirical research is currently available on how biased textbooks affect the achievement of ethnically diverse students. But personal stories from students of various ages and circumstances abound. Students, like Amy and Aaron from Chapter 1, tell of being insulted, embarrassed, ashamed, and angered when reading and hearing negative portrayals of their ethnic groups or not hearing anything at all. Some challenge these inaccuracies and exclusions, and intimidate teachers by doing so. Others recall being put on the spot when isolated events and individuals from their ethnic groups are singled out for special attention. On other occasions students are excited and amazed to learn new information about different ethnic groups, to discover what they have endured and accomplished, even though it is introduced in the classroom sporadically. This was the reaction of Amy and Aaron when they first watched *Roots* (Margulies & Wolper, 1977, 1978), the televised series of Alex Haley's (1976) book of the same title, and read *The Autobiography of Malcolm X* (Malcolm X & Haley, 1966).

A group of European American college students were rendered speechless after viewing *Something Strong Within* (Nakamura, 1994), a film composite of home movies taken by Japanese Americans in internment camps during World War II. Finally, after a long silence, one student said, "I never even thought of the people having regular lives in the camps. The video made me see them as human beings." This reaction represented the sentiments of many others in the class, and it was echoed in comments to the effect that the students felt their education had shortchanged them through information voids, thereby further dehumanizing and marginalizing Japanese Americans.

The observations Chun-Hoon (1973) made more than 45 years ago about the effects of these textbook inadequacies on the perceptions of ethnic groups are still applicable today. Omissions and myopic analyses of ethnically diverse peoples, issues, cultures, and experiences imply that they are irrelevant and even expendable. Although Chun-Hoon was concerned specifically about Asian Americans, his observations can be easily extended to other groups of color, as Sleeter and Grant (1991b) have done. They recommended that authors and publishers reorient their focus to deal with more authentic and substantial human experiences and contextualize specific subject-matter skills in more meaningful multicultural content. This is a better route to improving student achievement than using bland and fictitious stories, teaching decontextualized skills, and repeating excessive numbers of adventure stories about European American males.

The inadequacies of print and digital texts' coverage of cultural diversity can be avoided by including accurate, wide-ranging, and appropriately contextualized content about different ethnic groups' histories, cultures, and experiences in classroom instruction on a regular basis. The efforts need not be constrained by lack of information and materials. Plenty of resources exist about most ethnic groups, and in such variety that all subjects and grades taught from preschool through college can be served adequately. Since this information is not always in textbooks, teachers need to develop the habit of using other resources to complement or even replace them. Students also should be taught how to critique textbooks for the accuracy of their multicultural content and how to compensate for the voids these analyses reveal.

Furthermore, the more diversified the types of resources used and content taught, the greater the probability that students' interest will be peaked and their engagement with and mastery of knowledge and skills taught improved (Ginsberg, 2015). An example is the use of popular culture texts and artifacts, such as computer games, music, and movies popular among contemporary youth. Many of these social, cultural, and generational funds of knowledge are "crossovers" among various ethnic groups, thereby providing opportunities for developing intra- and intergroup cultural competencies and connections simultaneously. Hip-hop and spoken-word are graphic illustrations of these possibilities. These music genres are popular among producers and consumers in many different ethnic groups within the United States as well as throughout the world. Increasingly, education and social science scholars and practitioners are examining the viability of them as resources for improving the academic achievement of culturally diverse students (Chang, 2005; Dolberry, 2015; Emdin, 2010, 2016; Watkins, 2005).

STANDARDS, TESTING, AND DIVERSITY

Curricular forms and resources other than textbooks have powerful (and sometimes constraining) consequences for culturally responsive teaching. Prominent among them are recent emphases on achievement standards and standardized testing. Some scholars attribute their emergence to the *Nation at Risk* federal educational report released in 1983, and their elevation to the forefront of national attention to the No Child Left Behind Act of 2001 (NCLB). This act was a reauthorization of the 1965 Elementary and Secondary Education Act (ESEA). It was reauthorized again in 2015 with the Every Student Succeeds Act (ESSA), which replaced NCLB. Concerns about what students should know and be able to do at what levels of acceptability, and according to what evidence or measures of success (i.e., "standards"), existed long before then. They are recurrent throughout the history of U.S. education (Meier & Wood, 2004; Oliva, 2009; Sleeter, 2005; Tucker & Codding, 1998), although they were called something else, such as goals, objectives, outcomes, and basics. Mandated expectations for student learning, like other kinds of curriculum priorities, are strongly influenced by the social, cultural, political, and economic tenor and demands of the times of their creation.

Content standards, performance standardization, and testing have become inseparably linked. Content standards are what students are supposed to know and understand after specified units of instruction. These units of instruction may be courses (algebra, U.S. history, English, biology, etc.), grades (4, 8, 10), or levels of schooling (elementary, middle, high). Performance standards indicate what students should be able to do in association with selected content, and at what level of acceptability (basic, proficient, advanced). The Common Core State Standards (CCSS) are the latest iteration of academic performance criteria for students. Their focus is on mathematics and English language arts/literacy knowledge and skills that students are expected to meet at each grade level, and as indicators of how prepared high school graduates are for college, careers, and life. While the CCSS are, in effect, de facto national standards, they are not legally mandatory. To date, 42 states, Washington, DC, four U.S. territories, and the Department of Defense Education Activity (DoDEA) have adopted the Common Core (corestandards.org/about-the-standards/). Although the CCSS do not confront inequities directly, they are implied. If their intent to provide inclusive rigorous, relevant, and high-quality education for *all* students (i.e., a dual commitment to excellence and equity; Savage, O'Connor, & Brass, 2014) is to be taken seriously, then cultural responsiveness must be integral to implementing the Common Core and other forms of academic standards for students from different ethnic, racial, cultural, and economic backgrounds (Lindsey, Kearney, Estrada, Terrell, & Lindsey, 2015).

Educational standardization means using the same measures for all students to determine mastery of content and performance standards (Sleeter, 2005). In almost every instance the measure used is standardized testing. A guide for parents to the Ohio testing system issued by the Business Roundtable in 2004 explains the relationship between content standards and testing that is representative of the situation in most states. It declares that achievement measures are standardized tests, which means that they are

> the same for all students . . . based on the same materials . . . and all students take the tests based on the same guidelines and at approximately the same times. The statewide achievement tests . . . provide important results that are used to measure and compare student performance and progress across classrooms, schools, and districts, and across various student groups, such as racial and ethnic groups, gender groups, income status, disability status, or English language proficiency. (testingguideFINAL.pdf)

Additionally, standardized test results are used by governmental agencies and policymakers to determine school funding and other resource allocations. So far Nebraska is the only exception to this pattern. It, too, mandates content standards, but not standardized testing, and endorses local portfolio evaluations of student achievement through its School-based Teacher-led Assessment and Reporting System (STARS) (n.d.).

Most contemporary state achievement standards for students follow the lead and example of various national subject-area professional organizations that issue content standards for their particular disciplines. They include organizations inside and outside the educational profession (Kendall & Marzano, 1997). All of them are very powerful within, and frequently beyond, their respective arenas of influence on shaping the thoughts and actions of K–12 educators and policymakers about what students should know and be able to do. Among these organizations are the

- National Council of Teachers of Mathematics
- National Council of Teachers of English, and the International Reading Association

- National Geographic Society
- National Council for the Social Studies
- National Academy of Sciences
- Consortium of National Arts Education Associations
- International Society for Technology in Education

In most instances these two levels of standards are so similar that it appears as if the states merely adopted the organizations' versions with minor editorial modifications. As a result, a close reading of the content standards of one state provides a strong and dependable indication of standards of all states. This is especially the case for those areas of study often identified as "the academic core," "high-status knowledge and skills," and "high-stakes" content because of the consequences associated with students and schools that reach acceptable levels of achievement in them, or fail to do so. For all states these are reading and writing (which are treated separately or combined), mathematics, and science. Social studies is usually considered part of the "academic core" for secondary students as well, but is not assigned nearly the status and significance attributed to math, science, and English (or reading and writing). Nor is it tested as regularly or its performance levels considered as consequential for students. Somewhat more variance exists in the performance indicators and benchmarks associated with high-stakes content standards, and in other areas of expected student achievement (such as technology, fine arts, physical education, and health), but even then there is not a whole lot of real difference among states.

Two examples will suffice to illustrate this similarity of standards among states and professional organizations. The first is some variation of the same four common learning goals, applicable across subjects and grades, that are the foundation for the development of more specific content area standards. The 1993 Basic Education Act that created the Washington state "Essential Academic Learning Requirements" (EALRs) and the Washington Assessment of Student Learning (WASL) identified these goals as

- Reading with comprehension, writing with skill, and communicating effectively and responsively in a variety of ways and settings
- Knowing and applying the core concepts and principles of different subjects, including mathematics; social, life, and physical sciences; civics, geography, and history; arts; and health, wellness, and fitness
- Thinking analytically, logically, and creatively, and integrating knowledge and experience in forming reasoned judgments and solving problems
- Understanding the importance of work, and how performance, effort, and decisions affect future career and educational opportunities

The policy document gives credit to the National Council of Teachers of English (NCTE) as one of the primary source of these priorities.

The second example of the consensus of content standards across states and professional organizations is a sample of those for mathematics and reading. *The Connecticut Framework,* issued by the Connecticut Department of Education (1998), identified 10 categories of content standards for mathematics. They are number sense; operations; estimation and approximation; ratios, proportions, and percentages; measurement; spatial relationships and geometry; probability and statistics; patterns; algebra and functions; and discrete mathematics. Each of these content standards has several related performance standards of increasing complexity that are parallel but age-appropriate across school levels. For instance, one for Grades K–4 students is, "describe simple ratios when comparing quantities." For Grades 5–8, the same standard is, "understand and use ratios, proportions, and percentages in a wide variety of situations." Its equivalent for students in Grades 9–12 is, "use ratios, proportions, and percents to solve real life problems" (Connecticut Department of Education, 1998, p. 92). All states endorse the same four broad reading content goals, with each having multiple levels of the same kinds of specificity. They are

- Understand and use different strategies to read (such as developing vocabulary and fluency)
- Understand the meaning of what is read (i.e., comprehension, prediction, making inferences, analysis, synthesis, interpretation)
- Read different materials for a variety of purposes (to gain information, perform a task, have a literary experience)
- Set goals and evaluate own progress to improve reading proficiency (for self-improvement and to share reading interests and experiences with others)

Colorado deviates somewhat structurally from this trend by not separating reading from writing, but the substantive content of the combined standards is the same as that of the states that separate them.

Whatever the prior status of state standards, related assessments, and accountability expectations, NCLB embellished and expanded them through some of its regulations. A very powerful one was imposing fiscal sanctions on states whose students failed to achieve proficiency on their self-declared achievement expectations, and where there were significant disparities in the performance of students from different ethnic, racial, cultural, social, and linguistic groups. This could have been a viable entrée into culturally responsive teaching, but it did not materialize in actual practice. Many teachers are so preoccupied with teaching tested content that they have little time or motivation to do much else. They feel they cannot afford to risk teaching content about cultural diversity for fear that their students' performance on tests will be compromised and the consequences will be extreme for themselves and their students. Commercial publishers of textbooks and other instructional materials are responding to test-driven curricula in similar ways. State standards largely determine what content is included in many textbooks and how it is organized. Most state and national standardized tests seem to ascribe to a color-blind philosophy, as evident by avoiding any specific references to cultural diversity, social class, race, and ethnicity beyond the superficial, such as names of characters (Maria, Abdullah, Wei-ying, Ganaraj) in scenarios and prompts for test items. Therefore, the standards initiative that is supposed to be a major step forward in improving the academic achievement of low-performing ethnically and culturally diverse students actually is restricting rather than enhancing their learning opportunities.

The few explicit inclusions of content about cultural diversity in most state standards are restricted mostly to social studies, reading, English, and/ or language arts. One example of this trend is the Connecticut language arts standards. They include several references to specific kinds and dimensions of ethnic and cultural diversity in the performance standards related to each of the four content standards. One of the 12 performance standards for mastering "reading and responding" requires students to "demonstrate literacy and aesthetic appreciation for the text, awareness of the author's style, understanding of textual features, and ability to challenge the text and think divergently." A suggestion for these skills to be actualized in high school practice is, "Students read Ralph Ellison's *Invisible Man*, then engage in a discussion of . . . questions based on the text about its literary merit" (Connecticut Department of Education, 1998, p. 55). Culturally diverse examples used to illustrate what students can do to meet the standard of recognizing literary conventions and understanding how they convey meaning are *Hailstone and Halibut Bones*, Langston Hughes's poem "Mother to Son," and Wadsworth's sonnets in elementary, middle, and high school, respectively. Although these examples are intended only to suggest the diversity of learning possibilities and are not mandatory teaching strategies, they are instructive about how cultural diversity can be woven into learning standards. The National Council for the Social Studies (1994) includes a separate content standard on culture, as well as making frequent references to cultural diversity in its other nine standards.

Another illustration of the unfulfilled potential for incorporating cultural diversity into content and performance standards is apparent in the Washington state EALRs. In the introduction to the writing standards, an explicit commitment is made to culturally responsive teaching. Using ideas adapted from the National Board of Professional Teaching Standards, the declaration states:

Writing, by its nature, encompasses diverse subject matter and builds on the unique characteristics and cultures of each student writer. Accomplished teachers are aware of the unique role that language plays in dealing with cultural diversity, and they capitalize on the richness of languages that students bring to their learning and their writing to raise cultural awareness and to enrich the study of languages.

Writing teachers infuse their teaching with literature as examples and perspectives representing a broad range of cultures. They teach students to be aware of the cultural diversity of their audiences. Teachers appreciate and build on the diversity and commonalities they find in their classes so that those diverse and common elements become integral parts of their students' exploration of the world and human experience. ("K–10 grade level expectations," p. 5)

Unfortunately, these general commitments are not evident in the specific writing standards.

Even with these oversights, many of the states' standards, as well as those of professional organizations, could be extended to accommodate cultural diversity. Among these are literacy standards such as "reading different materials for a variety of purposes" and "understanding the meaning of what is read." In both instances, reading materials could include a variety of genres of writings by different ethnic authors, and about different ethnic groups' cultures, heritages, experiences, and contributions. Comprehension of these materials could be assessed by asking students to decipher or interpret culturally encoded messages, and convert them from one expressive form to another, such as from poetry to explanatory essays, and from narrative autobiography to conversational dialogue. Similar extensions of standards in other subject areas are possible as well. For instance, ethnically and culturally specific contexts, events, and situations (i.e., performance standards or benchmarks) could be used for students to demonstrate math standards like "using algebraic skills to describe real-world phenomena symbolically and graphically," and "using concepts of statistics and probability to collect and analyze data and test hypotheses."

The Alaska Assembly of Native Educators used another approach to accommodate cultural diversity in standards that could be replicated in other states as well. In 1998 it created a set of Standards for Culturally Responsive Schools to complement the state's subject-based content standards. They are based on the belief that a firm grounding in heritage language and indigenous culture of a particular place and group is fundamental to producing well-educated, healthy, responsible, and vibrant individuals and communities. They foster strong connections between students' lives in and out of school; teaching and learning through local cultures; and viewing different forms of knowledge and ways of knowing as being equally valid, adaptable, and complementary. Although the content and focus are different, the culturally responsive standards are organized in ways similar to the state standards. They address five areas (students, educators, curriculum, schools, and communities), each one has five or six standards, and several performance indicators accompany each standard. Some of the ones for learners declare that culturally responsive students

- are well grounded in the cultural heritages and traditions of their local communities
- build on local cultural knowledge and skills to achieve academic and personal success
- actively participate in various cultural environments
- engage effectively in learning activities based on traditional ways of knowing and learning (Lomawaima & McCarty, 2006)

In 2010 the Alaska Native Knowledge Network (ANKN) issued a comprehensive list of guidelines for dealing with the documentation, representation, and use of the cultural knowledge of indigenous Alaskans in educational contexts. These guidelines complement and extend the earlier recommendations made by the Alaska Assembly of Native Educators. They include suggestions for a variety of constituencies, including classroom teachers; curriculum developers; authors, illustrators, editors, and publishers; cultural elders and community organizers; and researchers. The general purpose of the guidelines is to encourage and facilitate the inclusion of accurate and authentic indigenous cultural content in teaching practices (ankn.uaf.edu/publications/knowledge.html).

Thus, the rhetoric of state standards; the No Child Left Behind Act; its successor, the 2015 Every Student Succeeds Act (ESSA); and the Common Core is enticing, but their actual practices are problematic for culturally responsive teaching. Too often standards-based curriculum reforms ignore the fact that students learn differently due in significant part to their cultural socialization, and that using this diversity as a resource in the educational process is fundamental to providing genuine educational equity and excellence for ethnically, racially, socially, and linguistically diverse students. There also is increasing evidence that the students who are supposed to be served most by the standards movement—that is, underachieving youth of color and poverty—are suffering more than they are benefiting. Their achievement levels are not increasing by leaps and bounds; the overall quality of their educational opportunities continues to be substandard; they do not have highly qualified teachers in all of their classrooms; uniform curriculum content is not tweaking their interest, developing their intellect, or enticing them to remain in school; the curriculum scope is narrowing; and the underresourced schools they attend are further compromised because they are sanctioned and penalized by losing funds for not reaching the levels of yearly average progress mandated by federal and state regulations (Darling-Hammond, 2007; Lomawaima & McCarty, 2006; Meier & Wood,

2004; Montaño & Metcalfe, 2003; Reyhner, 2006; Reardon, Greenberg, Kalogrides, Shores, & Valentino, 2013). The National Indian Education Association (NIEA) (2005) conducted a study on the effects of NCLB on Native American, Alaskan Native, and Native Hawaiian students. It applauded the policy for promoting equity and making schools accountable to indigenous students, but concluded that any success accomplished has been at the expense of Native languages and cultures, and the exclusion of Native voices in decisionmaking. Skerrett and Hargreaves (2008) found the same results in a comparative study of 4 decades of secondary school reform in the United States and Canada. They concluded that "standardization has become the enemy of diversity" (p. 913), because the "increasing trend toward curriculum standardization and high-stakes testing has significantly reduced teachers' flexibility in incorporating more culturally responsive practices into their classrooms" (p. 916). Valerie Strauss (2014) challenges the equity claims of the Common Core, arguing that this policy and its practices violate rather than promote equitable and fair learning opportunities for racial minorities, English language learners, and disabled students. Using test scores of students in New York City, she demonstrates that the performance of students in these three categories declined after the Common Core was initiated.

Despite the pressures of standards and increasing standardization in assessing student achievement, the best pedagogical response for ethnically diverse students is not to concede to them. There is no *one right* curriculum design, teaching style, and assessment procedure for all students. A better strategy is to understand how the encroachment of standardization confounds, erodes, and configures diversity in learning conditions and contexts, and develop culturally responsive instructional strategies in the midst of, and as alternatives to, it (Skerrett & Hargreaves, 2008). Rather than looking for silver bullets and magical answers, classroom teachers and school leaders should realize that achieving equity of educational opportunities, and higher levels of academic achievement for ethnically diverse students, resides in using a variety of curriculum content and designs, instructional materials and resources, teaching techniques, and assessment procedures that are responsive to their cultural heritages and personal experiences.

ETHNIC DIVERSITY IN LITERARY AND TRADE BOOKS

The inclusion of information about ethnic and cultural diversity in supplementary instructional materials, such as children's picture books, biographies and autobiographies, short stories, novels, and song lyrics, written by ethnic authors about ethnic groups, is both encouraging and discouraging. Several studies are presented here as illustrative of these trends, and as sample explanations of them. The first one deals with ethnic diversity authorship in the publishing industry of children' and young adult (YA) literature. The others examine portrayals of African Americans, Asian Americans, Native Americans, Mexican Americans, and multiethnic groups in child and adolescent literature.

The importance of including ethnic literature as curriculum content has been recognized by E. Kim (1976). She says fiction can provide valuable and otherwise unavailable insights into the social consciousness, cultural identity, and historical experiences of ethnic groups. Ramírez and Dowd (1997) add that high-quality authentic multicultural literature can help children "make connections to their personal experiences, provide role models, and expand their horizons" (p. 20). It also is a powerful way to expose students to ethnic groups, cultures, and experiences different from their own to which they may not have access in their daily lives. Multicultural literature can help students cross cultural borders and improve understanding of insider and outsider perspectives on cultural, ethnic, and racial diversity. It can "speak" thoughts, feelings, and beliefs about a wide variety of multicultural issues that people are unable or are not yet ready to do for themselves. Literature is a "window of opportunity" for authors, teachers, and students to contemplate what is and what can be regarding racially and culturally diverse attitudes and actions (Boyd, Causey, & Galda, 2015; Cai, 2002; Durden, Escalante, & Blitch, 2015). And it can be a "mirror" for reflecting images and representations of ethnic and cultural diversity (Botelho & Rudman. 2009; Wanless & Crawford, 2016).

Wanless and Crawford (2016) point out that literary texts can help young children visualize and develop positive racial identities, interracial relationships, and cognitive understanding of racial injustices. As part of the culturally responsive teaching agenda, it is important to include these issues in early childhood education because children begin forming ideas about their own and other people's racial identities at very young ages. This happens regardless of whether race is explicitly addressed or subtly ignored in early childhood classrooms, homes, and communities (Derman-Sparks & Edwards, 2010; Husband, 2012; Wanless & Crawford, 2016)

Michael Cart (2008) connects his assessment of the value of literature in teaching and learning to a specific category and a different readership (i.e., Young Adult or YA—literature targeted for high-school-age readers.). Speaking on behalf of the Young Adult Library Services Association (YALSA), he describes some of them as follows

> Young adulthood is, intrinsically, a period of tension. On the one hand young adults have an all-consuming need to belong. But on the other, they are also inherently solipsistic, regarding themselves as being unique, which—for them— is not cause for celebration but, rather, for despair. For to be unique is to be unlike one's peers; to be "other," in fact. And to be "other" is to not belong but, instead, to be outcast. Thus, to see oneself in the pages of a young adult

book is to receive the reassurance that one is not alone after all, not other, not alien but, instead, a viable part of a larger community of beings who share a common humanity.

Another value of young adult literature is its capacity for fostering understanding, empathy, and compassion by offering vividly realized portraits of the lives—exterior and interior—of individuals who are unlike the reader. In this way young adult literature invites its readership to embrace the humanity it shares with those who—if not for the encounter in reading—might forever remain strangers or—worse—irredeemably "other."

Still another value of young adult literature is its capacity for telling its readers the truth, however disagreeable that may sometimes be, for in this way it equips readers for dealing with the realities of impending adulthood and for assuming the rights and responsibilities of citizenship.

By giving readers such a frame of reference, it also helps them to find role models, to make sense of the world they inhabit, to develop a personal philosophy of being, to determine what is right and, equally, what is wrong, to cultivate a personal sensibility. To, in other words, become civilized. (Cart, 2008, n.p.)

Thus, multicultural literature and trade books are valuable content resources for culturally responsive teaching even if they are not always bias-free and culturally affirming for different ethnic groups. Teachers need to know how to assess the cultural accuracy and authenticity of these books, essays, poems, and short stories; correct their fallacies; and build upon their strengths in teaching. Some useful assistance in developing these skills is available from prior research studies and text analyses such as those summarized by Mendoza and Reese (2001) and the ones described below. For example, many techniques and criteria for evaluating child, adolescent, and young adult literature are easily accessible. One set that is easy to understand and use is provided by M. Perkins (2009) in the form of critical questions to ask about the realism of the characters; how race and ethnicity are addressed; congruity between narrative text and illustrations; who are the agents of change; and how beauty and aestheticism are portrayed.

Biases Persist in Child and Adolescent Literature

A major persistent bias in these sources of potential culturally responsive content is noted by Rothschild (2015). She identifies the underrepresentation of people of color as authors and characters in literature for children and young adults. This is not to suggest that European Americans should not be authoring books about minority people and issues, and/or including characters of color in other books. Rather, the problem is the lack of insider ethnic, racial, and cultural perspectives that occur when authors and characters of color are so few or nonexistent in literary books.

A study conducted by Deane (1989) of approximately 300 popular children's fiction books poses some serious questions about progress in including ethnically diverse content and characters. He concentrated on how African American characters are depicted in series written by European Americans that have dominated the fiction market for young readers from Grades 2 through 6 for generations. These are books "which involve the same major characters . . . in a successive series of actions, scenes, and situations" (p. 153), such as the Nancy Drew, Hardy Boys, Bobbsey Twins, Woodland Gang, and Sweet Valley High series. Deane concluded that most of the blatantly derogatory depictions of African Americans have vanished from these books, but so have many African American characters. Closer scrutiny of this "progress" revealed that extreme stereotypical images have been eliminated and more realistic portrayals of African American characters are presented. There also has been a tendency to overcorrect for stereotypes by not assigning any differentiating characteristics to the speech and actions of the African American characters (and other individuals of color in the storylines), or to eliminate them from the storyline entirely or make characters of color superhumanly good and supremely capable, while European Americans become the new-bred "bad guys" (Cai, 2002; Mendoza & Reese, 2001; M. Perkins, 2009).

J. Garcia, Hadaway, and Beal (1988) examined 33 trade books (16 fiction and 17 nonfiction) to determine whether the ethnic topics, themes, and personalities treated were "typical" or "new." "Typical" referred to topics, issues, and individuals that gained prominence in the civil rights movement and cultural/ethnic revolutions of the 1960s. "New" trade books were those that emphasized issues, themes, topics, and ideas that were identifiable in multicultural literature in the 1970s and early 1980s (such as cultural affirmation, unique ethnic identities, and political activism) but not necessarily included in works designed for children. The books were competitors for the 1986 Carter G. Woodson Award, sponsored by the National Council for the Social Studies. Since 1973 this award has been given to outstanding nonfiction trade books for their sensitive and accurate treatment of a topic related to ethnic minorities and race relations. J. Garcia and associates (1988) concluded:

> While stereotypic portrayals of ethnic and minority groups in children's tradebooks are no longer prevalent, contemporary writers continue to treat overused themes, topics, and personalities that, while providing some perspectives on ethnic and minority life, do little to expand into areas that would provide young learners with more creative interpretations of America's cultural diversity. (p. 71)

In a relatively rare research occurrence, Harada (1994) analyzed adolescent fiction books about Asian Americans and found characteristics that paralleled those identified by Garcia and associates. Twenty-four books published between 1988 and 1993, and targeted for 11- to 17-year-olds, were examined to determine how Asian characters from 11 countries of origin were treated. The countries were China, Japan, Taiwan, Korea, Laos, Cambodia, Burma, India, Thailand, Vietnam, and the Philippines. The books were analyzed for character portrayals, story development, language usage, historical authenticity, and cultural accuracy. Only 6 of the 11 Asian American groups were represented in the books. The largest numbers were Chinese Americans (32%), followed sequentially by Japanese Americans (20%), Korean and Vietnamese Americans (16% each), and Cambodian and Taiwanese Americans (8% each).

Biases and stereotypes were found in each of the five categories of analyses for 23 of the 24 books. Samples of these included presenting Asian Americans as being mysterious, inscrutable foreigners; all Asian ethnic groups as having the same physical traits; and both males and females as being exotic, alluring sex objects. In addition, Asians were presented as desiring and striving to be like European Americans, as model minorities, and as dependent on Whites for the resolution of conflicts. Speech behavior was parodied; token or superficial historical references that had little to do with the development of character or plot were included; and there was inaccurate or restricted mention of cultural details. These results caused Harada (1994) to suggest that the potential of fiction as a "powerful and natural vehicle for providing a thoughtful reflection of the values and beliefs of a culture" (p. 55) is not being realized in adolescent literature about Asian Americans. If this is to happen, authors must stop "recycling the super achiever and China doll images" (p. 55) and become much more responsible about "weaving authentic details and accurate cultural information into quality works for all young readers" (p. 56). Harada's admonishments and advice can be easily extended to all types of instructional materials and curriculum designs about all ethnic groups and for all levels of learners.

How Mexican American girls and women are portrayed in realistic fiction books for K–3 students was the focus of analysis in studies conducted by Rocha and Dowd (1993) and Ramírez and Dowd (1997). In the first study, two sets of realistic fiction books featuring female characters were examined. Nine of these were published between 1950 and 1969, and 20 between 1970 and 1990. Those in the Ramírez and Dowd study (a total of 21) were published between 1990 and 1997. Seven criteria were used to analyze the content of these books: characterization, plot, theme, point of view, setting, style of writing, and special features.

The findings of both studies are similar to those of research on the portrayal of other ethnic groups. Improvements have occurred across time in how Mexican American females are portrayed in books for young children. There are fewer stereotypes; a greater variety of roles, settings, and activities; and more modernity in profiling Mexican American people and culture.

Yet the major story themes of the 1990–1997 books are similar to those of the 1970–1990 period, with heavy emphasis on acculturation, satisfaction with self, Mexican heritage, privacy, goals and dreams, and the resolution of dilemmas. The recent books include more generic themes, such as relationships, individualism, and family. Ramírez and Dowd (1997) consider this an asset because universal experiences can make these books more readily understood by readers from other ethnic and cultural backgrounds. Increasingly, recent publications also are including special features that indicate the authors' cultural knowledge, Spanish language skills, and affiliation with Mexican American culture.

Despite these improvements, realistic fiction books about Mexican American females for young children are not as good as they need to be. The authors of both studies found that some significant stereotyping and traditional ethnic "typecasting" remain. Mexican American females too frequently are depicted in traditional hairstyles and clothing, and engaged in music, dancing, fiestas, and other celebrations. The characters are rarely shown participating in school activities or employment outside of the home. The story settings are more rural than urban (a reversal from books published in the 1970–1990 period); located away from permanent residences, such as at vacation sites; depict old-fashioned dwellings more than modern, contemporary ones; and never use an upper-class milieu (Ramírez & Dowd, 1997; Rocha & Dowd, 1993).

What accounts for these seemingly mixed results in how ethnic groups are portrayed in literary sources and textbooks? Ramírez and Dowd (1997) think they are a normal result of the developmental process of creating a rich body of multiethnic literature. They contend that

> With a proliferation of books comes more diversity in the literature as a whole. No one book has to present all of a culture—nor should it. For example, when so many books about Mexican Americans present facets of religion and religious practice, a book that seems to focus on what many see as superstition does not carry the negative weight it would if it were one of only two or three. In fact, its existence may very well enrich our understanding of diverse religious practices when read alongside other books. (p. 54)

Implicit in this explanation is some important advice for teachers. It is quite unlikely that any one author, book, or other reference is ever capable of providing a complete profile of ethnic groups and their cultures, contributions, and experiences. Therefore, teachers routinely should use a combination of resources and genres of various types to teach ethnic and cultural diversity.

The results of two other studies offer some implications for accomplishing these content extensions. In using literary resources, teachers are accustomed to engaging both written and pictorial content (e.g., illustrations) *within* books. Hart (2011) addresses another potentially valuable kind of content that can be derived from literary books (and other kinds, too!) for inclusion in culturally responsive teaching: book covers. They can be considered as symbolic, aesthetic, political, and cultural curriculum content. Hart examined the cover images of 624 young adult (YA) literary books released in 2011, and found that 90% of the images were of Whites and 79% were females. Latino and Asian images were radically fewer but equally represented, and occurred slightly more often than African Americans. Native Americans' images on books covers fared the worst of all ethnic groups; they were virtually invisible. The results of Hart's qualitative analysis were even more disheartening than the quantitative disparities. Ethnic minority book cover images most often did not depict people in full facial view looking outward as if facing the reader directly. Instead, they were presented in profile and silhouette. Over 15% of the books presented characters from rear views.

In a March 7, 2012, post on the Hello Ello Blog explaining "Why the pretty White girl YA book cover trend needs to end," Ellen Oh made some comments about the symbolic significance of book covers and the racial inequities present in them that have implications for culturally responsive curriculum content. She said,

> Putting pretty white girls on all [YA] book covers is the book equivalent of what all our fashion magazines do. An idealization of beauty that is unrealistic and dangerous to our youth. . . . To say that only pretty white girls can sell YA books is not a business model that publishers should approve of. . . . We need for publishing to break this trend . . . [and] act more responsibly. . . . We need to teach our youth the beauty of diversity. Beauty does not come in only one color. It does not come in only one size and one shape. And maybe when our teens grow up exposed to diversity, then they will grow into adults who embrace it. (Oh, 2012, n.p.)

Another study deals with ethnic diversity disparities in the authorship of literary books for children and young adults. Since 1994 the Cooperative Children's Book Center (CCBC) has been analyzing children and young adult fiction books "by" and "about" people of color published annually (see ccbc.education.wisc.edu/books/pcstats.asp#USonly). According to the statistics for 2016, of the 3,500 books reviewed and released by U.S. publishers, there were more "about" (265) but proportionally less "by" (90) African/African Americans than for other minority groups. The best "by/about" numbers and ratios were for Asian/Pacific Islanders (194:224) and Latinos (94:157), respectively. There were radically fewer children's books both by and about Native Americans, the numbers being 8 and 35, respectively. The CCBC review also included many books that were "about" minority groups and topics, but were not written "by" minority group authors. These data raise questions about the ethnic representation of the authorship, and the cultural accuracy and authenticity of trade and literary books that should be addressed in culturally responsive curriculum content selection and implementation. Similar analyses need to be conducted of other content sources as well, such as academic research and scholarship, personal narratives, oral histories, and various art forms.

Although the availability of multicultural literature is still not ideal, the following comments made by the CCBC Director Kathleen T. Homing are encouraging:

> publishing for children and teens has a long way to go before reflecting the rich diversity of perspectives and experiences within and across race and culture. . . . [But] numbers are far from the only important thing to consider when it comes to multicultural publishing for children and teens . . . . [E]very year we see amazing books by and about people of color and First/Native Nations people published. There just aren't enough of them. The more books there are, especially books created by authors and illustrators of color, the more opportunities librarians, teachers, and parents and other adults have of finding outstanding books for young readers and listeners that reflect dimensions of their lives, and give a broader understanding of who we are as a nation. (Homing, n.d.)

Some Improvements Are Evident

Other authors also have found positive results in how literary resources written for school-aged students portray cultural diversity. Two of these are Heller (1997) and Hafen (1997). Heller reviewed more than 50 children's picture books to determine how African American fathers were portrayed. Several themes emerged that conveyed positive characterizations. These include the role of the father in nurturing and childrearing; recreational activities with children; discipline; household maintenance and management; occupational and economic activities; and visits with children after absences caused by some crisis. Males in the extended family and community also were depicted in positive fathering roles and relationships. These findings are particularly noteworthy because of popular conceptions about the absence of fathers from African American families and the potential negative effects this can have on children's identity, self-concept, and various aspects of school achievement. Resources like the books on Heller's list can be used in classroom instruction to dispel myths and compensate for voids in Black father-child relationships.

The books cited in a study conducted by Hafen (1997) on popular images of Native Americans in contemporary literature were published between 1985 and 1996. The authors were successful in combining traditional tribal heritages with mainstream and contemporary cultures. They demonstrate how Native Americans are engaged in the reinterpretation and self-creation of a contemporary identity without forsaking traditional cultural values. These books also show how ethnic minority literature can be simultaneously particular and universal. Their positive portrayals are a welcome relief to the way Native Americans too often are presented in textbooks—as one-dimensional, exotic figures frozen in historical times, invisible in contemporary society, or restricted to statistical listings in the demographics of social problems such as crime, poverty, and unemployment. Resources such as these and the information they present are invaluable to culturally responsive teaching. They should be particularly comforting and helpful to teachers who are concerned about whether teaching multicultural education will create irresolvable tensions between unity and diversity, similarities and differences among the people of the United States.

However, Mihesuah (1996) warns against being overly optimistic about how Native Americans are portrayed in media readily accessible to children and youth, especially those produced from outside the ethnic communities. She suggests that distortions of Native Americans and their cultural identities can still be found "in every possible medium—from scholarly publications and textbooks, movies, TV shows, literature, cartoons, commercials, comic books, and fanciful paintings, to the gamut of commercial logos, insignia and imagery that pervade tourist locales throughout the Southwest and elsewhere" (p. 9). High school and college mascots can be added to this list of media that perpetuate stereotypes of Native Americans (Pewewardy, 1991, 1998). The stereotypes transmitted vary in range and intensity "from the extremely pejorative to the artificially idealistic, from historic depictions of Indians as uncivilized primal men and winsome women belonging to a savage culture, to present day . . . mystical environmentalists, or uneducated, alcoholic bingo-players confined to reservations" (Mihesuah, 1996, p. 9).

The quantity and variety of culturally validating books, written in authentic cultural voices and providing insider perspectives, are numerous for African, Asian, Native, and Latino Americans, as well as European Americans. But they are not of equal quality across all specific ethnic groups within these general categories. The *Multicultural Review* is a useful resource for some of these. It regularly publishes lists of recommended books, films, videotapes, and microfilm collections on a wide variety of ethnic groups, such as Southeast Asian Americans, Filipino Americans, Native Americans, Puerto Ricans, African Americans, Mexican Americans, Chinese Americans, Japanese Americans, Jewish Americans, Caribbean Americans, Arab Americans, biracial Americans, and immigrants from different countries. The topics examined vary widely, too. Among them are male and female characters and concerns; historical and contemporary issues, events, and perspectives; biographies, autobiographies, and picture books; short stories; fiction and nonfiction; myths and folklore; rhymes and poetry; literary critiques and scholarly treatises. These resources are valuable complements to textbooks, and have the potential to profoundly enrich learning experiences about the cultures, histories, heritages, and life experiences of ethnically diverse groups. But multicultural literature must be taught thoughtfully and critically, not merely as a form of cultural tourism in which it is showcased to students without any interpretative and reflective engagement. As M. Perkins (2009) explains:

> Our calling as educators and authors is to pay attention, both to the young people we serve, and to the books they're reading, and ask questions with them. Great stories, like their human counterparts, are beautiful, yet flawed, and discussing them in community can strengthen their power to enlighten, inspire, and let justice roll down.

MASS MEDIA AS CULTURAL CURRICULUM CONTENT

Mass media are powerful sources of curriculum content about ethnic and cultural diversity. As Bleich, Bloemraad, and Graauw (2015) explained, "the media inform the public, provide a communicative bridge between political and social actors, influence perceptions of pressing issues, depict topics and people in particular ways, and may shape individuals' political views and participation" (p. 857). Frequently the images and information they convey are contradictory to what is desirable and need to be corrected or countered by classroom instruction. Occasionally the reverse is true; some media presentations of ethnic peoples and experiences are positive and even complementary to school instruction. Either way, the images are too easily accessible and their influence too powerful for teachers to ignore how ethnic groups and issues are presented in television programming, films, newspapers, magazines, and music videos. Students bring this information and its effects to the classroom with them. Therefore, ethnic diversity in mass media should be part of the curriculum content of culturally responsive teaching.

The role that television alone plays is very extensive, with millions of viewers tuning in several hours each day. Because of its pervasiveness, K. Perkins (1996) calls television "omnipresent." This omnipresence is both quantitative and qualitative. The quantitative impact is indicated by the sheer number of hours children spend watching television daily. Common estimates are that they spend an average of 20–25 hours per week watching television. The programs they view include a wide range of cartoons, movies, music videos, news reports, documentaries, prime-time series, syndicated "family classics," and an avalanche of advertisements. At this rate, by the time students graduate from high school they will have spent more time viewing television than in formal classrooms (K. Perkins, 1996). Qualitatively, television programming is always involved in constructing knowledge, creating images, cultivating consumer markets, shaping opinions, and manipulating values and ideas about ethnic and cultural diversity.

Nadel (2005) notes that "television has contributed profoundly to solidifying what we could call a 'national imagining'" (p. 6). This is a set of common images that people share when they think of the United States as a nation, and themselves as its citizens. The imaginary America constructed by television (and other forms of mass media) is very distrustful of ethnic, linguistic, racial, and cultural plurality. It is a place where diverse individuals and groups exchange (voluntarily or through coercion) their heterogeneity for the opportunity to be part of an idealized homogeneous nation.

Although individual exceptions exist, as collectives ethnic American and immigrant groups of color are still stereotyped, exoticized, marginalized, homogenized, and made invisible in mass media. For example, too few distinctions are made among various social, cultural, linguistic, gender, and achievement variations within ethnic clusters. Latino and Asian Americans often are treated as "perpetual foreigners, or outsiders" regardless of how long they have lived in the United States, or the fact that many are indigenous citizens (Montaño & Metcalfe, 2003; Pang, Kiang, & Pak, 2004; Tuan, 1998). African American males are perceived as violent and economically and socially irresponsible, while females are considered to "always have attitude"—that is, being angry, mean, domineering, hostile, demanding, volatile, and unattractive. Native Americans are the most often "forgotten minority" in conversations about contemporary issues. What little consideration they receive frequently freezes them in historical time warps, dwells on the social problems they encounter, or treats them as "symbolized conquest" (defeated warriors, vanishing people, spiritual pacifists) (Harvey, 1994; Pewewardy, 1998). Individuals of Asian ancestry are thought to be "the model minority" who accomplish exemplary educational, professional, and economic success, without enough attention given to the wide diversity of cultures, ethnicities, social classes, and achievement levels that exist among and within the groups that constitute this ethnic category (S. Lee, 1996; Pang & Cheng, 1998; Pang et al., 2004; Park, Goodwin, & Lee, 2003). European Americans are presented as being responsible, dependable, and ingenious, and as succeeding in school and life because of their individual efforts and merits.

According to Horton, Price, and Brown (1999), ethnic and racial "profiling" in media is now less blatant and conspicuous, but still evident:

> The Paramount Pictures, NBC's, ABC's and Universal Studio's of the world . . . are the propagators of the negative stereotypes and inescapable stigmas that many thought were left behind once the shackles of segregation were broken. Unfortunately, they are resurfacing in our sitcoms, newscasts and big screen movies. . . . Whether it's appearing in disparaging roles or not appearing at all, minorities are the victim of an industry that relies on old ideas to appeal to the "majority" at the expense of the insignificant minority. (n. p.).

Researchers at the University of Southern California (Smith, Choueiti, & Pieper, 2016) released the results of a quantitative study that validated earlier observations made by Horton et al. and other analysts. Although their analyses were more comprehensive, only some data dealing with TV and film onscreen diversity are presented here. Smith, Choueiti, and Pieper analyzed over 10,000 speaking or named onscreen characters to ascertain their race and ethnicity, in 400 films and television shows released from September 2014 through August 2015. The results revealed that, generally, the media and entertainment industries do not reflect or match the demographic composition of the United States. Specifically, 71.7% of the onscreen speaking characters were White, 12.2% were Black, 5.8% were Latino, 5.1% were Asian, 2.3% were Middle Eastern, and 3.1% were Other. Less than one-fourth of leading characters in film (21.8%), and slightly more than a fourth (26.6%) in TV and digital products, were from underrepresented ethnic and racial groups. The vast majority of these leading characters were African American (65.6%); only 12.5% were Latino, while 6.3% were Asian. Gender distribution within race and ethnic groups revealed that Latina, Asian, and Other females were portrayed onscreen slightly more frequently than African American females. Females from underrepresented ethnic groups who are 40 years of age or older are largely invisible in film, television, and digital series. Based on these results, Smith and colleagues concluded that

> Overall, the landscape of media content is still largely whitewashed. Relative to the U.S. population, the industry is underperforming on racial/ethnic diversity of leads (film), series regulars (TV/digital), and all speaking characters. The number of shows missing two racial groups entirely is particularly problematic. The hashtag #OscarsSoWhite should be changed to #HollywoodSoWhite, as our findings show that an epidemic of invisibility runs throughout popular storytelling. (2016, p. 9)

C. Jones and Shorter-Gooden (2003) point out some of the effects that coping with "ethnic and racial image myths" and invisibility created and perpetuated in media have on groups targeted by them. Even though their conclusions derive from a study of the effects of racism and sexism on African American women, they are applicable to other ethnic groups and men as well. The participants in their study were 333 women, ages 18–88, in 24 states and Washington, DC, and from a variety of educational, social class, and marital status backgrounds. Ninety percent of the women surveyed said they had been victimized personally by racism and sexism. They have to spend inordinate amounts of time, thought, and emotional and intellectual energy monitoring themselves, managing an array of feelings, and altering their behavior. The consequences of this vigilant self-editing were

often ethnic shame, feelings of low self-esteem, lack of confidence and efficacy for success, and doubts, fears, and anxieties about whether they would
ever be accepted unconditionally by their middle-class European American
peers. They developed a coping strategy Jones and Shorter-Gooden called
"shifting"—that is, altering expectations, ways of thinking, outward ap-
pearances, speech, and behaviors to accommodate situations and audiences
dominated by privileged European Americans.

There is nothing inherently wrong with style-shifting as a strategy for
facilitating qualitative human interactions. The problem occurs when the
demands for and choices of style are always imposed by someone other
than self. The other message of this mandate is the negative effects it has on
the "shifting" individuals, and their implications for teaching and learning.
Some of these are symbolized by the women in Jones and Shorter-Gooden's
(2003) study. They felt

> pressured to present a face to the world that is acceptable to others even though
> it may be completely at odds with their true selves. . . . They try to cover up their
> intelligence with one group of friends and do everything possible to prove it
> with another. . . . They shift inward, internalizing the searing pain of going out
> into the world day after day and hitting one wall after the next solely because
> they are Black and female. . . . They become hyperalert, endlessly on patrol,
> scanning the environment for danger and ever prepared to respond. (pp. 61–63)

These reactions bring to mind, on a less graphic but nonetheless significant level, two other examples of the negative effects shifting has on
ethnically diverse students. One is the strong resistance of some Asian-
ancestry female students to being stereotyped as passive, quiet, cute, and
accommodating—that is, the "China and Japanese doll" image. The other
is Steele's (1997; Steele & Aronson, 1995) and Aronson's (2004) analyses
of how prejudices and stereotypes attributed to an ethnic group can derail
the academic performance of individuals within the group, even though they
do not believe the perceptions apply to them personally. Suárez-Orozco,
Suárez-Orozco, and Doucet (2004) highlight the psychological effects of
what they call "social mirroring" (p. 428) on immigrant Latino students,
and Nieto (2004) presents similar analyses for Puerto Ricans. People's sense
of self is affected profoundly by significant others in their lives, including
caretakers, teachers, peers, and media portrayals. Reflected images that are
positive generate feelings of worth, dignity, competence, and confidence
that can facilitate academic, personal, social, and professional achievement.
Negative ones lead to self-denigration, doubt, uncertainty, and feelings of
unworthiness that can be impenetrable barriers to school success. These are
powerful challenges and invitations for culturally responsive curricula and
instruction. Pewewardy (1998) makes a poignant statement in support of
cultural respect and responsiveness in educating Native Americans that puts

these needs in graphic perspective. He associates disrespect for the cultures, heritages, and experiences of indigenous peoples in mainstream U.S. society and schools with genocide, and warns that this "may prove to be one of the most destructive forces of oppression yet, as American racism steals precious mental and physical treasures of the soul. . . . Unless interrupted by healing grace, the atrocities of the past become ghosts within the cultural memory of . . . people crying out for justice" (p. 73). There is no doubt that negative images of ethnic groups in society and schools interfere with students' abilities to focus on academic tasks and cultural understanding as constructively as they should, and their achievement in both areas is negatively affected.

Creating Images and Constructing Knowledge About Ethnic Diversity

The images entertainment and news mass media convey about ethnic groups and issues are not always accurate, complimentary, malicious, or overt, but they are always powerful and have a strong influence on students' perceptions of different ethnic groups. A compelling example of these effects are the results of a study entitled "A Different World: Children's Perceptions of Race and Class in the Media." This survey was conducted by Lake Sosin Snell Perry and Associates, and involved 1,200 children between 10 and 17 years old, with equal representation of European, Asian, Latino, and African Americans. The important general findings indicated that children in all four ethnic groups (1) are not always encouraged by the ethnic images they see on television; (2) perceive that Latinos and African Americans are depicted more negatively than European and Asian Americans; (3) are aware of media stereotypes at an early age; and (4) understand the power of television to shape opinions. As one African American child stated, "People are inspired by what they see on television. If they do not see themselves on TV, they want to be someone else" (J. Allen, 1998, p. A8).

The Roper Organization (1993) found that most people in the United States depend on television for their news and consider it more credible than newspaper reporting. The portrayals TV presents about individuals easily become *uncontested* truth that is generalized to entire groups. But much of the information and many of the images about individuals and groups of color presented in news reporting are distorted, negative, and stereotypical. Research conducted by C. Campbell (1995) provides specific illustrations of these general tendencies. He did textual analyses of 39 hours of local newscasts from 29 cities to determine the symbolic and connotative cultural meanings they transmitted about racially and ethnically related issues. Campbell concluded that television journalism perpetuates invisibility, marginality, and erroneous conceptions, as well as a "myth of assimilation" about people of color. This is done by overembellishing the success of a few prominent ethnic individuals to show that racial inequalities, social injustices, and power differentials no longer exist, or are exceptions to the norm, or can be easily overcome by personal initiative. This kind of "ethnic type-casting" in mass media is reminiscent of the tendencies of textbooks to inflate the level of racial harmony, downplay conflicts between minority groups and mainstream society, and offer one-dimensional explanations of ethnic individuals, events, and experiences. They constitute a major challenge for culturally responsive teaching. While classroom teachers may not be in a position to transform mass media, they can teach students how to analyze them for racial and cultural stereotyping, as knowledge-constructors and image-makers, and to be critical consumers of what they see, hear, and read. According to Cortés (1995):

> The issue of media as multicultural information source goes well beyond the question of accuracy. In news, the constant reiteration of certain themes, even when each story is accurate in and of itself, may unjustifiably emphasize limited information about an ethnic group. . . . Similarly, the repetition of ethnic images by the entertainment media add to viewer's pools of "knowledge," particularly if news and entertainment coincide and mutually reinforce each other in theme, approach, content, perspective, and frequency. (p. 172)

These actions of entertainment and news mass media constitute a kind of *ideological management* (Spring, 1992). This is the deliberate exclusion or addition of information to create certain images, to shield consumers from particular ideas and information, and to teach specific moral, political, and social values. Two examples demonstrate the workings of ideological management in media. The first is the Public Broadcasting Service (PBS) production of *Ethnic Notions* (Biggs, 1987). It presents a poignant historical analysis of how stereotypical characterizations of African Americans were created and institutionalized by television and movies. The second example is *Killing Us Softly* (Lazarus, 1979) and its sequels, *Still Killing Us Softly* (Lazarus, 1987) and *Beyond Killing Us Softly* (Lazarus & Wunderich, 2000), produced by Cambridge Documentary Films. They demonstrate how sexist, exploitative, and degrading images, as well as suggested violence against women, are portrayed, cultivated, and disseminated through televised and print advertising. The first two films focus almost exclusively on European American women and girls, but the third one includes a broader and more balanced representation of ethnic diversity. It also presents on-camera analyses, commentaries, and recommendations of several gender-equity scholars and activists about the negative effects of media portrayals of women and how to resist them. It is a good instructional tool for teaching students critical consciousness and selective consumption of media materials and messages about ethnic, cultural, social, and gender diversity in advertising as well as prime-time programming, music videos, and the fashion industry.

K. Perkins (1996) provides another illustration of how television constructs knowledge that is important to culturally responsive teaching. She reviewed research on the influence of television on African American females' perceptions of their physical attractiveness. The conception of beauty presented in the mass media is based on Eurocentric standards—albeit idealized, sexist, and unrealistic ones. The ideal beauty is a tall, slim, lithe, debonair blue-eyed blonde with flawless hair, teeth, and skin, who radiates confidence, sexuality, and desirability on all fronts—intimately, socially, economically. The immutable racial characteristics (e.g., skin color, hair texture, bone structure, body type) of African American females make it impossible for them ever to achieve these ideals. Too frequently they are presented as large, nonsexual, overbearing, assertive, bold, and argumentative. These portrayals help to shape public opinion about what constitutes beauty and can negatively affect the social self-esteem of those deemed unattractive (Dates & Barlow, 1990).

Ideological management is not restricted to the mass media and popular culture. Educational media, including textbooks, films, and videos, do this, too. Their tone, topic, text, setting, format, and character development create a "viewing experience" that invites audiences to engage in particular kinds of social, political, and ideological involvements as the story, action, and discourse unfold (Ellsworth, 1990). Research in media studies over the past 35 years or so presents compelling evidence that educational film, video, and photographic representations are not neutral carriers of content. Instead, content reflects particular cultural, social, and political meanings (Ellsworth & Whatley, 1990).

Some media programs are genuine advancements in making society more ethnically inclusive and egalitarian, as is evident in the increasing numbers of men and women from different ethnic groups involved in more aspects of media programming—writing, producing, directing, and performing. Other programs are ambiguous and convey conflicting information about ethnic diversity. For example, why can Japanese, Chinese, and Filipino Americans participate in local and national news broadcasting but be virtually invisible in prime-time entertainment programs? Why can Native Americans be present in documentaries dealing with conflicts among ecology, traditional ethnic economies (such as fishing rights), and industrial development but otherwise be excluded from mainstream news and entertainment programs?

Subtle racial stereotypes transmitted through films, television, videotapes, and other popular media can leave deep emotional and psychological scars on children of the targeted ethnic groups, and on others as well (Pewewardy, 1996/1997). Mihesuah (1996) offers some alternative explanations and helpful advice for counterbalancing 24 commonly held stereotypes about Native Americans that are transmitted through mass media. Among them are that all Native Americans are alike; they were conquered because they were inferior; they were warlike and treacherous; they get a free ride from the government; they are stoic and have no sense of humor; and they contribute nothing of worth to U.S. society and culture.

Debunking these kinds of myths and other ethnic biases in mass media should be a central feature of culturally responsive teaching. It is also important for students and teachers to understand that curriculum content is not just the information taught in schools. The experiences students have outside of school, such as those provided by all forms of mass media, are also powerful influences on learning. These often are overlooked in schools because they do not have the official designation of "curriculum." Yet the only contact many students have with ethnically diverse people is through mass media. For others, media images are important gauges for how society views and values their ethnic groups. Either way, the "societal curriculum" (Cortés, 1991) comes to school with students, and teachers must contend with it as they struggle to make education more culturally responsive for diverse ethnic groups.

Uneven Progress in Treatment of Ethnic Diversity

For the most part, the numerical and qualitative presentation of groups of color in mass media follows trends in textbooks and literary materials. Portrayals of ethnic and cultural diversity are more numerous, positive, and varied now than in the past, but not without some remaining problems. Disparities exist among ethnic groups in favor of African Americans, and groups of color appear most frequently in programs with specific ethnic themes. Surfing national network, local, and syndicated television channels at any time of any day of the week produces many African Americans. In some cases, the entire cast and the setting of the programs are Black; in others, Blacks have recurrent supporting roles. African Americans also are highly visible in news programs—as reporters and subjects—on national networks and local affiliates. There is a growing presence of African Americans in the movie industry, both in front of and behind the cameras—as stars and in supporting roles; as writers, producers, directors, and technicians; in both all-Black and predominantly White productions.

The kind of treatment that African Americans are receiving in mass media does not exist to the same extent for Latinos, Native Americans, and Asian Americans. Individuals from these ethnic groups appear only occasionally as guest performers in entertainment television programs and movies dealing with specific ethnic-related topics. Asian American and Latino newscasters are more commonly found on local rather than national newscasts. Thus, Mexican Americans are familiar faces on local news programs in the southwest, and Japanese and Chinese Americans (especially females) are visible in such states as California, Hawaii, and Washington. Puerto Ricans may be on the air frequently in New York, but not elsewhere. In comparison to African Americans, the numerical representation of these ethnic groups is minuscule. Except for the exceptional individual actor here and there, selective historical documentaries, and special events, Native Americans are virtually invisible in these media.

Changes Are Not Always Improvements

Numerical ethnic representations in media do not ensure content quality. Ethnic groups may appear to be validated while simultaneously being subtly stereotyped. This can be done in many ways, including topic, focus, dialogue, personal image, and characterization. The recurrent plot of situation comedies in which the female character inevitably is the voice of resolution in family conflicts perpetuates traditional views of women as emotional anchors, peacekeepers, nurturers, and moral monitors in families. Slapstick comedy, gangs, crime-fighting, and in-vogue urban young adult and teen life are the themes of most television programs and movies in which African Americans are prominent. Violent crimes, more than any other single category, are what makes African Americans and Latinos subjects of the news. Some daytime talk shows are notorious for enticing African American, Latino, and European American teens and young adults to be guests on programs dealing with gangs, violence, and emotionally abusive, unstable male–female intimate relationships. Reality shows equate rudeness, insult, and crudeness with entertainment, and these depictions are not restricted to any one ethnic or racial group.

Even when mass media are used to offset negative stereotypes of ethnic groups, the results can be counterproductive, perpetuating that which they claim to dispel. A case in point is the 1995 Disney animated production of *Pocahontas*. In an instructive critique, Pewewardy (1996/1997) explains how this movie perpetuates some longstanding stereotypes about Native Americans. Pocahontas is portrayed as maidenly, demure, and so deeply committed to a White man that she violates the cultural rules of her own ethnic community. According to Pewewardy, this image of a young Native American woman was created to serve the purposes of European American mythology. For example, he suggests that the concept of "celestial princess" was probably an English, not a Native American, creation. Other stereotypes and racism in *Pocahontas* are transmitted through the language used to refer to Native peoples (e.g., "savages," "heathens," "devils," "pagans," "primitive") and the lyrics of the movie's song "Savages, Savages." Pewewardy (1996/1997) proposes that instead of countering a stereotype, Disney created "a marketable 'New Age' Pocahontas to embody our millennial dreams for wholeness and harmony, while banishing our nightmares of savagery and emptiness" (p. 22). Like textbooks, this movie avoids dealing with the uglier side of the English encounter with the indigenous peoples, such as their greed, dishonesty, and hegemony. The stereotypes embedded in *Pocahontas* are not overt or blatant. They can be undetected by people who do not thoroughly understand Native American cultures or their historical experiences with mainstream European American society.

Another example of attempts to compensate for damages inflicted by stereotyping Native Americans was the decision to place Sacagawea on a new $1 coin minted in 2000. U.S. Mint Director Philip Diehl saw this selection as bestowing honor specifically on Sacagawea, a Shoshone teenager, for her physical courage, generosity, hospitality, and interpreter skills in assisting Lewis and Clark in 1804 on their explorations of the western frontier, and more generally on Native Americans. The Assistant Director of the Bureau of Indian Affairs thought the coin would shape how future generations of young people viewed Native Americans. Some Native Americans agreed with these assessments and were pleased with the choice, while others probably considered it an act of tokenism and misplaced significance. Negative sentiments might have been prompted by questions about the merits of giving this "distinction" to a teenager (Sacagawea was thought to be 16 years old at the time she traveled with Lewis and Clark), and someone whose claim to fame was based on her service to European Americans, not contributions to her own ethnic community. Even her physical characteristics were unknown and could not be described with certainty, thereby making her visibility "opaque." Diehl initially thought this uncertainty could be countered by having the coin carry a design of "Liberty" as a Native American woman to represent Sacagawea (Figlar, 1998). The final image was selected from designs created by New Mexico sculptor Glenna Goodacre, who used a college student of Shoshone-Bannock heritage as a model (Axtman, 1999; Sonneborn, 2000). The production of the Sacagawea dollar for general circulation stopped in 2002 due to low demand. However, it is still minted for special purposes, and its reverse side is being redesigned for the Native American Dollar Series that will be produced between 2009 and 2012. The design for each year will commemorate a different contribution of Native Americans to the development of U.S. society and history. The first, in 2009, symbolizes agriculture (en.wikipedia.org/wiki/Sacagawea_dollar).

Undoubtedly, people questioned the reality of Sacagawea's significance (and by whose standards) and wondered whether the only way Native Americans can gain recognition is by *serving* mainstream European American individuals, culture, society, and ideology. What progress toward accomplishing cultural equity is there in honoring the contributions of individuals with ambiguous identity, and limiting significance to servitude? This scenario and the questions it brings to mind about "dubious distinctions" also apply to other groups of color. One example is the ironic and conflicting messages conveyed by the 1990 Academy Award nomination of Morgan Freeman (an African American male) as best supporting actor for his performance in *Driving Miss Daisy*, in which he played the chauffeur for a European American matriarch.

CULTURALLY DIVERSE CURRICULUM CONTENT EFFECTS

Discussion of the effects of culturally diverse or multicultural curriculum content on the performance of underachieving students of color is limited here to reading, writing, math, and science. These subjects and skills are selected for emphasis for five reasons. First, it is both politically expedient and pedagogically valid for the implementation and effects of culturally responsive teaching to be located in areas of school curricula generally considered most significant. Second, math, science, reading, and writing constitute the academic core in most educational settings and usually are used to assess student achievement. Third, reading abilities strongly influence performance in other academic tasks and subjects. Fourth, math and science (especially advanced-level courses) have high stakes and high status attached to them. They are considered the "gateways" to academic development and career opportunities beyond K–12 schooling for those students who have access to and high levels of performance in them. Fifth, more research and practice guidelines are available on multicultural curriculum content for reading and writing than for other school subjects, and more curriculum reforms have been undertaken to increase the participation of students of color (particularly Latinos and African Americans) and females in math and science than in other school subjects. As explained in Chapter 1, achievement is conceived broadly to include academics, standardized test scores, course grades, and other performance indicators and measures. Among these are increased enrollment in advanced-level, high-status courses; the quantity and quality of participation in instructional discourse; improved interest in and motivation for learning; feelings of efficacy among students; and meeting the criteria and expectations of specific programs of study.

Most information about culturally diverse curriculum and its effects on student achievement published in books and articles derives from "experimental" and "special" projects instead of regularly taught content, topics, skills, and courses. Although the number of programs on which research information is available is rather small, their results are consistently supportive of the theoretical claims about the pedagogical potential of culturally responsive teaching. A few of these are discussed here to demonstrate how they translate culturally responsive teaching principles into practice, and to illustrate their effects on student achievement. Unfortunately, many of these projects are no longer functioning, having closed down after funding ended. The current climate of standardization is not very amenable to extensive culturally diverse curricular and instructional programs, despite the fact that there appears to be increasing recognition (at least ideologically) of the expanding presence of ethnic, racial, cultural, and linguistic diversity in U.S. society, and the need for its inclusion in educational practice. It is still important for teachers to be familiar with culturally specific curricular projects and programs even if they no longer exist, because they provide insights that can be used to develop current and future culturally responsive curriculum and instruction. Hopefully, some of the principles and strategies of the special projects have been incorporated into regular classroom procedures, but it is difficult to determine with certainty. If they have not, this lack of normalization is a major problem in sustaining and extending efforts to provide culturally responsive education for ethnically diverse students.

Reading and Writing Achievement

One of the "special projects" that used culturally pluralistic content to teach reading and writing is the Multicultural Literacy Program (MLP) (Diamond & Moore, 1995). It was implemented in the Ann Arbor, Inkster, and Ypsilanti, Michigan, school districts over a 4-year period, with a multiethnic student population in Grades K–8. The program included multiethnic literature, whole-language approaches, and a socioculturally sensitive learning environment. The literature highlighted contributions of Asian Americans, Latino Americans, Native Americans, African Americans, and Native Hawaiians in a variety of traditional folktales, song lyrics, poems, fiction, essays, biographies, and autobiographies.

The program designers decided to use multicultural literature to teach reading and writing because it resonates with students' creative ways of thinking and illuminates common human connections among ethnically different people. Literature also is a powerful medium through which students can confront social injustices, visualize racial inequities, find solutions to personal and political problems, and vicariously experience the issues, emotions, thoughts, and lives of people otherwise inaccessible to them. These literary encounters help students "become critical readers, who learn to view the world from multiple perspectives as they construct their versions of the truth, . . . [and] make informed and rational decisions about the most effective ways to correct injustices in their community" (Diamond & Moore, 1995, p. 14).

The MLP provided a variety of group arrangements and social settings for learning. Among them were learning centers, peer interactions, multiple reality-based reading opportunities, different types of cooperative learning groups, and emotionally and academically supportive communities of learners. More specific teaching strategies included incorporating multicultural story features into read- and think-alouds, sustained silent reading (SSR), directed reading-listening-thinking activity (DRLTA), readers' theater, choral reading, personal response to literature, and dramatic interpretation (Diamond & Moore, 1995). Teachers in the Multicultural Literacy Program acted as:

(1) cultural organizers who facilitate strategic ways of accomplishing tasks so that the learning process involves varied ways of knowing, experiencing, thinking, and behaving; (2) cultural mediators who create opportunities for critical dialogue and expression among all students as they pursue knowledge and understanding; and (3) orchestrators of social contexts who provide several learning configurations that include interpersonal *and* intrapersonal opportunities for seeking, accessing, and evaluating knowledge. (Diamond & Moore, 1995, p. 35, emphasis in original)

No quantifiable data (such as increased standardized test scores and grade point averages) are available on how the MLP affected student achievement, but other powerful indicators of its success do exist. Its creators and facilitators cited classroom observations and analysis of samples of student work to indicate that the program had positive effects. On these measures of achievement, students exhibited:

- More interest and enjoyment in reading multicultural books
- More positive attitudes toward reading and writing in general
- Increased knowledge about various forms, structures, functions, and uses of written language
- Expanded vocabularies, sentence patterns, and decoding abilities
- Better reading comprehension and writing performance
- Longer written stories that reflect more clarity and cohesiveness
- Enhanced reading rate and fluency
- Improved self-confidence and self-esteem
- Greater appreciation of their own and others' cultures (Diamond & Moore, 1995)

These achievements were evident across groups of students who differed by ethnicity, cultural background, and intellectual ability. The results are consistent with the findings of other researchers, such as Mason and Au (1991), Bishop (1992), and Norton (1992). They, too, found that exposing children to literature that includes characters, settings, and events similar to their lived experiences produces positive academic, personal, and social results virtually identical to those generated by the Multicultural Literacy Program.

Another literature-based literacy program that produced many different kinds of academic improvements for the students involved is the Webster Groves Writing Project (WGWP). It included several different components of culturally responsive pedagogy, but only its curriculum content is examined here. This project was located in a small, suburban, economically diverse school district of approximately 4,400 students (three-fourths European American and one-fourth African American) that included five municipalities in Missouri: Webster Groves, Rock Hill, Warson Woods,

Glendale, and parts of Shrewsbury (Krater et al., 1994). At its peak, 14 English teachers and 293 students in Grades 6–12 were involved. Initially African Americans were targeted, but after the first 2 years the project was extended to all students in the participating teachers' classes who were performing below grade level.

The WGWP was organized around eight key principles and strategies that combined African American cultural characteristics and contributions with process and literature approaches to writing. The principles were: building on students' strengths; individualizing and personalizing instruction; encouraging cooperative learning; increasing control of language; using computers; enhancing personal involvement with reading and writing; building cultural bridges; and expanding personal horizons. Among the specific elements of African American culture woven into the curriculum content were short stories and personal narratives written in conversational styles; oral language interpretations; storytelling, script-reading, and playwriting; memorizing poetry, proverbs, and quotations; call–response and dramatic performance; language variation as demonstrated by a variety of literary forms; and factual information about African American history. Samples of literature produced by such distinguished authors as Langston Hughes, Virginia Hamilton, Alice Walker, Richard Wright, Paul Lawrence Dunbar, Gwendolyn Brooks, Toni Morrison, Sterling Brown, and Nikki Giovanni were used to teach these cultural features.

Effects of the WGWP on student achievement were determined by performance on standardized tests, analysis of student writing samples, and teacher observations of student behaviors. Significant improvements occurred on all these measures. At the end of its first year, the scores of the participating students on the district's writing assessment increased by an average of 2.0 points compared with a mean increase of 1.6 for all students. The scores for the African American students in the project increased by 2.3 points in middle schools and 1.7 points in high schools. Past writing assessments in the district had shown increases of 1.0 point from grade to grade over an academic year.

In the subsequent years of the project, all the participating students continued to make greater improvements in their writing skills than their counterparts. The performance of African Americans was comparable to that of other project students. Increases in their scores on the writing assessments ranged from 0.7 to 4.0 points across the first 4 years of the project. This achievement was equal to the improvement of other participating students, but slightly lower than the average growth for all students in the district, which ranged from 1.0 to 4.6 points. There was one deviation from these improvement trends. This occurred for grades 9 and 10 in the 2nd year of the project, when the achievement of all targeted and African American students declined. Despite these improvements, the total writing scores of the

African American students continued to be significantly lower than those of other students in the entire district (Krater et al., 1994).

During the fifth year of its existence, the Webster Groves Writing Project shifted from local district measures to the Missouri state writing test to assess student performance. Again, the results were positive. Sixty-seven percent of the 8th-graders (215) in the project scored above the state mean, and 14% (45) scored below the mean. Only 6% of all students taking the Missouri writing test scored 5 or 5.5 out of a possible score of 6 points; 20% of them were participants in the Webster Groves Writing Project (Krater et al., 1994). In addition to these test scores, there were other indicators of the positive effects of this project on student achievement. The writing samples demonstrated improvements in the development and organization of ideas, specific word choices, introductions and endings, and focused thinking and clarity of expression. The students themselves expressed greater confidence in and satisfaction with their writing. This was particularly true of the African Americans. The overall success of the Webster Groves Writing Project led the school district to adapt its principles and methods to K–9 mathematics, and two other districts to adopt the model for their writing programs.

Additional evidence of the successful use of ethnic literature to improve the literacy achievement of students is provided by Grice and Vaughn (1992). They studied the responses of African and European American 3rd-graders to African American culturally conscious literature; that is, picture books, novels, biographies, and poetry with African American topics, story lines, characters, and settings. These resources were selected to stimulate pride in cultural heritage; celebrate the triumphs of notable African Americans; develop commitment to community; value family life; and empower young readers by enhancing their self-confidence and decisionmaking skills. Four *qualitative* indicators were used to assess the effects of this curriculum on student achievement. They were (1) *comprehension* (did the students understand what the books were about?); (2) *authenticity* (did the students think the story and characters could be real?); (3) *identity* and *involvement* (could the students personally relate to and see themselves in the story?); and (4) *evaluation* (did the students like or dislike the books, and why?).

Twenty-one of the twenty-six books used in the project were categorized as "culturally conscious" and three were "melting pot" (the characters were middle-class and no explicit references were made to their racial identity). Of these, twenty were picture books, two were juvenile biographies, and four were realistic fiction works with characters close in age to 3rd-graders. They were varied across situation, textual focus, and genre to include African American heritage, biography, community, family ties, friendship, poetic verse, and male and female characters. The students who were selected to participate in the program read 2 years below grade level and had scored below the 25th percentile on the MAT-6 achievement test. Before the research began, they had demonstrated the ability to follow story lines, form opinions about the realism of characters and story plots, project themselves into stories, and explain their evaluation of books comparable in difficulty to the ones used in the study.

Regardless of ethnicity and gender, the students preferred books about family, community, and friends. The level of acceptance and identification was higher for African Americans (especially females) than European Americans. Both European and African Americans found the books about African heritage and those in poetic verse more difficult to understand and accept, but they were somewhat less problematic for the African American students. The contextual knowledge, prior experiences, and cultural background of students either facilitated or interfered with their ability to receive the messages from the books (Grice & Vaughn, 1992).

These findings support some general claims frequently made about culturally responsive pedagogy. Students from one ethnic group can learn and appreciate the cultures and contributions of other groups, and teaching students' their own cultural heritages is personally enriching (Aronson & Laughter, 2016; Sleeter, 2011). As Boyd, Causey, and Galda (2015) explained, it is important for diverse students to see themselves in curriculum content and instructional texts, but that is not enough. They also need to recognize themselves in others, and understand that they are part of a common humanity. Essential to this understanding and interconnectedness is realizing that no group or individual has a single story (Adichie, 2009). Attempts to reduce human complexity to one-dimensionality leads to stereotypes and dubious assumptions. Consulting a variety of texts about ethnically and culturally diverse individuals and groups in different times and contexts can prevent this from happening. However, without adequate background knowledge and contextual orientations, multicultural content can have negative effects. This was apparent in the reactions of the students in the Grice and Vaughn study to the books about African heritage. Both the European Americans and the African Americans rejected the stories about Africa because they did not have sufficient background knowledge to understand or appreciate them (Grice & Vaughn, 1992). Reactions such as these support L. Crawford's (1993) assertion that a mismatch between the intellectual, cultural, and experiential schemata of students and those represented in topics and texts of instructional materials impedes comprehension. Conversely, when academic and experiential schemata match, students find reading materials easier to understand and more useful in increasing mastery of other literacy skills. The results of Carol Lee's (2001, 2007, 2009) cultural modeling projects and use of cultural data sets to teach African American high school students literary interpretation skills and writing skills (described in detail in Chapter 4) substantiate Crawford's claims.

Other supportive evidence is provided by Schrodt, Fain, and Hasty (2015), this time from the vantage point of young children. They describe the content and effects of the Kindergarten Family Backpack Project, a classroom-based, teacher-parent partnership program to improve the language and literacy development of 5- and 6-year-olds. The ideological foundations of the project included the notion that diversity is a productive resource; that children have a wealth of culture, knowledge, and experience that can and should be used in teaching them; and that literary texts with positive depictions of diversity are more interesting, relevant, and engaging for both students and parents. Texts chosen for the students to read included a variety of diversity topics, perspectives, and experiences such as race, language, immigration, and adoption. These themes paralleled the experiences and identities of the students participating in the project. The students engaged in two-way sharing of the books read (school-to-home and home-to-school). In addition to verbally sharing their understanding of and responses to the texts, they kept written journals. These entries were subjected to content analyses to determine the effects of the texts and learning experiences on student performance. The results of these analyses indicated that the students experienced success in improved writing skills and reading comprehension. This general conclusion is validated by the following specifics:

> In their journals, children used a combination of responses that included narrating, recalling events in the story, making connections, and using phonemic awareness and phonics to write in emergent approximations, drawing pictures, expressing feelings and reactions to texts, and identifying relationships between characters and texts. Children's invented spellings allowed them to demonstrate what they already know about the writing code and inform teachers for future instruction. Through the framing, reading, and response to culturally relevant texts, the Kindergarten Family Backpack Project created a space where children can deconstruct harmful images and ideas and affirm positive self-images and cultures. Through open and meaningful discussion and written responses, children and families were able to challenge the status quo of the current social order . . . within the framework of an academically stimulating curriculum. (Schrodt, Fain, & Hasty, 2015, p. 596).

Since 1987, the Rough Rock Demonstration School on the Navajo Reservation in Arizona has used cultural content to increase the academic achievement of its students. The program designed for this purpose is the Rough Rock English–Navajo Language Arts Program (RRENLAP). This is a bilingual/bicultural initiative to improve students' language, literacy, and biliteracy skills (Dick, Estell, & McCarty, 1994; McCarty, 2002). The program began as an experiment with kindergartners and 1st-graders, eventually expanding to include Grades K–6. Its mission was to modify "cutting-edge" pedagogies, such as whole-language approaches, cooperative learning, and literature-based literacy instruction, to fit the linguistic and cultural contexts of students at the Rough Rock Demonstration School. An example of this adaptation was a 3rd-grade unit on wind that included the study of local and regional climatology, Navajo directional symbols and oral narratives, and journal-writing in Navajo and English. Over time, less reliance was placed on commercially published reading and language arts materials, and more on ones written by the students and teachers themselves that reflected local community culture (Dick et al., 1994).

RRENLAP produced significant improvements in student achievement. On locally developed criterion-referenced measures of reading comprehension, the K–3 students showed a gain of 12 percentage points, and their median percentile rank scores on the CTBS reading vocabulary test doubled, although they still remained below the national average. The first group of students who spent 4 years in the program made an average gain of 60 percentage points in their Navajo and English listening comprehension scores over 3 years. Teachers' qualitative assessments indicated consistent improvement and control of vocabulary, grammar, social uses of writing, and content-area knowledge for the RRENLAP students (Dick et al., 1994; Lipka & McCarty, 1994; McCarty, 2002). This project illustrated another important principle of culturally responsive teaching. That is, *sustained collaboration* among school staff with different capabilities, and between schools and community members, is a useful way to develop relevant curriculum content and instructional programs for ethnically diverse students.

The Kickapoo Nation in Kansas has tried to make the education available to children and youth of its tribal community more academically successful by instituting a reform plan called the "Circle of Learning" (Dupuis & Walker, 1988). Begun in 1985, it was designed to incorporate Kickapoo cultural characteristics into the educational process. Specific goals of the program included improving academic achievement; developing positive self-images; teaching competitive skills tempered with cooperation and sharing of resources; facilitating cultural maintenance and adaptation; and increasing participation of Kickapoo families and community in the educational process. Students learned their cultural values, native languages, histories, and contributions along with academic subject-matter content and skills. Some of the values taught included respect for the wisdom and dignity of elders, fortitude, community allegiance, bravery, caring and mutual assistance, generosity, and self-determination. In fact, "Kickapoo culture is woven into the total fabric of the curriculum" (Dupuis & Walker, 1988, p. 31). The only evidence of the effects of the Circle of Learning on student achievement comes from an attitude survey administered to the students 2 years after the program began. All the respondents felt that it had increased their interest and participation in school, self-confidence, feeling of efficacy in dealing with the non-Indian world, understanding of the importance of honoring their own cultural values, and pride in their ethnic identity (Dupuis & Walker, 1988).

Math and Science Achievement

The contributing authors to *New Directions for Equity in Mathematics Education* (Secada, Fennema, & Adajian, 1995) and *Culturally Responsive Mathematics Education* (Greer et al., 2009), as well as Moll and González (2004), O. Lee and Luykx (2006), and Leonard (2008), describe many short-term math and science projects, courses, units, and lessons that include elements of culturally responsive teaching. These tend to focus on mathematics but often include elements of science as well as other areas of learning, such as communication literacies, social studies, and technology. A common feature across the efforts is that student achievement across subjects, grades, and ethnic groups is improved by accepting the fact that mathematical and scientific knowledge is present in all cultural groups, extracting math and science knowledge and skills embedded in the everyday activities and cultural heritages of different ethnic groups, using these as resources and leverages to teach school-based mathematics and science, and connecting school knowledge with the funds of knowledge present in different cultural communities. As O. Lee and Luykx (2006) explain, while it may not be true in every ethnic group, for most the ways of knowing and talking students learn at home and in cultural communities are "continuous with these of scientific communities. . . . These students deploy sense-making practices—deep questions, vigorous augmentation, situated guesswork, embedded imagining, multiple perspectives, and innovative uses of everyday words to construct new meanings—that serve as intellectual resources in science learning" (p. 47). Yet, less progress has occurred in making science curriculum and instruction culturally responsive than in most other school subjects.

The cultural sites and sources used for teaching mathematical knowledge, concepts, and skills cover a wide range of imaginative and frequently untapped possibilities. Among these are the construction crafts; using urban transportation; taking trips; hair-braiding; shopping; star navigation; pattern designs in clothing, pottery, jewelry, blankets, quilts, and basket-weaving; music and art; cooking; and games. Two long-term programs are presented here to illustrate how some of the tenets of culturally responsive teaching are operationalized in mathematics curriculum and pedagogy. One of them involves Alaskan Natives, and the other African Americans. Two culturally based science projects for Native Americans are described as well.

Math in a Cultural Context (MCC) is a longstanding collaborative initiative for Alaskan Natives that was developed by mathematicians, math educators, Yup'ik community elders, Yup'ik teachers, and Alaskan school district officials (Lipka, 1994, 1998; Lipka & McCarty, 1994; Lipka, Yanez,

Andrew-Ihrke, & Adam, 2009). This integrated supplementary curriculum for elementary students was designed to incorporate indigenous cultural knowledge into the content and processes of reform-oriented mathematics teaching and to improve math achievement. It includes cultural content and contextual knowledge about Yup'ik patterns of communicating, relating, and teaching. The curriculum comprises seven modules about everyday activities in Yup'ik culture. They are Fish Racks, Berry Picking, Drying Salmon, Star Navigation, Parka Designs, Egg Island, and Smokehouse Construction. Information for the modules was collected by teams of classroom teachers and university-based teacher educators who observed demonstrations and listened to explanations presented by Yup'ik elders; participated in star navigations, building fish racks, and making model smokehouses; and collected traditional stories and games. As trust and equal-status engagements evolved between educators and community members, the project design team came to better understand the historical and cultural contexts of elders' knowledge; elders revealed more practices and procedures that previously were "hidden" from outsiders; and the mathematics embedded in everyday activities became more apparent, such as ways of measuring, numerating, estimating, designing, patterning, locating, and navigating. Cultural ways of communicating and teaching also emerged that subsequently were incorporated into MCC, such as storytelling, using symbols to represent ideas, expert–apprentice modeling, joint production activities, and cognitive apprenticeship. The program does not try to replicate indigenous knowledge in school contexts. Instead, it integrates Yup'ik everyday mathematical knowledge and teaching styles with Western math content and forms of pedagogy. This is done by situating school math teaching in cultural contexts familiar to Alaskan Native students, and using enough novelty to capture their interest and involvement in learning (Lipka, 1994, 1998; Lipka & McCarty, 1994; Lipka et al., 2009). Thus, "issues of culture, power, and creativity are [woven] together to form a third space—the newly recontextualized content and an environment that surrounds learning that content—without losing sight of the critical importance of improving student math learning" (Lipka et al., 2009, p. 266).

MCC is based on several assumptions that underlie culturally responsive teaching. Two of these are (1) greater access to and achievement in high-quality learning are possible when culturally diverse students identify on multiple levels with what is being taught, and have multiple ways of engaging with the content; and (2) using the knowledge, language, and culture of different ethnic groups in teaching has positive effects on students' identities that, in turn, improve academic achievement. These assertions have been confirmed by MCC and other culturally responsive curricula for Alaskan Natives (Demmert & Towner, 2003; Lipka, 1998; Lipka et al., 2009; Sternberg, 2006). Students in both rural and urban schools who learn the materials with cultural teaching techniques consistently outperform those who use conventional curricula of standard math concepts and skills.

For more than 40 years Bob Moses (Moses & Cobb, 2001; Moses, West, & Davis, 2009) has been directing the Algebra Project, designed to improve the participation and performance of middle school African American students in Algebra I, and their enrollment in advanced math classes in high school. It is a complement to rather than a replacement for other possible forms of math curriculum and instruction. Moses initiated the Algebra Project in Cambridge, Massachusetts, out of concern for the math learning opportunities of his own children, but it has since relocated to Jackson, Mississippi, with extensions in several other cities throughout the United States, including Chicago, San Francisco, Miami, and New York. By the late 1990s the project involved teachers in Grades 4–8 in 18 school sites in 12 states (Moses et al., 2009). Moses used his involvement in community political activism during the civil rights movement of the 1960s as the ideological grounding and methodological emphases to guide content selection and instructional practices. The goal of the Algebra Project is to use math embedded in the everyday knowledge and activities of marginalized students and communities of color, including African, Latino, and Native Americans, as well as some poor, underachieving European Americans, as bridges and conduits for teaching school-based mathematics. This development is facilitated through using transitional curriculum materials to help students move from arithmetic to algebraic thinking; placing a high value on student peer culture and collaborations; and connecting math literacy to social justice by having students actively engage in sociopolitical activism through the youth leadership development aspects of the program.

The Algebra Project curriculum materials and instruction are organized according to a five-step process for helping students move between their experiential worlds and social language, and the mathematization of their cultural experiences, or the creation of what Lipka and associates (2009) call a "third space" of intellectual engagement, and others have named crossing cultural borders in thought and action, scaffolding, and demystifying mathematics (Ernest, 2009; Gay 2009; Giroux, 1992). The five steps have students (1) engage in a physical experience; (2) represent it in their own words and visual images; (3) use everyday language in describing the experience; (4) translate these descriptions into more regimented language called "feature talk" that is amenable to mathematical expressions; and (5) convert feature talk to the symbolic representations of conventional mathematics (Moses & Cobb, 2001). A combination of specific cultural references from different ethnic-group experiences, local knowledge, and the universal human experience are woven throughout all of these procedures. Adaptations are made frequently to customize reference materials to local situations. For example, using the frequency and speed of subway train travel between different stations to teach algebraic concepts and skills is very appropriate for students in large urban areas who are familiar with this mode of transportation, but is meaningless and inappropriate for students in small rural communities (Moses & Cobb, 2001). The Algebra Project curriculum also uses dialogue scripts in almost all modules for secondary students that model mathematical discourse, and allows them to have conversations with mathematicians and to practice appropriate technical mathematical talk. Thus, experiential, culturally based learning occurs within a context of peer collaboration and classroom communities of mathematical practice.

The Algebra Project has had positive effects on student achievement consistently from its inception. More students of color who experience the project enroll in pre-algebra and algebra classes, pass the state-mandated tests the first time they are taken, and become activists for social justice than those who do not. Moreover, the cultural references incorporated in the program provide affirmation for disenfranchised students and increase their sense of academic efficacy, cultural identity, and ethnic pride (Moses & Cobb, 2001; Moses et al., 2009). Other non-math academic benefits are evident as well, such as those typically associated with literacy, for example, making inferences, comprehension, clarity and coherency of articulation, and audience-appropriate communication. The project exemplifies the culturally responsive principle of starting teaching with where students are, what they bring to the classroom, and their encounters with formal subjects taught; accepting that there is worth and value in this social and cultural capital; and using it as a bridge for making what is encoded in textbooks and classroom instruction more meaningful for ethnically diverse children and youth.

Matthews and Smith (1994) studied the effects of culturally relevant instructional materials on the interests, attitudes, and performance of Native American students in science and language arts. The participants in the study were 203 4th- through 8th-graders, 10 teachers, and 17 classes in 10 schools from eight Bureau of Indian Affairs (BIA) agencies. The students were distributed among 11 tribal affiliations: Navajo, Sioux, Tohono Odham (Pagago), Hopi, Kiowa, Cheyenne/Arapaho, Yakima, Comanche, Wichita, Caddo, and Ponca. The project covered a 10-week period during which teachers of the experimental group used Native American cultural content to teach 25 hours of science and 25 hours of language arts. Teachers in the control group taught the same number of hours and skills, but without the specifically designed materials. The culturally relevant content included biographical profiles of Native Americans in different careers who use science in their daily lives; math- and science-related activities developed by the Math and Science Teachers for Reservation Schools (MASTERS) Project; science activities from the Career Oriented Materials to Explore Topics in Science (COMETS) and the Outside World Science Projects (OWSP); and

12 sketches from the American Indian Science and Engineering Society (AISES) publications.

Achievement data were collected, using a pretest–posttest design, on students' attitudes toward Native Americans in science-related fields (measured by an Attitude Toward Indians in Science scale) and knowledge of science concepts (assessed by the Science Concept Questionnaire). The results indicated that students taught with Native American cultural materials had more positive attitudes and higher levels of achievement than those who were taught similar skills without the culturally relevant inclusions. No differences were apparent in these effects by the gender of students. More than two-thirds of the students taught with cultural materials said they learned more about science and that their teachers made science interesting to learn. There also was a positive, but low, correlation between attitude toward and achievement in science. The effects of the culturally relevant materials varied by ethnic groups, with non-Navajo students having higher achievement than Navajos but no significant differences in attitudes. These results prompted Matthews and Smith (1994) to suggest that curriculum content on Native Americans should deal explicitly with the cultural characteristics and contributions of specific tribal groups.

In her research Brown (2015) found that tailoring STEM education curriculum to the cultural backgrounds of diverse students improves their ability to learn content. One way of doing this is using science- and math-based application examples and cultural knowledge familiar to students. This reduces inconsistencies between students' home and school experiences, and thereby increases interest in and the authenticity of science content. The use of these cultural touchpoints generates multiple STEM education benefits, including students more eager to learn and more engaged in learning; improved relationships among teachers, students, and families; increased teacher credibility with diverse students; and higher academic performance. Culturally diverse connections in teaching techniques are fundamental to reducing the achievement gap and encouraging educational equity in science and math for underrepresented minority students.

Roehrig and Moore (2012) applied these general ideas in a culturally relevant STEM education program for Ojibwe students from the White Earth Reservation. Entitled Reach for the Sky (RFTS), the program integrated science into traditional Native American culture and routine ways of living, and included the use of Native American languages, spirituality, traditional activities and stories, and active participation of parents and elders. Roehrig and Moore maintain that combining cultural diversity with STEM makes good educational sense and builds on natural realities. The latter involves the fact that math, science, culture, and technology are natural parts of the daily lives of virtually every human being. They add that it is reasonable to begin teaching these interconnections in early childhood education because children are born scientists, have a natural curiosity, and are engaged in perpetual pursuits of discovery. The RFTS project produced other positive results as well. It energized community involvement. Reservation elders are now involved, along with university faculty and students, in teaching Native American youth that math, science, and engineering are part of their daily lives.

IMPROVING CULTURALLY DIVERSE CURRICULUM CONTENT

Much more cultural content is needed in all school curricula about all ethnic groups of color. The need is especially apparent in math and science and for ethnic groups other than African Americans. Also needed are multicultural literacy programs in secondary schools; more math and science programs at all grade levels; teaching explicit information about gender contributions, issues, experiences, and achievement effects *within ethnic groups*; and pursuing more sustained efforts to incorporate content about ethnic and cultural diversity in regular school subjects and skills taught on a routine basis.

Educators should be diligent in ensuring that curriculum content about ethnically diverse groups is accurate, authentic, and comprehensive. This goal can be accomplished by working in collaboration with ethnic scholars, community leaders, and "cultural brokers," as well as combining information from many disciplines to generate culturally relevant curriculum content for diverse ethnic groups. Culturally responsive curriculum content also should deal simultaneously with concepts, principles, and ideas (such as oppression, identity, powerlessness and privilege, culture, and struggle) generalizable across ethnic groups and knowledge about the particular lives, experiences, and contributions of specific groups (Banks, 1991, 2003; Gay, 1988, 1995, 2002). For example, students need to learn about Asian Americans in general and the many different ethnic groups usually included in this category, such as Chinese, Vietnamese, Filipino, Cambodian, Korean, Japanese, and East Indian Americans.

Several other important implications for culturally responsive pedagogical practices are embedded in the nature and effects of culturally diverse curriculum content examined thus far. One is the need to *regularly* provide students with more accurate cultural information about groups of color in order to fill knowledge voids and correct existing distortions. This information needs to be capable of facilitating many different kinds of learning—cognitive, affective, social, political, personal, and moral. It should be multiethnic, cover a wide range of perspectives and experiences, and encompass both tangible (artifacts) and intangible (values, beliefs) aspects of culture (Banks & Banks, 2010; Hilliard, 1991/1992; J. King, 1994; Nieto, 1999). No single content source is capable of doing all of this alone. Therefore, curriculum designers should always use a variety of resources from different genres and disciplines, including textbooks, literature, mass media, music, personal experiences, and social science research. Information derived from new and emerging ethnic-centered and feminist literary and social science scholarship also should be included.

Students should learn how to conduct ideological and content analyses of various sources of curriculum content about ethnic and cultural diversity. These learning experiences involve revealing implicit values and biases, modifying attitudes and perceptions, developing different evaluation criteria, and acting deliberately to first deconstruct and then reconstruct common ethnic and gender typecastings. Students can begin by compiling background information on the ethnicity, gender, expertise, experience, and motivation of textbook authors and media programmers. Then they might search for evidence of how these "positionality factors" affect the presentations writers and directors make about ethnic issues and groups. Phrases and words in dialogues of characters in TV programs and movies, themes, topics and scenarios depicted, and stories in textbooks that are age-, gender-, and ethnic-group-specific can be analyzed in search of this evidence. The students can compare different versions and interpretations of the same issues, such as African, Chinese, Latino, and Filipino American approaches to women's liberation.

These learning activities make manifest what is meant by knowledge being a social and situated construction, not a universal and absolute reality, and the influence of *contextuality* in meaning-making. They will be useful in counteracting the negative emotional and academic effects of the racism and sexism that continue to be embedded in both formal and informal curriculum content. The skills that students apply in these analyses, such as inquiry, critical thinking, collecting data, verifying evidence, perspective-taking, and comprehending and communicating information, represent significant academic achievement in and of themselves.

Teachers and students should conduct their own research on how textbooks, mass media, trade books, and other curriculum content sources affect knowledge, attitudes, and behaviors toward ethnic and cultural diversity and mastery of various academic skills. Many assertions exist about what these effects are, but too little actual data are available to substantiate them. Operating in the traditions of participatory observations, narratives, and collaborative action research, students and teachers should study themselves in their own classrooms on a routine basis. They might explore questions such as: What issues about ethnic groups and aspects of cultural diversity are most palpable, stress-provoking, difficult, and easy to master? How are receptivity and resistance to cultural diversity manifested by students, and how are these mediated? How are these reactions distributed by gender within ethnic groups and among different ethnic groups? What kinds of instructional materials work best for which students? What constitutes mastery of multicultural curriculum content and its associated evidence?

Shor and Freire (1987) speak convincingly about the educational values of these kinds of learning experiences. They see these experiences as foundations for high-quality, liberatory teaching. The critical reflection, uncertainty, curiosity, demanding inquiry, and action they demand and cultivate are indispensable to effective learning. This "research-teaching" also has practical value for improving student achievement. It helps teachers to develop curriculum content that is intrinsically motivating; places students and teachers in closer interaction with each other and facilitates better collaboration between them; and produces grassroots knowledge and perspectives that challenge the official ideologies marketed by schools (Shor & Freire, 1987).

Finally, students and teachers should become scholars of ethnic and cultural diversity, and generate their own curriculum content. They can do library research; conduct interviews and oral histories; participate in shadow studies; organize cultural exchanges; do site observations of ethnic communities and institutions; and collect personal stories covering a wide spectrum of individuals according to ethnicity, gender, age, generation, educational level, career, country of origin, and residential location. The information these inquiries produce can be used to contest, correct, supplement, and/or replace existing textbook and mass media content.

CONCLUSION

Students are exposed to a wide variety and quality of content about ethnic and cultural diversity. This exposure is both formal and informal, direct and tacit; it encompasses what is officially delivered in schools as well as what is offered through "societal curricula," especially as conveyed through mass media and tradebooks. Whether the images of ethnic diversity these content sources convey are positive or negative, they have powerful influences on students, including self-perceptions, attitudes toward others, what is considered "truth" and knowledge worth knowing, and how they respond to classroom instruction. Students who see their ethnic groups portrayed negatively in literary and trade books, television programs, movies, newspapers, and advertising may not value themselves or trust that schools will do anything differently. Unfortunately, their suspicions too often have been confirmed by racially biased instructional materials. Ethnically diverse students who feel invalidated in society and school are not likely to perform as well as they might on academic tasks, if for no other reason than that these prejudices interfere with their motivation to learn, time-on-task, and persistence in learning engagements. Consequently, all sources of curriculum content, both within and outside of schools, should be revised to be more accurate and inclusive in their representations of cultural diversity. Good information is a necessary element of culturally responsive teaching and the improvement in student achievement.

Some notable progress has been made over the past few decades in how the histories, lives, cultures, and contributions of African, Asian, Native, Latino, and European Americans are portrayed in textbooks, literary books, and mass media. The most blatant stereotypical characterizations have been eliminated. Yet these frequently used sources of curriculum content are not as good as they should be. Their flaws demand continuous improvements from all sectors of society and the educational profession. Teachers and students can and should be active participants in improving the quality of these instructional materials. Being directly involved in the construction of knowledge about ethnic and cultural diversity is an important way to practice culturally responsive pedagogy.

Curriculum sources and content that provide accurate presentations of ethnic and cultural diversity offer several other benefits for improving student achievement. First, they provide those who have never had close personal contact with members of ethnic groups other than their own with opportunities to communicate and engage with diverse people as well as to confront themselves. This experience alone will calm some fears, dispel some myths, and produce some learning that cannot be obtained from books and other media sources. Removing the threat and intimidation from new knowledge enhances receptivity toward and mastery of it. Second, students are actively involved in their own learning. Participatory engagement tends to have positive effects on achievement. Third, students have real power to help structure their own learning. They thus have some real control over their own academic destinies. Surely students will learn better that which is of their own creation.

Theory about the potential of multicultural curriculum content for improving the achievement of ethnically diverse students is rich and extensive, but supportive research is still rather sparse. My guess is that many teachers are doing culturally responsive teaching to some degree but that these practices are not recorded systematically or reported regularly in educational scholarship. Much more empirical research, observational studies, and documentation of practice are needed to support theoretical claims. In compiling this evidence, emphasis should be on specifying curriculum content effects on different types of achievements, such as grade point averages, test scores, participation in classroom discourse, and students' self-esteem and feelings of efficacy; how these effects are distributed within and across ethnic groups; and achievement effects derived from the incorporation of multicultural content into the curricula of all subjects and skills taught in school. Beyond the early elementary grades (K–2), students, along with their teachers, can contribute to the development of this fund of knowledge by "telling their own stories" about how exposure to multicultural curriculum content has affected them personally. Student commentaries are powerful evidence for determining the effectiveness of educational reforms, but they too often are overlooked. Culturally responsive teaching corrects this oversight by including the needs, knowledge, and participation of students in all aspects of the educational enterprise, including the selection, design, and analysis of curriculum content and the determination of its effects on achievement.

Several important messages for the future implementation of culturally responsive teaching can be derived from the curricular programs, practices, and research discussed in this chapter. To begin with, even curricula with minimum cultural content improve student achievement, according to a variety of indicators, across ethnic groups, grade levels, and subject or skill areas. The multiple achievement effects include higher scores on standardized tests, higher grade point averages, improved student self-concepts and self-confidence, and greater varieties and levels of student engagement with subject matter. The range of these effects is very encouraging, and it indicates that there are many ways in which teachers can design culturally responsive curricula for African, Asian, Native, and Latino American students. However, more evidence is needed to document the effects of multicultural content on student achievement in all subjects taught in schools, at all grade levels, and for all ethnic groups.

PRACTICE POSSIBILITIES

Like other aspects, curriculum content for culturally responsive teaching needs to be diversified (in form and substance) to reflect and maximize the knowledge, perspectives, experiences, and learning of students from different ethnic, racial, and social groups. The following content sources and examples can assist teachers in doing so. They also are helpful in countering frequently declared claims of not knowing where to locate valid information about cultural diversity, or not knowing how to use it effectively.

Culture Diversity and Social Justice Films and Videos

Compiled from carla.umn.edu/culture/resources/video.html and youtube.com

America Beyond the Color Line: Henry Louis Gates, Jr. travels to the East Coast, the deep South, inner-city Chicago, and Hollywood to investigate modern Black America and interview influential African Americans, including Colin Powell, Quincy Jones, Samuel L. Jackson, Alicia Keys, Maya Angelou, Willie Herenton, and others.

The Asianization of America: Describes the increasing role of Asians in U.S. business and society, and how this trend is affecting society.

Balablock: An animation depicting the various ways people react to others, strive for conformity, and are often intolerant of differences. It also shows the advantages that can be found in diversity.

Becoming American: The story of Laotian family members as they become refugees and are resettled in the United States. The film depicts their struggles entering a new country, such as culture shock, prejudice, and gradual adaptation.

Better Together Than A-P-A-R-T: Outlines fundamental concepts of intercultural communication. Some topics covered in this presentation are acculturation, stages of ethnocentrism, cultural values, cultural variation, verbal and nonverbal communication, styles of thinking, intercultural competence, and stereotyping.

Cold Water: A commentary on the experiences and feelings of international students who have studied in the United States. The focus is on their adjustment, value conflicts, and perceptions of Americans.

The Color of Fear: Examines the pain and anguish that racism has caused in the lives of North American men of Asian, European, Latin, and African descent. Out of their confrontations and struggles to understand and trust each other emerges an emotional and insightful portrayal into the type of dialogue most of us fear, but hope will happen sometime in our lifetime.

Coming Across: Five American students interview students who have immigrated to the United States from a variety of places. This film looks to develop empathy and understanding.

Communicating Across Cultures: This film discusses how misunderstandings can result from different communication styles. It also addresses the discomfort many people feel when dealing with issues of race and gender and suggests some ways to facilitate better communication.

The Danger of a Single Story: Novelist Chimamanda Adichie tells the story of how she found her authentic cultural voice, and warns that if only a single story or perspective about a person, country, or culture is told or heard, there is high risk of critical misunderstandings.

Differences: A collection of people from various minority groups within the United States discuss their experiences and conflicts as they deal with the unwritten rules of White, middle-class America. They discuss stereotypes, family traditions, and the biases they see in educational materials.

Ethnic Notions: Presents examples of the way that racism is depicted in American culture and the evolution of racial stereotypes.

Eye of the Storm: A public school teacher in Iowa divided her all-White third-graders into blue- and brown-eyed groups for a lesson in discrimination. On successive days, each group was treated as inferior and subjected to discrimination. *A Class Divided* and *Blue Eyed* are subsequent examinations of similar issues.

Hidden Figures: Oscar-nominated film about a team of female African American mathematicians who played a vital role in NASA during the early years of the U.S. space program.

How We Feel: Hispanic Students Speak Out: A group of successful high school students from Spanish-speaking backgrounds reflect upon their experiences in school and suggest ways to improve the experiences of minority students.

I Am Joaquin: Based on an epic poem published by Rodolfo "Corky" Gonzales in 1967. Gonzales's poem weaves together the diverse and complex roots of his Mexican, Spanish, Indian, and American parentage and a past mythology of pre-Columbian cultures. The film also spotlights the challenges they have endured because of discrimination.

More than Bows and Arrows: Documents the contributions of Native Americans to the United States and Canada.

Nuyorican Dream: Celebrates elements of community life—solidarity, sharing of resources, cultural citizenship—that make day-to-day survival possible, giving testimony to the central role played by Puerto Rican women in maintaining family and cultural ties.

A Place of Rage: Prominent African American women comment on their experiences of racial discrimination and the effects on U.S. culture, and make suggestions for improvements.

Precious Knowledge: Presents the struggles of students and teachers to save their high school Mexican American studies program against the opposition of elected state officials.

Race in the Classroom: Depicts moments when race and culture become major factors in classroom dynamics. It includes vignettes based on real incidents reported by students and teachers in a university environment.

Racial Stereotypes in the Media: Examines the relationship between mass media and social constructions of race from political and economic perspectives while looking at the effects media can have on audiences.

Shadow of Hate: A history of intolerance in the United States.

Skin Deep: Documents thoughts and feelings of several college students spending a weekend retreat together. It addresses issues of racism, prejudice, and cultural difference as seen through the perspectives of this very diverse group of students.

Something Strong Within: Shows insider perspectives of Japanese Americans during internment, and the strength of people surviving.

Take Two: Scenes of miscommunication are shown, followed by a demonstration of skills for alleviating the miscommunication. Interactions between U.S and nonnative speakers are used.

Telling It Like It Is: Reflections on Cultural Diversity: With candor and humor, Joan Fountain leads her audience through some of her own experiences as an African American woman, trainer, and teacher. She addresses issues such as how to deal with bigots and prejudiced remarks, racism and cultural identity, the power of words, post-discrimination trauma, nonverbal communication, etc.

Voices of Pain, Voices of Hope: This film shows a sociology class at the University of California, Los Angeles in which the ethnically and culturally diverse students find themselves confronting their own attitudes toward and experiences with prejudice and inequality in today's society. This confrontation forces them to come to terms with their own self-worth, self-image, and cultural pride, and encourage the transformation of their personal worldview.

Where Is Prejudice?: An intense film about youths from diverse backgrounds who gather together to discuss the nature of prejudice. They come to the realization that prejudice is embedded in each one of them.

Why Do People Misunderstand Each Other?: This film demonstrates how words are dynamic and often have different meanings for different people.

Working Together: Managing Cultural Diversity: In this video-book program, viewers learn how to monitor their words and body language to become more effective communicators within a multicultural setting.

Popular Culture, Social Justice, and Human Rights Songs

Abraham, Malcolm, and John by Dion
American Terrorist by Lupe Fiasco
Ball of Confusion by the Temptations
Black Dialogue by the Perceptionists
Black Man by Stevie Wonder
Blowin' in the Wind by Bob Dylan
Bury My Heart at Wounded Knee by Buffy Sainte-Marie
A Change Is Gonna Come by Sam Cooke
Change Myself by Todd Rundgren
Conversation Peace by Stevie Wonder
Deportee by Woody Guthrie
Equal Rights by Peter Tosh
Everyday People by Sly and the Family Stone
Fight Back by Holly Near
Fight the Power by the Isley Brothers
Fortunate Son by Creedence Clearwater Revival
Get Up, Stand Up by Bob Marley
Gimme Some Truth by John Lennon
Give the People the Right to Vote by Sweet Honey in the Rock

Have You Been to Jail for Justice by Anne Feeney
Higher Ground by Stevie Wonder
Indian Reservation by Paul Revere and the Raiders
Inner City Blues by Marvin Gaye
Just My Soul Responding by Smokey Robinson
Keep Ya Head Up by 2Pac
Living in the City by Stevie Wonder
Mississippi Goddam by Nina Simone
Peace, Love, and Understanding by Elvis Costello
People Are People by Depeche Mode
People Have the Power by Patti Smith
The Poverty of Philosophy by Immortal Technique
Propaganda by Dead Pres
The Revolution Will Not Be Televised by Gil Scott Heron
Say It Loud (I'm Black and I'm Proud) by James Brown
Stand Up by Flobots
Strange Fruit by Billie Holiday
This Land Is Your Land by Woody Guthrie
Time to Build by the Beastie Boys
We Shall Overcome by Pete Seeger
What's Going On by Marvin Gaye
When Will We Be Paid by Prince
Where Is the Love by The Black Eyed Peas
Words of Wisdom by Tupac Shakur
You Must Learn by KRS-One

Authors of Color of Children's and Adolescent Literature

African American

Lucille Clifton, Brenda Wilkinson, Eloise Greenfield, Jeanette Gaines, Rosa Guy, Patricia McKissack, Sharon Bell Mathis, Mildred Walter, Walter Dean Myers, Camille Yarbrough, John Steptoe, Rita Garcia-Williams, Mildred Taylor, Joyce Hansen, Angela Johnson, Emily Moore, Joyce Carol Thomas, Julius Lester, Nikki Grimes, Virginia Hamilton, Ernest J. Grimes, Faith Ringgold, Maya Angelou, Angela Johnson

Asian American

Yoshiko Uchida, Ed Young, Taro Yashima, Allen Say, Paul Yee, Tuan Ch'eng Shih, Laurence Yep, Arthur Bowie Chrisman, Elizabeth Forman Lewis, Jeanette Eaton, Elizabeth Seeger, Mildred Batchelder, Me Li, Rhoda Blumberg, Choi Ying Chang

Latino American

Pura Belpre, Carmen Lomas Garza, Nicholasa Mohr, Piri Thomas, Gary Soto, Ann Nolan Clark, Joseph Krumgold, Francis Kalnay, Jack Schaefer, Elizabeth Borton, Scott O'Dell, Maia Wojciechowski, Patricia Mora, Pam Munoz, Ryan Gary Soto, Victor Martinez, Francisco Jimenez, Sandra Cisneros

Native American

Virginia Driving, Hawk Sneve, John Bierhorst Te Ata, Jamke Highwater, Byrd Baylor, Gerald McDermott, William Apes, John Rollin Ridge, David Cusick, Charles Eastman, Elias Boudinot, Lois Lenski, Sharon Creech, Jean Craighead George, Sherman Alexie

Ethnic Minority Arts, Culture, and History Museums

National Civil Rights Museum, Memphis, TN
Skirball (Jewish) Cultural Center, Los Angeles, CA
National Museum of Mexican Art, Chicago, IL
National Museum of the American Indian, Washington, DC
Wing Luke Museum of the Asian Pacific American Experience, Seattle, WA
Arab American National Museum, Dearborn, MI
National Museum of Women in the Arts, Washington, DC
Japanese American National Museum, Los Angeles, CA
National Museum of African American History and Culture, Washington, DC
United States Holocaust Memorial Museum, Washington, DC
Smithsonian Institution Cultural Centers, Washington, DC
Chinese American Museum, Los Angeles, CA

CHAPTER 6

Cultural Congruity
in Teaching and Learning

"Culturally responsive teaching is never completely beyond context; nor is it ever totally replicable."

If teachers are to do effective culturally responsive teaching, they need to understand how ethnically diverse students learn. This is necessary because the processes of learning—not the intellectual capability to do so—used by students from different ethnic groups are influenced by their cultural socialization. Indeed,

> the sociocultural system of the child's home and community is influential in producing culturally unique preferred modes of relating to others . . . culturally unique incentive preferences, . . . as well as a preferred mode of thinking, perceiving, remembering, and problem solving. All of these characteristics . . . must be incorporated as the principal bases upon which programs for instituting changes in the school must be developed. (Ramírez & Castañeda, 1974, p. 32)

The mere mention of ethnically specific learning styles causes contention and resistance from many (Bendall, Galpin, Marrow, & Cassidy, 2016; Goodwin, 2017; Willingham, Hughes, & Dobolye, 2015). Opponents are quick to point out that "not everyone within a ethnic group learns like that." And right they are. There are exceptions to any cultural descriptions. Every individual in an ethnic group does not have to exhibit cultural characteristics as described for those characteristics to be valid. Characteristics of learning styles are pedagogically promising to the extent that they illuminate patterns of cultural values and behaviors that influence how children learn, and they provide functional directions for modifying instructional techniques to better meet the academic needs of ethnically diverse students (Bennett, 2007). Therefore, learning styles should be seen as tools for improving the school achievement of Latino, Native, Asian, and African American students by creating more *cultural congruity* in teaching–learning processes. Matching teaching styles with diverse learning styles is a way to build bridges among various cultures and communities of practice for students from different ethnic groups. It is essential to culturally responsive teaching. In examining learning styles, it is important to remember that they are constructs that have many different components, and are dynamic and fluid, not fixed and static. How, or whether, they are expressed by individual members of ethnic groups is influenced by many different variables. Critical among these are level of ethnic affiliation, social class, education, and degree of traditionalism. As explained in Chapter 1, cultural characteristics are likely to be more "pure" and come closer to approximating conceptual profiles among group members who have high levels of ethnic identification and affiliation, are poor, have low levels of education, and are rather traditional in their cultural expressions.

INTRODUCTION

Whereas Chapters 3 through 5 dealt with important and necessary components of culturally responsive teaching, this one focuses on the most fundamental aspect—that is, the process of instruction. The ethic of caring (Chapter 3) constitutes the *ideological grounding*, cultural communication (Chapter 4) is the *tool*, curriculum content about ethnic and cultural diversity (Chapter 5) is the *resource*, and instruction is the actual *praxis* of culturally responsive teaching. Instruction combines all the other components into coherent configurations and puts them into action to expedite learning. It is the *engagement*, the *interaction*, the *dialectic discourse* of students and teachers in the *processes* of teaching and learning. Interactional processes are absolutely imperative to the implementation of culturally responsive teaching. They can nullify, enrich, counteract, or complement other components of teaching.

Interactions between students and teachers may vary widely in form, function, and effect, but there is no question about their existence. Irvine and York (1995) explain that "teaching is an act of social interaction, and the resultant classroom climate is related directly to the interpersonal relationship between student and teacher" (p. 494). Whether direct or indirect, intellectual or emotional, physical or social, didactic or communal, literal or symbolic, verbal or nonverbal, interactions are the ultimate sites where teaching and learning happen—or do not happen.

Instructional effectiveness is often minimized by inconsistencies in the rules and protocols governing interactions in different cultural systems. In fact, mastering the substantive content of instruction may be jeopardized by students violating the procedural protocols about how learning processes are supposed to unfold (Holliday, 1985). For example, students may be denied credit for ideas offered in response to an intellectual inquiry because they did not wait to receive permission from the teacher before speaking, thus violating turn-taking rules. Therefore, establishing congruity between different aspects of the learning processes of ethnically diverse students and the strategies of instruction used by classroom teachers is essential to improving their academic achievement. This continuity requires that teachers contextualize the instruction of students of color in their various cultural forms, behaviors, and experiences (Irvine & York, 1995).

Culturally diverse instructional bridging and contextualizing—or scaffolding—exemplify several generally accepted principles of learning. These are summarized by Davis (2012), Doyle (2011), Glasgrow and Hicks (2009), Howe (1999), Ormrod (1995), and Rodriguez, Bellanca, and Esparza (2017). Among them are:

- Students' existing knowledge is the best starting point for the introduction of new knowledge (principle of similarity).
- Prior success breeds subsequent effort and success (principle of efficacy).
- New knowledge is learned more easily and retained longer when it is connected to prior knowledge, frames of reference, or cognitive schematas (principle of congruity).
- Reducing the "strangeness" of new knowledge and the concomitant "threat of the unfamiliar" increases students' engagement with and mastery of learning tasks (principle of familiarity).
- Organizational and structural factors surrounding how one goes about learning have more powerful effects on the mastery of new knowledge than the amount of prior knowledge one possesses per se (principle of transactionalism).
- Understanding how students' knowledge is organized and interrelated—their cognitive structures—is essential to maximizing their classroom learning (principle of cognitive mapping).
- Expectations and mediations affect performance. If students think they can learn, and receive competent assistance from supporters (e.g., teachers, parents, peers, and other mentors) in the process, they will learn (principle of confidence and efficacy).
- School achievement is always more than academics. Invariably learning takes place in context, and is influenced by the affective and caring climates of the places or settings where its efforts occur. The social, physical, emotional, psychological, cultural, political, and ethical dispositions, developments, and experiences of the participants in the learning process are significant contributing factors, and crucial targets for teaching (principle of holistic education).
- Out-of-school experiences matter, and are resources and filters for in-school learning. These "funds of knowledge, skill, and experience" are assets, building blocks, and leverage for subsequent learning (principle of scaffolding)

These principles suggest that it is not enough for teachers to know "what the learner knows about individual facts and concepts" (Howe, 1999, p. 78). They also need to understand how students come to know or to learn so that they can convey new knowledge through students' own learning systems. The goal of this chapter is to explain these "connections" and demonstrate the positive effects they have on student achievement. The discussion is organized into five sections. The first presents a brief summary of general aspects of ethnic learning styles. The emphasis is not on the debate about the validity of ethnic learning styles but on the constellation of components that constitute them.

Each of the four remaining sections of the chapter is devoted to discussions of instructional practices and research studies that amplify components of different learning styles. The second section deals with descriptions and effects of comprehensive instructional interventions. These are programs that encompass several different aspects of learning styles. Since they were designed as composites, to discuss their features separately would compromise the integrity of the programs. The third section of the chapter focuses on teaching techniques with different groups of color that are grounded in cooperative and collaborative learning, and the effects of these on student achievement. Instructional practices and research emphasizing active and affective engagement are discussed in the fourth section. The last section of the chapter examines the effects of ethnic-centered programs, such as African American and Native American schools and classes. Culturally responsive teaching does not advocate the physical separation of students by ethnic groups for instructional purposes. But, to the extent that these arrangements employ culturally situated teaching and learning, they can be seen as variations of culturally responsive teaching.

LEARNING STYLES BASELINE

By the time children begin their formal school career at 5 years of age, they already have internalized rules and procedures for acquiring knowledge and demonstrating their skills. These cognitive processing protocols are learned from their cultural socialization. They may be refined and elaborated over time, even superseded on occasion for the performance of certain tasks. But the core of these culturally influenced rules and procedures continues to *anchor* how individuals process intellectual challenges for the rest of their lives.

Learning styles are the processes individuals *habitually* use for cognitive problem-solving and for showing what they know and are capable of doing. They indicate preferences individuals have for perceiving and processing information, not the ability to learn the material. Thus, students with equal learning capabilities but different learning styles may experience different levels of success in the same learning situations (Boykin & Bailey, 2000b;

Hansen 1995; Riding & Rayner, 2000; Shade, 1997). Guild and Garger (1985) add that the essence of learning styles can be attained from analyzing what people routinely do when they interact with new ideas, people, situations, and information. This involves (1) cognition (ways of knowing); (2) conceptualizing (formulating ideas and thoughts); (3) affective reacting (feeling and valuing); and (4) acting (exhibiting some kind of behavior). Bennett (2007) and Guild (1997, 2001) agree that learning styles are the cognitive, affective, and behavioral ways that individuals perceive, interact with, and respond to learning situations. According to Shade and New (1993), learning styles have perceptual and thinking dimensions. The perceptual dimension deals with preference for sensory stimulation (e.g., sight, sound, touch, motion, etc.), and thinking patterns have to do with how information is processed, such as organizing, analyzing, inferring, appraising, and transforming. Many conceptualizations of learning styles describe them in terms of bipolarity. One end of the continuum is represented by analytical, reflective, abstract, field-independent, detail-specific, narrow, exclusive, and deductive approaches to learning; the other, by relational, impulsive, concrete, field-dependent, general, holistic, broad, inclusive, and inductive processes (more descriptive details and behavioral corollaries of these learning style features are provided by Barbe & Swassing, 1979; Dunn, Dunn, & Price, 1975; Hollins et al., 1994; Irvine & York, 1995; Morris, Sather, & Scull, 1978; Park, 2002; Ramírez & Castañeda, 1974; Riding & Rayner, 2000; Shade, 1997).

Mestre (2009) analyzed research on learning styles within the context of media and e-learning. According to her interpretations, students who exhibit learning preferences and habits that are the equivalent of field dependency and field independency respond to electronic-based teaching differently. Those who are field-independent tend to be more confident, self-sufficient, and proficient in computer search and navigation tasks because they are logical and sequential thinkers, and are less interested in social dimensions of learning. Field-dependent learners are likely to be less adaptable to and more disoriented by hyper-mediated learning prompts and interactions. They do better in face-to-face interactions that take place in social contexts. However, the prominence of computers and other media in the lives of students may be blurring the lines between these archetypal learning preferences, and students are blending elements of both more often. In acknowledging these possibilities. Mestre (2009) noted that millennials, or Generation Y,

> are used to multitasking, tend to be visual learners, and benefit from lots of tactile experiences, . . . prefer to do what is of personal interest to them, and are motivated by authentic . . . and self-selected tasks. . . . They prefer a lot of interactivity, the use of mobile tools, and social networking. Therefore, providing

them interactive multimedia that allows them to choose their topics and customize their paths online may motivate and engage them more (p. 30).

As educators explore the feasibility of using web-based and online techniques in culturally responsive teaching, individual and ethnic group learning styles should be considered. In doing so, Mestre (2009) suggested that media and program designers "accommodate a broad range of learning styles, move beyond text-based interactions, and include visual or kinesthetic modalities, as well as intuition and thinking exercises" (p. 32).

Overall characterizations of learning styles suggest that they are multidimensional and dynamic processes, and the "central tendencies" of how students from different ethnic groups engage with learning encounters, rather than static descriptors of finite behaviors in all situations. According to Riding and Rayner (2000), a learning style is "an 'umbrella construct' defining several aspects of an individual's approach to learning. It is made up of a 'core,' a cognitive style, which in turn influences a secondary set of processes, including learning strategies, learning preferences, motivation, and self-perception as learner" (p. 116). This means that students may function outside of their dominant learning style core in some learning situations, and well within the heart of it at other times. But learning styles do not ever cease to exist because they are closely related to cultural values and traits. For example, Boykin and Bailey (2000a, 2000b), Watkins (2002), and Boykin, Coleman, Lilja, & Tyler (2004) have found strong correlations between African American cultural values of communalism, verve, rhythmic movement, and performance, and preferences in learning environments and behavioral styles of low-income, elementary-age African American students.

Learning styles encompass eight key dimensions, but they are not necessarily evenly evoked in learning activities or among individuals within ethnic groups. Yet in most learning situations individuals apply many if not all of them. The same is true for multiple intelligences. As Howard Gardner (2006) explained, "As human beings, we all have a repertoire of skills for solving different kinds of problems" (p. 20). Furthermore, "as nearly every cultural role requires several intelligences, it becomes important to consider individuals as a collection of aptitudes rather than having a single problem-solving faculty." No ranking of importance is intended by the order in which these learning style dimensions are presented. Conceptually, they should be understood as an interactive composite. Operationally, their separate identities provide different opportunities for designing culturally compatible instruction for ethnically diverse students. These dimensions are:

- *Procedural*—the preferred ways of approaching and working
  through learning tasks. These include pacing rates; distribution of
  time; variety versus similarity; novelty or predictability; passivity or

activity; task-directed or social; structured order or freedom; and preference for direct teaching or inquiry and discovery learning.

- *Communicative*—how thoughts are organized, sequenced, and conveyed in spoken and written forms, whether as elaborated narrative storytelling or precise responses to explicit questions; as topic-specific or topic-chaining discourse techniques; as passionate advocacy of ideas or dispassionate recorders and reporters; whether the purpose is to achieve descriptive and factual accuracy or to capture persuasive power and convey literary aestheticism.

- *Substantive*—preferred content, such as descriptive details or general pattern, concepts and principles or factual information, statistics or personal and social scenarios; preferred subjects, such as math, science, social studies, fine or language arts; technical, interpretative, and evaluative tasks; preferred intellectualizing tasks, such as memorizing, describing, analyzing, classifying, or criticizing.

- *Environmental*—Preferred physical, social, and interpersonal settings for learning, including sound or silence; room lighting and temperature; presence or absence of others; ambiance of struggle or playfulness, of fun and joy, or of pain and somberness.

- *Organizational*—preferred structural arrangements for work and study space, including the amount of personal space; the fullness or emptiness of learning space; rigidity or flexibility in use of and claims made to space; carefully organized or cluttered learning resources and space locations; individually claimed or group-shared space; rigidity or flexibility of the habitation of space.

- *Perceptual*—preferred sensory stimulation for receiving, processing, and transmitting information, including visual, tactile, auditory, kinetic, oral, or multiple sensory modalities.

- *Relational*—Preferred interpersonal and social interaction modes in learning situations, including formality or informality, individual competition or group cooperation, independence or interdependence, peer–peer or child–adult, authoritarian or egalitarian, internal or external locus of control, conquest or community.

- *Motivational*—Preferred incentives or stimulations that evoke learning, including individual accomplishment or group well-being, competition or cooperation, conquest or harmony, expediency or propriety, image or integrity, external rewards or internal desires.

Some ethnic group members exhibit "purer" learning style characteristics than others. The degree of purity is affected by such variables as levels of in-group identification and affiliation, education, social class, and gender. For instance, highly ethnically affiliated African Americans will exhibit strong preferences for "group-ness" across procedural, motivational, relational, and substantive dimensions of learning because of the values their culture places on working collaboratively to accomplish tasks, emotionalism, and informal social interactions. Independence and self-initiation will permeate the various learning-style dimensions for middle-class European Americans, since their culture values competition, individualism, and upward mobility. Culturally traditional Japanese and Chinese American students may be more bi-stylistic. Because of the emphases their cultures place on familial obligations and harmonious relationships (Fox, 1994; B. Tong, 1978), their motivation and preparation for academic performance tends to be communal and group-focused, but they are quite individualistic in actual performance delivery. They also tend to perform well on mechanistic, technical, and detail-specific learning tasks instead of the more humanistic, socially oriented, and holistic emphases that usually are preferred by communal learners (B. Kim, 1978; Leung, 1998; Nakanishi & Nishida, 1995; Pai et al., 2006).

Additional assistance in understanding the learning styles of students of color and designing compatible instructional strategies can be gained from theory, research, and practice on teaching through sensory modalities (Barbe & Swassing, 1979), multiple intelligences (Armstrong, 2000; L. Campbell, Campbell, & Dickinson, 2004; H. Gardner, 1983, 2006; Lazear, 1991, 1994; Silver, Strong, & Perini, 2000), and brain lateralization (Farmer, 2004; McNeil, 2009; Springer & Deutsch, 1998). Although these models were not created specifically with people of color in mind, there is a great deal of parallelism between them and ethnic learning styles. They can be easily overlaid on one another as well as on various approaches to improving teaching effectiveness. For example, Armstrong (2000) illustrated connections among Gardner's nine intelligences (logical, verbal, visual, kinesthetic, musical, interpersonal, intrapersonal, naturalist, existentialist) and the taxonomy of cognitive objectives (knowledge, comprehension, application, analysis, synthesis, evaluation) developed by Bloom (1956). He demonstrated how multicultural curriculum content can be taught by organizing ethnic individuals and their contributions by type of intelligence. The chapter ends with some practical possibilities for actually doing culturally responsive teaching.

FUNDS OF KNOWLEDGE AND CULTURAL SELF-STUDY

Three highly successful programs are discussed here to illustrate the effects of instructional interventions that incorporate multiple elements of cultural compatibility on the achievement of students of color. Their achievement effects are also multiple and varied. These programs are the Foxfire Project, the Kamehameha Early Education Program (KEEP) and the Hawaiian Cultural Influences in Education (HCIE) Study, and the Webster Groves

Writing Project (WGWP). They involve poor rural European Americans, Native Hawaiians, and African Americans, respectively. None of these programs self-identified as culturally responsive teaching, but in effect they were, or at least they were precursors. They suggest that culturally relevant and responsive instructional actions may exist without being so named. The reverse is true, too. Sometimes actions claimed as culturally responsive really are not. These three large examples may help educators to better make these critical distinctions.

Foxfire

Like the Cultural Modeling Narrative Project discussed in Chapter 4, the Foxfire Project used "cultural data sets," social and cultural capital, localized funds of knowledge, and self-study to teach a combination of academic, literary, cultural pride, personal efficacy, and self-knowledge skills. It grew out of one teacher's desire to make classroom instruction more meaningful for 9th- and 10th-grade Appalachian students. This goal was accomplished by the students learning communication and language arts skills in the process of conducting ethnographies of their own everyday lives and cultural heritages, traditions, and experiences. The project reached its peak between 1967 and 1984, but continues on a lesser scale even today, over 50 years later. It began as a class in journalism and eventually expanded into an academic program of 16 courses; a series of *Foxfire* magazines; 21 published books compiled from the oral history research of the participating students; community development initiatives; Teacher Networks for professional development; recordings and videotapes; lecture series in which students were co-presenters; student exchange programs; the creation of a Foxfire Museum and Heritage Center composed of authentic replicas of Appalachian log cabins; the inspiration for a Broadway play based on the first three *Foxfire* books; the Foxfire Fund; and being a prototype for over 200 similar projects throughout the United States and in other countries (Boucher, 2013; Danovich, 2017; Oliver, 2011; Puckett, 1989; Wigginton, 1985, 1991). Students played pivotal roles in most of these activities, including providing the primary content and being decisionmakers and leaders. For example, they were speakers in the lecture series and served as consultants to the authors of the Broadway play and to the producers of films, articles, and books about their learning projects.

Fifty years after it began, the *Foxfire* magazine is still being published by public high school students at the same school of its inception (Glaser, n.d.). Accolades for the program and its success are still occurring. For example, Foxfire won the 2015 Georgia Governor's Award for Arts and Humanities for its sustained contributions to the welfare of schools and communities (Glickman, 2016). In her reflective analysis Glaser said that the program taught the Appalachian students "to appreciate the power of the written word within the context of their own experience," and she described the *Foxfire* magazine as an "unprecedented source of information that was at once a sociological study, instructional pamphlet, and archival log" (n.d.). Walls (2017) agrees with Glaser's assessment in applauding the community members and students who were the conveyors and recipients of Appalachian culture and knowledge that made Foxfire possible. She noted that although many of the people the students interviewed and observed were illiterate, they had broad-based funds of survival knowledge, ingenuity, and skills that were passed down orally and practically from generation to generation. Walls gives praise to both in the comment, "How fitting that a culture that passed its wisdom down from the old to the young is being passed on to the world by the young recipients of this mountain culture."

Like many marginalized and underachieving students today, the participants in the Foxfire Project were initially alienated, disinterested, and unmotivated by conventional school programs and teaching methods. Wigginton, the project teacher and director, countered these attitudes by collaborating and sharing responsibility with students about what to teach and how to learn, by developing their individual and collective talent potential, and by using the cultural funds of knowledge of the Appalachian communities surrounding the school. These actions were based on beliefs that students should help construct their own educational destinies and be actively engaged in useful, productive, positive, rewarding, stimulating, and exciting learning experiences. Pursuing these objectives led to an instructional technique that came to be known as *cultural journalism* (Glickman, 2016; Puckett, 1989; Wigginton, 1985, 1991), and embodied in practice as *Foxfire*, a student-produced magazine. Its major features were the collecting and reporting of local Appalachian culture, history, folklore, customs, traditions, and artifacts. The students researched, catalogued, codified, and disseminated their own family, cultural, and community competencies, or funds of knowledge.

Several culturally responsive objectives were embedded in the Foxfire Project. They included developing knowledge of and sustaining cultural heritage; the validity of individual, group, and culture self-study; legitimizing the family and community funds of knowledge of culturally diverse students; contextualizing academic learning in the lived experiences of diverse students; using community cultural resources and students' prior social experiences as conduits for classroom teaching; honoring the cultural heritages and experiences of ethnically, racially, and socially diverse students; teaching academic and cultural competencies simultaneously; and students and teachers being genuine partners in the learning process. Many of these sociocultural assets were lacking in many of the Appalachian students, as is the case with some members of other ethnic groups who are ashamed of and embarrassed by their cultural heritages, ethnic identities, and lived experiences.

Wigginton (1985) thought that turning a positive spotlight onto students' cultural backgrounds, making them active procurers and conservationists of their own culture, appealing to different skills and interests, and promoting self-reflection, would counteract these negative perceptions, develop personal agency and efficacy, and improve academic achievement. His beliefs were confirmed by the effects of the Foxfire Project. The participating students learned regular English and language arts skills in the process of collecting and reporting data on their cultural communities, customs, and artifacts. They were taught units on grammar, formal letter-writing, poetry, interviewing, superstitions, writing for clarity, and magazine and newspaper production. Some of the first products published in the *Foxfire* magazine and books resulted from homework assignments associated with these units. The students used their transcriptions of the oral histories they collected from local residents to practice the Georgia state academic language arts standards. Their performance on a multitude of academic skills increased radically (including mastery of English, writing, and oral speech mechanics, action research and community-based data collection, decision-making, and collaborative leadership and accountability); their self-confidence and cultural pride soared; truancy and school nonattendance virtually disappeared; and interpersonal, civic, and social relationship skills grew exponentially (Knapp, 1993). In the following statement, Wigginton (1985) explained how the students developed English skills as they documented their cultural attributes, traditions, beliefs, and practices:

> In their work with photography (which must tell the story with as much impact and clarity as the words), text (which must be grammatically correct except in the use of pure dialect from tapes that they transcribe), lay-out, make-up, correspondence, art and cover design, and selection of manuscripts from outside poets and writers—to say nothing of related skills such as fund raising, typing, retelling, advertising, and speaking at conferences and public meetings—[my students] learn more about English than from any other curriculum I could devise. (p. 13)

Kamehameha Early Education Program (KEEP)

KEEP began in 1972 (and lasted for 24 years) as a multidisciplinary educational research and development effort to create a language arts program that would improve the reading performance of underachieving Native Hawaiian children in Grades K–3 (Jordan, 1985). In addition to improving academic performance, KEEP intended to increase these students' ownership, investment, pride, and engagement in the educational enterprise (Jordan, Tharp, & Baird-Vogt, 1992). From its beginning, several researchers (Au, 1993; Au & Kawakami, 1994; Boggs et al., 1985; Cazden et al., 1985; Tharp & Gallimore, 1988; Wong Fillmore & Meyer,

1992) investigated the achievement effects of matching teaching styles to the Polynesian-based discourse, activity, participation, performance structures, values, beliefs, and behaviors of Native Hawaiian students.

Among the key instructional features of KEEP were small cooperative learning groups, highly interactive discussion processes using an E–T–R sequence (experience–text–relationship), and student engagement in "talk-story" or "co-narration" to construct and communicate meaning in the classroom. The classroom was arranged in activity centers that provided many opportunities for students to participate in collaborative efforts and instructional conversations with the teacher and one another. In these centers, kindergartners engaged in peer interactions 50% of the time and 1st-graders as much as 70% of the time (Tharp & Gallimore, 1988). KEEP also used a natural-context approach to language development that was strongly shaped by how discourse skills were acquired and applied in Native Hawaiian homes, communities, and culture. While the greatest emphasis in reading instruction was on comprehension, attention also was given to developing vocabulary, sight phonetics, and decoding skills.

The achievement effects of KEEP were profound. For several years the program consistently met its primary goal of achieving mean scores near or at the 50th percentile on standardized tests of reading achievement. After the program had been in existence for 15 years, the percentile mean of reading achievement of the 1st-graders was 55.7 compared with 31.7 for students in non-KEEP classes. The performance of participating and non-participating 2nd-graders was 52.5 and 28.8, and for 3rd-graders it was 47.8 and 25.5, respectively. These levels of achievement represent major improvements from the 13th percentile average when the program first began. Two other achievement effects are noteworthy. First, KEEP teachers gave significantly more praise and less criticism to students than did other teachers. Of the three types of praise feedback used most often in the classrooms—*management* for deportment behaviors, *academic* for learning task-related behaviors, and *verbal negatives* (scolds and desists) for unacceptable behavior—the means for KEEP teachers were 21.80 for management, 13.87 for academics, and 2.07 for verbal. The comparative means for other teachers on these types of feedback were 6.03, .65, and 6.01, respectively. Second, KEEP students had an average of 85% engaged time on academic tasks, which was 20 percentage points higher than the means of comparison classrooms (Tharp & Gallimore, 1988).

The Hawaiian Cultural Influences in Education (HCIE) study examined aspects and effects of culturally responsive teaching for Native Hawaiian students more broadly than KEEP. It provides quantitative data derived from surveys of 600 teachers, 2,969 students, and 2,264 parents at 62 participating public and private schools (Kana'iaupuni, Ledward, & Jensen, 2010). Some specific examples of culturally responsive teaching for Native Hawaiian students identified in the study are:

project-based and place-based teaching and learning for children, integrating culture, community and the natural environment. Some of the schools use Hawaiian language as the medium of instruction, but all use the language routinely and offer language classes. Students engage in authentic experiences at wahi pana (sacred places) and other community outdoor learning laboratories. They conduct science experiments to assess the relative successes of various methods to revive endangered endemic species or water resources. Their curriculum includes learning about the lifestyles, knowledge, and values of Native Hawaiians. In this way, connections to the land, culture, and community create a rich educational environment that nourishes spiritual, physical, and educational well-being. (Kana'iaupuni, Ledward, & Jensen, 2010, p. 3)

The findings of the Hawaiian Cultural Influences in Education Study are consistent with prior qualitative studies, indicating that culture-based educational strategies produce multiple positive outcomes for Native Hawaiian students. Among them are:

- positive impacts on student socio-emotional well-being (e.g., identity, self-efficacy, social relationships).
- enhanced socio-emotional well-being positively affected math and reading test scores.
- culture-based instruction that had especially strong positive effects for students with low socio-emotional development.
- greater indigenous cultural affiliation, civic engagement, school motivation, community connections, sense of belonging at school, and higher levels of trusting relationships with teachers.
- the mitigation of negative experiences of cultural and ethnic identity by increasing self-confidence, self-esteem, and resiliency.
- despite demonstrated positive results, a decrease in culture-based education as the normative approach to teaching with Native Hawaiian students.
- teachers going above and beyond conventional best practice in culture-rich environments to achieve educational relevance and rigor by blending culture-based and research-based teaching strategies (or best practices).
- general principles of effective teaching, such as contextualization and joint productive activity, that are most often achieved by teachers using culturally relevant strategies.

The HCEI study had some other important effects for culturally responsive teaching in general. According to Kana'iaupuni, the data it produced

help to debunk some myths associated with culture-based education such as: the use of CBE [culture-based education] is limited to only "Hawaiian teachers" or "Hawaiian schools", CBE is radically different from conventional best practices, or there is no added value of CBE to educational outcomes. In fact, the data support the hypothesis that cultural approaches strongly enhance relevance and relationships at school, while also supporting positive academic outcomes. (Kana'iaupuni et al., 2011, p. 17)

Consequently, "One-size-fits-all education models make no sense at the community level, where scripted approaches could be replaced by those that harness the wonders, the fullness, and the richness of cultural practices, values, and knowledge" (Kana'iaupuni et al., 2011, p. 18). More socio-emotional well-being and academic success for underachieving culturally diverse students can be accomplished with differentiated cultural-based teaching.

Webster Groves Writing Project

The culturally responsive instructional dimensions of the Webster Groves Writing Project fall within four of its eight principles and strategies—building on students' strengths, individualizing and personalizing instruction, encouraging cooperative learning, and building bridges and expanding horizons. The teachers in this project translated cues derived from African American cultural values, communication and social interaction patterns, and performance styles into compatible instructional techniques to improve students' writing skills. A set of more specific strategies emerged that applied across the general categories, including:

- Affirming the strong personal voice in African American informal interactions and formal writing
- Building on oral discourse habits and interpretation
- Incorporating performance and role-playing as regular features of teaching and learning
- Validating African American dialect and expressive modes as a functional communication system and assisting students in analyzing and appreciating them
- Valuing and using African American culture habitually, rather than just on special occasions
- Developing a sense of trust, community, and mutual responsibility for learning among students and with teachers
- Consistently combining individual and group efforts and accountability for task performance
- Creating classroom climates and opportunities for collaborative composing, revising, and editing tasks
- Using a system of peer response, tutoring, and study buddies
- Affirming personal responses to reading (Krater et al., 1994)

While the existing frames of reference of students were always the starting points or anchors, instruction did not end there. The WGWP teachers used the confidence that affirmation of these orientations generated to entice and obligate students to "expand their horizons" (Krater et al., 1994; Zeni & Krater, 1996). These expansions took the form of "code-shifting" to learn the writing and speaking conventions of mainstream society and schools; connecting their oral creative strengths to the demands of academic reading and writing; and using their skills in storytelling, oral interpretation, role-playing, improvisation, script-reading, and call–response to improve performance in school-based reading and writing. Hanley (1998) used similar techniques with middle school African Americans to examine their knowledge construction within the context of drama production and performance.

Other reading and writing skills also were contextualized within African American cultural, performance, and learning styles. The expressive verbal technique of "rapping" (for an explanation, see Baber, 1987; Kochman, 1972; Smitherman, 1986) was used for book talks, character development, and advertisements. Sermonizing motifs of speaking and call–response discourse patterns frequently were employed by students to demonstrate their understanding of the cultural techniques and embedded conventional literary skills (e.g., topic selection, purpose, clarity of development, point of view, and audience appropriateness). They learned by doing, and frequently in cooperative groups, "in the familiar" before broaching the unfamiliar, or alternative, communicative modes. Consequently, speech and performance preceded writing narratives and reading texts, since these were the cultural strengths and the "expressive anchors" of African American culture. Instead of using a static grammatical structure, language variations were learned by performing aloud and fine-tuning the voice (dialogue within a narrative) and discourse features (Krater et al., 1994). The WGWP teachers hastened to explain that European American students responded positively as well to the dramatic, performance, expressive, participatory, and collegial ambiance of these teaching styles.

In addition to the improvement in test scores and writing skills discussed in Chapter 5, the Webster Groves Writing Project produced some noteworthy results in personal and social achievement. The thinking of the students was more focused, as evidenced in writing samples that had more details and clearer explanations. Students expressed more confidence in their ability to write and more enjoyment of writing. These reactions were particularly apparent in self-selected writing topics, a finding consistent with those of Chapman (1994). More African Americans than European Americans (two-thirds compared with one-half) were satisfied with and surprised by the skills and self-disclosures their writings revealed. These results confirmed the project staff's assertions that:

Some of the joys of writing are clarifying what you already think, discovering feelings you didn't know you had, surprising yourself with a well-turned phrase, and unearthing a relationship between ideas. Self-satisfaction during the process is the immediate reward; communicating clearly to others is a delayed fulfillment. (Krater et al., 1994, p. 398)

The WGWP also had significant effects on the participating teachers in ways that are important for culturally responsive teaching. They learned (and modified their thinking and instructional behaviors accordingly) that effective teaching and learning really are *informed, dialectic, and dynamic processes* in which roles are fluid and even reversible—where, frequently, teachers become students and students become teachers (Krater et al., 1994; Zeni & Krater, 1996). Indeed, culturally different students are often the best teachers about themselves if teachers learn how to recognize and receive the knowledge they have to give. By the end of the project, attitudes of the WGWP teachers had changed significantly. They no longer believed specific teaching methods made the most difference in improving the writing achievement of underachieving African American students. Instead, they mused:

Our interactions with, our concern for, and our immersion with our students as *persons* are the key. . . . We began as teachers who wanted to learn how to help our students write better. Now we want to learn what our students have to teach us. We are still teachers of writing, but first we are teachers of students. (Krater et al., 1994, p. 415, emphasis in original)

COOPERATIVE LEARNING

Cooperation, collaboration, and community are prominent themes, techniques, and goals in educating marginalized Latino, Native, African, and Asian American students. Two major reasons help to explain these pedagogical trends. First, underlying values of human connectedness and collaborative problem-solving are high priorities in the cultures of most groups of color in the United States. Second, cooperation plays a central role in these groups' learning styles, especially the communicative, procedural, motivational, and relational dimensions. Therefore, they should be key pillars of culturally responsive teaching. Several research projects and instructional programs have demonstrated the feasibility of community, collaboration, and cooperation for improving the achievement of students of color (Boykin & Bailey, 2000b; Boykin et al., 2004; Cohen, Brody, & Sapon-Shevin, 2004; Fashola et al., 1997). Some focus on the processes of cooperative learning in general, and others emphasize cooperative learning in specific subject or skill areas.

General Cooperative Processes and Achievement Effects

Findings of the eight research studies reviewed by Losey (1997) provide support for the pedagogical power of cooperative learning for Latino students. These studies demonstrated that the academic achievement of Mexican Americans improved when they helped design their own assignments, discussed assigned tasks, worked collaboratively with one another in small groups, had "informal, almost familial" relationships with teachers (p. 310), perceived that they belonged to a classroom community, and felt that their cultural experiences and the use of both Spanish and English were validated. These kinds of learning environments and techniques led to greater reasoning and clarity of expression in writing and reading as well as higher scores on school district writing proficiency tests.

Slavin (1987, 1992, 2015), Stevens and Slavin (1995), Fashola and associates (1997), and Gillies (2007, 2014) offer additional evidence about the pedagogical power of cooperative learning. They report that, for the most part, this instructional technique has similar positive effects for students across ethnic, gender, and ability groupings; achievement measures; and intervention scale (classroom or school, short- or long-term). These include more interethnic group social interactions and friendships; increased academic achievement in a variety of subjects; improved academic self-concepts; higher levels of confidence and efficacy for students of color; and better engagement in learning tasks, retention of class materials, time on task, and intrinsic motivation. Similar results are reported by Johnson and Johnson (1999), Dotson (2001), and Morgan (2012).

Dotson (2001) included social skills and academic achievement as indicators of success in her review of 67 studies on the effects of cooperative learning. So did Johnson and Johnson (1999) in their meta-analysis of 158 studies. Both reviews confirmed the theory that cooperative learning is advantageous for student outcomes in both social and academic domains of school performance. Collectively, most of the research Dotson and Johnson and Johnson reviewed produced positive results for both academic performance and interpersonal relationships in all major subjects; at all grade levels (elementary, secondary, and college); in urban, rural, and suburban settings; and for high, average, and low achievers. The value and power of cooperative learning was highlighted further by Karl Smith in his statement that

> The importance of cooperative learning experiences goes beyond improving instruction, increasing student achievement, and making life easier and more productive for teachers, although these are worthwhile activities. Cooperation is as basic to humans as the air we breathe. The ability of all students to cooperate with other people is the keystone to building and maintaining stable families, career success, neighborhood and community membership, important values

and beliefs, friendships, and contributions to society. Knowledge and skills are of no [value] if . . . [one] cannot apply them in cooperative interaction with other people. . . . There is nothing more basic than learning to use one's knowledge in cooperative interaction with other people. (Smith, 2009, p. 73)

According to Morgan (2012), research on the effectiveness of cooperative learning has considerable validity and generalizability because of its magnitude (over 900 studies), longevity (over 110 years), multiple perspectives and methodologies (conducted by a wide range of researchers with different orientations and working in various settings and countries), varied targets of analysis (diverse cultural, ethnic, economic, age, and gender participants), and many data sources (research tasks, variables, and measures). The results of Morgan's review of research and scholarship (like those of other meta-analysts, such as Warfa, 2016; Laal & Ghodsi, 2012; and Lin, 2006) showed that students gain multiple benefits from cooperative learning, which he categorized as academic, social, and psychological. The academic effects were the same as those named in earlier reports by scholars, such as Slavin, Fashola et al., Johnson and Johnson, and Gillies. Social benefits included improved understanding of diversity, and better helping, caring, and supportive relationships with peers. Psychologically, cooperative learning has generated for participating students higher self-esteem, more friends, greater involvement in classroom activities, and improved attitudes toward learning

Results from Stevens and Slavin's (1995) 2-year study of five cooperative elementary schools in suburban Maryland, involving 1,012 students in grades 2–6, indicate that cooperative learning works as well at the school level as in individual classrooms. Students in these schools performed better than their peers in traditional schools on reading vocabulary and comprehension, language expression, and mathematics computation as measured by subscales of the California Achievement Test (CAT), Form C. The findings in this study are not disaggregated by ethnic groups, so we do not know who is accounting for what kind of performance.

For several years Cohen and her colleagues (Cohen, 1984; Cohen et al., 2004; Cohen, Kepner, & Swanson, 1995; Cohen & Lotan, 1995, 1997) at Stanford University conducted studies on the internal structure and dynamics of cooperative learning groups. Specifically, they examined the effects of status differences in the interactional dynamics of heterogeneous cooperative groups and how equalizing status among ethnically diverse members would affect achievement. This research is significant because students of color often are assigned lower status with respect to achievement expectations, and most of the participating students were Latinos, low-income European Americans, and Southeast Asian immigrants. As part of the Program for Complex Instruction, Cohen and associates developed several techniques for modifying academic-status differences and patterns of classroom participation for students of color. Among these were students using one another as resources in mixed-gender cooperative learning groups; the use of multiple-ability, higher-order thinking and problem-solving tasks that require a wide range of intellectual abilities and skills; publicly assigning competence in *valued abilities* to low-status students; and validation, with practice opportunities, of multidimensional intelligence and academic ability.

In one of the studies involving 13 classrooms in grades 2–6, the students used Finding Out/Descubrimiento (FO/D), which is an English–Spanish math and science curriculum. Completion of the learning tasks required reading, writing, and computing; the use of manipulatives; reasoning, hypothesizing, and visual and spatial thinking; careful observation; and interpersonal skills (Cohen et al., 1995, 2004; Cohen, Brody, et al., 2004; Cohen & Lotan, 1995, 1997). Cohen and associates (1995) explained the value of these teaching techniques, noting that "multiple-ability tasks enable a much wider range of students to make important contributions; they set the stage for challenging the assumption that there is only one way to be smart" (p. 23). As this lesson was learned and status attitudes shifted accordingly, the level of participation in learning experiences of low-status students increased, which, in turn, led to higher academic achievement. Findings from research by Boykin and associates (2004) and Boykin and Bailey (2000a, 2000b) also attest to the positive effects of variability in teaching styles and cooperative learning on the academic performance of African American students. Their focus has been limited to low-income students and different literacy skills in the elementary grades.

The results of these studies and reviews of cooperative learning are particularly instructive for teaching ethnically, racially, and culturally diverse (both native and immigrant) students. Many of them are adrift and estranged from their communal connections and from academic affiliation by the typical ways schools and classrooms are conducted. Cooperative teaching and learning techniques and classroom climates can create psychoemotional "safe spaces" and culturally responsive "grace spaces" (or protective devices), can "re-center" students, and can increase congruence among students' preferred ways of personal being, intellectual engagement, and academic task performance. In effect, cooperative learning is an important instrumental tool of culturally responsive teaching. Four specific projects (two each in mathematics and literacy) are described next to illustrate how cooperative teaching and learning operate in actual classroom practice.

Cooperative Mathematics Learning and Achievement

The Calculus Project (TCP) was initiated in 2009 by Adrian Mims in Brookline, MA, public schools to increase the participation and success of African American, Latino, and low-income students in high school geometry and other advanced math courses. It has since expanded to other schools in Massachusetts, Florida, and New York. The project is grounded in the belief that a growth mindset (believing abilities can develop and grow rather than being "given" and fixed)—which allows all students to meet the rigorous demands of advanced math, cooperative efforts among students, and trusting, supportive relationships with teachers—leads to academic success (Colannino. 2016). Students begin the project in 8th grade with 4 weeks of intensive summer study, followed by cohort enrollments in advanced math classes during the regular academic year. These study arrangements continue throughout their senior year. The summer sessions preview the upcoming mathematics curriculum, and include field trips focusing on careers in science, technology, engineering, and math (STEM). The summer work is reinforced with after-school tutoring during the academic year. Creating feelings of community, connectedness, and belonging among minority students in high-status, advanced mathematics curriculum is as important as mastering the curriculum content in The Calculus Project. To respond to these needs, TCP schools group low-income and students of color in the some classes. This apparent academic segregation occurs often and seemingly unintentionally in gifted and talented or advanced classes, but in TCP it is intentional—a way to compensate for ethnic isolation and ensure the creation of cooperative learning communities. This feature of the project was inspired by Mims's memories and observations of his successful peers in college working together in groups to solve difficult math problems, share their work, and learn from each other. It also is consistent with research on the effects of racial prejudice and isolation on learning (Steele, 2010), which shows that a critical mass of diverse students in classrooms creates a more comfortable and productive academic environment for them.

In the first year of TCP (school year 2010–2011), all participants scored proficient or advanced on the Massachusetts Comprehensive Assessment System Math Test (MCAS), one of the most rigorous standardized tests in the nation. Also, the student who received the highest math score at Brookline High School for that year was an African American who went through the Calculus Project (Colannino, 2016). Chen (2015) reports that the project now serves 200 students at Brookline High School, but when participants in other cities and states are combined the yearly total rose to about 700. And involvement is continuing to increase. For example, in Orlando, Florida, during the 2016–2017 academic year, 1000 students in 41 schools took part (Larkin, 2017). Another encouraging result of the TCP is that the number of African American students at Brookline High who scored "advanced" on the math section of the MCAS tests increased from 18% in 2013 to 53% in 2015 (Chen, 2015).

Jamie Escalante did for high school Latino students what Mims did for African Americans. He reversed their achievement patterns in calculus by incorporating elements of their cultural values, work habits, learning styles, and background experiences into teaching. All the participants in the

Escalante Math Program (Escalante & Dirmann, 1990; Mathews, 1988), which was implemented from 1978 to 1991 (Barham & Thomas, n.d.; Sanchez, 2010), were considered highly "at-risk" for academic failure, and most teachers felt they were incapable of succeeding in advanced placement (AP) courses. At Garfield High School in East Los Angeles, when Escalante began his Math Program, no Latinos were enrolled in calculus or took the AP tests, and the school staffed only 6 Algebra I and 10 Geometry and/or Algebra II classes. Ten years later more than 500 students had successfully taken the AP calculus tests, and the school was staffing 25 Algebra I and 30 Geometry and/or Algebra II classes, and offering AP physics, chemistry, and biology. In 1978, 10 AP tests were given in the school and one Latino student took the calculus exam. In 1987 alone, Garfield High School produced 27% and 22% of all Mexican Americans in the United States who scored 3 (average) in AP Calculus AB and Geometry BC, respectively. Thirteen other calculus students scored 5 (highest possible) and 19 scored 4. More than 87% of all Garfield's test-takers in 1987 were Latinos, and the remainder were Asian Americans. No other inner-city school had ever produced that many students who took as many Advanced Placement tests or scored so well on them. In fact, of 15 public schools with the greatest numbers of students taking AP calculus tests in May 1987, Garfield ranked fourth and was the only one with predominantly lower-class Latino students (Escalante & Dirmann, 1990; Mathews, 1988).

Escalante's success, which was popularized in the feature film *Stand and Deliver* (Menendez, 1988), resulted from the teacher's personal convictions, commitment, and influence, combined with cooperation, camaraderie, caring, hard work, and ethnic pride among the students (Mathews, 1988). Sanchez (2010) added that Escalante inspired, cajoled, and even taunted often troubled Latino youth to envision themselves as who they could be instead of the limitations of their current circumstances. Escalante and his students worked together in small teams in a climate that cultivated intellectual champions, and where mutual assistance, fun, humor, serious intellectual work, accountability, and cultural responsiveness were always present. He gave this explanation for why creating this instructional ethos and community of caring was imperative to student success:

> I am trying to give my students two things: "roots" and "wings." I feel a great responsibility to teach my students respect for values that will sustain their families, their school, their community, their race, their culture, and their country; to a large extent, students discover their cultural heritage in the classroom. . . . I do not merely teach math, I teach respect for American democratic values and institutions. . . . We owe it to our succeeding generations to ensure that our students learn these aspects and become full participatory citizens in our country. With these roots firmly in place, they are more likely to develop wings to fly to success, even greatness. (Escalante & Dirmann, 1990, p. 419)

Unfortunately the exemplary program and phenomenal progress that Escalante and his team members accomplished with poor urban Latino students over 13 years began to deteriorate soon after he resigned from the faculty of Garfield High School in 1991. But, like Wigginton with the Foxfire Project, he left a legacy that prevails and a powerful example of culturally responsive teaching worthy of emulation. In recognizing this contribution, Barham and Thomas (n.d.) noted:

> Jaime Escalante focused on results. His pupils had been told all their lives that they weren't good enough. Because they were poor Latinos, no one expected them to excel at advanced mathematics. Escalante believed that anyone with *ganas*, a Spanish term meaning "drive" or "desire," could grasp math principles and use them as the key to a well-paying career. He was dedicated to doing whatever it took to make that happen.

Cooperative Literacy Learning and Achievement

Sheets (1995a, 1996) achieved success in AP Spanish language and literature with Latino students reminiscent of what Escalante did in calculus. Over a 3-year period in the Seattle, Washington, public schools, 20 of the 29 "at-risk" students who participated in a class designed to prepare them to take the AP Spanish language and literature tests passed with scores high enough (3 or above) to receive college credit. The students involved were high school sophomores, juniors, and seniors who were considered "at-risk" for academic failure. They were native Spanish speakers but had no formal skills in reading or writing the language. Sheets credited the students' achievement to the combination of instructional strategies she used. They included

> the use of the Spanish language as the medium of instruction, affirmation and validation of ethnic identity, development of self-esteem, curricular content emphasis on the students' cultural heritage, history, and literature, and implementation of learning strategies that matched their preferred learning styles (e.g., oral language, cooperative learning, peer support, and family involvement). (1995a, p. 189)

In addition to remarkable academic improvement, other high-level achievements resulted from Sheets's efforts. For example, a strong system of peer mentoring evolved in which students bartered other services in exchange for the academic assistance they received from one another. Out of this reciprocity emerged "feelings of togetherness, unity, community, and family. The class was never an individual effort! . . . Cooperation was actualized and internalized" (Sheets, 1995a, pp. 192, 191). Confidence in and efficacy of individual skills also increased, as did cultural knowledge,

Spanish language competence, pride in cultural heritage, and school attendance and behavioral records.

Another cooperative learning program designed to make entry to and success in high-status literacy courses more accessible to poor, urban students of color is the Advancement Via Individual Determination (AVID) Project (AVID, n.d.; Mehan, Hubbard, Lintz, & Villanueva, 1994; Mehan et al., 1996; Swanson et al., 1995; Watt, Johnston, Huerta, Mendiola, & Alkan, 2008; Watt, Powell, & Mendiola, 2004; Watt, Powell, Mendiola, & Cossio, 2006). It grew out of one English teacher's concerns (at Clairemont High School in San Diego County) in 1980 for the academic plight of Latino and African American urban students bused to her school. They were not assigned to the kinds of courses, or achieving at levels, that would gain them entry into California's leading colleges and universities. This teacher persuaded 30 of these students, with grade point averages (GPAs) of 1.5 to 2.5, to enroll in academically rigorous courses for which they had no prior preparation. The intent was to teach them academic coping skills, improve their achievement levels through Advanced Placement course enrollments, achieve higher GPAs, and increase college attendance. These continue to be AVID's primary goals, although opportunities to participate in the program have been extended to include European Americans, Asians/Pacific Islanders, and Native Americans, and students with a wider range of performance levels. However, Latino and African Americans who are middle-level and low achievers are still the dominant participants. AVID has grown from one class of one subject (high school English) in one school to a widely used program in many subjects and in numerous school districts. As of the 2016–2017 school year, there were 6,200 elementary, secondary, and higher education AVID programs through the United States. (avid.org).

Pedagogically, AVID practices "untracking" by placing low- and middle-income, low-achieving students in college preparatory biology, algebra, English, and foreign language courses with middle-class, high-achieving European Americans (Mehan et al., 1996). Initially, the participants also enroll in an elective college readiness class that meets daily throughout the school year. Peer and college tutors work with them in study groups and individually to reach levels of academic achievement that meet college expectations. Trained teachers instruct the students in lessons from the Maximum Competency Materials developed specifically for AVID. College instructors of first-year survey courses teach mini-lessons to acclimate them to college-level academic work. The participants also receive lessons in note-taking, study skills, test-taking, time management, preparation for college entrance/placement and SAT exams, effective textbook reading, library skills, and preparing college admission and financial applications. They are expected and taught how to work collaboratively, build on one another's strengths, engage in inquiry methods of academic problem-solving, and develop an ethos of success. Cooperative learning is used to teach students to take responsibility for their own and one another's academic success, and to improve their listening, thinking, speaking, and writing skills. In these learning situations, teachers act as coaches and facilitators (AVID, n.d.; Mehan et al., 1994, 1996; Swanson et al., 1995; Watt, Johnston, et al., 2008; Watt et al., 2004, 2006). Many of these operational features continue to be foundational aspects of AVID (Matthews, 2015; Parker, Eliot, & Tart, 2013; Pugh & Tschannen-Moran, 2016). For example, after almost 40 years of existence, AVID's goal is still to ensure that all students, and most especially those often marginalized and least served, are well prepared for college and success in a global society (avid.org).

The AVID staff and coordinators contend that student placements and academic instruction alone are not sufficient to realize the project's achievement goals. A network of personal supports, or what Mehan and associates (1996) called "social scaffolding," has been developed to complement the instructional interventions. These supports are reduced gradually as the students become more personally competent and academically self-sufficient. Specific aspects of this scaffolding include training in thinking critically and talking analytically about learning problems; developing a sense of camaraderie and community; teaching the social knowledge and skills needed to operate effectively in the school culture; and encouraging students to display identifying markers that link them to the AVID program, such as spending time in a specially designated classroom, using notebooks decorated with an AVID logo, and wearing badges of distinction. The staff act as academic, social, and personal advocates for the participating students while they are in high school, and serve as mediators or liaisons for them between high school and college. In other words, this program explicitly teaches low-income, linguistically and ethnically different students the *cultural and social capital* that leads to school success that middle- and upper-class students learn implicitly at home (Matthews, 2015; Mehan et al., 1994, 1996; Pugh & Tschannen-Moran, 2016; Swanson et al., 1995; Watt, Johnston, et al., 2008; Watt et al., 2004, 2006).

AVID has produced some impressive improvements in the academic achievement and learning climate of the participants. They vary somewhat by ethnic group, school level, and measurement variable, but more in degree than in kind. For example, the academic performance of recent Mexican immigrant students does not always show as much improvement as that of Native Americans, and the length of time involved in AVID across grades does not seem to affect African American students' school attendance positively or negatively (Pugh & Tschannen-Moran, 2016). However, overall, AVID produces positive results. These include benefits in performance on standardized tests, school attendance rates, GPAs, enrollment in algebra and Advanced Placement classes, and acceptance and enrollment in 4-year colleges. Students who participate in the program also point to the personal bonds, family-style atmosphere, institutional identity and affiliation, feelings of belonging, and intellectual and social mentoring as salient features that contribute to their academic success and overall feelings of intellectual empowerment or academic self-efficacy (Matthews, 2015; Parker, Eliot, & Tart, 2013; Pugh & Tschannen-Moran, 2016; Watt, Johnston, et al., 2008; Watt et al., 2004).

Mehan and associates (1996) identified yet another important achievement of AVID students. Latinos and African Americans develop the kind of linguistic styles, academic skills, and social behaviors needed to succeed in mainstream high schools and colleges *without sacrificing their cultural and ethnic identities*. They become effective "cultural border crossers" (p. 187) by engaging in academic pursuits with their AVID peers at school and recreational and social activities with their neighborhood friends after school. Because AVID uses students' own cultures and experiences as instructional resources, in conjunction with the professional expertise of different types of teachers, participants can better accomplish the "two interrelated goals [AVID has] found to be important in their academic achievement: maintaining their street identity while developing their academic identity" (Mehan et al., 1996, p. 209). This accomplishment is especially noteworthy because of observations such as those made by Fordham and Ogbu (1986) and Fordham (1993, 1996) that some students of color may sabotage their own academic achievement to avoid compromising their friendships with low-achieving peers or being accused of "acting White."

Effects of communal contexts and cooperative learning produced by AVID are multiracial in that the program activities and their analyses include students from different ethnic groups, including African Americans, Latino Americans, immigrants from different ethnic and national backgrounds, and European Americans. Other research that examines cooperation and communalism in teaching and learning on the school performance of African Americans only have been conducted by several different scholars (Albury, 1992; Boykin, 1994; Boykin & Bailey, 2000b; Boykin et al., 2004; Dill & Boykin, 2000). Albury's work is illustrative of this research and the results it produced. He asked low-income African and European Americans from the same neighborhoods to match 25 words with definitions. After a baseline score was established, the students were organized into three-member, same-race teams and assigned to one of four performance arrangements. Those in the "individual criteria" option were advised to study alone, and they would receive a reward if they got 15 of the 25 definitions correct. In the "interpersonal competitive" structure, students were told to study alone, and only the team that got the highest score would be rewarded. Students in the "group competition" setting were informed that their group was competing with others, and if they got the highest score of all the groups, they would be rewarded. The "communal" learning team members were not offered any rewards but were reminded of their shared community backgrounds and told that they needed to work together, share responsibility, and help one another so that their group could receive a better score. After studying the word list, the students were given a post-test. The European American students who studied under the "individual criteria" had the highest performance, followed by those in the "interpersonal competitive" learning context. African Americans in the "communal" study option performed best, followed by those in the "group competition" learning context.

Cooperative Learning Within Culturally Responsive Teaching

A very important message for culturally responsive teaching derives from these cooperative learning instructional programs and research projects. Cooperative learning works well for underachieving students of color on multiple levels. However, participation of all individual members of cooperative learning groups cannot be assumed to be of comparable quality, even when students have free choice in organizing the groups. Deliberate efforts are needed to ensure that this happens. Some teachers may try to accomplish this by unilaterally assigning students to groups, and tasks and roles to individuals within groups. This will not work for an obvious reason: If teachers make all the decisions in the groups, then these are neither student nor cooperative groups; they are the teachers' groups.

A more constructive course of action is for teachers and students to work together to develop criteria for selection of group members, performance accountability, and monitoring of the groups' process dynamics. Then students should be allowed maximum choice within these parameters. *This is structured rather than total free choice.* Concerted efforts should be undertaken to build ethnic, racial, gender, social, and ability diversity into the organization and task assignments of groups. Heterogeneous groups work best and are consistent with the underlying values and explicit goals of culturally responsive teaching. However, in some settings and for some learning tasks, groups of the same ethnicity and gender may be desirable—or unavoidable, given the demographics of some schools and classrooms.

This similarity can be compensated for somewhat by ensuring ability diversity within each group. Cohen and her colleagues (1995, 1997, 2004) offered some guidance for how this can be accomplished. They recommended using complex learning tasks that require multiple abilities for their successful completion. Group members can then complement one another's strengths and compensate for one another's weaknesses. H. Gardner's (2006) multiple intelligences, Barbe and Swassing's (1979) sensory modality strengths, and various ethnic learning style characteristics (Shade, 1997) are helpful guides for selecting members so that "multiple intellectual ability" is as much a feature of group membership as it is of the tasks to be learned. Another way to compensate somewhat for minimum diversity on variables important in forming cooperative groups is to change the composition of the groups often. Then, even groups of the same ethnicity can experience different ability configurations.

Although the pedagogical potential of cooperative learning is powerful, it can be aborted or distorted if students and teachers do not know how to work in groups. Teachers should not assume that students (or they themselves) automatically know how to do cooperative learning. Many have not had any prior experiences with it, or their experiences have been negative. Working in groups is a skill that has to be learned by both students and teachers. Initially, some students may resist it; others may use it as an excuse to avoid working and assuming their fair share of the learning responsibilities. Still others may be threatened about the possibility of not receiving due recognition and "credit" for their individual efforts. Some teachers may see this learning arrangement as threatening their authority and classroom control, consuming too much time, and being pedagogically inefficient because the students undoubtedly will not analyze topics exactly as the teachers would.

These issues can be negotiated and managed as students and teachers become more skilled in group dynamics. Some effective ways to diminish the doubts about cooperative learning (especially for students and teachers who prefer to learn in individual arrangements) are to (1) create a climate and ethos of valuing cooperation and community in the classroom that operates at all times, not just when cooperative tasks are performed; (2) start small and phase cooperative learning into instruction gradually on the levels of both frequency and magnitude; (3) allow time and provide opportunities for students and teachers to become comfortable with and skilled at cooperative learning; (4) initially use a combination of individual, small-group, and whole-class learning activities; and (5) use multidimensional tasks and be very clear in explaining these to students. The last strategy allows students to attach themselves to specific tasks within a group context according to learning style preferences and intellectual abilities, thereby satisfying their need for individual task responsibility and recognition.

ACTIVE AND AFFECTIVE ENGAGEMENT

Emotionality, variability, novelty, and active participation are important aspects of the learning styles of some ethnic groups and the ways in which they demonstrate what they know. For them, teaching and learning are more than cognitive and technical tasks; they are also active and emotional processes. Consequently, all these are critical features of culturally responsive teaching.

Boykin and his colleagues at Howard University have conducted a series of studies (see B. Allen & Boykin, 1992; Boykin, 1994; Boykin & Bailey, 2000b; Ellison et al., 2000) demonstrating the effects of teaching strategies that include these features on the achievement of African American students. Together they address several elements of traditional African American culture as well. The pertinent ones for this discussion are a vivacious and exuberant rather than a mechanistic approach to living; behavioral expressiveness that integrates movement, rhythm, music, and dance; verve, or high levels of energy and sensory stimulation; emphasis on emotions and feelings; communal and social connectedness that transcends individual privileges; spontaneity in thought and behavior; preference for oral and aural communication modalities; and social time orientations.

Varied Formats and Multiple Sensory Stimulation in Teaching

Boykin (1978, 1982), Tuck (1985), and Tuck and Boykin (1989) examined the effects of varied and intense sensory stimulation (verve) on the academic task performance of African American students. Their studies are grounded in the findings of previous researchers, such as Guttentag (1972), Guttentag and Ross (1972), Morgan (1990), and Shade (1994). They found that many African American students preferred learning situations that are active, participatory, emotionally engaging, and filled with visual and physical stimulation. For example, Guttentag and Ross found that when spontaneous and directed physical performances, or "acting out ideas," were used in teaching preschool African Americans, they learned basic concepts such as big–small, over–under, and above–below quickly, easily, and thoroughly.

Howard (1998) examined how culturally relevant pedagogical principles are manifested in the actual behaviors of elementary teachers of African American students during reading instruction. He observed a strong presence of movement, affectivity, and emotionality in the teaching behaviors of the African American teachers. "Dramatic performance" was a prominent feature of their teaching repertoires. One participant was especially adept at and consistent in dramatizing her teaching. Howard (1998) described her talents and techniques as follows:

> Louise used pedagogical practices filled with emotion and passion, and connected students to the learning process through her theatrical performances. . . . It was not unusual for [her] . . . to go into five-to-ten minute performances that included hopping around the classroom, raising her voice several octaves, acting out various characters, and becoming completely immersed in a scene, character, or story. (p. 133)

This dramatic performance style of teaching had positive effects on the learning motivation, interest, efforts, and achievement outcomes of students. Howard's perceptions were confirmed by the reactions and comments of students. Many followed Louise's example and encouragement to read with feeling, emotion, and conviction, and their recitations became "performances" as they acted out meanings of words and comprehension of reading passages. These performances provoked rich intellectual discourse as students asked numerous questions about the passages read and engaged in analyses of story plots, events, and role characterizations. Many of the students found Louise's teaching style funny, exciting, and engaging; it also made understanding and remembering what was taught much easier (Howard, 1998).

In their studies, Tuck and Boykin (1989) used experimental designs in which 3rd-, 4th-, and 6th-graders were exposed to problem-solving tasks presented in unvaried and varied formats. In the unvaried format, all tasks of one type were presented before any tasks of a different type were introduced. In the varied format, tasks were presented in random order, with no more than two of the same kind occurring sequentially. These studies also compared how students from home environments with different levels of sensory stimulation reacted to variations in learning task formats. The results revealed that (1) African American students perform significantly better in learning contexts and tasks with high variability; (2) children from home environments with high levels of sensory stimulation perform better in high-variability contexts, while children from homes with low levels of sensory stimulation perform the same across varied and unvaried task presentations; (3) European American students perform better than African Americans on constant-format tasks; (4) European and African Americans perform better on varied-format tasks, but the amount of improvement was substantially greater for African Americans; (5) the preference of African Americans for varied task formats is not a function of academic ability, since it was the same for both high and low achievers; and (6) African American students engage in more off-task and nonpersistent behaviors in unvaried learning formats than European Americans.

Using Music and Movement in Learning

Another teaching technique for improving the academic performance of African Americans is to incorporate rhythmic patterns, music, and movement into learning activities. This has been demonstrated by B. Allen (1987), B. Allen and Boykin (1991, 1992), and B. Allen and Butler (1996) in two experimental studies. Allen and Allen and Boykin examined the effects of music and movement on a picture-pairing task and analogical reasoning performed by low-income elementary school European and African Americans. In one experimental condition, the learning tasks were accompanied by music, physical actions, and hand-clapping, and music was played while the students were tested on these skills. In the other no music was present. The African American students performed much better to the accompaniment of music and movement, while the European Americans did better without. Informal classroom observations provided additional support for these findings. B. Allen and Boykin (1992) noticed that the African American students exhibited signs of restlessness and boredom during the learning sessions devoid of music and movement. Their eyes frequently wandered away from the task, and they attended to their hands and feet more than to the learning materials and tasks. These results led the researchers to conclude that the academic achievement of low-performing African American students improves significantly when their cultural experiences are incorporated into learning tasks (Allen & Boykin, 1992).

Further support of the positive effects of using rhythm, motion, and movement in teaching African American students comes from the experiences of teachers in actual classrooms. Four examples illustrate these strategies. One is of an urban middle school language arts teacher in Long Beach, California. She tells about the unsuccessful struggle of trying to teach grammar to academically "at-risk" African American students using traditional methods. To overcome these obstacles, she created a "rap" about the parts of speech, shared it with the students, and asked them for their input to improve the quality. Together, she and the students created a modified version. Using the rap, all the students learned the parts of speech with 100% accuracy with little effort, and they significantly improved their ability to use them correctly in both academic and social writing and speaking.

The second example is of a middle school math teacher in a poor suburban school district near St. Louis, Missouri. The situation involved teaching fractions to an 8th-grade class comprised entirely of African Americans. The teacher had been involved in a long sequence of unsuccessful efforts to get a particular female student to understand fractions based on eighths (e.g., 1/8, 4/8, 7/8, etc.). Apparently acting spontaneously and without forethought, he asked eight students, including the targeted one, to come to the front of the room and form a circle. He then demonstrated the various fractions, in relationship to the whole, by moving the students in and out of different configurations. The students were shifted around (actually moving about) several times to form 1/8, 2/8, 3/8, and so forth, with the student who was having difficulty understanding the concept being a part of all of the changing configurations. The teacher then pointed out what the formation was and its relation to the remainder of the whole. Thus, the targeted student could *see* that when she alone was moved from the circle, she was 1/8 (one of eight), while those remaining in the circle symbolized 7/8 (seven of eight).

Within a matter of minutes, and by physically acting out the ideas, the student had mastered the concept that had totally baffled her only a short time earlier. The other students who actively participated in the "performance," as well as the rest of the class, were captivated by the experience and were learning along with her. Once the targeted student's understanding became obvious, the teacher commented, "Now, you see what I mean." The student responded rather nonchalantly, "Of course! Why didn't you say it this way earlier?" Embedded in this situation is instructional compatibility with multiple aspects of African American culture and learning styles—movement, performance, dramatic flair, cooperative learning, group context, personalization, rhythm, emotionality, and holistic engagement.

The third illustration of how music and movement can be used to improve African American students' academic performance is a preschool class of 4-year-olds being taught vowel sounds. The children were accustomed to a set routine for their class. Upon arrival at school (the time varied somewhat for different students), the children went individually to a designated chalkboard and read to one of the co-teachers the posted current day, date, month, and year. This ritual was followed by work on individual study plans. After these were completed, the children gathered in a circle for large-group reading instruction. During a lesson on vowel sounds a group of four girls began a rhythmic pattern of hand-clapping, rhyming, and chanting for each vowel, which they repeated several times (somewhat like the chorus in a song). The other students applauded their performance, but the teacher made no comment about this student-initiated behavior. After the lesson ended she complimented the clapping students on how well they knew their letters and vowel sounds. What at first appeared to be totally impromptu was a technique (rhythm and rhyming) commonly used by this class, and the four students simply were applying it to this lesson, using their own creative style.

The fourth example comes from the Ron Clark Academy in Atlanta, Georgia. After thoroughly examining the 2008 Presidential election candidates and campaigns, a group of 6th- and 7th-grade mostly African American students culminated their study by writing a song in the tradition of hip-hop and rapping, and performing it to music and a dance routine. The content of the song, entitled "You Can Vote However You Like" (2008), addressed issues and differences between Barack Obama and John McCain, as well as Democrats and Republicans in general. It was written and performed, along with the dance routine, in the form of a challenge with half of the class endorsing McCain, and the other half promoting Obama. The general refrain of the song was:

> Obama on the left
> McCain on the right
> We can talk politics all night
> And you can vote however you like
> You can vote however you like, yeah

Part of the McCain endorsement stated:

> McCain's the best candidate
> With Palin his running mate

They will fight for gun rights, pro life
The conservative right
Our future is bright
Better economy in sight
And all the world will feel our military might

The Obama supporters responded with:

But McCain and Bush are real close right
They vote alike and keep it tight
Obama's new, and he's younger too
The Middle Class he will help you
He'll bring a change, he's got the brains
McCain and Bush are just the same
You are to blame, Iraq's a shame
Four more years would be insane.

In the process of doing this project the students combined rhythm, rhyme, music, and movement with intellectual inquiry and academic knowledge. They explained that the teaching technique was interesting, motivating, challenging, exciting, creative, and validating because it used motifs for learning familiar to them. It made the Presidential election campaign more meaningful and relevant to the students; taught them reading, writing, research, civic participation, and collaborative skills; and piqued their interests in politics generally.

SOCIAL AND EMOTIONAL LEARNING (SEL)

In the last 20 years or so, increasing attention has been given to the psycho-emotional challenges (such as stress, trauma, and bullying) of students, and the need to address them in the educational agendas along with academic development. The American Institutes for Research webpage included a recent statement that "fostering social and emotional well-being is a key component in improving conditions for learning" (air.org/topic/social-and-emotional-learning). Instructional proposals for responding are often classified as developing social and emotional competence. While this innovation is not targeted primarily at ethnically and racially diverse students, it can and should be accessible to them, and thus a major aspect of culturally responsive teaching. It is particularly apropos because of its primary targets for reform (social and emotional skill development) and its correlations with various forms of positive school performance. Research and experience documenting the psycho-emotional attacks that ethnic, racial, linguistic, and economic minority students habitually encounter (in the form of prejudices, discrimination, isolation, alienation, marginalization, and various inequities) attest to the need for their education to include social and emotional competence, along with academic and cultural.

The Collaborative for Academic, Social, and Emotional Learning (CASEL) described the intent of SEL programs as creating learning environments that meet the needs of students for belonging, safety, and community, and thereby provide ideal conditions for high-quality academic, relational, and personal wellness. In its 2015 guide to "Effective Social and Emotional Learning Programs—Middle and High School Edition," CASEL explained further that

> Social and emotional learning (SEL) is the process through which children and adults acquire and effectively apply the knowledge, attitudes, and skills necessary to understand and manage emotions, set and achieve positive goals, feel and show empathy for others, establish and maintain positive relationships, and make responsible decisions. Social and emotional skills are critical to being a good student, citizen, and worker, and many risky behaviors (e.g., drug use, violence, bullying, and dropping out) can be prevented or reduced when multi-year, integrated efforts are used to develop students' social and emotional skills. (secondaryguide.casel.org/casel-secondary-guide.pdf, p. 1)

Several research studies, reviews, and meta-analyses (for example, Brackett & Rivers, 2013; Brackett, Rivers, & Salovey, 2011; Durlak, Domitrovich, Weissberg, & Gullotta, 2015; Jones, Greenberg, & Crowley, 2015) produced similar results that validate the theoretical explanations of CASEL about the need for and effects of social and emotional learning. The findings are consistent across both locations (urban, suburban, and rural) and levels (elementary, middle, high school, and college) of education. They include:

- more positive attitudes toward self and others,
- enhanced self-efficacy, confidence, persistence, and empathy,
- better connections and commitment to schools,
- clearer sense of purpose,
- more positive social behaviors and relationships with peers and adults,
- reduced conduct problems and risk-taking behaviors,
- decreased emotional distress,
- improved test scores, grades, and school attendance,
- better overall mental health,
- increased likelihood of high school graduation, readiness for postsecondary education, career success, and family relationships,
- reduced criminal behavior, and
- more engaged citizenship.

Since these elements and effects of social and emotional learning have positive effects on academic performance, are valid dimensions of high-quality comprehensive education, and are the ultimate goals of culturally responsive teaching, the two interventions are interconnected. SEL also has a strong affinity with many of the aspects of culturally responsive caring described in Chapter 3. Some educational initiatives for Native American and African American students are included here to illustrate the integration of some elements of SEL into culturally responsive teaching that have been implied in earlier discussions.

SEL in Culturally Responsive Teaching for Native American Students

Some empirical support for how cultural compatibility responds to the social and emotional learning needs and improves the academic performance of Native American students is provided by Coggins, Williams, and Radin (1997) in their work with the Ojibwa Nation in northern Michigan. Their study of 19 families revealed that the identification of mothers with the traditional Native American values of sharing, other-centeredness, harmony with nature, noninterference, and extended family had positive effects on their children's academic and social functioning in school. Elementary school students from these family backgrounds performed well in reading, language arts, science, and math. Other studies have shown positive relationships between the retention of traditional Native American values and the academic success of Sioux college students (Huffman, Sill, & Brokenleg, 1986) as well as high school completion and academic achievement among Northern Cheyenne girls (Ward, 1994). Because of these results Coggins and associates recommended integrating cultural revitalization programs and learning activities for different Native American groups into routine educational experiences. Knowledge of traditional cultural values and heritages can be an important anchor for Native American students as they navigate their community and school cultures, expectations, responsibilities, and performances. Thus, being bicultural can facilitate academic achievement. These suggestions fit well within the purview of culturally responsive pedagogy.

Another study that substantiated the power of Native American-centric pedagogy to improve students' socioemotional competence and academic achievement was conducted by Deyhle (1995). She studied Navajo students in two high schools over 10 years—one was a reservation school and one was not. Contrary to the claims of some that performance will be lower in "racially isolated" schools populated by students of color, Deyhle observed the opposite. Students at the reservation school performed much better than those at the nonreservation school, as indicated by lower dropout rates, greater satisfaction with school, and stronger feelings of support from school personnel. Similar patterns were also apparent for the reservation students who attended the nonreservation school, compared with the students who lived in the town. Deyhle (1995) attributed these differences to the degree of cultural affiliation students had with their ethnic community and the amount of cultural integrity present in school programs and practices. She noted:

> The more academically successful Navajo students are more likely to be those who are firmly rooted in their Navajo community . . . are not alienated from their cultural values and who do not perceive themselves as inferior to the dominant group. . . . In contrast, those who are not academically successful are both estranged from the reservation community, and bitterly resent the racially polarized school context they face daily. (pp. 419–420)

The curricular and instructional practices of the Native American Community Academy (NACA) present other illustrations of how social and emotional learning are woven into culturally responsive teaching (McCarty & Lee, 2014). This is a public Native American-operated charter school in Albuquerque, NM, that serves middle and high school students. It applies a holistic approach to education that is consistent with Indigenous (Native American) cultural philosophies and psychological wellness. It focuses on developing students' intellectual, physical, emotional, social, and leadership competencies within community and cultural contexts. These priorities are anchored in the core values of respect, responsibility, community, service, culture, and perseverance, which reflect those of the different tribal communities of NACA students, They are intended to develop strong, capable, committed, and autonomous (or sovereign) culturally sustaining individuals and communities. At a fundamental level these instructional orientations and practices promote the overall well-being and competence of students, in part to counter psychoemotional and structural residues of colonizing influences that are often internalized by Native American youth (Klug, 2012; McCarty & Lee, 2014).

Native American heritage colleges demonstrate how culturally responsive teaching can be implemented in higher education. One of their major goals is to create culturally embedded climates for learning, and to promote cultural reconciliation, maintenance, and pride as part of educational excellence for their students. In doing so they integrate social, emotional, cultural, and academic knowledge and skill development. Haskell Indian Nations University (HINU) in Kansas is a compelling example of how this is done. It is a 4-year intertribal institution for Native Americans and Alaskan Natives, and is one of the 34 federally recognized tribal colleges and universities (TCUs) located in 14 (mostly Midwestern and Southwestern) states that serve over 30,000 students (tribalcollegejournal.org/map-of-tribal-colleges/). Although HINU has been in existence since 1884, when it began as an elementary school with 22 students, it transitioned into a high school and then a junior college before officially gaining its current status as a university in 1993. It now enrolls over 1000 students per term from federally recognized nations from across the United States. It is committed to empowering Native American and Alaskan Native students for leadership and service to Native communities and the world. This is accomplished by promoting Native sovereignty and self-determination through culturally based holistic learning environments and programs that uphold traditional Native American and Alaskan Native cultural values of respect, cooperation, honesty, and communal responsibility (haskell.edu; McCarty, 2002). The programs of study offered at Haskell combine "the intellectual, physical, social, emotional, and spiritual components of American Indian life into a unique university experience." Part of this uniqueness is that all students are required to take courses in American Indian/Alaskan Native citizenship and contemporary issues, along with general liberal arts and the requirements of specific degrees (education, business, sociology, psychology, computer science, etc.) typically offered by universities. The "cultural citizenship" curriculum includes Environmental Protection in Indian Country; Indian Law and Legislation; Indian Real Estate and Land Management; Fundamentals of Tribal Sovereignty; Tribal Resources and Economic Development; Cherokee and Choctaw Languages; and courses in American Indian poetry, art, film, history, rhetoric, and literature (haskell.edu). These courses are designed to develop cultural knowledge; a strong sense of cultural kinship and respect; more genuine ethnic and cultural pride; and a commitment to, and related skills for, cultural community service. Formally and informally, Haskell cultivates an ambience of authentic "Indianness" through its curriculum, system of supports for students, recreational and social events, and faculty and staff relationships with students. However, little information is available on the actual instructional strategies used in classes or the specific effects of these learning experiences on student achievement while in college and beyond.

SEL in Culturally Responsive Teaching for African American Students

Supporters of African American-centric programs suggest they are needed because conventional education does little if anything to teach African Americans their history and culture. This void causes students to be culturally dislocated or disaffiliated, which can interfere with academic achievement and social, psychological, and emotional well-being. Molefi Asante (1991/1992), a leading Afrocentrist, asserted that students "may learn, but, without cultural grounding, the learning will have destroyed their sense of place" and personal integrity (p. 30). Asa Hilliard (1991/1992), another well-known proponent of Afrocentricism, proposed that "schools must . . . accept the fact that some racial and ethnic groups have endured hundreds of years of systematic defamation that has distorted, denied, and deformed the truth of their cultural and historical reality" (p. 14). Conversely, when students are centered in their own cultural heritages and performance styles, they are more motivated to learn, perform better academically, and are better disciplined (Asante, 1991/1992, 2014; Sampson & Garrison-Wade, 2011; Sheffield, 2014).

Regardless of geographic location, school level (elementary or middle), type (entire school or classes within schools), or targeted population (male, female, or both), African American-centered (or Afrocentric) educational programs have a three-part instructional agenda. They aim to improve academic achievement in basic literacy (reading, writing), intellectual (critical thinking, problem-solving), and subject-specific (history, calculus, biology) skills; contribute to the cultural socialization of students by teaching African and African American history, heritage, and culture; and facilitate individual development through improved self-concepts, self-expression, self-reliance, and self-confidence (J. Foster, 1994; Lipman, 1995; Watson & Smitherman, 1996). A climate for learning is created in which students are validated, held in high esteem, expected to achieve high performance, and supported in meeting expectations. The principal of the Robert W. Coleman School in Baltimore called this ambiance a "conspiracy of caring" (Lipman, 1995). Collin Williams (personal interview) spoke similarly about the African American Academy in Seattle, which he described as a "a place of success, where students are not put down, and there is no blame or shame at being African American."

Afrocentric programs for elementary and secondary school students produce improvements on all measures of achievement, and the students' performance is generally better than that of their peers in other schools within their districts. Among these achievements are: higher scores on standardized tests and GPAs; better attendance records; lower disciplinary infractions, detentions, and suspensions; increased feelings of academic capability and confidence; stronger personal self-concepts; and more frequent acknowledgment of being genuinely respected, supported, and cared for by teachers (Asante, 2014; Hudley, 1995; Rayford, 2014; Sheffield, 2014).

Afrocentric, culturally responsive, and social and emotional teaching and learning for African American students in higher education is done most broadly and effectively by historically Black colleges and universities (HBCUs). HBCUs have a long legacy of achieving success for the students who attend them. They combine academic and disciplinary knowledge with cultural competence, civic responsibility, leadership development, modeling and mentoring, and personal caring. I asked 10 graduates of HBCUs to explain why these institutions are successful in educating African Americans from their own personal experiences and perspectives. They had attended a wide range of colleges in different states at different times, and pursued different areas of study. However, there were some common themes across institutional, temporal, and individual contexts. All 10 individuals agreed that HBCUs are diligent about meeting the *multidimensional needs* of students, by promoting positive growth in intellectual abilities, personal self-esteem, psychosocial development, cultural knowledge, community service, and economic productivity. Their responses reaffirmed the findings reported by Fleming (1991) and Gasman and Tudico (2008), as well as proposals for education that is culturally sustaining for African Americans and other students of color (Paris, 2012; Paris & Alim, 2014, 2017). Comments from six of these HBCU alumni explain why and how these objectives were accomplished by their respective colleges and universities.

Jesolyn recalled that she and her peers at Tougaloo were reminded repeatedly by their teachers that they were intellectually the "cream of the crop" (i.e., the academic vanguard) and as such they were expected to contribute to the betterment of local, state, and national African American communities and causes. They were taught that responsibilities come with their intellectual and educational privilege as college students. These involved doing something to help less fortunate African Americans, such as volunteer community service and participating in political activism. The moral edict underlying this teaching at different HBCUs, according to Jesolyn, Terri (at Spelman), and Ayana (at Spelman) is, "To whom much is given, from those much is expected."

Tanisha did not take any specific courses in African American history and culture at Grambling University, but she was immersed in an environment where "Black people counted. Everything was focused on my race, my people, and how I could contribute to them. I never felt ashamed of being Black. Grambling helped me to see, know, and accept myself." This was a critical form of cultural capital for Tanisha because she arrived at college with ambivalent feelings about her ethnicity and limited formal knowledge of African American heritage. Her experience at Grambling pulled Tanisha out of these feelings of ambiguity, uncertainty, and ignorance, and "hooked her up" with her own culture, ethnicity, and other African Americans as she learned the knowledge required for her selected area of academic study.

Jesolyn's cultural learning was more explicit at Tougaloo. African American heritage and contributions to the state of Mississippi and the national civil rights movement were stressed. All students were required to take courses in African American history and culture. Ayana and her peers at Spelman received explicit instruction in African American culture as well. She recalled a yearlong required course on African Diaspora in the World. It included examinations of interactions between Black men and women, and a variety of readings about African and African American histories, cultures, experiences, and societies. This learning experience validated Ayana's ethnic and cultural identities, and helped her develop a strong sense of self, which relieved her from "having to be self-defensive without any protection" in mainstream societal settings.

Terri did not experience that particular course at Spelman (having attended several years before Ayana), but African American culture was still a vital and pervasive feature of her education. She remembered learning about African American women in the Bible and historical individuals who were strong social activists, and being reminded to "always act like a lady because you never know who might be on campus" (and there were always famous folks and former Spelman women dropping in). She added that "we had access to high-profile and accomplished African American women and other individuals in all fields of study who were focused on doing significant things. It was instilled in us that we must live up to and carry on this legacy of success." Shedrick had similar expectations, teachings, and encounters at Morehouse. Being a "Morehouse Man" was a badge of honor, and everyone was taught to give the identity the respect it deserved by demonstrating high levels of academic accomplishment, social decorum, impeccable public personae, and active political engagement. Ed remembered fondly how Southern University socialized him and other students to look, behave, and dress in a manner becoming African American college men and women.

All HBCUs are not equally effective or remembered as fondly. But they do an admirable job in educating African American students in multiple ways, including academically, culturally, personally, and civically. Many students are able to receive college degrees who would not be admitted to or succeed at predominantly White institutions (PWIs). After graduation many go on to advanced degrees at prestigious PWIs, and highly esteemed careers and influential positions in the African American and national communities. The comments of the alumni quoted here speak persuasively to J. Davis's (1998) contention that HBCUs are sites for explicitly teaching African American cultural and social capital because the students acquire cultural knowledge, establish ethnic community connections, and adhere to culturally acceptable lifestyles and behaviors, along with academic achievement. They also are illustrative of proposals scholars make for the education of students of color to be culturally sustaining—that is, to preserve and perpetuate the practices, languages, literacies, legacies, and ways of being of their cultures and communities as a means of promoting educational justice, equity, and excellence (Paris, 2012; Paris & Alim, 2014, 2017).

CONCLUSION

Several important general instructional messages emerge from the specific culturally responsive programs and practices discussed in this chapter. The praxis of culturally responsive teaching confirms the theory. When instructional processes are congruent with the cultural orientations, experiences, and learning styles of marginalized African, Asian, European, Latino, and Native American students, their school achievement improves significantly.

This success is most evident in learning spaces where culturally relevant content, teacher attitudes and expectations, and instructional actions converge.

Different culturally responsive programs and practices have similar positive overall achievement effects for students from different ethnic groups. Furthermore, better academic achievement occurs when different types of learning (e.g., intellectual, social, emotional, psychological, cultural, political, ethical) take place at the same time. This explains why ethnically, racially, and culturally diverse students involved in these experiences speak with as much praise about acquiring cultural knowledge, feelings of cultural community, and social and emotional competence, and developing self-respect and ethnic pride, as they do about increasing academic performance. Nurturing the total human condition of diverse students is the mission and the ultimate indicator of the success of culturally responsive teaching.

The following specific effects of teaching to and through ethnic, racial, and cultural diversity (sometimes called ethnic studies–ES; culturally relevant education–CRE; culturally relevant pedagogy–CRP) are derived from original studies, reviews, and synthesis of research and scholarship by Aronson and Laughter (2016), Dee (2015), Dee and Penner (2017), Hanley and Noblit (2009), Sleeter (2011), and Tintiangco-Cubales et al. (2015). They examined curriculum and teaching in different educational levels (elementary, secondary, and college), school settings (mostly urban), ethnic groups (single and multiple), and subjects (one and several). The results indicate

- higher grades and standardized test scores
- increased student interest, excitement, engagement, motivation, comfort, and confidence in learning
- improved "democratic outcomes," such as cross-racial relations, interest and involvement in social justice initiatives, and concerns about inequities
- increased commitment to cooperative learning
- classroom environments more conducive to learning and feelings of belonging for culturally diverse students
- more consciousness of bias in subject-matter content and knowledge typically taught in school
- increased knowledge of the cultures and contributions of peoples of color to society, their own communities, and humanity
- increased understanding of the individual and communal agency of individuals and groups of color throughout history
- classrooms that are "safe places" to pursue alternative pathways to teaching and learning
- heightened creativity for both students and teachers
- positive effects on behavioral performance, such as fewer school and classroom distractions, higher attendance rates, and more attention and efforts given to assignments

- more opportunities for cross-racial and intercultural interactions, which are positively related to higher levels of general knowledge, critical thinking, problem-solving, and perspective taking
- improved student self-esteem, self-confidence, self-efficacy, identity development, political activism, civic responsibility, community participation, and overall social engagement

These general effects of culturally responsive teaching, along with ones specific to subjects, school location, and student population, are further validated by commentaries from researchers and scholars. A few excerpts are provided here to illustrate these verifications. Hanley and Noblit observed that "In-school and out-of-school programs can be designed to develop [academic success and resilience] and to more generally promote the wider project of racial uplift in ALANA [African, Latino, Asian, and Native American] communities. The approach will need to be systemic and directly address issues of racism and deficit thinking" (2009, p. 11). Ruggs and Hebi (2012) associated perspective-taking among students of different racial, cultural, and gender backgrounds with increasing feelings of equality with peers, which, in turn improves self-confidence, particularly in domains in which students may be stereotyped. Sleeter highlighted the consistency of positive effects of different variations of culturally responsive teaching across contexts. She noted that "different research methodologies . . . involving students at middle school through university levels, in different regions of the U.S. consistently find a relationship between academic achievement, high level of awareness of race and racism, and positive identification with one's own racial group" (2011, p. 8). Aronson and Laughter (2016) explicated benefits of culturally responsive education for teachers as well as students—a needed and worthy addition to the discourse because teacher benefits tend to be assumed or implied rather than made explicit. Research by Zirkel (2008) revealed that academic and relational outcomes of cultural diversity education are interwoven, such that improvements in one produce improvements in the other. This research result validates the idea that quality education for ethnically and racially diverse students involves more than academics. Dee and Penner (2017) concluded their study of a 9th-grade culture-centered program that involved Asian, Latino, and African American at-risk students with the observation that the

> findings provide a compelling confirmation of the extensive literature that has emphasized the capacity of CRP [culturally relevant pedagogy] to unlock the educational potential of historically marginalized students . . . our results are consistent with other theoretical frames as well. In particular, . . . social psychology has shown that quite modest interventions that buffer students against stereotype threat can . . . dramatically improve student outcomes. (p. 158)

Students of color come to school having already mastered many cultural skills and ways of knowing. To the extent that teaching builds on these capabilities, academic success will result. In other words, *the successful succeed*. This principle suggests the need for educators to redirect their orientation to teaching students of color who are not doing well in school away from the "don't have, can't do" orientation toward a "do have, can do" growth mindset—that is, to engage in asset- rather than pathology-based teaching and learning. Translating it into instructional action begins with accepting the cultural knowledge and skills of ethnically diverse students as valuable teaching–learning resources, and using them as scaffolds or bridges to academic achievement. This has been done successfully by the Kamehameha Early Elementary Program for Native Hawaiians; the Webster Groves Writing Project, the Calculus Project, and HBCUs for African Americans; the Escalante Math Program and AVID for Latinos; the Rough Rock Demonstration School and tribal colleges for Native Americans and Alaska Natives; and the Foxfire Project for poor rural European Americans. Other instructional interventions should follow suit.

A single area of achievement (such as academic performance) is maximized when multiple areas of learning (e.g., academic, cultural, personal, social, civic) are facilitated at once and different teaching techniques are used, all within the cultural contexts of various ethnic groups. This applies to skills within subjects, different subjects across school curricula, and different levels of schooling. The comprehension of factual information, problem identification, and critical and moral reflection complement one another. Reading improves when writing skills are taught at the same time. Mathematical calculations make more sense when they are embedded in problem-solving exercises about issues relevant to the life experiences of different ethnic groups. Mastery of academic skills is easier when social, emotional, and psychological learning is considered as well. Thus, multiplicity and diversity are the mainstays of culturally responsive teaching and the venues for enhanced academic achievement for students of color.

Culturally responsive instructional practices unveil some solutions to the seemingly unsolvable mystery of the perpetual underachievement of marginalized students of color. They are not being taught in school like they learn in their cultural communities. This discontinuity interrupts their mental schemata and makes academic learning harder to achieve. Filtering teaching through the cultural lens of Native, Latino, African, and Asian American students can lead to much greater school success. These students deserve nothing less. The programs and practices discussed in this chapter point to some instructional techniques that work and provide directions for others to follow. It remains for more teachers to heed the clarion call and approach teaching with diligence, devotion, imagination, knowledge, will, and skill based in cultural responsiveness to make educational equity and excellence realities for students of color. Teaching does not have to replicate the cultural features and procedures of different ethnic groups in their entirety. But it should *begin* with being informed by and reflective of them. After African, Asian, Latino, and Native American students have been affirmed and grounded in their respective cultural ways of knowing, they are then better able to explore new knowledge horizons and different avenues of learning without their human dignity and cultural identities being demeaned or compromised.

PRACTICE POSSIBILITIES

There are many ways for teachers to initiate, revise, revitalize, and validate culturally responsive teaching. The suggestions offered here are some helpful hints for how to do so. They include ideas for both teachers' personal and instructional engagements. Additional suggestions and supports can be derived from the professional journals listed below, which concentrate primarily on educating ethnically and racially diverse students and explicating culture-centered teaching and learning.

Ideas for Imagining and Actualizing Culturally Responsive Instruction

(Based on ideas derived from nea.org/home/16711.htm; middleweb.com/9471/culturally-responsive-classrooms/; and ascd.org/publications/books/107003/chapters/Diverse-Teaching-Strategies-for-Diverse-Learners.aspx)

Engage in self-monitoring, self-regulation, and self-reflection: Start by asking yourself questions such as: Do I know the cultural backgrounds of my students? Do I integrate resources from their cultures into my lessons? Do I consistently begin my lessons with what students already know from their homes, communities, cultures, and schools? Do I understand the differences between academic language and my students' social language, and do I find ways to bridge the two?

Don't depend on old assumptions: Encourage students to talk about elements of their cultures, both positive and negative, and thus remove the onus from you to speculate about or ask questions that you fear might be too probing. Have students describe what they enjoy doing outside of school, with whom they spend most of their time, and whom they admire. Having children elaborate on their culture is a shortcut to learning more about them, while they practice academic skills.

Get out of the classroom and go beyond the textbook: Parent-teacher meetings are valuable tools, but the culturally responsive teacher moves beyond the traditional framework for such get-togethers, considering, for example, the schedule of parents working more than one job. Find out if your district has translators or cultural interpreters available and invite them to attend. Or consider meeting with parents at a location in their community, and attend community cultural events.

Begin teaching culturally diverse students of color using what they already know: Some general theories of good teaching, such as using prior frames of reference, existing knowledge schemas, and scaffolding, are applicable to ethnically, racially, and culturally diverse contexts. Also consider the experiences of minority and low-income students as valuable resources, assets, or building blocks for cultural preservation, individual agency and resilience, and academic achievement.

Use the work of predecessors, colleagues, and allies: Don't try to reinvent the wheel when it comes to selecting appropriate culturally responsive content and instructional strategies. Reach out to those who have come before you to share their strategies for successfully teaching ethnic minority students.

Recognize that you are not alone: Identify and connect with some individuals, agencies, and organizations that regularly promote culturally responsive teaching ideas, resources, and actions.

Modify existing curriculum content and instructional strategies: Culturally responsive lessons available in books and online can often be adapted to address different purposes, cultures, grades, and subjects.

Appreciate and accommodate similarities and differences among students' cultures: Identify these differences in a positive manner. Social skills such as respect and cross-cultural understanding can be modeled, taught, prompted, and reinforced in your teaching.

Build relationships with students: Develop an understanding of students' lives outside of school. This helps to increase the relevance of lessons and make examples more meaningful.

Focus on the ways students learn and identify their task orientations: Once students' orientations are known, learning tasks can be designed that take them into account. Provide time for students to prepare, offer advance organizers, and announce how much time will be given for preparation and when the task will begin. This is a positive way to honor diverse students' rhythms of work and needs for preparation, rituals, and customs.

Teach students to shift behaviors according to settings or contexts: We all behave differently in different settings and for different purposes. Therefore, teach students behaviors appropriate for different contexts such as home, community, school, and various relationships.

Be deliberate and intentional in teaching about ethnically, racially, culturally, and socially diverse issues and experiences: Students need guidance and assistance in dealing with cultural diversity, racism, and inequities. Do not avoid these issues or sanitize them. With careful analysis of these issues students can develop resilience and agency for social change.

Embed teaching about ethnic and cultural diversity into the rituals, routines, and subjects regularly taught and practiced in schools: Avoid relegating the study of race, ethnicity, cultural diversity, and associated issues to special times and events, or addendums to academic content and skills. Instead, incorporate multicultural perspectives and multiethnic experiences into regularly taught subjects such as math, literacy, science, social studies, and computer science, and classroom protocols.

Teach cultural consciousness and critical analysis of beliefs and assumptions about self and others: Teachers and students need to understand why they are cultural beings, and how their cultural socialization and orientations are manifested in values, attitudes, and behaviors toward self and others.

Provide structured and guided activities for students to engage in cross-cultural and interracial interactions: Students need to practice these engagements, along with acquiring academic knowledge about different ethnic, racial, cultural, and social groups, events, perspectives, and experiences. These interactions can be actual and vicarious, and can be facilitated through person-to-person interactions, literature, film, cultural exchanges, online connections, and student-conducted action research.

Habitually use multiple perspectives, resources, and methodologies that are multiethnic and multicultural to teach general academic and subject-specific knowledge and skills: Culturally diverse examples, scenarios, and vignettes used to illuminate the meaning of abstract academic ideas, concepts, and skills improve competence and comprehension for students from different ethnic, racial, socioeconomic, gender, and national origin groups.

Use symbols, signs, images, and icons in the classroom to personify value commitments to cultural diversity, social justice, equality, and anti-oppression: Sometimes these ideas, values, and beliefs need to be visualized for students at various levels of learning. This can be done through classroom decorations, book and artifact collections, proverbial statements, and teacher modeling.

Differentiate instructional strategies to accommodate culturally diverse learning styles: Research studies have produced salient attributes of learning styles common among African, Asian, European, Latino, and Native American students that reflect elements of their cultural heritages. Match teaching practices to these learning styles.

Teach students at all levels of learning to embrace and respect their differences (and one another's) as a natural part of their humanity: Dealing with cultural diversity and maximizing different students' individual potential (as so many educators claim is their intention) are interrelated, since culture and difference are inherent to the human condition. Thus, difference should be considered as an individual asset and a human normalcy.

Use culturally diverse curricula and instructional materials that include the historical and contemporary heritages, experiences, and contributions of various ethnic groups and individuals: All students need to acquire more knowledge about and appreciation of their own and other ethnic groups' contributions to U.S. society and humankind. Such knowledge contributes to developing self-pride; ethnic, racial, and gender group uplift; and a more accurate understanding of the synergistic construction of U.S. history, life, and culture.

Teach students knowledge, skills, and the will to be change agents for equity, social justice, human dignity, and sociopolitical, cultural, and personal empowerment: Knowledge of and respect for ethnic, racial, and cultural diversity are necessary but not sufficient. Students need to learn how to engage systematically and persistently in transformative actions that personify these values and intentions.

Create physical, intellectual, and relational learning environments that are culturally congruent for ethnically, racially, socially, and linguistically diverse students: Students learn better in classroom settings that are caring, supportive, and reflective of who they are. These psycho-emotional contexts generate more energy, efforts, and outcomes in academic task performance as well.

Capitalize on ethnically and racially diverse students' cultures, languages, and experiences: Even very young children have broad repertoires of social and cultural capital, or funds of knowledge, that are very functional outside of schools if not within. These "contextual competencies" can be scaffolded in school for academic purposes, and students can be authors and authorities on themselves. That is, they can be teachers, too!

Use innovative and multiple forms of performance assessment: Just as culturally diverse students have different learning styles, they demonstrate competence in different ways, too. Therefore, a wide variety of verbal, written, visual, and action tools and techniques should be used to diagnose their needs and access the quality and levels of their learning accomplishments. Since high-quality learning for culturally diverse students includes more than academics, so should indicators of achievement.

Journals about Race, Diversity, and Equity in Education

Asia Pacific Education Review
Asia Pacific Journal of Education

Asia-Pacific Journal of Teacher Education
Association of Mexican American Educators Journal
Education and Urban Society
Gender and Education
Intercultural Education
International Journal of Inclusive Education
International Journal of Multicultural Education
Journal of Latina/o Psychology
Journal of Multicultural Counseling and Development
Journal of Multilingual and Multicultural Development
Journal of Negro Education
Journal of Urban Learning, Teaching, and Research
Multicultural Education
Multicultural Education Review
Multicultural Learning and Teaching
Multicultural Perspectives
Race, Ethnicity and Education
Tribal College Journal of American Indian Higher Education
Urban Education
Urban Review: Issues and Ideas in Public Education

CHAPTER 7

A Personal Case of Culturally Responsive Teaching Praxis

"Modeling in culturally responsive teaching is a moral imperative and a professional necessity."

Thus far I have functioned primarily as an "offstage" narrator for the story of culturally responsive teaching that was constructed in Chapters 1–6. I shift roles for this chapter. I will now step onto center stage to share some personal experiences. They are about some of the characteristics of my own teaching beliefs and practices that I think exemplify culturally responsive praxis. The story these experiences convey is incomplete in that it illustrates some but not all principles of culturally responsive teaching, and my conceptual understanding, multicultural knowledge, and instructional capabilities are continuing to grow.

INTRODUCTION

Invariably, teaching is a personal endeavor, and what it looks and feels like in actual practice is best conveyed through personal stories. These stories transmit an affective ambiance and level of clarity that defy even the best of abstract or conceptual descriptions. They inform, enforce, and encourage with a potency that is impossible in reporting research, explaining theory, and summarizing collective practices. Sherrelle Walker (2012) says that humans are storytelling creatures who habitually use stories to transmit information, share histories, and teach important messages. In the spirit of this human habit, the mini-stories of my own culturally responsive teaching presented in this chapter are intended to embody culturally responsive teaching more in action than idea, in practice rather than in theory. And the focus is more on my instructional processes than on students' performance products.

Personal stories of practice move understanding of concepts and principles beyond cognition to embrace the psychoemotional energy, the exuberance, and the ethical convictions that are embedded in all good teaching. As Joseph Catapano (n.d.) explained, "There's something about stories that stick with us. Something about an organized narrative teaching strategy that serves as a unique kind of glue, lingering with us long after the facts and formulas fade away." He elaborates further that stories in teaching

> humanize learning. [They] offer us the opportunity to connect to like-minded characters, or see the world literally from within someone else's skin. Stories touch our emotions and make us laugh, cry, fear, and get angry. . . . Plus, no matter how organized or detailed a textbook might be, there's something about the shape of a narrative—the exposition, the problem, the quest for a solution, the resolution—that resonates with our mental makeup.

The power of the personal story, then, provides the reasons for this chapter. While other discussions have provided a wealth of varied information about culturally responsive teaching, they have looked at it largely from the outside. This discussion provides some glimpses of it from the inside out. In other words, it takes the reader into the *dynamics of teaching*, where the essence of culturally responsive pedagogy lies. Hopefully my stories add that "glue" Catapano talks about that will cause culturally responsive teaching to "linger on" indefinitely in the minds, hearts, values, beliefs, and actions of classroom teachers and other educators.

The ideas and actions described constitute, in part, my *pedagogical creed* for teaching ethnically, racially, and culturally diverse students. Concern for marginalized students of color in pre-K–12 schools, such as African, Asian, Latino, and Native Americans, is the primary motivating force for my teaching ideas and actions. These beliefs and their concomitant behaviors (or close approximations) are appropriate for the preparation of prospective and practicing teachers in professional development programs, and for improving equity of learning experiences and achievement outcomes in their classroom instruction. Teachers at all educational levels should create, clarify, and articulate clearly defined beliefs about cultural diversity generally and in education specifically because personal beliefs drive instructional behaviors. If teachers have positive beliefs about ethnic and cultural diversity, they will act in accordance with them, and vice versa. Therefore, beliefs are critical components of culturally responsive teaching.

My students are predominantly European Americans, especially those in teacher education. However, my graduate students include a wide variety of ethnic groups, both nationally and internationally. They are Taiwanese, Chinese, and Chinese Americans, Japanese and Japanese Americans, Africans, Caribbeans, and African Americans, Filipino Americans, Latino Americans, Korean and Korean Americans, Cambodian Americans, Jordanian and Greek citizens, biracial and biethnic Americans, and European Americans. The students also are in various stages of their professional education. Some are enrolled in teacher certification programs. Others are experienced teachers who are returning to school for master's and doctoral degrees. Of these, some will remain in classroom teaching, some will assume administrative positions in K–12 education, and others will become college professors. Many of my students are interested in cultural diversity and social justice issues. They also are concerned about how they can teach differently to improve the learning outcomes for students from a variety of ethnic, cultural, social, and linguistic backgrounds. Consequently, culturally responsive teaching is an important item on their professional agendas. It is for me, too, as well as modeling the methods and messages in my own teaching that I expect of others.

BEING SUPPORTIVE AND FACILITATIVE

Whether in formal classroom settings, advising situations, or informal contacts on and off campus, I try to be supportive and facilitative of students' intellectual, personal, social, ethnic, cultural, and pedagogical development. Students working on assignments often want to know, "What exactly do you want us to do?" When I respond, "I don't know other than for you to put forth genuine effort, do your best, and address all aspects of the assigned tasks within the context of our class goals, readings, and discussions," they are puzzled. My assignments never deal with merely reproducing factual information; they focus on application, analysis, interpretation, and transfer of knowledge. For instance, my students are not asked to learn about the cultural values and stages of ethnic identity development among Latino, Asian, Native, and African Americans as an end in itself. They are to derive from this knowledge implications for improving the quality of teaching and learning. While I do not have a single specific end product in mind that everyone is to accomplish, I do provide the students with parameters within which they are expected to perform. For example, I might specify several questions to guide their analyses, such as the number and types of learning activities they need to develop in creating simulated lesson plans. Or I will identify the categories of information (e.g., person, event, place, image, etc.) to be included in an observation log on "cultural diversity in our daily lives" and the kind of information that should accompany each entry (such as multiethnic samples, descriptions, cultural traits the observations illustrate, and how the observations can be used to teach what).

Even my doctoral students initially want me to tell them what to do for their research of issues of ethnic and cultural diversity in education. They often ask, "What should I do?" My response is, "This is your degree and/or dissertation, so the question is not for me to tell you what to do, but to help you do what you want to do to the best of your ability." Then I invite them to pose questions and think about challenges and opportunities of engaging in culturally responsive and social justice research in different communities of color and/or sites of difference. These responses are not meant to be insensitive, but to let students know from the outset that I want to help them find their own focus and develop their own skills, rather than imposing my professional priorities onto them. Unlike some professors who expect their graduate advisees to conduct research that is a continuation of their own, I discourage this. Nor do I try to direct students toward one methodological approach over another, or expect or even want them to become "replications of Me." But whatever their choices are relative to research topics and procedures, I do insist on high-quality performance. In the dissertation-writing process, I am notorious among my advisees for demanding "do-overs." I give generously of my time, support, and other resources to ensure that my students achieve highly. In many instances, this means going the extra mile with them and mobilizing professional networks to access expertise that is beyond my personal capabilities. For me, this is within the normal duties of an adviser, if he or she is genuinely an advocate of and caring learning partner with students.

I think graduate school is the time for students to begin developing their own professional interests and intellectual independence. In working with them toward these ends, I try to be simultaneously friend, mentor, model, critic, teacher, and confidante. This does not mean that I aim to be a "buddy" and neglect my teaching responsibilities. Rather, I try to model the importance of students and teachers interacting with one another in multiple ways and on many different levels. This, to me, is essential to effective teaching and learning, since both encompass more than academic skill development. In performing these diverse roles, I hope to help students grow in similar directions and act accordingly in their own careers.

I think living and learning should be filled with significance, enjoyment, inquiry, and action. And I believe that all of these are best achieved when personal struggles for academic betterment and the joys of achievement are shared with others. In trying to facilitate these accomplishments for myself and my students, I am driven more by the need to abide by my own professional ethics and personal morality than by any policies and practices recommended by external sources. Personally, this means being genuine and authentic in all that I do. Professionally, it means making my classes and other teaching endeavors intellectually stimulating and exciting. It also means empowering students by teaching them how to improve their own decisionmaking, cognitive-processing, problem-solving, imaginative and creative, and self-reflecting skills. A persistent commitment to ethnic and cultural consciousness of self and others, and how that contributes to improving teaching and learning, permeates all of these efforts.

RITUALS AND ROUTINES

Some common rituals exist across my classes that are symbolic of my values and pedagogical priorities about preparing teachers to work well with ethnically and culturally diverse students (especially African, Latino, Asian, and Native Americans) who are marginalized and underachieving. One of them is to build a sense of community among students and create a classroom ambiance characterized by inquiry, discourse, personal involvement, novelty, and reciprocity. I begin doing this on the first day of classes with some mind-boggling and very unorthodox ice-breaking conversations and experiences. On one occasion I asked the students to form pairs and to look at each other closely enough to identify subtle physical features. This excluded things like hair and eye color, height, race, and gender. After a short period of time, the pairs took turns describing each other to the rest of the class. On the surface, this sounds like a simple task to do; in fact, it is very difficult and unnerving. Many people in the United States do not look closely enough at one another to discern individual traits. This is especially so cross-racially. The exercise was intended to convey the idea that teachers really do have to look closely to see *individual differences within ethnic and cultural groups,* and to teach this lesson through experience.

In another first-day exercise, I asked several randomly selected students to publicly declare their ethnic identities and give "personal evidence" of their claims of ethnic ownership. If they said, "I am Italian American, or Korean-African American," then they had to provide some examples of values, beliefs, and behaviors that signal these ethnic identities. Each student was probed in depth about his or her ethnicity before the next one was asked anything. The first student asked to share was someone who had had another class with me. She was familiar with my routines, and I knew she would handle the exercise very well. She served as a model for the other students who followed. Her modeling was not so much about the content of what she shared as it was a signal to the other students that they would live through the "inquisition." After all the students shared, I asked the rest of the class what they thought was going on, whether other people's revealing of their ethnicity prompted them to do likewise, and whether there were any messages in this exercise for teaching K–12 students about ethnic and cultural diversity.

Therefore, on the very first day of class students are introduced to some key elements of my pedagogical style. They learn from the outset that every teaching exchange involves describing, documenting, and analyzing experiences or events; sharing individually and communally; engaging in personal and professional reflections; learning by doing; and constantly seeking to improve classroom instruction for the benefit of underachieving students of color. This is my advocacy in all of my teaching, and it is always made evident. In explaining what is happening in class, why, and how it relates to which aspects of culturally responsive teaching, I am engaging in what some other scholars call "transparent teaching" and still others refer to as "praxis," that is, combining knowledge acquisition with ideological declarations, illustrative actions, and critical analysis. These ice-breaking activities also are intended to (1) let students know that my classes are going to be conducted in a manner that may be quite different from what they are accustomed to in most of their other college learning experiences; (2) provide a demonstrated example of how I engage with issues and relate to students, and how I expect students to interact with me and one another; and (3) begin creating a sense of camaraderie, an esprit de corps, a climate of caring, and a community of practice where we assist one another in the struggle to know and share in the celebration of our success. These features of my instruction are continually developed in all subsequent instructional interactions.

Teachers need to use an established routine to give order and direction to their instruction. It provides a framework for students to make better sense of what is happening, and a set of dependable guidelines or parameters for moving through learning engagements. Three examples of possibilities are provided. My instructional mantra is "know, think, feel, do, and reflect." These phases of learning do not have to occur in the same sequence all the time, but for me all need to happen before a teaching exchange is completed. In examining issues related to race, culture, ethnicity, and education, my students are expected to acquire some knowledge; examine their own and others' thoughts about the knowledge acquired; clarify feelings and beliefs about the issues and topics being studied; consider some ways to convert their knowledge, feelings, and opinions into transformative actions; and review and critique their learning processes to discern broader insights, messages, and implications for improvement embedded in them. Esteem, empathy, and equity are the organizing principles for Tiedt's and Tiedt's (2010) culturally responsive pedagogy. The esteem emphasis is designed to validate students and improve their perceptions of themselves. Equality activities develop understanding of and appreciation for multiple ways of living and learning. Equity recognizes that all students do not come to learning situations with the same resources and preparation. This diversity is acceptable as a natural feature of humanity and is a consistent criterion for selecting a wide variety of learning opportunities and experiences for culturally diverse students. Weber's (2005) approach to teaching is a five-phase process that includes (1) *questions* to identify diverse learning possibilities; (2) *targets,* or specifically stated goals to avoid confusion about what is to happen in learning activities and how; (3) *expectations* that convey intended performance quality levels; (4) *moves or actions* that engage students in the creative construction and application of knowledge; and (5) *reflections*, which are opportunities to revisit learning tasks for guidance in future activities and growth potential. Teachers do not have to adopt any of these particular teaching routines, but they should create some recurrent protocol that provides order, regularity, and dependability to their instructional procedures. These routines help students make better sense of and engage in teaching encounters, as well as ensure that they will participate in different types of learning. I believe teaching is better when it takes place within well-established conceptual and procedural frameworks that include multiple and diverse layers of learning opportunities, especially about topics that are new and troubling to students, as is often the case with ethnic, racial, and cultural diversity in education.

LEARNING COOPERATIVELY AND SUCCESSFULLY

I do not believe in competitive learning or punitive grading. Rather than encouraging students to compete with one another for grades and using grades as controlling devices, I design my classes for all students to be maximally successful. I try to provide opportunities for every student to achieve the highest grade possible (although I would prefer not to give grades at all). I do this by designing learning experiences and projects to demonstrate learning that has several different components at multiple levels of complexity. None are about merely regurgitating factual information. I am more interested in students understanding what they read, analyzing critical issues, and applying the knowledge they acquire to teaching situations. When we examine principles of multicultural curriculum design, students are expected to understand them conceptually and then create some examples of how these can be translated to actual practice in classroom instruction about and for cultural, racial, and cultural diversity. Embedded in class projects are some aspects that every student should be able to accomplish with relative ease. Therefore, even novices should never complete a task without getting some portion of it correct. Conversely, there are other parts of the assignments that all students should find intellectually challenging—but not the same ones for everybody.

I believe very strongly in the power of cooperative learning, learning by doing, and prospective teachers learning in ways similar to how they should teach their own students (i.e., modeling). Consequently, these are distinguishing features of my classroom dynamics. My students and I share teaching tasks and trade student–teacher roles. As small groups take on the responsibility to teach different topics to the class, I become an ex officio student/teacher member of each one to assist in getting the tasks done. Members of small study groups are always expected to be diversified on some level. Sometimes it is not possible to have racial and gender diversity among the membership of every small study group because of the population demographics in the programs of study. Then we look for "invisible" diversifying factors, such as longevity of U.S. residence for immigrant and/or international students, students who grew up in different regions of the United States, or students of African ancestry who are racially Black but are ethnically and culturally different (such as non-Spanish-speaking Puerto Ricans, Jamaican Americans, and African Koreans). We learn about cooperative learning by engaging in it as we learn. Using this format also increases the chances for students to be more actively involved in multicultural interactions and classroom dynamics, at different levels and in different ways. Thus, *diversity* and *modeling* are both pedagogical anchors and learning outcomes of my teaching. I strongly believe that no learners ever learn alone; that cooperative learning is inherently human; that implicit aspects of our individual and collective humanity should be made explicit; and that different kinds of quality teaching and learning are easier to accomplish when students with diverse identities, skills, and repertoires of being work together for each other's personal and academic betterment. This cross-cultural collaboration is essential for building genuine multicultural community, improving experiential knowledge of different cultures, and thereby actualizing some fundamental component of culturally responsive teaching and learning. My goal is to practice what I teach/preach, or demonstrate my instructional messages as much as possible. If I tell prospective teachers they should use cooperative learning with ethnically diverse students in pre-K–12 schools, then I feel morally and pedagogically obligated to do so in my teacher education classes in ways similar to those I recommend for elementary and secondary classrooms.

Another way that I try to guarantee success for all students is to have them design a self-growth project that represents their commitment to the causes we are pursuing and in which they make a contract with themselves and me to do something for their own individual development. For example, in one case, when we were studying "prejudice reduction," a student made a personal contract with herself to stop being a tacit supporter (through silence and nonresistance) of her father's habitual use of racial slurs when referring to Latino, Japanese, Chinese, and African Americans. All the students have to do in order to receive maximum credit for the self-growth contracts is fulfill the terms they themselves have specified, document the fulfillment of the terms, provide a reflection on how the experience affected them, and explain how this activity or some facsimile can be used in teaching K–12 students.

CHOICE AND AUTHENTICITY ARE ESSENTIAL TO LEARNING

When I give tasks to students that require mastery of key concepts we have explored in class, there are always opportunities for them to choose from a variety of options. One of these options is to propose a task of their own. The only stipulation is that whatever they propose to do has to be similar in magnitude, focus, and intent to the options I have provided. Thus, variety of tasks and personal participation in the decisionmaking process about how to demonstrate mastery are hallmark features of the "partnership in learning" principle that informs my teaching. It constitutes a form of empowerment and agency that are fundamental elements of culturally responsive teaching.

In one class that was studying multicultural curriculum and instruction, the students were given an assignment to apply the principles we had examined by developing a micro-multicultural curriculum on a selected issue. The list of issues included ones that they were likely to encounter in actual school and societal situations. Among them were "the changing images of ethnic diversity in mass media," "cultural conflicts in social interactions," "mainstream consumption of cultural diversity," "quality of public transportation for different ethnic groups and communities," and "ethnically diverse patterns of consumerism." To complete these projects, the students were to simulate the steps that commonly are involved in curriculum development. They began by forming small design committees and collecting data about these issues prior to designing their curricula. For example, the students working on the transportation topic collected information on bus routes and schedules; took bus rides through different communities; made observations about the advertisements, decorations, and cleanliness of the buses; noted the demeanor of the bus drivers; and talked with some of the regular passengers. The group working on mass media decided to focus on billboards. They scanned billboards in several different communities before beginning to create their curriculum. The decision to go on these "scouting" expeditions was the students'. I only advised them that their curricula needed to be "realistic." The results of these preliminary analyses informed the curriculum decisions; made their final projects more authentic with respect to what was designed for hypothetical K–12 students; and provided opportunities for them see how common issues and experiences (such as public transportation, or advertising for products and services) are manifested in different ethnic, racial, cultural, and socioeconomic communities. These types of learning experiences also allow students to immerse themselves in cultural diversity as lived daily and routinely beyond the walls of classroom, and to observe concepts like resource inequities and disparities based on race, ethnicity, and residence in actual practice.

In creating their micro-curricula, my students had to complete several different tasks. These involved:

- Choosing a targeted student audience and school context (such as 7th-graders in an urban multiracial school or 10th-graders in a rural monoracial European American school), and providing an explanation for these choices that addressed multicultural education needs. These choices created some baselines to help me determine the quality of the subsequent tasks.
- Selecting a goal for the focus of the curriculum from a list common to multicultural education, such as acquiring knowledge about ethnic and cultural diversity, reducing prejudices, engaging in social action to promote social justice, and developing critical political and cultural consciousness.

- Including several different content samples and learning activities (specified by number and type), such as geographic, reading, and mathematical skills, as well as cognitive, affective, and action experiences.
- Developing some creative techniques for marketing the completed micro-curricula to selected audiences. These could be commercials, slogans, logos, jingles, or public announcements.
- Anything else the students decided to use to make their micro-curricula uniquely and persuasively illustrative of the mission of multicultural education.

In completing these tasks the students had to combine knowledge and skills of culturally responsive teaching and commonly accepted standards of curriculum development.

Another technique I use for prospective teachers to practice authentic choice-making about cultural diversity in their own learning is to have them multiculturalize some aspects of regular classroom dynamics. First, they choose as a target of change something that typically is done in classrooms by many teachers, such as displaying symbols of subjects (e.g., maps in a social studies class, pictures of prominent authors in a literature class, alphabet streamers in a kindergarten classroom, etc.), cueing signals to refocus students' attention on tasks and reduce noise levels, and sending correspondence to parents. Then, my students reconstruct their selections to make them multicultural and multiethnic. They make their own choices about the specific content to include, but it must be consistent with the content areas selected and fundamental principles of multicultural education. One group did a phenomenal job of multiculturalizing the alphabet for primary teachers. They created a multimedia multicultural alphabet book that included a noteworthy individual from a different ethnic group for each letter of the alphabet, along with a visual image and a brief statement about the individual's achievements that was age-appropriate for kindergarten and 1st-grade students. Another group chose to demonstrate how to multiculturalize correspondence with bilingual working-class parents, many of whom were recent immigrants. My students began by translating school information from professional jargon into a language they felt was more user-friendly and accessible for their targeted audiences. Then they "wrote" their correspondences in different formats, including typical letters in Standard English, Spanish, Vietnamese, Chinese, and Tagalog; made an audiotape of the message for parents who might have difficulty reading any language; and created a videotape with a teacher speaking personally to parents or guardians of specific children, on the assumption that this would be a more warm and welcoming approach to communicating with parents unfamiliar with the U.S. education system. Authenticity is apparent in these examples because my students' suggested reforms focused on things that happen in actual classrooms and were compatible with principles of culturally responsive teaching and their selected areas of schooling. An important embedded message in these learning activities is for prospective teachers to understand culturally responsive teaching as an integral part of all teaching, not something reserved for special occasions.

TEACHING TO ENABLE AND EMPOWER

Periodic "process-checking" is also a regular part of my classroom discourse. I review with students the requirements of assigned tasks prior to completion to determine how well their group dynamics are going. The purposes of these reality checks are to see whether what is expected is clear to them; to find out whether the students are experiencing any major substantive problems with the tasks; to see how their community-building is coming along; to bolster their confidence; and to reaffirm, through public declaration, my faith in their ability to complete the tasks successfully. To me, being very public and genuine about conveying confidence in students' ability to accomplish high-quality performance, and standing in readiness to assist in their accomplishments, are fundamental to effective teaching and learning. This is true whether the students are in kindergarten or doctoral programs, members of majority or minority, achieving or nonachieving demographics.

I do not believe I should use the power of my position as professor to threaten or intimidate students, or to keep the knowledge I am supposed to know shrouded in mystery. My task should be to make knowledge accessible to students and to diffuse the threat and anxiety that are often part of the learning process. I try to do this by teaching my students how to "read between the lines" of professional writings by learning how to locate the authors' central streams of thought; discerning assumptions and beliefs embedded in their ideas and explanations; locating cues that reveal authors' disciplinary frames of reference and preferred metaphors (these are very revealing indicators of value emphases); and, whenever possible, sharing something personal about the authors. I constantly explain the motivations behind my own actions as a scholar, theorist, researcher, and pedagogue.

What does this have to do with culturally responsive teaching? Everything. Scholars, like classroom teachers, are ethnic and cultural beings. Their attitudes and values are nested in their writings, research, and teachings. These need to be revealed and then analyzed to better understand their particular positions, analytical emphases, and points of view. Learning to discern how the "positionality" of authors affects their analyses of educational issues during their preparation programs may become a habit that teachers take into the classroom and pass on to their students. Furthermore, it is an excellent way to dispel the notion that scholars are infallible or the only ones with legitimate claims to expertise. In the process of revealing the constraints of one's positionality, the power of another's perspectives is unfolded. The intellectual give-and-take that results is a compelling illustration and reinforcement of the need for multiple, *culturally diverse* voices and perspectives in cultivating the intellectual competence, and capturing the experiential realities of different ethnic and racial individuals and groups. This is something that I particularly want my students to understand and include in their teaching.

As part of a class I teach on "Teaching African American Students and Culture," we examine cultural characteristics that affect teaching and learning. Because many of my students have no personal interactions with African Americans, they find these descriptions to be abstractions that are difficult to visualize or to consider as anything but stereotypes. To help them break through these barriers to understanding, I try to exemplify some of the cultural features we are reading and talking about. I may intersperse bits of Ebonics (such as topic-chaining talk, storytelling, sermonizing, dramatic wordplay) into my regular teaching discourse without any warning of what is about to happen. After a while, I shift back to more typical academic language. I may then stop the conversation and do a reflective analysis with the students on what they have just experienced. I ask whether they were aware of any differences in language usage, whether they understood the information being transmitted, and how they felt about what happened. Now that they have a "living example" of a cultural behavior, we can compare the theory with the practice—and possibly achieve a better understanding of both. I use similar processes in analyzing other people's narratives and dialogues, observations, film, and other types of media. We begin with conceptualization, followed sequentially by an illustrative behavioral experience, new information, debriefing, and reconceptualization. This habit of teaching is based on my belief that explicit connections need to be made between ideas and corresponding actions; many aspects of cultural and ethnic diversity need to be visualized for teachers, especially those who have had little or no practical experiences with it in their personal lives; and guided practice improves learning quality. Furthermore, my African American cultural behaviors may be facsimiles of what they will encounter from African American students in their classes. Having experienced a variation of these behaviors, they may not be so quick to judge them negative, inappropriate, or invalid.

At first most of my students do not know what is going on, or they are captivated by my "performances," or they are too polite to challenge or differ with the professor. But with time, practice, and knowledge they become very adept in their observations and analyses, as well as their willingness to probe me about the implications of my culturally expressive behaviors for their own teaching. They seek clarifications about whether these "performances" are authentic, whether they are generalizable across person and place, and how to translate insights derived from them into better classroom instruction. These teaching techniques are very effective in demonstrating the importance and principles of culturally responsive teaching. Teacher education students who do not understand me when I speak Ebonics to them now have a personal experience with what it feels like to be intelligent but still not know what your teacher is talking about. This experience may enable them to better empathize with ethnically diverse students in their own classrooms who are in similar situations. They also have some experience with the concepts and related skills of "cultural style-shifting," "cultural hybridity," and "cultural border-crossing." These are important in teaching students from different ethnic backgrounds to function more effectively in school situations without having to forsake their cultural heritages. They are skills that are especially important for students of color whose cultural socialization may be very different from that which prevails in mainstream schools.

KNOWLEDGE PLUS PRACTICE IS IMPERATIVE

I often give assignments that require students to take an advocacy position on some issue directed toward a specific audience. One of these asks students in teacher education courses to select a "constituent audience" and explain the benefits of human differences and cultural diversity to it. The choices might include a member of the Moral Majority; a potential advocate who is willing to promote cultural diversity but lacks sufficient knowledge; a Latina grandmother who just wants her grandchildren to learn to be good members of the culture, community, and society in which they live; a group of Southeastern Asian immigrants new to the United States; or an elementary, middle, or high school European American student who declares that, "My parents say this stuff about diversity is a waste of time and will interfere with me getting a good-quality education." We discuss the importance of "contextualizing" pedagogical explanations and actions, and making them audience-appropriate. I then explain how this task illustrates the culturally responsive premise of being able to communicate and relate in different ways in different situations with different individuals and groups. The quality of students' responses to the assignment is determined more by how well they "speak in a voice" that is appropriate for their intended audiences than solely by the factual information provided.

In completing this assignment, one student responded to hypothetical 5th-graders who were aggressively resisting a teacher's efforts to embrace cultural diversity. She began by acknowledging that the students' skepticism was not exceptional, explaining that they were already learning a lot about ethnic, racial, and cultural diversity implicitly, and providing examples of how awareness of cultural diversity was present in their immediate lives. Her tone was informative in a nonthreatening, nonjudgmental, and non-dictatorial way. Thus, she demystified and diffused some of the threat of diversity in a way that is very appropriate for 5th-graders, and for culturally responsive teaching, by making it a natural and routine occurrence in daily life. My student's advocacy statement declared in part:

I want you to know that you're not the first to declare that you shouldn't have to learn about different ethnic groups, and you probably won't be the last. But, let me explain why this is important.

First of all, let me say that you already are learning about ethnic groups whether you realize it or not. Do you watch TV? If you see people you think might be different from you on TV, you're already forming opinions of them. Do you read newspapers and magazines? If you do, you're gathering information and developing beliefs about other ethnic and cultural groups and individuals. How do you know that the information is correct or that the opinions and beliefs you're forming are fair? You'll never know if you don't learn about other ethnic groups. . . .

The question then becomes whether or not what and how you are learning is a positive or negative experience for yourself and others. Is it accurate? Is it going to help or hinder you and others? Let me give you an example that might demonstrate how not having information could hinder or prevent you from knowing what you need to know.

You are learning to play a new game. There are ten rules to follow, but at home you decide to play by only five. You learn these five rules very well and you win a lot. Later on you go to a friend's house to play the same game. He has learned all of the rules. You lose and lose but can't figure out why. Not having all of the information prevented you from playing the game as well as you might have once you were outside of your home. It might even have caused you to argue with or distrust your friend. Once you learn the other rules of the game, you find that you win some of the time and have much more fun playing the game.

In this class, we want to look at a lot of different information around us. We want to think about the stories we read and hear. We want to look at pictures of many different experiences and peoples, and talk about them. We want to speculate about how others feel and why. We want to try different things in different ways. We want to learn in ways that will better prepare us for the "game of life." Since ethnic and cultural diversity is an important part of life now and in the future, you need to know about it to be able to play the game better. As we prepare for the "game of life," we will be learning about our own as well as others' cultural differences. . . . And, we're going to discover that learning about differences is exciting. So give it a try before you decide it is unnecessary.

I also use role-playing and simulations frequently to provide students with opportunities to translate theory into practice in relation to understanding information and being more pedagogically responsive to cultural diversity in classrooms. These instructional techniques are especially useful for students who have not had any actual teaching experiences. Two examples illustrate how the learning activities operate and the range of opportunities they provide. In the first case, I told my students that representatives from the state department of education had asked me to consult with them about improving the school performance of at-risk students, a high percentage of whom were African, Latino, and Native Americans. To respond to this request I had volunteered this group of students, who, at the time, were enrolled in a class on "Multiethnic Curriculum and Instruction." Their task was to develop a prototype curriculum on "Essential Multicultural Citizenship Skills for 'At-Risk' Students in the State of Washington." The underlying assumptions of the simulation were (1) elementary and secondary students throughout the state are at-risk multiculturally because they are not taught adequately about ethnic and cultural diversity, and (2) any students can be at-risk under some circumstances. I wanted my students to be cautious about accepting simplistic explanations for complex issues involved in teaching ethnically diverse students and to understand the importance of "contextuality" in educational decisionmaking. Thus, being at-risk should not be understood as an identifier for particular groups of students, but a condition that is contextually specific. My students had to begin the task by rethinking what it meant to be at-risk if all students in Washington were affected, determining what was the best focus and tone for a curriculum for a state department of education, and deciding what constituted a "curriculum prototype." They needed to make these preliminary decisions in order to make their curriculum prototype more audience and culturally appropriate. This learning experience invited students to engage critically with the idea that effective culturally responsive teachers must challenge and transform some prevailing normative educational assumptions, ideologies, practices, and protocols.

The second example of using role-playing and simulation to bring an aura of practical reality to my teaching about cultural diversity involved the students in translating knowledge from one form to another. This process was a powerful testament to the quality and depth of understanding that students had acquired. The students were asked to assume the role of producers and consumers of art and mass media while we were studying philosophical beliefs about what being responsive to ethnic, racial, cultural, and social diversity means and why it is important to include it in school curricula and instruction. The motif adopted for the discussion was the opening day of an art exhibition. In small groups, the students became "artists" by creating visual images of the messages they had derived from reading samples of different authors' ideas about the whats and whys of culturally responsive education. We then converted the classroom into an art museum, and the students hung their artworks throughout. When the exhibition opened, half the students were artists who were there to talk with the audience about their artistic renditions. After some time, the roles were reversed. Those students who had been artists became audience, and the audience became artists to explain their works.

At the close of the exhibition (which coincided with the end of the class period), the students switched to another role. They became "journalists" to report on what they had seen and experienced at the "Multicultural Philosophical Art Exhibition." Each small group chose a section common to newspapers and wrote about their experiences in its "voice"; for instance, a headline story, editorial, obituary, human interest page, advertisement, classified ad, comic, horoscope, and entertainment review. After all the selected parts of the newspaper were composed, representatives from the small groups arranged themselves in the proper order and then "read themselves aloud" to the rest of the class.

One small group that chose to write about their experiences in the form of a birth announcement wrote:

The world's most awaited child finally arrived here in Seattle with the birth of "multicultural education." Father, True Democracy, and mother, Necessity, are the proudest of parents. After nearly 300 years of racism and inequality, Multicultural Education was conceived in the 1960s. After a long and tenuous labor, Multicultural Education was finally born on June 28, 1999 [the date of the class assignment], and made her first public appearance at the grand opening of the art museum named in her honor. Famous artists awaiting her prepared a fabulous multimedia presentation for the public to herald her arrival. The thought-provoking exhibitions and presentations captured the colorful, complex, creative, and challenging personality of Multicultural Education in all of her expressive dimensions. The artists' works also alluded to the hopes, expectations, and potentials of Multicultural Education for a millennium of cooperation and collaboration among ethnically diverse groups in schools and society. Multicultural Education's older siblings, Justice and Social Activism, also were on hand for the festivities.

Another group of students selected weather forecasting as the motif for writing about their perceptions of the multicultural education philosophical art exhibition. Their creative rendition stated:

Upon entering the Museum of Multicultural Education this past Monday, June 28th, one could not help but notice the dramatic change in the *weather*. The *cloudy skies* outside were apparently no match for the *warm front* of high hopes and expectations in the gallery. Participants in the exhibition found success in clarifying the *foggy* misconceptions that have long nourished the *storms* of controversy surrounding multicultural education. Their presentations included a *downpour* of information unearthing *sunny* prognoses for the future of education grounded in culturally relevant approaches to teaching and learning. These cleansing *deluges* were followed by brilliant *sunshine* of insights and a dazzling *rainbow* of pedagogical possibilities.

In order to correct the *climate* characterized by a barrage of misunderstandings and misapprehensions, the artists for multicultural education produced a *flood* of positive anecdotal and research-based data that are sure to *precipitate* great changes in the minds of the public. With the *cold front* of misinformation in check, it looks like nothing but *clear skies* ahead.

The ten-year forecast includes a period of continued scattered *clouds* of controversy early on that will eventually develop into greater *visibility* and a hopeful *air index* of multicultural education policy formation and implementation. Finally, our *satellite weather* shows the end of the decade immersed in the *sun belt* of cultural diversity infusion. A few *thunderstorms* of doubt and back-peddling might pop up occasionally on the national *radar screens* as we work out the glitches. But, overall it looks like calm *seas,* warm *temperatures,* and only moderate *rainfall* ahead. No *natural catastrophes,* such as *earthquakes, hurricanes, droughts,* or *tornadoes* are expected. So make your plans now to celebrate the increasing success of multicultural education.

A class was assigned the task of experientially examining two related ideas. One was that everyday life in the United States is fraught with inequities, cultural hegemony, taken-for-grated habits of being, and marginalizing practices toward ethnically and culturally diverse people and communities. The other was that culturally responsive teaching can, and must, occur in sites other than schools, classrooms, and formal academic curricula. The former involves the iconic symbolism in U.S. society, such as the flag, the national anthem, and national holidays, and the "proper" decorum associated with them. Rarely (if ever) do educators examine how various marginalized populations may react to them. An example is recent incidents of professional African American athletes refusing to stand (an expected signal of honor and respect) or kneeling for the playing of the national anthem before the beginning of games. It is reminiscent of the Black Power salute medalists Tommie Smith and John Carlos executed during the playing of the U.S. national anthem for awarding their medals at the 1968 summer Olympic games in Mexico City. The flag is another revered symbol that for many citizens deserves high honor. Others, whose ancestors suffered genocidal practices under these symbols of significance, find them and the normal expected deference to them problematic. With these and similar context-framing comments, students were asked to reconstruct some of the typical U.S. Independence Day (July 4) festivities to make them more inclusive and reflective of culturally diversity.

The class was organized into five study groups. Each group self-selected a categorical activity or event routinely included in U.S. Independence Day (July 4) festivities, and developed plans for multiculturalizing it. One group designed a "Memory Promenade" along the main walkway of the events center where the celebration usually takes place. It included posters of visual images and brief explanatory text of individuals across time and ethnic identity who were and are activists in struggles for independence (broadly defined). These were to be displayed at intervals along the entire walkway. Another group concentrated on fireworks, which is a highlight and the culminating event of the celebration. This group envisioned the fireworks occurring in a series of montages composed of color combinations symbolizing the countries of origin of major ethnic groups in the United States. A third group planned a menu for an "authentic" multicultural barbecue that included the content and presentation of foods characteristic of the five major ethnic clusters in the United States (African, Asian/Pacific Islanders, European, Latino, and Native Americans), plus others who do not fit neatly into these categories, such as Middle Easterners and recent immigrants from various nations. The fourth group of students acted as entertainment managers and planned a musical concert composed of different genres of freedom songs performed by a host of multiethnic musicians of various ages and styles, live and video-recorded, historical and contemporary. The fifth group created a game center where children and adults could participate in individual and group games, including social dancing, created by or associated with different ethnic groups. No individual or computerized games were allowed. Instead, their games were all group-based, physical, and kinetically interactive.

In order to create transformative proposals for making the U.S. Independence Day celebrations more culturally and ethnically inclusive, my students had to do thorough and extensive research by collecting pertinent information in order to ensure that their ideas were based on cultural accuracy. Skills cultivated and applied in the learning process included creativity, collaboration, building confidence and efficacy, embracing novelty in learning, self-assessment, creating criteria for and implementing quality control, and engaging in continuous critique and reflection. The students also extrapolated key culturally responsive teaching principles and criteria from their simulated practical experiences. They took teaching "beyond the classroom" and began to realize that much quality learning, including academic skills, cultural competence, and socioemotional development, can occur in apparently noneducational contexts, and that all aspects of culturally diverse living have the potential to teach.

These are beautiful examples of the creativity and high-quality performance of prospective teachers. They attest to the incredible capability of students for imagination and mastery if teachers create opportunities, convey high expectations, and provide facilitative assistance. Although these performances were produced by adult learners in college, elementary and high school students also have the ability to be highly creative in learning activities if they are provided ample opportunities. In addition to tapping creativity and providing practical experiences for preservice teacher education students, simulated learning opportunities offered several other benefits that are consistent with theoretical ideas of culturally responsive teaching. Among them are:

- Getting students personally involved in their own learning
- Using varied formats, multiple perspectives, and novelty in teaching
- Responding to multiple learning styles
- Modeling in teaching and learning
- Using cooperation and collaboration among students to achieve common learning outcomes
- Learning by doing
- Incorporating different types of skill development (e.g., intellectual, social, emotional, moral) in teaching and learning experiences
- Transferring knowledge from one form or context to another
- Combining knowledge, concepts, and theory with practice (i.e., engaging in praxis)
- Having students reflect critically on their knowledge, beliefs, thoughts, and actions
- Building capacity, confidence, and efficacy in students as agents of pedagogical, intellectual, moral, and social justice changes related to cultural diversity

CULTIVATING CRITICAL ORIENTATIONS IS IMPORTANT

The intellectual processes that students go through in my classes are designed to engage and enhance their own knowing potential. I want them to be independent, critical, reflective, and quality thinkers and decisionmakers who are deliberate and intentional in constructing their personal pedagogical positions, and in monitoring and assessing the quality of their culturally diverse beliefs and behaviors. Consequently, my students are challenged to reconfigure and integrate knowledge segments from several sources to serve new purposes; to be analytical about sources of knowledge; to push the boundaries of their present knowledge frames by looking for deeper meanings and principles in descriptive texts; and to create new ways to organize and categorize information and insights. I constantly prompt them to "think about," to wonder "what if," to explain why. When I do this myself, I frequently stop the dialogue to explain how I arrived at my new categories and why I think the information should be sorted accordingly. This "explanation of processing" is intended to be an instructive model for my students to emulate in their intellectual operations with their own students.

I encourage and assist students to deconstruct conventional assumptions about and paradigms for teaching marginalized students of color and to search for more viable alternatives. In one of my classes, "Multiethnic

Curriculum and Instruction," a routine activity undertaken to accomplish this task is to expose the cultural underpinnings of explanations for low academic achievement, such as lack of motivation, devaluing education, at-riskness, limited intellectuality, and parental nonparticipation. We consider alternative paradigms that promise possibilities for different solutions. Among them are cultural incongruity, stress and anxiety, existential distance between students and teachers, situational competence, and transitional trauma caused by having to shift from home to school cultural systems. Each of these is examined to determine different explanations for why students are not achieving well in school and new implications for classroom instruction. In another class, on "Teaching African American Students," we consider the principles of Kwanzaa (Riley, 1995) as a pedagogical paradigm. In exploring this possibility, my students engage in activities such as translating Kwanzaa principles to the arena of teaching and learning; explaining how Kwanzaa principles exemplify African American cultural values and characteristics; and delineating how these can function as educational ideologies and classroom practices. They also develop teaching strategies and learning activities that illustrate the Kwanzaa principles in a variety of subjects, skills, grades, and school settings. These kinds of instructional activities are based on the premises that (1) positive beliefs about ethnic and cultural diversity produce positive teaching and learning behaviors, and (2) educational interventions for ethnically diverse students based on prior success (not failure) generate subsequent learning successes.

In this same course, but with a different group of students, we used literature as our motif for culturally responsive teaching. I wanted my students to acquire a deeper understanding of the process of writing and publishing literary books, so that they could, in turn, use their knowledge to teach students about culturally diverse literature and the processes of its construction to teach other academic and social skills, such as publishing, authorship, cultural retentions through literature, interdisciplinary skill development, and targeted issue analysis. After analyzing children's picture books as cultural artifacts and mechanisms for transmitting cultural information, my students had to write a picture book. To make them as contextually authentic as possible, the books had to have an African American cultural theme and include the attributes of this genre of literature, such as having little word text but much visual text or illustrations. Since the creation and production of books are never a one-person enterprise (including those that appear to be single-authored!), my students had to "write" their books in small groups. Other performance criteria included the students being both authors and artists/illustrators; researching the cultural issue, individual, or attribute that centered the book so that it could be more culturally accurate and authentic; developing a publication release statement to cultivate interest and define the audience; and creating a short "How to Use" set of suggestions to accompany the book and help readers use it as a catalyst for additional learning.

Like culturally responsive teaching at its best, this assignment had several purposes and appealed to a variety of different learning options and styles. First, students had to collaborate and work together to accomplish the task. Second, knowledge acquired in one format had to be converted into other formats. Third, students had to pursue additional learning on their own initiative beyond that which was taught in the classroom. Fourth, multiple kinds of learning took place, including academic research, analyzing samples of prior publications, using creativity, developing community and collaboration among students, and blending different competencies for high-quality task accomplishment. The books produced were phenomenal!— and were yet another verification of the transformative potential and multiple positive effects of culturally responsive teaching.

THE PERSONAL IS POWERFUL

I think interpersonal relations have a tremendous impact on the quality of teaching and learning. Students perform much better in environments where they feel comfortable and valued. Therefore, I work hard at creating a classroom climate and ambiance of warmth, support, caring, dignity, informality, and enjoyment. Yet these psychoemotional factors do not distract from the fact that my classes are very demanding intellectually. Students are expected to work hard and at high levels of quality. I, too, am at my best in these kinds of settings. So I try to bond with my students as teacher, friend, and advocate, and to get them to accept me and one another in a similar manner. One way I do this is by legitimizing personal experiences as significant sources of knowledge. As a result, "telling our personal stories" plays a prominent part in our conversations as we work to capture the essence of culturally responsive educational ideas, theories, principles, and practices.

It is not always easy to get students (even those in graduate studies programs) to self-declare and share their personal stories. They are often reluctant to discuss their experiences, impressions, and thoughts about racial discrimination, ethnic inequities, and cultural hegemony. Some are uncertain about their own ethnic and cultural identity as well as about their role in advocating for cultural diversity in teaching and learning. Their reluctance is fueled further by the fact that they are predominantly European Americans and I am African American. Many of my students are initially anxious about how their comments will be received by me. I think this hesitancy is driven by a combination of intimidation by my ethnicity, fear of showing ignorance and insult, and respect for my position of dual authority (personal and professional).

To help students break out of this reluctance, during the early part of courses I talk about, critique, and even make fun of myself a lot. I share many scenarios about mistakes I have made in the past and the tentativeness and incompleteness of my early efforts to engage with the issues we are examining in class. I share successes, too, as well as experiences I am ambivalent about, and areas of growth I am currently pursuing (or need to be). My purposes in these self-disclosures are threefold: to model sharing one's own experiences and how these illustrate the pedagogical principles under study; to lead the way for my students to follow and prepare the classroom climate to make it easier for them to function in telling and analyzing their own stories; and to demonstrate that competence is not something that happens instantaneously, but rather develops over time and shifts according to contexts. In other words, I use my own stories to show how I came to be, and how I am still in the process of becoming, with respect to competence in teaching for, about, and to cultural and ethnic diversity.

As the students become more comfortable and confident about sharing their stories, I share fewer of mine and increasingly vary how this sharing is done. I may wait for the students to share their stories first before declaring my own. Or I may use the students' stories as a catalyst to prompt a memory of my own, and tie it to their stories, as an obvious secondary narrative. On other occasions I defer the telling of stories totally to students, and I restrict my participation to extrapolating pedagogical principles from them. I also change how I react with the students' stories. Initially, I simply encourage the class members to "receive" the stories and compliment the "authors" of them for sharing. Next, I begin to invite the storyteller and other students to analyze the stories, looking for pedagogical messages within them or ways in which they illustrate specific principles of, or the potential for, culturally responsive teaching. Finally, I, along with the students, "evaluate" the stories as they are told. By this I mean that we make judgments about whether the stories offered are appropriate to the ongoing discourse and as illustrations of the bigger issues or ideas being developed in class. Sometimes this approach to dealing with the stories of students as pedagogical content evolves over many weeks. At other times it occurs within the duration of a single class, and may even unfold within a scenario provided by one student.

I also use a variety of techniques to dialogue with students, to capture their attention, and to engage their deep feelings and thoughts, both in and outside of the classroom. For example, when I give feedback on their papers, I share whatever thoughts or feelings their ideas prompt at the moment I read them. Sometimes it is a new insight, a question, a memory, a smile, a new thought, a gladness that they have mastered a task, or a criticism that they are performing at a level below their potential. In other words, my feedback on written assignments becomes an "interactive conversation" with my students through their papers, and a means for me to continue the instructional process on a level that is more personal than the classroom sometimes allows.

My personalized approach to culturally responsive teaching is manifested in several other ways, and for many additional reasons. But only three are presented here to make the point. First, there are many autobiographical nuances in my cultural responsiveness advocacy and actions. Once upon a time I was that poor, rural, and marginalized student who did not fit in with her classmates, and felt very uncomfortable in the presence of teachers and the content they taught (even through most of my K–12 teachers were African American; in undergraduate college they were all White, with one exception). I was ashamed of my racial identity, ethnicity, and culture. When I was not trying to run away for them or disguise them, I spent much intellectual time and psychic energy attempting to be hypercorrect according to my understanding of mainstream White norms and expectations. Many of the children in my family are still "at-risk" in schools; they struggle academically and from feelings of not belonging or of being interlopers. Somewhere along my educational, professional, and life journeys, I literally reconstructed myself, claimed self-acceptance, and developed unequivocal pride in being African American. As my ownership of self increased, so did my academic agility. This "reconstruction of self" did not come easily, instantaneously, or by my efforts alone. Teachers contributed significantly to the process. I often convey the effects of the transformation in the statement, "I did not become really intellectual until I became genuinely Black." Therefore, in many ways *I am my advocacy,* and I know personally the truth of research findings and theoretical claims about the personal and educational empowerment potential of cultural diversity in teaching and learning for students of color. In sharing this story of my ethnic identity transformation and its correlation with improved academic performance, I put a personal "face" on the socioemotional and academic effects of embracing and promoting cultural diversity. Hopefully it also makes it easier for students to reveal their own stories about similar challenges and establish bonds of affinity in culturally diverse classrooms. All of these are key elements of culturally responsive teaching.

Second, just as I write to teach, I teach to learn. In both writing and teaching I want to demystify and defuse the threat of academic and cultural discourse so that students (and readers of my scholarship) can get to the "inside" of my ideas, explanations, and analyses. Rather than simply stating them and expecting their merits to be a foregoing conclusion "because I, the expert and author, said so," I always provide descriptive and explanatory details of the ideas and analyses presented. Invariably, I begin the writing and teaching discourse with conceptualization, followed by some kind of illustrations of the idea or concept in action. Thus, for me, examples in teaching are the bridges between conceptual abstraction and experiential relevance. The use of prolific examples in my teaching is also a means of translating theory into practice. In putting this practice in the context of culturally responsive teaching, I am deliberate and diligent about systematically using examples from different ethnic, racial, and cultural groups, disciplinary orientations, socioeconomic locations, and time periods. This is an effort to model equity and egalitarian inclusion of multicultural and multiethnic diversity in a small way. I want students to learn from my example and do likewise in their own culturally responsive teaching.

In a 2013 article I made the following statement about the autobiographical and personal presence in my scholarship and teaching:

> My ethnic, racial, and cultural identity as African American is the primary anchor and explanation for what I emphasize in analyzing current educational realities and future possibilities for marginalized students of color. I know from personal experiences the transformative benefits of culturally responsive teaching, and the devastating effects of perpetual failure due to educational irrelevance and ineffectiveness. So, my advocacy for teaching to and through cultural diversity to improve the achievement of ethnically diverse students is both a personal priority and a more generalized educational mandate. It is infused with a conviction that extends beyond intellectual competence and accumulated professional experience. I am neither apologetic for these autobiographical nuances in my scholarship, nor do I pretend they do not exist. While I do not always make these declarations explicit, their presence is not difficult to discern. I am not unique in writing (and teaching) through my own filters of identity and affiliation. This is a common occurrence among scholars of cultural diversity and for classroom teachers in general. (Gay, 2013, p. 53)

Third, in teaching ethnically diverse students I expect to learn about their cultural differences, too. There is no doubt in my mind that students from different ethnic groups and backgrounds can teach me a lot about their cultures, heritages, and experiences. I don't abdicate my responsibilities as teacher, or expect my students to do my job. I just believe that teachers must always be learners too, and continually develop, refine, and update their competencies. I invite students to share their ethnic and cultural selves by doing so myself. These are not revelations of intimacies, or religious confessionals, or psychoanalytical therapy sessions; they are simply invitations for students to explain their ethnic and cultural selves and how they came to be. There are some things about cultural, racial, and ethnic differences that are best learned experientially, and my culturally diverse students are the resources and authorities on themselves in these ventures. The relationship I build with them is based on reciprocity—we co-teach and help each other learn. Therefore, I expect students to be teachers as well as learners, as I teach and learn simultaneously. We share the power and privilege of expertise and authorship. This is a helpful disposition and strategy in culturally responsive teaching because it recognizes that diverse students have assets to be acknowledged, respected, accessed, and incorporated into teaching and learning. It also visualizes their experiences and heritages, develops cultural pride and significance, and fits well with the mandate of "getting to know our students" as a condition of effective teaching.

CONCLUSION

The themes that run through all of my culturally responsive teaching and other interactions with students are "we are partners in the quest for learning" and "the better we can combine our resources, the better all of us will be. I will teach better and you will learn better."

I approach teaching as if it is an unfolding drama, a story in the making that is never finished. Each class session is a new episode in this drama. It has its own unique texture and function, yet is a critical contribution to the construction of the larger story. I am responsible for creating the sets, props, and the rough draft of the scripts for the learning encounters that take place. But how these actually unfold is beyond my unilateral control because the students play crucial roles in my teaching. I neither dictate nor control exactly what these roles will be. I simply cast the parts, and the students construct the characters. Together, we create teaching and learning dynamics that work best for us and what we are trying to accomplish.

Consequently, completing learning tasks is simultaneously a cause for celebration and an invitation for us to return to the stage once again and add yet another segment to the continuing drama of teaching and learning. We compile our efforts, resources, experiences, and intellects to making learning ventures the best possible for everyone involved. Thus, my students and I work closely together to develop learning experiences that are simultaneously personally validating, academically enriching, socially empowering, morally uplifting, and pedagogically transforming. Sometimes the unfolding script and drama work well for my students and me, but not always. Although I wish otherwise, when my teaching is less than desirable I am not incapacitated by imperfection. I know well that there is no end to learning, that I do not know all there is to be known about ethnic and cultural diversity, that good teachers are always learning, and that there are no guarantees or infallible formulas for perpetual success in teaching. I welcome the uncertainty and imperfections as invitations to be imaginative and innovative, to reaffirm that culturally responsive teaching is a continuous process of development, and to embrace the reality stated so eloquently by William Ayers (2004) that "teaching is never twice the same" (p. 43).

CHAPTER 8

Epilogue: Looking Back and Projecting Forward

"Cultural responsiveness in teaching is always in the process of becoming, rather than a fixed destination or a set of finished skills."

Will culturally responsive teaching reverse the trends of school achievement for Amy and Aaron's younger siblings, their children, and the future generations of all marginalized students of color? "Yes, but . . ." The equivocation of this response is prompted by considering the question from the double perspectives of theory and practice, moral courage and political power, transformation and conservation, potential and reality. The theory, morality, and transformative answer is "yes," without a doubt. Its certainty stems from the ideas that culture, teaching, and learning are interconnected and that school achievement increases to the extent to which teaching employs the cultural referents of the students to whom it is directed. The practice and political power answer is "yes," too, but somewhat qualified.

Research findings and classroom practices indicate that culturally responsive teaching improves different kinds of achievement. The only problem is that the body of evidence about these classroom practices is still relatively small. In their synthesis of research on the effects of culturally relevant education (or Culture-Based Education—CBE; their preferred nomenclature), Aronson and Laughter (2016) conceded this state of affairs, but still declared that there is a sufficient body of research to provide significant insights regarding the consistency and persistence of its effectiveness. More research will probably continue to be forthcoming, but whether the scope and magnitude will broaden, and the implementation of the findings will prevail and widen in face of other school reform initiatives (such as standardized testing and recurrent searches for instructional panaceas to fit all students), is unpredictable. Will most teachers have the courage, competence, and confidence to do what they must to make their instruction more culturally responsive for students of color from marginalized groups, poverty, linguistically diverse backgrounds, and recent immigration experiences? Will other dimensions of schooling that should complement classroom instruction, such as administrative, policy, staffing, and assessment reforms, be forthcoming? Will changes in society at large soon end longstanding racial discrimination and social inequities? If such changes are not made, then the achievement of students of color will not be maximized. The unfortunate precedents from existing educational practices will prevail, and yet another generation of students will experience disproportionate failure in and unpleasant memories of schools.

INTRODUCTION

The preceding chapters demonstrate how and why teachers who use culturally responsive approaches to teaching underachieving African, Latino, Asian, and Native American students improve their school performance, even in the midst of school and societal contexts that are not moving in similar directions. These experiences should encourage other teachers to do likewise. Several ideas gleaned from the discussions in Chapters 1–7 provide some important directions to follow in increasing the implementation of culturally responsive pedagogy in schools. These are discussed in this chapter. The emergence of these ideas is somewhat like the Sankofa principle of looking back to the past to make better sense of the present, and to construct a more desirable future. Literally, Sankofa means "we should reach back and gather the best of what our past has to teach us, so that we can achieve our full potential as we move forward. Whatever we have lost, forgotten, forgone or been stripped of, can be reclaimed, revived, preserved and perpetuated" (duboislc.net/SankofaMeaning.html). The previous chapters in this book are "the past"; this chapter is "the present" (although a very transient and fleeting one for the author); and the effects of all the chapters and their associated recommendations and invitations symbolize "the future" for culturally responsive teaching.

CULTURALLY CENTERED INCREMENTAL EFFORTS MAKE A DIFFERENCE

While systemic, multidirectional educational equity and culturally responsive teaching are most desirable, individuals do not have to wait for these to happen before taking action on their own. Micro-level changes, such as those that take place within classrooms, are important, too. Their effectiveness needs to be determined *within context*. Otherwise, some of their positive results may be overlooked. The descriptions, proposals, and practices of culturally responsive teaching described throughout this book are types of micro-educational reforms that have improved the academic, social, and emotional development of many ethnically diverse students of color.

An important question is whether the progress made by micro-level changes will endure over time, especially since the initiatives that produce them may have short life spans or operate in relative isolation from other aspects of schooling. For example, curriculum and instructional reforms may produce improvement in student achievement at the classroom level that do not show up in standardized test scores. This may happen because the content of the national and state tests is not aligned with culturally responsive teaching in classrooms.

Something fundamentally different from what currently is happening must occur in how large numbers of students of color are taught if their school achievement is ever to improve significantly. This is a necessity, not a choice, and it is urgent. The patterns of disproportionate underachievement for some segments of the African, Native, Latino, and Asian American student populations are too persistent to be chance occurrences or to respond to sporadic, cosmetic, and selective reforms. The changes need to be sustained, substantive, and comprehensive. This is another reason why classroom teachers, however dedicated and capable they may be, cannot do the job alone. Nor can schools. Concomitant changes to provide higher-quality and equitable opportunities for people of color must occur in all segments of society. Yet within their primary domain of influence, teachers can (and do) make significant contributions to student achievement through what and how they teach. Therefore, culturally responsive pedagogy is essential to improving the performance of underachieving students of color.

Some teachers are already achieving remarkable success with academically marginalized Latino, Native, African, and Asian American students. They deserve to be applauded, as some were in the preceding chapters. Undoubtedly, there are many other teachers who should be complimented, but their stories were not readily accessible for inclusion here. And there are some teachers who are not doing as well as they could in implementing culturally responsive teaching. With some cultural knowledge, pedagogical skills, encouragement, and support, they would do much better. *Culturally Responsive Teaching* is for all these individuals. For those teachers who are succeeding, it is validating. For those willing to try different approaches to teaching ethnically diverse students but somewhat hesitant, it should be encouraging. For teachers who resist doing culturally responsive teaching with low-achieving students of color, the programs and practices presented in Chapters 1–7 represent mandates for change. The need to improve the achievement of these students is too pressing for teachers to ignore pedagogical techniques that can make a difference.

There is no big mystery about what the changes should be. Students of color should always be the center—the source, focus, and effect—of instructional programs and practices designed for them. Since they are ethnically and culturally diverse, their educational opportunities and experiences must be likewise. This culturally sensitive, pedagogical variability and plurality should become the new normative standards of accountability for teaching effectiveness.

CONFRONTING CONVENTION AND RESISTING RESISTANCE

To act on these ideas, teachers need to deconstruct and transform some longstanding pedagogical assumptions, beliefs, and practices, and to understand and counter opposition. Most educational conventions are not *deliberately* intended to discriminate against students of color, but in fact they do. They are deeply embedded within the fabric of educational routines. These assumptions and practices may be considered as "just the ways things are done" in mainstream educational processes, but they can be powerful obstacles to changing teaching to make it more effective for underachieving African, Latino, Native, and Asian American students. Culturally responsive educators should not make their advocacy and actions contingent on popularity and mass approval. Equity and social justice in education (and other aspects of U.S. society) for the different and marginalized are still very problematic for large segments of the population generally and educators specifically. Classroom teachers and other educators need to understand what the obstacles are and how they are manifested behaviorally before they can effectively reveal, resist, and resolve them. Several of these educational conventions and obstacles are discussed below.

Tradition

One of the most recalcitrant of these obstacles is the *tenacity of tradition*. U.S. educational institutions are notoriously conservative and resistant to change. They pride themselves on being consistent over time, and the recurring appeal for the resurrection of the nostalgic past (e.g., "back to the basics") in opposition to innovations (especially after the novelty pales without leaving behind miraculous changes) is not surprising. A case in point is the current resurgence of phonics-focused, skill-and-drill reading programs such as DISTAR and Open Court, after experimentation with whole-language instruction and writing-to-read did not produce radical improvements in reading performance. Another is the preoccupation with standardized testing, which has a long history of failure for improving the academic achievement of students of color, with the possible exception of some East Asian American groups such as Japanese, Chinese, and South Koreans. The problem with these kinds of appeals is the selective memory on which they are based. That memory conveniently forgets that "the past" was not very glorious for students of color. They were not performing well then, as they are not now. Nor were the cultures and contributions of their ethnic groups honored in the curricula taught in schools. The "good times" in education for members of mainstream society—the tradition—that some wish to resurrect were the worst of times for many marginalized ethnic minorities.

However, there are other "pasts" and "traditions" that are often overlooked that could empower, rather than obstruct, culturally responsive teaching. Many different groups of new ethnic immigrants to the United States have created neighborhood, cultural, and/or language schools to teach and preserve their cultural heritages, help themselves and their children adapt to a new country and culture, and compensate for the failure of mainstream schools. A graphic example of these initiatives are the forerunners to historically Black colleges and universities (HBCUs), many of which began as high schools and vocational training institutions to educate African American who were denied access to even the basic education offered in mainstream schools. Their longevity alone is a testament to their success, but other confirming evidence exists, too. Other examples of historical community- and culturally-based schools and instructional programs created by different ethnic communities that could be instructive for mainstream schools and teachers vested in contemporary culturally responsive teaching are: street corner and political academies (such as the Student Nonviolent Coordinating Committee—SNCC—of the 1960s and 1970s, for college political activists primarily) to resist racism and discrimination; language and cultural schools for immigrant Italians and Germans in the 1920s; Filipino community centers and neighborhood networking; and contemporary Japanese and Chinese language schools in various cities throughout the United States. For these ethnic community-based education traditions to be of value to mainstream educators today, much work will need to be done. This work will have to include: acknowledging that there is not one, but many, educational traditions in the United States, in the past and the present; conceding that individuals and communities of color can, and do, make valuable contributions to their own uplift and well-being; and rescuing these historical educational legacies for the archives of mainstream silence, marginalization, and denigration toward ethnically, culturally, and racially diverse groups and communities.

Volunteerism

Another obstacle to implementing culturally responsive teaching at the scale that is needed for it to make a sustainable difference is the practice of *professional volunteerism*. Teacher educators, inservice staff developers, administrative and supervisory personnel, policymakers, and accrediting agencies must stop promoting or tolerating the idea that dealing with ethnic and cultural diversity in the educational process is a choice, or that teachers can attend to ethnic diversity in their classrooms and professional development if they have any time left after other tasks have been accomplished. Nothing is further from the truth. If the patterns of achievement among ethnic students of color are to be reversed, culturally responsive teaching preparation and practice have to be required of everyone.

Teachers are not allowed to formally teach subjects for which they have no academic preparation. Professional regulations do not even allow teachers educated in cultures and countries different from U.S. society to teach without additional preparation in the United States. For instance, the employment status of individuals who were high-level educational leaders in Cambodia, Nigeria, or Sri Lanka prior to immigrating does not transfer into U.S. schools. If they wish to teach at all, they have to start over by completing new professional preparation programs and accepting entry-level positions. The imposition of these conditions on employment for teachers is not considered harsh or unusual because of the beliefs we hold about knowledge of sociocultural content and contexts being essential to teaching effectiveness. Since the achievement of many students of color is dependent on their ethnic and cultural differences being embraced in the classroom, teachers cannot be allowed or enticed to think that culturally responsive teaching is anything other than an obligatory and necessary part of their professional preparation and performance accountability. Thus, culturally responsive teaching for ethnically, racially, socially, and residentially diverse students is a normative and pedagogical requirement for their educational equity and excellence.

Professional Racism

Yet another obstacle to moving forward effectively with the widespread implementation of culturally responsive teaching is a subtle form of *professional racism*. It occurs in the guise of dealing with teaching ethnically different students by underscoring the need for more teachers of color. The need for more Latino, Asian, Native, and African American teachers in U.S. schools is unquestionable. But to make improving the achievement of students of color contingent only on fulfilling this need is based on a very fallacious and dangerous assumption. It presumes that membership in an ethnic group is necessary or sufficient to enable teachers to do effective culturally competent pedagogy. This is as ludicrous as assuming that one automatically knows how to teach English to others simply because he or she is a native speaker, or that a person has to be a time-warp traveler between modern times and antiquity to teach ancient Greek, Aztec, or Egyptian history. These assumptions also ignore the lessons learned from research that knowledge and use of the cultural heritages, experiences, and perspectives of ethnic groups in teaching are far more important to improving student achievement than is shared group membership. Furthermore, teachers of color may not identify or be affiliated strongly with their ethnicity; nor are they automatically skilled in culturally responsive teaching simply because of their ethnic-group membership. Admittedly, similar ethnicity between students and teachers may be potentially beneficial, but it is not a guarantee of pedagogical effectiveness.

In fact, some African American teachers are better at teaching European American than African American students. Some European American teachers achieve stellar success with African American, Native American, Asian American, and Latino American students. Some Japanese American teachers are very effective in teaching students from a variety of Asian backgrounds (e.g., Japanese, Chinese, Filipino, Cambodian, Vietnamese, East Indian), as well as European, Native, Latino, and African Americans. Others may not be very good at teaching any of these groups. Other teachers really are best at teaching students from their own ethnic background. In all of these examples (and many others unnamed), the ability of teachers to make their instruction personally meaningful and culturally congruent for students accounts for their success, not their ethnic identity per se. Many of the individuals introduced in Chapters 3–6 are these kinds of "cultural and ethnic border-crossers" (such as Vida Hall in Chapter 3 and Lois in Chapter 2, and the AVID project teachers in Chapter 6) in that they are members of one ethnic group and successful teachers of students from other ethnic and racial groups.

Making culturally responsive teaching contingent on the presence of more teachers of color is justified on the basis that underachieving students need more successful ethnic role models to identify with and emulate. On first hearing, this may sound like a plausible pedagogical idea and one that many educators of color endorse. Closer scrutiny may reveal a deeper, subtle message (whether intended or not) that teachers of color can be experts only on themselves. Yet when they self-initiate support for ethnic-group-specific schools or programs (such as African-centered academies and separate courses of study on various ethnic groups), the same individuals often are accused by their mainstream peers of being "separatists" or "reverse racists." What other explanation is there but racism when the empowered mainstreamers make essentially the same proposal for teachers of color to teach students from their own ethnic groups and are applauded for it, while their peers of color are vehemently opposed? Sure, the European American arguments are more subtle, and those of the proponents of color are more overt, but the message of both is very similar—teachers of color should assume the primary responsibility (and, by extension, blame) for the achievement of students from their own ethnic groups.

The idea of students of color being taught only by teachers from their own ethnic groups is also untenable because it is undoable. Even if all teachers of color were highly competent and willing advocates of culturally responsive pedagogy (of course, this is not the case), there are not enough of them to take on the task by themselves and make a real difference in student achievement. Their current proportional representation in the profession, and in relation to the number of students of color in schools, is not going to increase significantly in the foreseeable future. The fact of life is that the overwhelming majority of U.S. teachers are European Americans. Even if it were wise to do so, they simply cannot be absolved or excused from the responsibility of effectively teaching students of color. Therefore, ethnic and racial identity itself cannot be used as the "scapegoat" for why either teachers or students are not performing maximally in their respective roles. All teachers, regardless of their ethnic-group membership, must be taught how to do, and held accountable for doing, culturally responsive teaching for diverse students, just as students from all ethnic and racial groups must be held accountable for high-level academic achievement and provided feasible means to accomplish it.

Individualism and Compartmentalization

The emphases given to individuality and compartmentalization in conventional schooling also can be obstacles to effective culturally responsive teaching. Many educators genuinely believe that it is only the individual, not his or her race, ethnicity, culture, or gender, that counts in the learning process. However much those who take this stand may wish it so, these variables cannot be ignored in designing and implementing pedagogical practices for improving student achievement. Individuals cannot be separated from the contexts of their lives (invariably some form of groupness) if their human integrity is to be honored and their achievement potential maximized. Cultural heritages, social contexts, and background experiences, along with individual attributes, count in critical ways for both teaching and learning.

As the educational process has become increasingly complex, rampant specialization has emerged as the way to effectively manage this complexity. Thus, learning experiences, teaching responsibilities, and instructional programs are organized according to specialization of subjects or disciplines (e.g., math, science, literature) and areas within these (e.g., algebra and calculus, biology and chemistry, American and English literature). Curriculum content and instructional activities are separated according to whether they are designed to facilitate intellectual or emotional development. Some content and skills are perceived as paramount functions of the educational enterprise (intellectual development), while others are considered less so, if at all (cultural, moral, and spiritual development). Even the impassioned claim that "it's the individual that counts" is a kind of compartmentalization.

In actuality, the best potentials for and actual levels of learning achieved are holistic. They deal simultaneously with multiple aspects of the phenomena to be learned (such as facts, opinions, feelings, critiques, applications, reconstructions, and reconfigurations), and the various dimensions of humanness (e.g., intellectual, social, personal, emotional, physical, ethical, etc.). John Dewey (1902) presented a compelling argument for this fact more than a century ago, yet it is still pertinent today. Although he was not speaking specifically about educating ethnically and culturally different students, his cogent ideas can be applied to this challenge, and they are worth repeating. He said, in part:

> The child's life is an integral, a total one. He passes quickly and readily from one topic to another, as from one spot to another, but is not conscious of translation or break. . . . The things that occupy him are held together by the unity of the personal and social interests which his life carries along. Whatever is uppermost in his mind constitutes to him, for the time being, the whole universe. That universe is fluid and fluent; its contents dissolve and re-form with amazing rapidity. But, after all, it is the child's own world. It has the unity and completeness of his own. He goes to school, and various studies divide and fractionalize the world for him. (pp. 8–10)

Educational fractionalization is exacerbated for students of color who bring to school cultural heritages, experiences, needs, and capabilities that frequently are not recognized and rewarded by schools. The resulting division of loyalties and cultural inconsistencies provoke high levels of intrapsychic disequilibrium and intellectual/emotional stress. No wonder so many students of color are not performing as well as they could. To prevent these negative consequences, instructional programs and practices should deal simultaneously with the realities of their human wholeness, their ethnic and cultural particularities, and their individual uniqueness. These priorities are neither dichotomous nor synonymous. Instead, a symbiotic interaction exists among, as well as within, these different levels of learning. Teachers cannot claim to have attended sufficiently to all by dealing with one of them, as some are inclined to believe, when they pridefully point out that they are committed to educating *individual* students.

Cultural Hegemony

The greatest of all obstacles to culturally responsive teaching is mainstream ethnocentrism and hegemony. They effectively block the acquisition and application of new, culturally relevant pedagogical knowledge, skills, and will in teaching African, Latino, Native, and Asian American students. Some educators fail to realize that the assumptions, expectations, protocols, and practices considered normative in conventional education are not universal and immutable. They are based on the standards of the cultural system of one ethnic group—European Americans—that have been imposed on all others. This cultural system is a human creation and, as such, is fallible and mutable. Its biggest fallibility is its assumed universality and "that's the right way" justifications for its beliefs, values, and behaviors. Hymes's (1985) observation that "what man has made, man can change" is instructive here for reconceptualizing the normative cultural foundations of schooling (p. xxxiii).

The imposition of Eurocentric values and orientations on everyone else is un-American and unhuman, not to mention being morally suspect and pedagogically unsound. U.S. society and culture, in fact, is comprised of a multitude of multiethnic and multivaried peoples, contributions, and influences. This obligates school programs and practices to likewise be multicultural. Furthermore, research evidence (although not as inclusive and extensive as it needs to be) consistently demonstrates that when teaching and learning are filtered through the cultural frameworks of students of color, their achievement (of many kinds) improves dramatically. Why, then, are schools en masse not hastening to make the necessary changes? Probably because these changes require transforming prevailing paradigms of power, privilege, and normalcy within the educational enterprise. However discomforting this challenge may be to the guardians of pedagogical traditions, the change must occur if the performance of ethnically diverse students is to be reversed, and if better-quality, relevant, and honorable education is to be available to all students. The failure to do so can cause irreversible damage to the intellectual, social, emotional, psychological, cultural, and academic achievement of some students. As the United Negro College Fund's promotional motto admonishes, "a mind is a terrible thing to waste," meaning it is too precious to be undernourished. Two equally important ideas particularly relevant to culturally responsive teaching can be added to this caution. They are that the best indication of the genuine quality of an educational system is how well it serves students with the greatest needs, and the future of a society is as good as the present it provides for its children. Cultural diversity is a plausible means for accomplishing all of these in the United States.

CULTURALLY RESPONSIVE TEACHING'S COMPREHENSIVE BENEFITS

Culturally responsive teaching produces positive results in many ways for many different constituencies, including society writ large. When done appropriately, its theory and practice promote the idea that educational excellence for all students is more inclusive than mastery of academic knowledge deemed mandatory in schools. Ultimately, both students who are victimized by and the perpetrators of inequities, the marginalized and the mainstream, the minority and the majority, the economically privileged and underprivileged, the female and the male, the native and the immigrant, need to be liberated from the consequences of the unfair distribution of power, resources, and opportunities, and learn to engage more humanely with themselves and each other. For example, students who perform highly on academic content and standardized tests but are racist, sexist, and unethical in their personal, social, and civic behaviors would be considered intolerable and educationally "unfinished." Conversely, many individuals who are adroit community members, active advocates for social justice, culturally knowledgeable and affiliated, live by high moral and ethical standards, and are economically successful, would be considered very accomplished, even if their formal education is only average.

However, the point is not to value one type of growth and development to the exclusion of all others, but to develop multiple abilities simultaneously. Youth and adults thusly skilled and knowledgeable contribute to making society more equitable, receptive, and reflective of diverse peoples, experiences, perspectives, and contributions. Hence, an individual's, community's, school's, classroom's, and society's diversity is made manifest without equivocation or apology; it is normative and distinguishable in every facet of living and learning.

WHERE TO BEGIN AND WHEN TO END

The quick answer to these questions are "Very Young," "Everywhere," and "Never." These questions, or some facsimile of them, are often asked by educators who still have some doubts about the validity and viability of culturally responsive teaching beyond very restricted contexts. They fail to understand that culturally responsive teaching is not a temporary, quick-fix measure that can be abandoned after a short time, allowing schools and teachers to then return to business as usual. Instead, it should be considered as the "new normative" and permanent criteria for providing equitable and excellent education for the demographically diverse students in U.S. schools. Since teaching and learning are always nested in culture, and both processes are populated by multiple cultures, as long as teachers teach and students learn, culturally responsive education should be occurring. In other words, if high-quality and valid learning experiences are to always be available to ethnically and racially diverse students, then culturally responsive teaching has to always be; its presence is permanent! It also has to be "everywhere," since students learn throughout the entire infrastructure of schooling, sometimes formally and at other times informally, sometimes intentionally and at other times not, sometimes purposefully and at other times by happenstance, sometimes as a result of forethought but at other times incidentally, and sometimes through direct personal experience at and other times vicariously. All of these "ways of learning" are opportunities for culturally responsive teaching—thus, when fully in force, it is everywhere, all the time! It certainly belongs in all parts of the educational enterprise, all subjects taught, and all levels of schooling.

The other part of this dilemma is when is the best time, developmentally, to begin culturally responsive teaching with students. Some educators feel that some of the issues that this innovation deals with, such as racism and discrimination, are too harsh for very young preschool and kindergarten students. Others signal, through deliberate exclusion or simple oversight, that college students of color and poverty do not need this intervention because being in college is evidence of their academic success. Their educational focus should instead be on developing higher-order academic expertise. Both arguments overlook some major issues that could be remediated with culturally responsive teaching for young children and for college students. Research indicates that children are aware of race and racism at a very young age. Wanless and Crawford (2016) and Derman-Sparks and Edwards (2010) explain that children's ideas about their own and others' race are being shaped in early childhood, regardless of whether the topic is directly addressed, completely ignored, or actively suppressed in their classrooms. The common practice among many early childhood educators of attempting to ignore race and other human differences is untenable. Instead, intentional and routine teaching about ethnic, racial, and cultural diversity in early childhood education can circumvent future dilemmas and negative consequences.

Young children, even babies, are very curious about everything as they are discovering, encountering, and interacting with the world that surrounds them for the first time in their lives—they are explorers and adventurers! Their insatiable desire to know, to see, to do, can be the ideal framework to address ethnic, racial, and cultural diversity within their naturalistic discovery learning. Culturally responsive teaching during these formative years can access young children's natural curiosity and ensure that they acquire accurate information about, positive attitudes toward, and effective relationships with different ethnic, racial, and cultural individuals and experiences. It also can help these children understand, from the very beginning, that human differences are natural and normal, and should always be acknowledged, respected, and valued as part of dignifying the humanity of self and others.

In promoting the arts as a medium for teaching early childhood education students, Purnell, Ali, Begum, and Carte (2007) mention some other attributes of both that can act as entry points for culturally responsive teaching for this age group. According to these authors, young children have a natural inclination to be storytellers, actors, and artists; for them the arts—drawing, moving, singing, and creative play—are a unique language. The inherent characteristics of the arts are very compatible with the ultimate objective (and many of the methods) of culturally responsive teaching, which are to maximize the human dignity, capacities, and possibilities of diverse students. As Purnell et al. explain, the arts

> provide opportunities to think and learn in new ways; they allow us to communicate when other forms of language fail; and they enrich the spaces in which we live. When we apply these benefits to the classroom we broaden the scope of our teaching to include all of our students' senses, learning styles, intelligences,

and backgrounds. The arts are both a method of communication and one of the most important ways that people develop a sense of cultural and personal identity. . . . For young children multicultural stories can act as a mirror, reflecting and validating the students' cultural identity. For children from diverse backgrounds, these stories are windows into a new realm of experiences. (2007, p. 421)

Since young children are naturalistic and uninhibited artists and explorers, this stage of life seems like an ideal time for them to begin deliberately incorporating knowledge of ethnic, racial, and cultural diversity into their evolving funds of knowledge, ethical standards, and repertoires of being and behaving.

At the other end of the education spectrum is the question of whether culturally responsive teaching in college is necessary. The assumption claimed by many that undergraduate and graduate college students of color have "made it" is not necessary true. Mainstream college campuses, or PWIs (Predominately White Institutions), are often hostile and unfriendly toward them; and many students of color, immigrants, and internationals feel isolated and culturally adrift in these environments, even when they are performing adequately academically. In other words, their on-campus quality of life is far from desirable or culturally affirming. Consequently, they could benefit from the social, emotional, political, and cultural sustaining dimensions of culturally responsive teaching, even if the academic may not be necessary, but that, too is debatable.

ALTERNATIVE PARADIGMS FOR PRACTICE

The legitimacy and viability of cultural diversity in teaching and learning for ethnically diverse students are far from being commonly accepted among educators. Even those who are receptive to them often do not have the depth of knowledge, competence, and confidence needed to guide pedagogical practices. A notion frequently expressed by teachers is the importance of "awareness, sensitivity, appreciation, and respect" for cultural diversity in racially and ethnically pluralistic classrooms. Others confess to feeling guilty about the educational and societal injustices that have been imposed upon people of color, and fearful of making mistakes and being inadvertently insulting in interracial and intercultural interactions. Others are sympathetic to the cause for justice and equity in education for students and communities of color, but feel incapable of doing anything about it beyond "being aware." Or they are intimidated by the prospect of "going against the system," and prevailing educational policies and priorities (such as the Common Core Standards and standardized testing). These declarations give the appearance of change, but, in fact, they are more illusionary than real.

Personal awareness and empathic feelings about ethnic and cultural diversity without accompanying pedagogical actions do not lead to instructional improvements for students of color. Positive recognition of and attitudes toward ethnic and cultural diversity are necessary but not sufficient for dealing effectively with the educational needs and potentialities of ethnically diverse students. Some teachers may know very well that attitudes are not enough to accomplish sound pedagogical reforms but still focus energy and attention on them to avoid really *doing* anything.

Culturally competent instructional action is essential to achieving genuine commitment to educational equity, justice, and excellence for students of color. Teachers who truly care about students are persistent in their expectations of high performance from them and are diligent in their efforts to ensure that these expectations are realized. They know that a genuine commitment to transforming educational opportunities for their ethnically diverse students requires that they have knowledge of the cultural characteristics of different ethnic groups and of how culture affects teaching and learning, as well as pedagogical skills for translating this knowledge into new teaching–learning opportunities and experiences. They also must have the moral courage and the will to stay the course in efforts to make the educational enterprise more multiculturally and multiethnically responsive, even in the face of the opposition that is surely to come from somewhere. As Dillard (1997) suggests:

> Learning how to live and teach through diversity, including the inevitable struggles and contradictions, seems especially important. . . . [and] becoming a literate teacher, in relation to diversity, means doing more than writing and reading *about* culture—it means learning to *be* diverse in perspectives, skills, and knowledges. It means understanding, influencing, and participating in the lives of diverse students, schools, and the wider society. Thus, the integration and valuing of diverse and multiple literacies is [*sic*] crucial to the philosophy, pedagogy, and practice of teacher education and preparation. (p. 94, emphasis in original)

Cultivating the competence and confidence needed to implement culturally responsive teaching should begin in preservice teacher education programs and continue in inservice professional development. During preservice it should include acquiring information about cultural characteristics and contributions, pedagogical principles, and methods and materials for ethnic and cultural diversity. This knowledge should be complemented with learning experiences for teacher education students to critically examine existing paradigms of educational thought and practice to determine whether they can be modified to accommodate ethnic and cultural diversity, or whether they need to be replaced. These analyses should be supplemented with supervised practices in designing and implementing replacement models; for example, determining what "authentic assessment" means within the context of ethnic diversity and culturally responsive teaching. How might portfolio assessment be modified to better accommodate the components of the learning styles of different ethnic groups? Or what changes are needed in structured academic controversy (SAC) approaches to problem-solving to make them illuminate culturally responsive teaching ideologies and methodologies?

Infrastructures also need to be created to support inservice teachers who are trying to implement culturally responsive teaching. These may need to include several different components, such as (1) staff development to acquire knowledge of ethnic diversity and culturally responsive teaching; (2) availability of necessary instructional materials; (3) systematic ways in which teachers can receive constructive feedback on their efforts and recognition for their accomplishments in implementing culturally responsive teaching; (4) activities in other aspects of the educational enterprise, such as administration, counseling, curriculum design, performance evaluation, and extracurricular activities, comparable to (but jurisdictionally appropriate) culturally responsive classroom teaching; and (5) clearly defined techniques for meeting the opposition that culturally diverse people and programs may encounter in both the school and the community.

The absence of any one of these elements of cognitive, pedagogical, and political agency is likely to lead to underestimating the challenges of making education better for students of color. This possibility brings to mind prospective teachers who optimistically but naively think that their "desire to be caring and appreciative of cultural diversity" and novel multicultural curriculum designs will automatically expedite radical improvements in student learning, only to be disappointed soon after entering the classroom. This kind of hopefulness and optimism is important in teaching underachieving students of color, but it needs to be anchored in and augmented by preparation for and commitment to diligent struggle. The struggle requires *caring*, to be complemented by content and pedagogical *competence*, personal and professional *confidence*, and moral and ethical *conviction*. How these lessons were implemented by creators of the Webster Groves Writing Project (Krater et al., 1994) is useful for others to emulate. Four years into the project, the participating teachers realized they had to change themselves if they hoped to improve the writing performance of their students. The masks and myths of cultural neutrality and color-blindness in teachers, and cultural invisibility in students, needed to be deconstructed. The teachers in the project came to realize that

> we could make no headway solving our problems [improving writing achievement] until we looked carefully at ourselves, studied what we saw, changed the vision, and realized a new solution—one out of the realm of what we already

knew . . . we had to move out of our comfort zone, . . . stretching ourselves to brand-new, out-of-the-ordinary solutions. We did this through self-study, kid watching, and reflection. (Krater et al., pp. 426–427)

The most compelling and instructive points in this story are that the teachers stopped blaming and trying to "fix" the students, validated the worth of the students' cultural heritages, accepted the inevitability of cultural influences on their own beliefs and behaviors, disavowed the sanctity of educational conventions, and placed the burden of change upon themselves. Additional support for the power of these contentions and orientations toward teaching students of color is evident in the research, programs, and practices discussed in Chapters 3–6. They provide powerful lessons that all teachers should learn and use to guide their instructional actions with ethnically and culturally different students.

Culturally responsive teachers also "go where they have not been before" by expanding their pedagogical repertoires, sometimes into novelty and unorthodoxy. Teaching to different ethnic and cultural learning styles demands this. Additionally, teachers have to be willing to experiment, to use novel approaches, to engage in "leaps of faith" in instructional practices. Sometimes innovative teaching and learning unleashes creativity and expedites mastery by, as Maxine Greene would say, "making the unfamiliar familiar" and demystifying academic content. Teaching culturally diverse content and students through the motifs and substance of film, photography, fiction, poetry, biography and autobiography, games, actual and vicarious experiences, drama, online relationships, and travel are exciting and viable pedagogical possibilities for teachers to pursue in order to improve their effectiveness.

CHALLENGES AND INVITATIONS

The research, theory, and practice presented in the previous chapters are not exhaustive; rather they are illustrative of developments in culturally responsive teaching to date. As need continues and demand increases, more explanations and proposals for practice are forthcoming. It was impossible to include everything that is now available and/or in the making. Hopefully, as teachers and other users of this "unfinished story" of culturally responsive teaching, you will still find it validating, enticing, and instructive in your pursuit of additional insights and opportunities. It also should encourage you to contribute your own analyses, interpretations, and creations. The field, and the students it serves, are continually evolving. We need new knowledge and actions for all students' further growth and development.

NOW IS THE TIME

Teachers and other educators should act now, without a moment's hesitation and with deliberate speed, to revise the entire educational enterprise so that it reflects and responds to the ethnic and cultural diversity that characterizes U.S. society and its schools. The underachievement of marginalized African, Asian, Native, and Latino American students is too pervasive to do anything less. The question is not whether to act, but how soon and in what ways. Acting with deliberate speed does not mean being capricious, impulsive, or irresponsible. Nor does it mean trying to operate on good intentions alone. Instead, teachers should be trained in the knowledge and skills of culturally responsive pedagogy for ethnic diversity, systematically supported in their praxis efforts, and held accountable for quality performance within the context of cultural diversity.

Reform cannot wait until teachers and other educators are comfortable with the idea of culturally responsive pedagogy or are certain of their mastery of the skills necessary for its implementation. Change is never easy, and its effects cannot be predicted with absolute certainty. But the consequences for not doing so should be sufficient to sustain teachers as they make the transition to new ways of teaching if they genuinely care (as described in Chapter 3) about the comprehensive well-being of students of color. If this is not adequate to motivate their pedagogical movement, then firmly applied accountability mandates should. Mastery is a developmental phenomenon that is acquired over time. And the only absolute certainty in the arena of teaching in general, and of teaching marginalized students of color in particular, is that many things done in the past must not continue in the future.

Failures and mistakes are not self-correcting; they must be deliberately transformed. Teachers can expedite this transformation for themselves and their ethnically diverse students by embracing, with diligence and enthusiasm, culturally responsive pedagogy. For a time, their training for and practice of it probably will have to occur in tandem. This notion is not unorthodox or unprecedented. There is much support in certain educational arenas for "teaching by doing," "combining theory, research, and practice," "field-based, situated teacher education," and "place-based teaching and learning for diverse students." The benefit of training for and trying out culturally responsive teaching at the same time is how knowledge and praxis can reinforce and refine each other.

PILLARS FOR PROGRESS

Teachers need guidance in their attempts to do multiculturally responsive teaching. Some general principles can be extrapolated from the specific programs and practices discussed in detail in the preceding chapters that may be inspirational and instructive for teachers. They are offered here as "pillars for progress," or assessment benchmarks by which the adequacy of efforts to implement culturally responsive teaching can be determined. Ideally, all will occur at once, but a few are better, by far, than continuing tradition. Culturally responsive teaching has all of the following characteristics:

- It is a part of all subjects and skills taught at all grade levels.
- It has multiple benefits for all students. Of all the curricular programs, instructional practices, and research projects discussed in the preceding chapters, there was no instance in which improvements occurred for some ethnic groups or area of academic functioning but not for others.
- It cannot be a happenstance, sporadic, or fragmentary occurrence. Instead, it has to be deliberate and explicit, systematic and sustained. This is not something that happens only as notations of special events; it must *characterize* children's learning opportunities and experiences at all times.
- It has multiple emphases, features, and effects. It simultaneously addresses development of academic, psychological, emotional, social, moral, political, and cultural skills; it cultivates school success without compromising or constraining students' ethnic identity and cultural affiliation. In fact, it develops competence, confidence, and efficacy in these latter areas as well.
- It uses comprehensive and integrative approaches to teaching and learning, all of which are informed by the contexts and content of the cultures and lived experiences of different groups of color.
- It cultivates an ethos of academic success as well as a sense of community, camaraderie, kindredness, and reciprocity among students who work collaboratively for their mutual personal well-being and academic achievement.
- It requires a combination of curriculum content, school and classroom learning climates, instructional strategies, and interpersonal interactions that reflect the cultures, experiences, and perspectives of different ethnic groups of color.
- It deals with the general and the particular of ethnic and cultural diversity simultaneously; that is, it encompasses concepts and principles, patterns and trends that apply to all ethnic groups and the ways in which these are uniquely manifested in the cultures and experiences of specific ethnic groups and individuals.
- It includes accurate information about the cultures and contributions of different ethnic groups, as well as moral and ethical dilemmas about their treatment in the United States, the

redistribution of power and privilege, and the deconstruction of educational and societal racism and hegemony.

- It teaches ethnic students of color the "cultural capital" (i.e., the informal, tacit knowledge, skills, and behaviors to negotiate the rules, regulations, protocols, and demands of living within educational institutions) needed to succeed in schools.
- It considers achievement to be multidimensional and uses multifocal indicators in assessing the levels of accomplishment for students. Both the acquisition and demonstration of the various dimensions of achievements are synchronized with different ethnic groups' preferred learning, performance, participation, and communication styles.
- It engages students perpetually in processes of self-knowing and self-assessment.
- It demonstrates genuine caring and concern for students of color by demanding high levels of performance and facilitates their living up to these expectations.
- It creates cultural bridges, or scaffolds, between academic learning in school and the sociocultural lives and experiences of different groups of color outside of school.
- It teaches students to envision and develop the skills needed to construct more desirable futures and to be integral, active participants in these creations.
- It develops in students an intolerance for all kinds of oppression, discrimination, and exploitation, as well as the moral courage to act in promoting academic, social, cultural, and political justice among ethnic groups.
- It requires the professional development of teachers that includes cultural knowledge and instructional skills, in concert with personal self-reflection and self-monitoring techniques for teaching to and about ethnic diversity.
- It commits institutional and personal resources, along with creative imagination, to facilitating maximum achievement for students of color.

CONCLUSION

Children are our most valuable resource and investment for the future. They are far more precious than limitless amounts of money, unchallenged fame, or the most expensive gems. They are our best investments in the future. If they do not receive a high-quality education, the promise of a rich future will be unfulfilled. Let us act now to prevent such an unthinkable catastrophe by ensuring the best education possible for all children. The way to do this is to implement culturally responsive teaching for students from various ethnic groups now and always.

All our children deserve to be empowered on multiple levels. Empowerment encompasses competence, accomplishment, confidence, and efficacy. Their achievement needs to be academic, social, emotional, psychological, cultural, moral, and political. Children of color deserve to receive this kind of empowerment from their educational experiences so that the dream of a secure and successful future for them will no longer be deferred, minimized, or vanquished, but realized and maximized. Educators need to contribute to this realization by providing students with the best possible learning opportunities. This is a nonnegotiable moral imperative and a mandatory professional responsibility. The stakes are too high and the consequences too enduring to take chances on continuing to perpetuate underachievement among students of color.

The Quality Education for Minorities Project ended its 1990 policy statement, *Education That Works*, with a strong reaffirmation of the faith that ethnic groups of color have in the redemptive power of education. The explanations for why this is so are a fitting way to bring to a close this story of the need for, nature of, and effects of culturally responsive teaching for students of color. Speaking in a register of affiliation and kindredness with the constituent groups for whom they were advocates (Alaskan Natives, Native Americans, Mexican Americans, Puerto Ricans, and African Americans), the authors of *Education That Works* declared, "The gateway to a better life for us has always been education. . . . For us, education is freedom's foundation, and the struggle for a quality education is at the heart of our quest for liberty" (p. 1)—the ultimate achievement. Furthermore,

> The one force that has sustained and empowered *all* our people, has been the power of education. It has been our schools that have equipped individuals to take their places in the great work of transforming visions into realities. . . . Minority children, who by right and by virtue of their unlimited potential, surely deserve their own roles as visionaries and builders, are being shut out. If, indeed, education is the way we deal with the future before it arrives, then we are truly casting our future aside if we do not bend every effort to open opportunities for minority children. The door to the future for every child is first and foremost the door to the schoolhouse. (p. 89, emphasis in original)

This "doorway" is more metaphorical than literal, symbolizing access to opportunities for children and adolescents to learn to the very best of their capabilities, and in ways and environments that dignify their humanity. Teachers and other educators must have as much faith in the abilities of children to learn as children have in the power of education—and act accordingly. These shared beliefs open the way to improved student performance. But they will not be realized without *culturally responsive pedagogical competence*. Teachers cannot reasonably be expected to meet these challenges if they have not been adequately prepared for them. Therefore, both preservice and inservice education agents and agencies must include skills for culturally responsive teaching in their professional development programs for teachers. This is as crucial to improving the performance of underachieving students of color as is teachers being culturally responsive in K–12 classroom instruction.

References

AAUW report: How schools shortchange girls. (1995). The AAUW [American Association of University Women] Educational Foundation, Wellesley College Center for Research on Women.

Abrahams, R. D. (1970). *Positively Black.* Englewood Cliffs, NJ: Prentice-Hall.

Abrahams, R. D., & Troike, R. C. (Eds.). (1972). *Language and cultural diversity in American education.* Englewood Cliffs, NJ: Prentice-Hall.

Adichie, C, N. (2009). The danger of a single story. *Youtube*, Retrieved from youtube.com/watch?v=D9Ihs241zeg.

Alaska Native Knowledge Network (ANKN). (2010). Guidelines for respecting cultural knowledge. Retrieved from ankn.uaf.edu/publications/knowledge.html

Albury, A. (1992). *Social orientations, learning conditions, and learning outcomes among low-income Black and White grade school children.* Unpublished doctoral dissertation, Howard University, Washington, DC.

Alim, H. S., & Baugh, J. (Eds.). (2007). *Talkin' Black talk: Language, education and social change.* New York, NY: Teachers College Press.

Allen, B. A. (1987). *The differential effects of low and high movement and sensate stimulation affordance on the learning of Black and White working class children.* Unpublished doctoral dissertation, Howard University, Washington, DC.

Allen, B. A., & Boykin, A. W. (1991). The influence of contextual factors on Afro-American and Euro-American children's performance: Effects of movement opportunity and music. *International Journal of Psychology, 26*(3), 373–387.

Allen, B. A., & Boykin, A. W. (1992). African-American children and the educational process: Alleviating cultural discontinuity through prescriptive pedagogy. *School Psychology Review, 21*(4), 586–598.

Allen, B. A., & Butler, L. (1996). The effects of music and movement opportunity on the analogical reasoning performance of African American and White school children: A preliminary study. *Journal of Black Psychology, 22*(3), 316–328.

Allen, J. E. (1998, May 6). Children see minorities stereotyped on TV. *Seattle Times*, p. A8.

American Association of Colleges of Teacher Education. (1973, November). No one model American: A statement on multicultural education. Retrieved from eric.ed.gov/?id=ED143631

American Evaluation Association. (2011). American Evaluation Association statement on cultural competence in evaluation. Retrieved from eval.org/ccstatement

American Textbook Council. (2003). Islam and the textbooks: A report of the American Textbook Council. *Middle East Quarterly, 10*(3), 69–78

Anyon, J. (1988). Schools as agents of social legitimization. In W. F. Pinar (Ed.), *Contemporary curriculum discourses* (pp. 175–200). Scottsdale, AZ: Gorsuch Scarisbrick.

Anyon, J. (1997). *Ghetto schooling: A political economy of urban educational reform.* New York, NY: Teachers College Press.

Anzaldua, G. (2004). Linguistic terrorism. In O. Santa Ana (Ed.), *Tongue tied: The lives of multilingual children in public education* (pp. 270–271). Lanham, MD: Rowman & Littlefield.

Apple, M. W. (1985). The culture and commerce of the textbook. *Journal of Curriculum Studies, 17*(2), 147–162.

Aragon, J. (1973). An impediment to cultural pluralism: Culturally deficient educators attempting to teach culturally different children. In M. D. Stent, W. R. Hazard, & H. N. Rivlin (Eds.), *Cultural pluralism in education: A mandate for change* (pp. 77–84). New York, NY: Appleton-Century-Crofts.

Arciniega, T. A. (1975). The thrust toward pluralism: What progress? *Educational Leadership, 33*(3), 163–167.

Armstrong, T. (2000). *Multiple intelligences in the classroom* (2nd ed.). Alexandria, VA: Association for Supervision and Curriculum Development.

Aronson, B., & Laughter, J. (2016). The theory and practice of culturally relevant education: A synthesis of research across content areas. *Review of Educational Research, 86*(1), 163–206

Aronson, J. (2004). The threat of stereotype. *Educational Leadership, 62*(2), 14–19.

Asante, M. K. (1991/1992). Afrocentric curriculum. *Educational Leadership, 49*(4), 28–31.

Asante, M. K. (1998). *The Afrocentric idea* (rev. and exp. ed.). Philadelphia, PA: Temple University Press.

Asante, M. K. (2014). *Facing south to Africa: Toward an Afrocentric critical orientation.* Lanham, MD: Lexington Books.

Ascher, M. (1992). *Ethnomathematics.* New York, NY: Freeman.

Ashton, P. T., & Webb, R. B. (1986). *Making a difference: Teachers' sense of efficacy and student achievement.* New York, NY: Longman.

Au, K. H. (1980). Participation structures in a reading lesson with Hawaiian children: Analysis of a culturally appropriate instructional event. *Anthropology and Education Quarterly, 11*(2), 91–115.

Au, K. H. (1993). *Literacy instruction in multicultural settings.* New York, NY: Harcourt Brace.

Au, K. H., & Kawakami, A. J. (1985). Research currents: Talk story and learning to read. *Language Arts, 62*(4), 406–411.

Au, K. H., & Kawakami, A. J. (1991). Culture and ownership: Schooling of minority students. *Childhood Education, 67*(5), 280–284.

Au, K. H., & Kawakami, A. J. (1994). Cultural congruence in instruction. In E. R. Hollins, J. E. King, & W. C. Hayman (Eds.), *Teaching diverse populations: Formulating a knowledge base* (pp. 5–23). Albany, NY: State University of New York Press.

Au, K. H., & Mason, J. M. (1981). Social organizational factors in learning to read: The balance of rights hypothesis. *Reading Research Quarterly, 17*(1), 115–152.

August, D., & Shanahan, T. (Eds.). (2006). *Developing literacy in second-language learners: Report of the National Literacy Panel on language-minority children and youth*. Mahwah, NJ: Erlbaum.

Austin, A. M. B., Salehi, M., & Leffler, A. (1987). Gender and developmental differences in children's conversations. *Sex Roles, 16*(9–10), 497–510.

AVID. (n.d.). Retrieved from avidonline.org

Axtman, K. (1999, January 15). Native American to shine from new coin. *The Christian Science Monitor*, 4.

Ayers, W. (2001). *To teach: The journey of a teacher* (2nd ed.). New York, NY: Teachers College Press.

Ayers, W. (2004). *Teaching the personal and the political: Essays on hope and justice*. New York, NY: Teachers College Press.

Baber, C. R. (1987). The artistry and artifice of Black communication. In G. Gay & W. L. Baber (Eds.), *Expressively Black: The cultural basis of ethnic identity* (pp. 75–108). New York, NY: Praeger.

Ball, A. F., & Muhammad, R. J. (2003). Language diversity in teacher education and in the classroom. In G. Smitherman & V. Villanueva (Eds.), *Language diversity in the classroom: From intention to practice* (pp. 76–88). Carbondale, IL: Southern Illinois University Press.

Banks, J. A. (1974). Cultural pluralism and the schools. *Educational Leadership, 32*(3), 163–166.

Banks, J. A. (1991). A curriculum for empowerment, action, and change. In C. E. Sleeter (Ed.), *Empowerment through multicultural education* (pp. 125–141). Albany, NY: State University of New York Press.

Banks, J. A. (2003). *Teaching strategies for ethnic studies* (7th ed.). Boston, MA: Allyn & Bacon.

Banks, J. A. (Ed.). (2009). *The Routledge international companion to multicultural education*. New York, NY: Routledge.

Banks, J. A. (Ed.). (2012). *Encyclopedia of diversity in education* (Vols. 1–4). Thousand Oaks, CA: Sage.

Banks, J. A., & Banks, C. A. M. (Eds.). (2010). *Multicultural education: Issues and perspectives* (7th ed.). New York: Wiley.

Bankston, C. L., III, & Zhou, M. (1995). Effects of minority-language literacy on the academic achievement of Vietnamese youths in New Orleans. *Sociology of Education, 68*(1), 1–17.

Barbe, W. B., & Swassing, R. H. (1979). *Teaching through modality strengths: Concepts and practice*. Columbus, OH: Zaner-Bloser.

Barham, J., & Thomas, A. (n.d.). Jaime Escalante in the 21st century: Still standing and delivering. Retrieved from thebestschools.org/magazine/jaime-escalante-21st-century-still-standing-delivering/

Baron, N. (2016, July 20). Do students lose depth in digital reading? *The Conversation*. Retrieved from theconversation.com/do-students-lose-depth-in-digital-reading-61897

Bartell, T. G. (2011). Caring, race, culture, and power: A research synthesis toward supporting mathematics teachers in caring with awareness. *Journal of Urban Mathematics Education, 4*(1), 50–74.

Basic Education Act. (1993). Olympia, WA: State Department of Education. Retrieved from k12wa.us/curriculumInstruct/default.aspx

Baugh, J. (1999). *Out of the mouths of slaves: African American language and educational malpractice*. Austin: University of Texas Press.

Baugh, J. (2000). *Beyond Ebonics: Linguistic pride and racial prejudice*. New York, NY: Oxford University Press.

Belenky, M. F., Clinchy, B. M., Goldberger, N. R., & Tarule, J. M. (1986). *Women's ways of knowing: The development of self, voice, and mind*. New York, NY: Basic Books.

Bendall, R. C. A., Galpin, A., Marrow, L. P., & Cassidy, S. (2016). Cognitive style: Time to experiment. *Frontiers in Psychology, 7*(1786), 1–4.

Bennett, C. I. (1995, April). *Teacher perspectives as a tool for reflection, partnerships, and professional growth*. Paper presented at the annual meeting of the American Educational Research Association, San Francisco, CA.

Bennett, C. I. (2007). *Comprehensive multicultural education: Theory and practice* (6th ed.). Boston, MA: Pearson/Allyn & Bacon.

Bensman, D. (2000). *Central Park East and its graduates: "Learning by heart."* New York, NY: Teachers College Press.

Berman, L. M. (1994). What does it mean to be called to care? In M. E. Lashley, M. T. Neal, E. T. Slunt, L. M. Berman, & F. H. Hultgren (Eds.), *Being called to care* (pp. 5–16). Albany, NY: State University of New York Press.

Bernardo, A. (1996). *Fitting in*. Houston, TX: Arte Publico.

Biggs, M. (Producer & Director). (1987). *Ethnic notions* [Video]. San Francisco, CA: California Newsreel.

Biklen, S. K., & Pollard, D. (Eds.). (1993). *Gender and education. Part I (Ninety-second yearbook)*. Chicago, IL: National Society for the Study of Education.

Bishop, R. (1992). Extending multicultural understanding. In B. Cullinan (Ed.), *Invitation to read: More children's literature in the reading program* (pp. 80–91). Newark, DE: International Reading Association.

Bleich, E., Bloemraad, I., & Graauw, E. (2015). Migrants, minorities, and the media: Information, representations and participation in the public sphere. *Journal of Ethnic and Migration Studies, 41*(6), 857–873).

Bloom, B. (1956). *Taxonomy of educational objectives*. New York, NY: David McKay.

Boggs, S. T. (1985). The meaning of questions and narratives to Hawaiian children. In C. B. Cazden, V. P. John, & D. Hymes (Eds.), *Functions of language in the classroom* (pp. 299–327). Prospect Heights, IL: Waveland.

Boggs, S. T., Watson-Gegeo, K., & McMillen, G. (1985). *Speaking, relating, and learning: A study of Hawaiian children at home and at school*. Norwood, NJ: Ablex.

Bondy, E., & Ross, D. D. (2008). The teacher as warm demander. *Educational Leadership, 66*(1), 54–58.

Botelho, M. J., & Rudman, M. K. (2009). *Critical multicultural analysis of children's literature: Mirrors, windows, and doors*. New York, NY: Routledge.

Boucher, P. (2013). The spirit of Foxfire is alive in Appalachia. Retrieved from appvoices.org/2013/10/03/the-spirit-of-foxfire-is-alive-in-appalachia/

Bowers, C. A., & Flinders, D. J. (1990). *Responsive teaching: An ecological approach to classroom patterns of language, culture, and thought*. New York, NY: Teachers College Press.

Bowers, C. A., & Flinders, D. J. (1991). *Culturally responsive teaching and supervision: A handbook for staff development*. New York, NY: Teachers College Press.

Bowie, R., & Bond, C. (1994). Influencing future teachers' attitudes toward Black English: Are we making a difference? *Journal of Teacher Education, 45*(2), 122–118.

Boyd, F. B., Causey, L. I., & Galda, L. (2015). Culturally diverse literature: Enriching variety in an era of Common Core State Standards. *Reading Teacher, 68*(5), 378–387.

Boyd, H. (1997). Been dere, done dat. *Black Scholar, 27*(1), 15–17.

Boykin, A. W. (1978). Psychological/behavioral verve in academic task performance: Pretheoretical considerations. *Journal of Negro Education, 47*(8), 343–354.

Boykin, A. W. (1982). Task variability and the performance of Black and White schoolchildren: Vervistic explorations. *Journal of Black Studies, 12*(4), 469–485.

Boykin, A. W. (1986). The triple quandary and the schooling of Afro-American children. In U. Neisser (Ed.), *The school achievement of minority children: New perspectives* (pp. 57–92). Hillsdale, NJ: Erlbaum.

Boykin, A. W. (1994). Afrocultural expression and its implications for schooling. In E. R. Hollins, J. E. King, & W. C. Hayman (Eds.), *Teaching diverse populations: Formulating a knowledge base* (pp. 243–256). Albany, NY: State University of New York Press.

Boykin, A. W. (2002). Talent development, cultural deep structure, and school reform: Implications for African immersion initiatives. In S. J. Denbo & L. M. Beaulieu (Eds.), *Improving schools for African American students: A reader for educational leaders* (pp. 81–94). Springfield, IL: Charles C Thomas.

Boykin, A. W., & Bailey, C. T. (2000a). *Experimental research on the role of cultural factors in school relevant cognitive functioning: Description of home environmental factors, cultural orientation, and learning preferences* (Report No. 43). Baltimore, MD: Johns Hopkins University, Center for Research on Education on Students Placed At Risk (CRESPAR).

Boykin, A. W., & Bailey, C. T. (2000b). *The role of cultural factors in school relevant cognitive functioning: Synthesis of findings on cultural contexts, cultural orientations, and individual differences* (Report No. 42). Baltimore, MD: Johns Hopkins University, Center for Research on the Education of Students Placed At Risk (CRESPAR).

Boykin, A. W., Coleman, S. T., Lilja, A. J., & Tyler, K. M. (2004). *Building on children's cultural assets in simulated classroom performance environments: Research vistas in the communal learning paradigm* (Report No. 68). Baltimore, MD: Johns Hopkins University, Center for Research on the Education of Students Placed At Risk (CRESPAR).

Brackett, M. A., & Rivers, S. E. (2013). Transforming students' lives with social and emotional learning. Retrieved from ei.yale.edu/wp-content/uploads/2013/09/Transforming-Students%E2%80%99-Lives-with-Social-and-Emotional-Learning.pdf

Brackett, M. A., Rivers, S. E., & Salovey, P. (2011). Emotional intelligence: Implications for social, academic, and workplace success. *Social and Personality Compass, 5*(1), 88–103.

Bravo, E. (2007). *Taking on the big boys: Or why feminism is good for families, business, and the nation.* New York, NY: Feminist Press at CUNY.

Brisk, M. E. (2006). *Bilingual education: From compensatory to quality schooling* (2nd ed.). Mahwah, NJ: Erlbaum.

Brown, J. C. (2015, September 4) .Reach your students with culturally responsive STEM education methods. Retrieved from cehdvision2020.umn.edu/blog/culturally-responsive-stem-education/

Bruner, J. (1996). *The culture of education.* Cambridge, MA: Harvard University Press.

Burnett, C. (Director). (1998). *The wedding* [Film]. Chicago, IL: Harpo.

Byers, P., & Byers, H. (1985). Nonverbal communication and the education of children. In C. B. Cazden, V. P. John, & D. Hymes (Eds.), *Functions of language in the classroom* (pp. 3–31). Prospect Heights, IL: Waveland.

Byrne, M. M. (2001). Uncovering racial bias in nursing fundamentals textbooks. *Nursing and Health Care Perspectives, 22*(6), 299–303.

Cai, M. (2002). *Multicultural literature for children and young adults: Reflections on critical issues.* Westport, CT: Greenwood Press.

Campbell, C. P. (1995). *Race, myth, and the news.* Thousand Oaks, CA: Sage.

Campbell, L., Campbell, B., & Dickinson, D. (2004). *Teaching and learning through multiple intelligence* (3rd ed.). Boston, MA: Pearson/Allyn & Bacon.

Canagarajah, S. (2003). Foreword. In G. Smitherman & V. Villanueva (Eds.), *Language diversity in the classroom: From intention to practice* (pp. ix–xiv). Carbondale, IL: Southern Illinois University Press.

Carhill, A., Suárez-Orozco, C., & Páez, M. (2008). Explaining English language proficiency among adolescent immigrant students. *American Educational Research Journal, 45*(4), 1155–1179.

Carlson, P. E. (1976). Toward a definition of local-level multicultural education. *Anthropology & Education Quarterly, 7*(4), 28–29.

Carroll, J. B. (Ed.). (1956). *Language, thought, and reality: Selected writings of Benjamin Lee Whorf.* Cambridge, MA: MIT Press.

Cart, M. (2008). The value of young adult literature. *Young Adult Library Services Association (YALSA).* Retrieved from ala.org/yalsa/guidelines/whitepapers/yalit

Case, K. A., & Hemmings, A. (2005). Distancing strategies: White women preservice teachers and antiracist curriculum. *Urban Education, 40*(6), 606–626.

Catapano, J. (n.d). Storytelling in the classroom as a teaching strategy. Retrieved from teachhub.com/storytelling-classroom-teaching-strategy

Cazden, C. B. (1988). *Classroom discourse: The language of teaching and learning.* Portsmouth, NH: Heinemann.

Cazden, C. B., John, V. P., & Hymes, D. (Eds.). (1985). *Functions of language in the classroom.* Prospect Heights, IL: Waveland.

Champion, T. B. (1997). "Tell me something good": A description of narrative structures among African American children. *Linguistics and Education, 9*(3), 251–286.

Champion, T. B. (2003). *Understanding storytelling among African American children: A journey from Africa to America.* Mahwah, NJ: Erlbaum.

Chan, S. (Ed.). (1991). *Asian Americans: An interpretative history.* Boston, MA: Twayne.

Chang, J. (2005). *Can't stop, won't stop: A history of the hip hop generation.* New York, NY: St. Martin's Press.

Chapman, I. T. (1994). Dissin' the dialectic on discourse surface differences. *Composition Chronicle, 7*(7), 4–7.

Chen, C. (2015). Starting in Brookline, a math project quickly adds up. Retrieved from bostonglobe.com/metro/regionals/west/2015/10/02/starting-brookline-math-project-quickly-adds-up

Christian, D. (2011). Dual language education. In E. Hinkel (Ed.), *Handbook of research in second language teaching and learning* (Vol. II, pp. 3–20). New York, NY: Routledge.

Chun-Hoon, L. K. Y. (1973). Teaching the Asian-American experience. In J. A. Banks (Ed.), *Teaching ethnic studies: Concepts and strategies* (pp. 118–146). Washington, DC: National Council for the Social Studies.

Class divided, A. [Film]. (1986). Washington, DC: PBS Video.

Coggins, K., Williams, E., & Radin, N. (1997). The traditional tribal values of Ojibwa parents and the school performance of their children: An exploratory study. *Journal of American Indian Education, 36*(3), 1–15.

Cohen, E. G. (1984). Talking and working together: Status interactions and learning. In P. Peterson, L. C. Wilkinson, & M. Hallinan (Eds.), *Instructional groups in the classroom: Organization and processes* (pp. 171–188). Orlando, FL: Academic Press.

Cohen, E. G., Brody, C. M., & Sapon-Shevin, M. (Eds.). (2004). *Teaching cooperative learning: The challenge to teacher education.* Albany, NY: State University of New York Press.

Cohen, E. G., Kepner, D., & Swanson, P. (1995). Dismantling status hierarchies in heterogeneous classrooms. In J. Oakes & K. H. Quartz (Eds.), *Creating new educational communities* (Ninety-fourth Yearbook of the National Society for the Study of Education) (pp. 16–31). Chicago, IL: University of Chicago Press.

Cohen, E. G., & Lotan, R. A. (1995). Producing equal-status interaction in the heterogeneous classroom. *American Educational Research Journal, 32*(1), 99–120.

Cohen, E. G., & Lotan, R. A. (Eds.). (1997). *Working for equity in heterogeneous classrooms: Sociological theory in practice.* New York, NY: Teachers College Press.

Colannino. A. (2016, March 15). The Calculus Project: A growth mindset success story. Retrieved from blog.mindsetworks.com/entry/the-calculus-project-a-growth-mindset-success-story

Collier, V. P. (1992). A synthesis of studies examining long-term language minority student data on academic achievement. *Bilingual Research Journal, 16*(1&2), 187–212.

Collier, V. P., & Thomas, W. P. (2014). *Creating dual language schools for a transformed world: Administrators speak.* Albuquerque, NM: Fuente Press.

Collins, B. A. (2014). Dual language development of Latino children: Effect of instructional program type and the home and school language environment. *Early Childhood Research Quarterly, 29*(3), 389–397.

Collins, M. (1992). *Ordinary children, extraordinary teachers.* Norfolk, VA: Hampton Roads.

Connecticut Framework: K–12 Curricular Goals and Standards. (1998). State of Connecticut, Department of Education.

Cortés, C. E. (1991). Empowerment through media literacy: A multicultural approach. In C. E. Sleeter (Ed.), *Empowerment through multicultural education* (pp. 143–157). Albany, NY: State University of New York Press.

Cortés, C. E. (1995). Knowledge construction and popular culture: The media as multicultural educator. In J. A. Banks & C. A. M. Banks (Eds.), *Handbook of research on multicultural education* (pp. 169–183). New York, NY: Macmillan.

Crawford, J. (1997a). English plus. Retrieved from ourworld.compuserve.com/homepages/jwcrawford/langleg.htm

Crawford, J. (1997b). The official English question. Retrieved from ourworld.compuserve.com/homepages/jwcrawford/langleg.htm

Crawford, J. (2000). Anatomy of the English-Only movement. Retrieved from ourworld.compuserve.com/homepages/JWCRAWFORD/anat

Crawford, J. (2003). Language legislation in the U.S.A. Retrieved from ourworld.compuserve.com/homepages/jwcrawford/langleg.htm

Crawford, L. W. (1993). *Language and literacy learning in multicultural classrooms.* Boston, MA: Allyn & Bacon.

Crawford, M. (1995). *Talking difference: On gender and language.* Thousand Oaks, CA: Sage.

Crichlow, W. C., Goodwin, S., Shakes, G., & Swartz, E. (1990). Multicultural ways of knowing: Implications for practice. *Journal of Education, 172*(2), 101–117.

Crum, M. (2015, February 27). Sorry, Ebooks. These 9 studies show why print is better. *Huffington Post.* Retrieved from huffingtonpost.com/2015/02/27/print-ebooks-studies_n_6762674.html

Cuban, L. (1972). Ethnic content and "White" instruction. *Phi Delta Kappan, 53*(5), 270–273.

Cullen, C. (1970). Incident. In A. Murray & R. Thomas (Eds.), *The journey* (p. 93). New York, NY: Scholastic.

Cummins, J. (1989). *Empowering minority students.* Sacramento, CA: California Association of Bilingual Education.

Dandy, E. B. (1991). *Black communications: Breaking down the barriers.* Chicago, IL: African American Images.

Daniels, J. (2012). Race and racism in Internet studies: A review and critique. *New Media and Society, 15*(5), 1–25.

Darling-Hammond, L. (2007). The flat earth and education: How America's commitment to equity will determine our future. *Educational Researcher, 36*(6), 319–335.

Danovich, T. (2017). The Foxfire book series that preserved Appalachian foodways. Retrieved from npr.org/sections/thesalt/2017/03/17/520038859/the-foxfire-book-series-that-preserved-appalachian-foodways

Dates, J. L., & Barlow, W. (1990). *Split image: African Americans in the mass media.* Washington, DC: Howard University Press.

Davis, B. M. (Ed.). (2012). *How to teach students who don't look like you: Culturally relevant teaching strategies* (2nd ed.). Thousand Oaks, CA: Corwin.

Davis, J. E. (1998). Cultural capital and the role of historically Black colleges and universities in educational reproduction. In K. Freeman (Ed.), *African American culture and heritage in higher education research and practice* (pp. 143–153). Westport, CT: Praeger.

Davis, O. L., Jr., Ponder, G., Burlbaw, L. M., Garza-Lubeck, M., & Moss, A. (1986). *Looking at history: A review of major U.S. history textbooks.* Washington, DC: People for the American Way.

Deane, P. (1989). Black characters in children's fiction series since 1968. *Journal of Negro Education, 58*(2), 153–162.

Dee, T. S. (2015). Social identity and achievement gaps: Evidence from an affirmation intervention. *Journal of Research on Educational Effectiveness, 8*(2), 149–168.

Dee, T. S., & Penner, E. K. (2017). The causal effects of cultural relevance: Evidence from an ethnic studies curriculum. *American Educational Research Journal, 54*(1), 127–166.

De Jesus, A. (2003). "Here it's more like your house": The proliferation of authentic caring as school reform at El Puente Academy for Peace and Justice. In B. C. Rubin & E. M. Silva (Eds.), *Critical voices in school reform: Students living through change* (pp. 133–151). New York, NY: Routledge.

Delain, M. T., Pearson, P. D., & Anderson, R. C. (1985). Reading comprehension and creativity in Black language use: You stand to gain by playing the sounding game. *American Educational Research Journal, 22*(2), 155–173.

Delgado-Gaitan, C., & Trueba, H. (1991). *Crossing cultural borders: Education for immigrant families in America.* New York, NY: Falmer.

Delpit, L. (2006). *Other people's children: Cultural conflict in the classroom* (2nd ed.). New York, NY: New Press.

Delpit, L., & Dowdy, J. K. (2002). (Eds.). *The skin that we speak: Thoughts on language and culture in the classroom.* New York, NY: New Press.

Demmert, W. G., Jr., & Towner, J. C. (2003). A review of the research literature on the influences of culturally based education on the academic performance of Native American students. Portland, OR: Northwest Regional Educational Laboratory. Retrieved from docstoc.com/docs/2391651

Denman, G. A. (1991). *Sit tight, and I'll swing you a tail . . . Using and writing stories with young people.* Portsmouth, NH: Heinemann.

Derman-Sparks, L., & Edwards, O. J. (2010). *Anti-bias education for young children and ourselves.* Washington, DC: National Association for the Education of Young Children.

Dewey, J. (1902). *The child and the curriculum.* Chicago, IL: University of Chicago Press.

Deyhle, D. (1995). Navajo youth and Anglo racism: Cultural integrity and resistance. *Harvard Educational Review, 65*(3), 403–444.

Deyhle, D., & Swisher, K. (1997). Research in American Indian and Alaska native education: From assimilation to self-determination. In M. W. Apple (Ed.), *Review of research in education* (Vol. 22, pp. 113–194). Washington, DC: American Educational Research Association.

Diamond, B. J., & Moore, M. A. (1995). *Multicultural literacy: Mirroring the reality of the classroom*. New York, NY: Longman.

Dick, G. S., Estell, D. W., & McCarty, T. L. (1994). Saad naakih bee'enootiltji na'aikaa: Restructuring the teaching of language and literacy in a Navajo community school. *Journal of American Indian Education, 33*(3), 31–46.

Digest of Education Statistics, 2007. (2008). Washington, DC: Department of Education, National Center of Education Statistics.

Dill, E., & Boykin, A. W. (2000). The comparative influence of individual, peer tutoring, and communal learning contexts on the text recall of African American children. *Journal of Black Psychology, 26*(1), 65–78.

Dillard, C. B. (1997). Placing student language, literacy, and culture at the center of teacher education reform. In J. E. King, E. R. Hollins, & W. C. Hayman (Eds.), *Preparing teachers for cultural diversity* (pp. 85–96). New York, NY: Teachers College Press.

Dolberry, M. E. (2015). From "they" science to "our" science: Hip hop epistemology in STEAM education [Dissertation]. University of Washington, Seattle, WA. Retrieved from digital.lib.washington.edu/researchworks/handle/1773/33734

Dotson, J. M. (2001). Cooperative learning structures increase student achievement. Retrieved from kaganonline.com/free_articles/research_and_rationale/increase_achievement.php

Doyle, T. (2011). *Learner-centered teaching: Putting the research on learning into practice*. Sterling, VA: Stylus Publishing.

Dunn, R., Dunn, K., & Price, G. E. (1975). *Learning style inventory*. Lawrence, KS: Price Systems.

Dupuis, V. L., & Walker, M. W. (1988). The circle of learning at Kickapoo. *Journal of American Indian Education, 28*(1), 27–33.

Durden, R., Escalante, E., & Blitch, K. (2015). Start with us! Culturally relevant pedagogy in the preschool classroom. *Early Childhood Education Journal, 43*(3), 223–232.

Durlak, J. A., Domitrovich, C. E., Weissberg, R. P., & Gullotta. T. P. (Eds.). (2015). *Handbook of social and emotional learning: Research and practice*. New York, NY: Guilford Press.

Duval, C. A. (2005). Navajo bilingual language and cultural education programs: Will the Navajo be able to revitalize and maintain their language and culture? Retrieved from bunkyo.ac.jp/faculty/lib/kiyo/Int/it150206.pdf

Dyson, A. H., & Genishi, C. (Eds.). (1994). *The need for story: Cultural diversity in classroom and community*. Urbana, IL: National Council of Teachers of English.

Eaker-Rich, D., & Van Galen, J. (Eds.). (1996). *Caring in an unjust world: Negotiating borders and barriers in schools*. Albany, NY: State University of New York Press.

Education Commission of the States. (2012). Teacher expectations of students: A self-fulfilling prophecy? Retrieved from ecs.org/clearinghouse/01/05/51/10551.pdf

Education that works: An action plan for the education of minorities. (1990). Cambridge, MA: Quality Education for Minorities Project, Massachusetts Institute of Technology.

Education Week. Retrieved from edweek.org/ew/articles/2015/04/15/k-12-schools-still-mix-print-and-digital.html

Eisenhart, M., & Cutts-Dougherty, K. (1991). Social and cultural constraints on students' access to school knowledge. In E. Hiebert (Ed.), *Literacy for a diverse society: Perspectives, programs, and policies* (pp. 28–43). New York, NY: Teachers College Press.

Ellison, C. M., Boykin, A. W., Towns, D. P., & Stokes, A. (2000). *Classroom cultural ecology: The dynamics of classroom life in schools serving low-income African American children.* Report No. 44. Washington, DC: Center for Research on the Education of Students Placed At Risk (CRESPAR), Howard University.

Ellsworth, E. (1990). Educational films against critical pedagogy. In E. Ellsworth & M. H. Whatley (Eds.), *The ideology of images in educational media* (pp. 10–26). New York, NY: Teachers College Press.

Ellsworth, E., & Whatley, M. H. (Eds.). (1990). *The ideology of images in educational media.* New York, NY: Teachers College Press.

Emdin, C. (2010). *Urban science education for the hip hop generation: Essential tools for the urban science educator and researcher.* Boston, MA: Sense Publishers.

Emdin, C. (2016). *For White folks who teach in the hood . . . and the rest of y'all too: Reality pedagogy and urban education.* Boston, MA: Beacon Press.

Erickson, F. (1987). Transformation and school success: The politics and culture of educational achievement. *Anthropology and Education Quarterly, 18*(4), 335–383.

Erickson, F. (2010). Culture in society and in educational practices. In J. A. Banks & C. A. M. Banks (Eds.), *Multicultural education: Issues and perspectives* (7th ed., pp. 33–56). Hoboken, NJ: Wiley.

Ernest, P. (2009). New philosophy of mathematics: Implications for mathematics education. In B. Greer, S. Mukhopadhyay, A. B. Powell, & S. Nelson-Barber (Eds.), *Culturally responsive mathematics education* (pp. 43–84). New York, NY: Routledge.

Escalante, J., & Dirmann, J. (1990). The Jamie Escalante math program. *Journal of Negro Education, 59*(30), 407–423.

Estes, L., & Rosenfelt, S. (Producers). (1998). *Smoke signals* [Film]. New York, NY: Miramax Films.

Expectations of excellence: Curriculum standards for the social studies (Bulletin 89). (1994). Washington, DC: National Council for the Social Studies.

Eye of the storm [Video]. (1970). Washington, DC: ABC Media Concepts.

Fairview Capital. (2015). The value of ethnic and gender diversity in private equity and venture capital. Retrieved from fairviewcapital.com/download_file/view/32/192

Farmer, L. S. J. (2004). Left brain, right brain, whole brain. *School Library Activities Monthly, 21*(20), 27–28, 37.

Farrell, J. P. (n.d.). Overview, school textbooks in the United States. *Education Encyclopedia.* Retrieved from http://education.stateuniversity.com/pages/2507/Textbooks.html

Fashola, O. L., Slavin, R. E., Calderón, M., & Durán, R. (1997). *Effective programs for Latino students in elementary and middle schools* (Report No.

11). Baltimore, MD: Johns Hopkins University, Center for Research on Education of Students Placed At Risk (CRESPAR).

Fass, P. S. (1989). *Outside in: Minorities and the transformation of American education*. New York, NY: Oxford University Press.

Figlar, G. (1998, June 27). Sacagawea likely choice for dollar coin. *The Denver Post*, pp. 25A, 27A.

Figueroa, A. (2004). Speaking Spanglish. In O. Santa Ana (Ed.), *Tongue tied: The lives of multilingual children in public education* (pp. 284–286). Lanham, MD: Rowman & Littlefield.

First, J. C., & Carrera, J. W. (1988). *New voices: Immigrant students in U.S. public schools: A NCAS research and policy report*. Boston, MA: National Coalition of Advocates for Students

Fives, H., & Gill, M. G. (Eds.). (2015). *International handbook of research on teachers' beliefs*. New York, NY: Routledge

Fleming, J. (1991). *Blacks in college: A comparative study of students' success in Black and White institutions*. San Francisco, CA: Jossey-Bass.

Flippo, R. F., Hetzel, C., Gribouski, D., & Armstrong, L. A. (1997). Creating a student literacy corps in a diverse community. *Phi Delta Kappan, 78*(8), 644–646.

Fogel, H., & Ehri, L. C. (2000). Teaching elementary school students who speak Black English Vernacular to write in Standard English: Effects of dialect transformation practice. *Contemporary Educational Psychology, 25*(2), 212–235.

Forbes, J. D. (1973). Teaching Native American values and cultures. In J. A. Banks (Ed.), *Teaching ethnic studies: Concepts and strategies* (43rd Yearbook, pp. 200–225). Washington, DC: National Council for the Social Studies.

Fordham, S. (1993). "Those loud Black girls": (Black) women, silence, and gender "passing" in the academy. *Anthropology and Education Quarterly, 24*(1), 3–32.

Fordham, S. (1996). *Blacked out: Dilemmas of race, identity, and success at Capital High*. Chicago, IL: University of Chicago Press.

Fordham, S., & Ogbu, J. U. (1986). Black students' school success: Coping with the "burden of 'acting white.'" *Urban Review, 18*(3), 176–206.

Fortune, T. W. (2014). What the research says about immersion. Center for Advanced Research on Language Acquisition. Retrieved from carla.umn.edu/immersion/documents/ImmersionResearch_TaraFortune.html

Foster, J. T., Jr. (1994, Spring). The Songhai Empire: An Afrocentric academy for science, math, and technology. *Sine of the Times*, pp. 26–27.

Foster, M. (1989). It's cooking now: A performance analysis of the speech events of a Black teacher in an urban community college. *Language in Society, 18*(1), 1–29.

Foster, M. (1991). Just got to find a way: Case studies of the lives and practice of exemplary Black high school teachers. In M. Foster (Ed.), *Readings on equal education: Vol. 11. Qualitative investigations into schools and schooling* (pp. 273–309). New York, NY: AMS Press.

Foster, M. (1994). Effective Black teachers: A literature review. In E. R. Hollins, J. E. King, & W. C. Hayman (Eds.), *Teaching diverse populations:*

Formulating a knowledge base (pp. 225–241). Albany, NY: State University of New York Press.

Foster, M. (1995). African American teachers and culturally relevant pedagogy. In J. A. Banks & C. A. M. Banks (Eds.), *Handbook of research on multicultural education* (pp. 570–581). New York, NY: Macmillan.

Foster, M. (1997). *Black teachers on teaching.* New York, NY: New Press.

Fowler, L. C. (2006). *A curriculum of difficulty: Narrative research in education and the practice of teaching.* New York, NY: Peter Lang.

Fox, H. (1994). *Listening to the world: Cultural issues in academic writing.* Urbana, IL: National Council of Teachers of English.

Franklin, W. J., & Dowdy, J. K. (2005). Storytelling. In J. K. Dowdy (Ed.), *Readers of the quilt: Essays on being Black, female, and literate* (pp. 119–136). Cresskill, NJ: Hampton Press.

Freire, P. (1980). *Education for critical consciousness.* New York, NY: Continuum.

Friedman, A. (2015, July 9). Can we just, like, get over the way women talk? Retrieved from thecut.com/2015/07/can-we-just-like-get-over-the-way-women-talk.html

Fuligni, A. J. (2007). *Contesting stereotypes and creating identities: Social categories, social identities, and educational participation.* New York, NY: Russell Sage Foundation.

Fullilove, R. E., & Treisman, P. U. (1990). Mathematics achievement among African American undergraduates at the University of California, Berkeley: An evaluation of the Mathematics Workshop Program. *Journal of Negro Education, 59*(3) 463–478.

Gallimore, R., Boggs, J. W., & Jordan, C. (1974). *Culture, behavior and education: A study of Hawaiian Americans.* Beverly Hills, CA: Sage.

Garcia, C., & Chun, H. (2016). Culturally responsive teaching and teacher expectations for Latino middle school students. *Journal of Latina/o Psychology, 4*(3), 173–187.

Garcia, E. (1999). *Student cultural diversity: Understanding and meeting the challenge* (2nd ed.). Boston, MA: Houghton Mifflin.

Garcia, J., Hadaway, N. L., & Beal, G. (1988). Children's multicultural literature: Promoting pluralism? *Ethnic Forum, 8*(2), 62–71.

Garcia, O., & Wei, L. (2014). *Translanguaging: Language, bilingualism, and education.* New York, NY: Palgrave MacMillan.

Garcia-Vasquez, E., Vasquez, I. A., & Lopez, I. C. (1997). Language proficiency and academic success: Relationships between proficiency in two languages and achievement among Mexican American students. *Bilingual Research Journal, 21*, 334–347.

Gardner, H. (1983). *Frames of mind: The theory of multiple intelligences.* New York, NY: Basic Books.

Gardner, H. (2006). *Multiple intelligences: New horizons.* New York, NY: Basic Books.

Gardner, J. W. (1984). *Excellence: Can we be equal and excellent too?* (rev. ed.). New York, NY: Norton.

Garza, R., Alejandro, E. A., Blythe, T., & Fite, K. (2014). Caring for students: What teachers have to say. *International Scholarly Research Notices (ISRN).* Retrieved from hindawi.com/journals/isrn/2014/425856/

Gasman, M., & Tudico, C. L. (Eds.). (2008). *Historically Black colleges and universities: Triumphs, troubles, and taboos.* New York, NY: Palgrave Macmillan.

Gay, G. (1975). Organizing and designing culturally pluralistic curriculum. *Educational Leadership, 33*(3), 176–183.

Gay, G. (1988). Designing relevant curricula for diverse learners. *Education and Urban Society, 2*(4), 327–340.

Gay, G. (1995). Bridging multicultural theory and practice. *Multicultural Education, 3*(1), 4–9.

Gay, G. (2002). Preparing for culturally responsive teaching. *Journal of Teacher Education, 53*(2), 106–116.

Gay, G. (Ed.). (2003a). *Becoming multicultural educators: Personal journey toward professional agency.* San Francisco, CA: Jossey-Bass.

Gay, G. (2003b). Deracialization in social studies teacher education textbooks. In G. Ladson-Billings (Ed.), *Critical race theory perspectives on social studies: The profession, policies, and curriculum* (pp. 123–148). Greenwich, CT: Information Age.

Gay, G. (2009). Preparing culturally responsive mathematics teachers. In B. Greer, S. Mukhopadhyay, A. B. Powell, & S. Nelson-Barber (Eds.), *Culturally responsive mathematics education* (pp. 189–205). New York, NY: Routledge.

Gay, G. (2013). Teaching to and through cultural diversity. *Curriculum Inquiry, 43*(1), 48–70.

Gay, G. (2015). Teachers' beliefs about cultural diversity: Problems and possibilities. In H. Fives & M. G. Gill (Eds.), *International handbook of research on teachers' beliefs* (pp. 436–452). New York, NY: Routledge.

Gee, J. (1985). The narrativization of experience in oral style. *Journal of Education, 167*(1), 9–15.

Gee, J. P. (1989). What is literacy? *Journal of Education, 171*(1), 18–25.

Genesee, F., Lindhom-Leary, K., Sanders, W. M., & Christian, D. (2006). *Educating English language learners: A synthesis of research evidence.* New York, NY: Cambridge University Press.

Gentemann, K. M., & Whitehead, T. L. (1983). The cultural broker concept in bicultural education. *Journal of Negro Education, 52*(2), 118–129.

Gewertz, C. (2017, February 15). National testing landscape continues to shift. *Education Week, 36*(21), pp. 1, 8.

Giamati, C., & Weiland, M. (1997). An exploration of American Indian students' perceptions of patterning, symmetry, and geometry. *Journal of American Indian Education, 36*(3), 27–48.

Giarrizzo, T. (2013). History losing its value: Representation of minorities within high school history [Master's Degree Thesis], Rochester, NY. St. John Fisher College. Retrieved from fisherpub.sjfc.edu/education_ETD_masters/213/

Gillies, R. M. (2007). *Cooperative learning: Integrating theory and practice.* Los Angeles, CA: Sage.

Gillies, R. M. (2014). Cooperative learning: Developments in research. *International Journal of Educational Psychology, 3*(2), 125–140.

Gilligan, C. (1982). *In a different voice: Psychological theory and women's development.* Cambridge, MA: Harvard University Press.

Ginsberg, A. E., Shapiro, J. P., & Brown, S. P. (2004). *Gender in urban education: Strategies for student achievement.* Portsmouth, NH: Heinemann.

Ginsberg, M. B. (2015). *Excited to learn: Motivation and culturally responsive teaching.* Thousand Oaks, CA: Corwin.

Giroux, H. (1992). *Border crossings: Cultural workers and the politics of education.* New York, NY: Routledge.

Glaser, S. (n.d.). The Foxfire project. Retrieved from porterbriggs.com/the-foxfire-project/

Glasgrow, N. A., & Hicks, C. D. (2009). *What successful teachers do: 101 research-based classroom strategies for new and veteran teachers.* Thousand Oaks, CA: Corwin.

Glickman, C. (2016). Whatever happened to Foxfire: Still glowing? *Phi Delta Kappan, 97*(5), 55–59.

Goldblatt, P. (2008). Reciprocity between life and art: Telling stories. *Multicultural Review, 17*(3), 23–28.

Gonzales, R. (1972). *I am Joaquin.* New York, NY: Bantam.

González, N., Moll, L. C., & Amanti, C. (2005). *Funds of knowledge: Theorizing practices in households, communities, and classrooms.* Mahwah, NJ: Erlbaum

Good, T. L., & Brophy, J. E. (1978). *Looking in classrooms* (2nd ed.). New York, NY: Harper & Row.

Good, T. L., & Brophy, J. E. (1994). *Looking in classrooms* (6th ed.). New York, NY: HarperCollins.

Good, T. L., & Brophy, J. E. (2003). *Looking in classrooms* (9th ed.). Boston, MA: Allyn & Bacon.

Goodlad, J. I. (1984). *A place called school: Prospects for the future.* New York, NY: McGraw-Hill.

Goodman, D. J. (2013). Cultural competency for social justice. Retrieved from acpacsje.wordpress.com/2013/02/05/cultural-competency-for-social-justice-by-diane-j-goodman-ed-d/

Goodwin, B. (2016). "High touch" is crucial for "high tech" students. *Educational Leadership, 74*(1), 81–83.

Goodwin, B. (2017). Learning styles: It's complicated. *Educational Leadership, 74*(7), 79–80.

Goodwin, M. H. (1990). *He-said she-said: Talk as social organization among Black children.* Bloomington, IN: Indiana University Press.

Gordon, B. M. (1993). African American cultural knowledge and liberatory education: Dilemmas, problems, and potentials in a postmodern American society. *Urban Education, 27*(4), 448–470.

Gordy, L. L., & Pritchard, A. M. (1995). Redirecting our voyage through history: A content analysis of social studies textbooks. *Urban Education, 30*(2), 195–218.

Goto, S. T. (1997). Nerds, normal people, and homeboys: Accommodation and resistance among Chinese American students. *Anthropology & Education Quarterly, 28*(1), 70–84.

Gougis, R. A. (1986). The effects of prejudice and stress on the academic performance of Black-Americans. In U. Neisser (Ed.), *The school achievement of minority children: New perspectives* (pp. 145–158). Hillsdale, NJ: Erlbaum.

Graham, M., & Dutton, W. H. (Eds.). (2014). *Society and the Internet: How networks of information and communication are changing our lives*. New York, NY: Oxford University Press.

Gray-Schlegel, M. A., & Gray-Schlegel, T. (1995/1996). An investigation of gender stereotypes as revealed through children's creative writing. *Reading Research and Instruction, 35*(2), 160–170.

Greenbaum, P. E. (1985). Nonverbal differences in communication style between American Indian and Anglo elementary classrooms. *American Educational Research Journal, 22*(1), 101–115.

Greene, J. P. (1998). *A meta-analysis of the effectiveness of bilingual education*. Claremont, CA: Thomas Rivera Policy Institute.

Greer, B., Mukhopadhyay, S., Powell, A. B., & Nelson-Barber, S. (Eds.). (2009). *Culturally responsive mathematics education*. New York, NY: Routledge.

Grice, M. O., & Vaughn, C. (1992). Third graders respond to literature for and about Afro-Americans. *The Urban Review, 24*(2), 149–164.

Grossman, H., & Grossman, S. H. (1994). *Gender issues in education*. Boston, MA: Allyn & Bacon.

Guild, P. B. (1997). Where do the learning theories overlap? *Educational Leadership, 55*(1), 30–31.

Guild, P. B. (2001). Diversity, learning style and culture. Retrieved from newhorizons. org/strategies/styles/guild.htm

Guild, P. B., & Garger, S. (1985). *Marching to different drummers*. Alexandria, VA: Association for Supervision and Curriculum Development.

Gullicks, K. A., Pearson, J. C., Child, J. T., & Schwab, C. R. (2005). Diversity and power in public speaking textbooks. *Communication Quarterly, 53*(2), 247–258.

Gutiérrez, K. D. (2005). The persistence of inequality: English language learners and educational reform. In J. Flood & P. L. Anders (Eds.), *Literacy development of students in urban schools: Research and policy* (pp. 288–304). Newark, DE: International Reading Association.

Guttentag, M. (1972). Negro-White differences in children's movement. *Perceptual and Motor Skills, 35*(2), 435–436.

Guttentag, M., & Ross, S. (1972). Movement responses in simple concept learning. *American Journal of Orthopsychiatry, 42*(4), 657–665.

Hafen, P. J. (1997). "Let me take you home in my one-eyed ford": Popular imagery in contemporary Native American fiction. *Multicultural Review, 6*(2), 38–44.

Haley, A. (1976). *Roots: The saga of an American family*. Garden City, NY: Doubleday.

Hall, W. S., Reder, S., & Cole, M. (1979). Story recall in young Black and White children: Effects of racial group membership, race of experimenter, and dialect. In A. W. Boykin, A. J. Franklin, & J. F. Yates (Eds.), *Research directions of Black psychologists* (pp. 253–265). New York, NY: Russell Sage Foundation.

Hampton, H. (Executive Producer). (1987). *Eyes on the prize*, I–VIII [Video]. Los Angeles, CA: PBS.

Hanley, M. S. (1998). *Learning to fly: Knowledge construction of African American adolescents through drama*. Unpublished doctoral dissertation, University of Washington, Seattle.

Hanley, M. S., & Noblit, G. W. (2009). Cultural responsiveness, racial identity, and academic success: A review of literature. Retrieved from heinz.org/userfiles/library/culture-report_final.pdf

Hansen, J. W. (1995). Student cognitive styles in postsecondary technology programs. *Journal of Technology Education, 6*(2), 19–33. Retrieved from scholar.lib.vt.edu/ejournalsjte/v6n2/jhansen.jte/html

Harada, V. H. (1994). An analysis of stereotypes and biases in recent Asian American fiction for adolescents. *Ethnic Forum, 14*(2), 44–58.

Harlin, R., Sirota, E., & Bailey, L. (2009). Review of research: The impact of teacher expectations on diverse learners' academic outcomes. *Childhood Education, 85*(4), 253–256.

Harry, B. (1992). *Cultural diversity, families, and the special education system: Communication and empowerment.* New York, NY: Teachers College Press.

Hart, K. (2011). Uncovering YA covers: 2011. Retrieved from katehart.net/2012/05/uncovering-ya-covers-2011.html

Harvey, K. (Ed.). (1994). *American Indian voices.* Brookfield, CT: Millbrook Press.

Haskins, J., & Butts, H. F. (1973). *The psychology of Black language.* New York, NY: Barnes & Noble.

Heath, S. B. (1983). *Ways with words: Language, life, and work in communities and classrooms.* Cambridge, UK: Cambridge University Press.

Hecht, M. L., Jackson, R. L., II, & Ribeau, S. A. (2003). *African American communication: Exploring identity and culture.* Mahwah, NJ: Erlbaum.

Hegi, U. (1997). *Tearing the silence: On being German in America.* New York, NY: Simon & Schuster.

Hein, J. (2006). *Ethnic origins: The adaptation of Cambodian and Hmong refugees in four American cities.* New York, NY: Russell Sage Foundation.

Heller, C. (1997). Selecting children's picture books with strong Black fathers and father figures. *Multicultural Review, 6*(1), 38–53.

Hilliard, A. G., III. (1991/1992). Why we must pluralize the curriculum. *Educational Leadership, 49*(4), 12–14.

Hogben, M., & Waterman, C. K. (1997). Are all of your students represented in their textbooks? A content analysis of coverage of diversity issues in introductory psychology textbooks. *Teaching of Psychology, 24*(2), 95–100.

Hoijer, H. (1991). The Sapir–Whorf hypothesis. In L. A. Samovar & R. E. Porter (Eds.), *Intercultural communication: A reader* (6th ed., pp. 244–251). Belmont, CA: Wadsworth.

Holliday, B. G. (1981). The imperatives of development and ecology: Lessons learned from Black children. In J. McAdoo, H. McAdoo, & W. E. Cross, Jr. (Eds.), *Fifth conference on empirical research in Black psychology* (pp. 50–64). Washington, DC: National Institute of Mental Health.

Holliday, B. G. (1985). Towards a model of teacher–child transactional processes affecting Black children's academic achievement. In M. B. Spencer, G. K. Brookins, & W. R. Allen (Eds.), *Beginnings: The social and affective development of Black children* (pp. 117–130). Hillsdale, NJ: Erlbaum.

Hollins, E. R. (1996). *Culture in school learning: Revealing the deep meaning.* Mahwah, NJ: Erlbaum.

Hollins, E. R., King, J. E., & Hayman, W. C. (Eds.). (1994). *Teaching diverse populations: Formulating a knowledge base.* Albany, NY: State University of New York Press.

Homing, K. T. (n.d.). Publishing statistics on children's books about people of color and First/Native Nations, and by people of color and First/Native Nations authors and illustrators. Madison, WI: Cooperative Children's Book Center, School of Education, University of Wisconsin. Retrieved from ccbc.education. wisc.edu/books/pcstats.asp#USonly

Horton, Y., Price, R., & Brown, E. (1999, June 1). Portrayal of minorities in the film, media and entertainment industries. Retrieved from web.stanford.edu/ class/e297c/poverty_prejudice/mediarace/portrayal.htm.

Houston, M. (2000). Multiple perspectives: African American women conceive their talk. *Women and Language, 23*(1), 11–17.

Howard, T. C. (1998). *Pedagogical practices and ideological constructions of effective teachers of African American students.* Unpublished doctoral dissertation, University of Washington, Seattle.

Howe, M. J. A. (1999). *A teacher's guide to the psychology of teaching* (2nd ed.). Malden, MA: Blackwell.

Hoyenga, K. B., & Hoyenga, K. T. (1979). *The question of sex differences: Psychological, cultural, and biological issues.* Boston, MA: Little, Brown.

Hudley, C. A. (1995). Assessing the impact of separate schooling for African American male adolescents. *Journal of Early Adolescence, 15*(10), 38–57.

Huffman, T. E., Sill, M. L., & Brokenleg, M. (1986). College achievement among Sioux and White South Dakota students. *Journal of American Indian Education, 25*(2), 32–38.

Hurston, Z. N. (1990). *Their eyes were watching God: A novel.* New York, NY: Perennial Library.

Husband, T., Jr. (2012). "I don't see color": Challenging assumptions about discussing race with young children. *Early Childhood Education Journal, 39*(6), 365–371.

Hymes, D. (1985). Introduction. In C. B. Cazden, V. P. John, & D. Hymes (Eds.), *Functions of language in the classroom* (pp. xi–xvii). Prospect Heights, IL: Waveland.

Igoa, C. (1995). *The inner world of the immigrant child.* New York, NY: St. Martin's Press.

Irvine, J. J. (1990). *Black students and school failure: Policies, practices, and prescriptions.* New York, NY: Greenwood.

Irvine, J. J., & Foster, M. (Eds.). (1996). *Growing up African American in Catholic schools.* New York, NY: Teachers College Press.

Irvine, J. J., & York, D. E. (1995). Learning styles and culturally diverse students: A literature review. In J. A. Banks & C. A. M. Banks (Eds.), *Handbook of research on multicultural education* (pp. 484–497). New York, NY: Macmillan.

Jackson, J. J. (1997). On Oakland's Ebonics: Some say gibberish, some say slang, some say dis den dat, me say dem dumb, it be mother tongue. *Black Scholar, 27*(1), 18–25.

Johnson, D. W., & Johnson R. T. (1999). *Learning together and alone: Cooperative, competitive, and individualistic learning* (5th ed.). Boston, MA: Allyn & Bacon.

Johnstone, B. (1993). Community and contest: Midwestern men and women creating their worlds in conversational storytelling. In D. Tannen (Ed.), *Gender and conversational interaction* (pp. 62–80). New York, NY: Oxford University Press.

Jones, C., & Shorter-Gooden, K. (2003). *Shifting: The double lives of Black women in America*. New York, NY: HarperCollins.

Jones, D. E., Greenberg, M., & Crowley, M. (2015). Early socio-emotional functioning and public health: The relationship between kindergarten social competence and future wellness. *American Journal of Public Health*, *105*(11), 2283–2290.

Jones, F. (1981). *A traditional model of educational excellence*. Washington, DC: Howard University Press.

Jordan, C. (1985). Translating culture: From ethnographic information to educational reform. *Anthropology & Education Quarterly, 16*(2), 105–123.

Jordan, C., Tharp, R. G., & Baird-Vogt, L. (1992). "Just open the door": Cultural compatibility and classroom rapport. In M. Saravia-Shore & S. F. Arvizu (Eds.), *Crosscultural literacy: Ethnographies in communication in multiethnic classrooms* (pp. 3–18). New York, NY: Garland.

Journal of Black Psychology, 23(3). (1997, August). K–10 grade level expectations: A new level of specificity (writing). Olympia, WA: Office of Superintendent of Public Instruction. Retrieved from wsipp.wa.gov/rpt-files/07-01-2201.pdf

Kahn, A., & Onion, R. (2016, January 6). Is history written about men, by men? *Slate*. Retrieved from slate.com/articles/news_and_politics/history/2016/01/popular_history_why_are_so_many_history_books_about_men_by_men.html

Kana'iaupuni, S., Ledward, B., & Jensen, U. (2010). Culture-based education and its relationship to student outcomes. Retrieved from ksbe.edu/_assets/spi/pdfs/CBE_relationship_to_student_outcomes.pdf

Kane, J. (1994). Knowing and being. *Holistic Education Review, 7*(12), 2–4.

Kanganis, C. T. (Director). (1996). *Race the sun* [Film]. Culver City, CA: TriStar Pictures.

Kendall, J. S., & Marzano, R. J. (1997). *Content knowledge: A compendium of standards and benchmarks for K–12 education*. Retrieved from mcrel.org/standards-benchmarks/

Kiang, P. N., & Kaplan, J. (1994). Where do we stand? Views of racial conflict by Vietnamese American high school students in Black-and-White context. *The Urban Review, 26*(2), 95–119.

Kim, B. L. (1978). *The Asian Americans: Changing patterns, changing needs*. Montclair, NJ: Association for Korean Christian Scholars of North America.

Kim, B. S. K., & Park, Y. S. (2015). Communication styles, cultural values, and counseling effectiveness with Asian Americans. *Journal of Counseling & Development, 93*(3), 269–279

Kim, E. (1976). *Survey of Asian American literature: Social perspectives*. Unpublished doctoral dissertation, University of California.

Kim, Y., Roehler, L., & Pearson, P. D. (2009). Strength-based instruction for early elementary students learning English as a second language. In H. R. Milner (Ed.), *Diversity and education: Teachers, teaching, and teacher education* (pp. 103–115). Springfield, IL: Thomas.

King, J. E. (1994). The purpose of schooling for African American children: Including cultural knowledge. In E. R. Hollins, J. E. King, & W. C. Hayman (Eds.), *Teaching diverse populations: Formulating a knowledge base* (pp. 25–56). Albany, NY: State University of New York Press.

King, J. E., Hollins, E. R., & Hayman, W. C. (Eds.). (1997). *Preparing teachers for cultural diversity*. New York, NY: Teachers College Press.

King, J. E., & Wilson, T. L. (1990). Being the soul-freeing substance: A legacy of hope in Afro humanity. *Journal of Education, 172*(2), 9–27.

King, N. (1993). *Storymaking and drama: An approach to teaching language and literature at the secondary and postsecondary levels*. Portsmouth, NH: Heinemann.

Kitano, H., & Daniels, R. (1995). *Asian Americans: Emerging minorities* (2nd ed.). Englewood Cliffs, NJ: Prentice-Hall.

Klein, S. S. (Ed.). (1982). *Handbook for achieving sex equity through education*. Baltimore, MD: Johns Hopkins University Press.

Kleinfeld, J. (1973). Effects of nonverbally communicated personal warmth on the intelligence test performance of Indian and Eskimo adolescents. *Journal of Social Psychology, 91*(1), 149–150.

Kleinfeld, J. (1974). Effects of nonverbal warmth on the learning of Eskimo and White students. *Journal of Social Psychology, 92*(1), 3–9.

Kleinfeld, J. (1975). Effective teachers of Eskimo and Indian students. *School Review, 83*(2), 301–344.

Klug, B. (Ed.). (2012). *Standing together: American Indian education as culturally responsive pedagogy*. Lanham, MD: Rowman and Littlefield.

Knapp, C. E. (1993). An interview with Eliot Wigginton: Reflecting on the Foxfire approach. *Phi Delta Kappan, 74*(10), 779–782.

Kochman, T. (Ed.). (1972). *Rappin' and stylin' out: Communication in urban Black America*. Urbana, IL: University of Illinois Press.

Kochman, T. (1981). *Black and White styles in conflict*. Chicago, IL: University of Chicago Press.

Kochman, T. (1985). Black American speech events and a language program for the classroom. In C. B. Cazden, V. P. John, & D. Hymes (Eds.), *Functions of language in the classroom* (pp. 211–261). Prospect Heights, IL: Waveland.

Kohn, A. (1999). *The schools our children deserve: Moving beyond traditional classrooms and "tougher" standards*. Boston, MA: Houghton Mifflin.

Kozol, J. (1991). *Savage inequalities: Children in America's schools*. Boston, MA: Houghton Mifflin.

Kozol, J. (2007). *Letters to a young teacher*. New York, NY: Crown.

Krater, J., Zeni, J., & Cason, N. D. (1994). *Mirror images: Teaching writing in black and white*. Portsmouth, NH: Heinemann.

Kuykendall, C. (2004). *From rage to hope: Strategies for reclaiming Black and Hispanic students* (2nd ed.). Bloomington, IN: Solution Tree Press.

Laal, M., & Ghodsi, S. M. (2012). Benefits of collaborative learning. *Social and Behavioral Sciences, 31*, 486–490.

LaBelle, J. (2010). Selecting ELL textbooks: A content analysis of ethnicity depicted in illustrations and writing. Retrieved from epublications.marquette.edu/cgi/viewcontent.cgi?article=1175&context=edu_fac

Ladson-Billings, G. (1992). Reading between the lines and beyond the pages: A culturally relevant approach to literacy teaching. *Theory Into Practice, 31*(4), 312–320.

Ladson-Billings, G. (1995a). But that's just good teaching! The case for culturally relevant pedagogy. *Theory Into Practice, 34*(3), 159–165.

Ladson-Billings, G. (1995b). Multicultural teacher education: Research, practice, and policy. In J. A. Banks & C. A. M. Banks (Eds.), *Handbook of research on multicultural education* (pp. 747–759). New York, NY: Macmillan.

Ladson-Billings, G. (1995c). Toward a theory of culturally relevant pedagogy. *American Educational Research Journal, 32*(3), 465–491.

Ladson-Billings, G. (2009). *The dreamkeepers: Successful teachers for African-American children* (2nd ed.). San Francisco, CA: Jossey-Bass.

Ladson-Billings, G., & Henry, A. (1990). Blurring the borders: Voices of African liberatory pedagogy in the United States and Canada. *Journal of Education, 172*(2), 72–88.

Lakoff, R. (1975). *Language and women's place.* New York, NY: Harper & Row.

Lakoff, R. (2004). *Language and woman's place: Text and commentaries.* New York, NY: Oxford University Press.

Landrine, H., & Klonoff, E. A. (1996). The schedule of racist events: A measure of racial discrimination and a study of its negative physical and mental health consequences. *Journal of Black Psychology, 22*(3), 144–168.

Larke, P. J., Webb-Hasan, G., & Young, J. L. (Eds.). (2017). *Cultivating achievement, respect, and empowerment (CARE) for African American girls in Pre-K–12 Settings: Implications for access, equity, and achievement.* Charlotte, NC: Information Age Publishing.

Larkin, M. (2017, April 14). This teacher's mission is readying minority students for calculus class. Retrieved from wbur.org/edify/2017/04/14/calculus-project-mims

Lazarus, M. (Producer & Director). (1979). *Killing us softly* [Video]. Cambridge, MA: Cambridge Documentary Films.

Lazarus, M. (Producer & Director). (1987). *Still killing us softly* [Video]. Cambridge, MA: Cambridge Documentary Films.

Lazarus, M., & Wunderich, R. (Producers & Directors). (2000). *Beyond killing us softly: The impact of media images on girls and women* [Video]. Cambridge, MA: Cambridge Documentary Films.

Lazear, D. (1991). *Seven ways of knowing: Teaching for multiple intelligences: A handbook of techniques for expanding intelligence.* Palatine, IL: Skylight.

Lazear, D. (1994). *Multiple intelligence approaches to assessment: Solving the assessment conundrum.* Tucson, AZ: Zephyr.

Lee, C. D. (1991). Big picture talkers/words walking without masters: The instructional implications of ethnic voices for an expanded literacy. *Journal of Negro Education, 60*(3), 291–304.

Lee, C. D. (1993). *Signifying as a scaffold to literary interpretation: The pedagogical implications of a form of African-American discourse* (NCTE Research Report No. 26). Urbana, IL: National Council of Teachers of English.

Lee, C. D. (2000). Signifying in the zone of proximal development. In C. D. Lee & P. Smagorinsky (Eds.), *Vygotskian perspectives on literacy research: Constructing meaning through collaborative research* (pp. 191–225). New York, NY: Cambridge University Press.

Lee, C. D. (2001). Is Charlie Brown Chinese: A cultural modeling activity system for underachieving students. *American Educational Research Journal, 38*(1), 97–142.

Lee, C. D. (2007). *Culture, literacy, and learning: Taking bloom in the midst of the whirlwind.* New York, NY: Teachers College Press.

Lee, C. D. (2009). Cultural influences on learning. In J. A. Banks (Ed.), *The Routledge international companion to multicultural education* (pp. 239–251). New York, NY: Routledge.

Lee, C. D., Rosenfeld, E., Mendenhall, R., Rivers, A., & Tynes, B. (2004). Cultural modeling as a frame for narrative analysis. In C. Daiute & C. Lightfoot (Eds.), *Narrative analysis: Studying the development of individuals in society* (pp. 39–62). Thousand Oaks, CA: Sage.

Lee, C. D., & Slaughter-Defoe, D. T. (1995). Historical and sociocultural influences on African American education. In J. A. Banks & C. A. M. Banks (Eds.), *Handbook of research on multicultural education* (pp. 348–371). New York, NY: Macmillan.

Lee, J., & Bean, F. D. (2010). *The diversity paradox: Immigration and the color line in twenty first century America.* New York, NY: Russell Sage Foundation.

Lee, J., & Zhou, M. (2015). *The Asian American paradox.* New York, NY: Russell Sage Foundation.

Lee, O., & Luykx, A. (2006). *Science education and student diversity: Synthesis and research agenda.* New York, NY: Cambridge University Press.

Lee, S. J. (1996). *Unraveling the "model minority" stereotype: Listening to Asian American youth.* New York, NY: Teachers College Press.

Lee, S. J. (2009). *Unraveling the "model minority" stereotype: Listening to Asian American youth* (2nd ed.). New York, NY: Teachers College Press.

Lenkei, A. (2016, March 7). Students prefer print. Why are schools pushing digital textbooks? *Education Week.* Retrieved from blogs.edweek.org/edweek/bookmarks/2016/03/students_prefer_print_schools_pushing_digital_textbooks.html?qs=Lenkei

Leonard, J. (2008). *Culturally specific pedagogy in the mathematics classroom: Strategies for teachers and students.* New York, NY: Routledge.

Leung, B. P. (1998). Who are Chinese American, Japanese American, and Korean American children? In V. O. Pang & L-R. L. Cheng (Eds.), *Struggling to be heard: The unmet needs of Asian Pacific American children* (pp. 11–26). Albany, NY: State University of New York Press.

Levmore, S., & Nussbaum, M. (Eds.). (2010). *Offensive Internet: Speech, privacy, and reputation.* Cambridge, MA: Harvard University Press.

Lin, E. (2006). Cooperative learning in the science classroom. Retrieved from nsta.org/publications/news/story.aspx?id=52116

Lindsey, D. B., Kearney, K. M., Estrada, D., Terrell, R. D., & Lindsey, R. B. (2015). *A culturally proficient response to the Common Core.* Thousand Oaks, CA: Corwin.

Lipka, J. (1994). Culturally negotiated schooling: Toward a Yup'ik mathematics. *Journal of American Indian Education, 33*(3), 14–30.

Lipka, J. (with Mohatt, G. V., & the Ciulistet Group). (1998). *Transforming the culture of schools: Yup'ik Eskimo examples.* Mahwah, NJ: Erlbaum.

Lipka, J., & McCarty, T. L. (1994). Changing the culture of schooling: Navajo and Yup'ik cases. *Anthropology & Education Quarterly, 25*(3), 266–284.

Lipka, J., Yanez, E., Andrew-Ihrke, D., & Adam. S. (2009). A two-way process for developing effective culturally based math: Examples from Math in a Cultural Context. In B. Greer, S. Mukhopadhyay, A. B. Powell, & S. Nelson-Barber (Eds.), *Culturally responsive mathematics education* (pp. 257–280). New York, NY: Routledge.

Lipman, P. (1995). "Bringing out the best in them": The contribution of culturally relevant teachers to educational reform. *Theory Into Practice, 34*(3), 202–208.

Loewen, J. W. (1995). *Lies my teacher told me: Everything your American history textbook got wrong.* New York, NY: New Press.

Lomawaima, K. T., & McCarty, T. L. (2006). *To remain an Indian: Lessons in democracy from a century of Native American education.* New York, NY: Teachers College Press.

Longstreet, W. (1978). *Aspects of ethnicity: Understanding differences in pluralistic classrooms.* New York, NY: Teachers College Press.

Lopez, F. A. (2017). Altering the trajectory of the self-fulfilling prophecy: Asset-based pedagogy and classroom dynamics. *Journal of Teacher Education, 68*(2), 193–212

Lopez, N. (2003). *Hopeful girls, troubled boys: Race and gender disparity in urban education.* New York, NY: Routledge.

Losey, K. M. (1997). *Listen to the silences: Mexican American interaction in the composition classroom and community.* Norwood, NJ: Ablex.

Maccoby, E. E. (1988). Gender as a social category. *Developmental Psychology, 24*(6), 755–765.

MacSwan, J. (2017). A multilingual perspective on translanguaging. *American Educational Research Journal, 54*(1), 167–201.

Malcolm X, & Haley, A. (1966). *The autobiography of Malcolm X.* New York, NY: Grove.

Maltz, D. N., & Borker, R. A. (1983). A cultural approach to male-female miscommunication. In J. J. Gumperz (Ed.), *Communication, language, and social identity* (pp. 196–216). Cambridge, UK: Cambridge University Press.

Mandelbaum, D. G. (Ed.). (1968). *Selected writings of Edward Sapir in language, culture and personality.* Berkeley, CA: University of California Press.

Margulies, S., & Wolper, D. L. (Producers). (1977). *Roots,* Parts I–VII [Video]. Burbank, CA: Warner Home Video.

Margulies, S., & Wolper, D. L. (Producers). (1978). *Roots: The next generation,* Parts I–VII [Video]. Burbank, CA: Warner Home Video.

Masland, S. W. (1994). Gender equity in classrooms: The teacher factor. *Equity & Excellence in Education, 27*(3), 19–27.

Mason, J. M., & Au, K. H. (1991). *Reading instruction for today*. Glenview, IL: Scott Foresman.

Mathews, J. (1988). *Escalante: The best teacher in America*. New York: Henry Holt.

Matthews, C. E., & Smith, W. S. (1994). Native American related materials in elementary science instruction. *Journal of Research in Science Teaching, 31*(4), 363–380.

Matthews, J. (2015). *Questioning everything: The rise of AVID as America's largest college readiness program*. San Francisco, CA: Jossey-Bass.

Mayeroff, M. (1971). *On caring*. New York, NY: Harper and Row.

McCarthy, A., Lee, K., Itakura, S., & Muir, D. W. (2006). Cultural display rules drive eye gaze during thinking. *Journal of Cultural Psychology, 37*(6), 717–722.

McCarty, T. L. (2002). *A place to be Navajo: Rough Rock and the struggle for self-determination in indigenous schooling*. Mahwah, NJ: Erlbaum.

McCarty, T. L., & Lee, T. S. (2014). Critical culturally sustaining/revitalizing pedagogy and Indigenous education sovereignty. *Harvard Educational Review, 84*(1), 101–124.

McCarty, T. L., Wallace, S., Lynch, R. H., & Benally, A. (1991). Classroom inquiry and Navajo learning styles: A call for reassessment. *Anthropology & Education Quarterly, 22*(1), 42–59.

McDonnell, T. L., & Hill, P. T. (1993). *Newcomers in American schools: Meeting the educational needs of immigrant youth*. Santa Monica, CA: Rand.

McFadden, A. C., Marsh, G. E., Price, B. J., & Hwang, Y. (1992). A study of race and gender in the punishment of school children. *Education and Treatment of Children, 15*(2), 140–146.

McNeil, F. (2009). *Learning with the brain in mind*. Los Angeles, CA: Sage.

Mehan, H., Hubbard, L., Lintz, A., & Villanueva, I. (1994). *Tracking untracking: The consequences of placing low track students in high track classes*. San Diego: University of California, San Diego, National Center for Research on Cultural Diversity and Second Language Learning.

Mehan, H., Hubbard, L., Villanueva, I., & Lintz, A. (1996). *Constructing school success: The consequences of untracking low-achieving students*. New York, NY: Cambridge University Press.

Meier, D., & Wood, G. (Eds.). (2004). *Many children left behind: How the No Child Left Behind Act is damaging our children and our schools*. Boston, MA: Beacon Press.

Mendoza, J., & Reese, D. (2001). Examining multicultural picture books for early childhood classrooms: Possibilities and pitfalls. *Early Childhood Research and Practice, 3*(2). Retrieved from ecrp.uiuc.edu/v3n2/mendoza.html

Menendez, R. (Director). (1988). *Stand and deliver* [Film]. Burbank, CA: Warner Home Video.

Mercado, C. I. (1993). Caring as empowerment: School collaboration and community agency. *The Urban Review, 25*(1), 79–104.

Mestre, L. (2009). Accommodating diverse learning styles in an online environment. *Reference & User Services Quarterly, 46*(2), 27–32.

Michaels, S. (1981). "Sharing time": Children's narrative styles and differential access to literacy. *Language in Society, 10*(3), 423–442.

Michaels, S., & Cazden, C. B. (1986). Teacher/child collaboration as oral preparation for literacy. In B. B. Schieffelin & P. Gilmore (Eds.), *The acquisition of literacy: Ethnographic perspectives* (pp. 132–154). Norwood, NJ: Ablex.

Mickelson, R. A. (1990). The attitude–achievement paradox among Black adolescents. *Sociology of Education, 63*(1), 44–61.

Mihesuah, D. A. (1996). *American Indians: Stereotypes & realities.* Atlanta, GA: Clarity Press.

Miller, P. S. (1991). Increasing teacher efficacy with at-risk students: The sine qua non of school restructuring. *Equity & Excellence, 25*(1), 30–35.

Min, P. G. (1995). Major issues relating to Asian American experiences. In P. G. Min (Ed.), *Asian Americans: Contemporary trends and issues* (pp. 38–57). Thousand Oaks, CA: Sage.

Moll, L. C., Amanti, C., Neff, D., & Gonzalez, N. (1992). Funds of knowledge for teaching: Using a qualitative approach to connect homes and classrooms. *Theory into Practice, 31*(2), 132–141

Moll, L. C., & Combs, M. C. (2015). Funds of knowledge as a multicultural project. In H. P. Baptiste, A. Ryan, & B. Araujo (Eds.), *Multicultural education: A renewed paradigm of transformation and call to action* (pp. 149–161). San Francisco, CA: Caddo Gap Press.

Moll, L. C., & González, N. (2004). Engaging life: A funds-of-knowledge approach to multicultural education. In J. A. Banks & C. A. M. Banks (Eds.), *Handbook of research on multicultural education* (2nd ed., pp. 699–715). San Francisco, CA: Jossey-Bass.

Montagu, A., & Matson, F. (1979). *The human connection.* New York, NY: McGraw-Hill.

Montaño, T., & Metcalfe, E. L. (2003). Triumphs and tragedies: The urban schooling of Latino students. In V. I. Kloosterman (Ed.), *Latino students and American schools: Historical and contemporary views* (pp. 139–151). Westport, CT: Praeger.

Montecel, M. R., & Cortez, J. D. (2002). Successful bilingual education programs: Development and the dissemination of criteria to identify promising and exemplary practices in bilingual education at the national level. *Bilingual Research Journal, 26*(1), 1–21.

Morgan, B. M. (2012). Teaching cooperative learning with children's literature. *National Forum of Teacher Education Journal, 22*(3), 1–12.

Morgan, H. (1990). Assessment of students' behavioral interactions during on-task activities. *Perceptual and Motor Skills, 70*(2), 563–569.

Morris, L., Sather, G., & Scull, S. (Eds.). (1978). *Extracting learning styles from social/cultural diversity: A study of five American minorities.* Washington, DC: Southwest Teacher Corps Network.

Moses, R. P., & Cobb, C. E. (2001). *Radical equations: Math literacy and civil rights.* Boston, MA: Beacon Press.

Moses, R., West, M. M., & Davis, F. E. (2009). Culturally responsive mathematics in the Algebra Project. In B. Greer, S. Mukhopadhyay, A. B.

Powell, & S. Nelson-Barber (Eds.), *Culturally responsive mathematics education* (pp. 239–256). New York, NY: Routledge.

Mun Wah, L. (Producer and Director). (1994). *The color of fear* [Film]. Berkeley, CA: Stir Fry Productions.

Murdock, T. B., & Miller, A. (2003). Teachers as sources of middle school students' motivational identity: Variable-centered and person-centered analytic approaches. *The Elementary School Journal, 103*(4), 383–399.

Nadel, A. (2005). *Television in Black and White America: Race and national identity*. Lawrence, KS: University Press of Kansas.

Nakamura, L. (2002). *Cybertypes: Race, ethnicity, and identity on the Internet*. New York, NY: Routledge.

Nakamura, L. (2014). Race and gender online. In M. Graham & W. D. Dutton (Eds.), *Society and the Internet: How networks of information and communication are changing our lives* (pp. 81–98). New York, NY: Oxford University Press.

Nakamura, L., & Chow-White, P. (Eds.). (2012). *Race after the Internet*. New York, NY: Routledge.

Nakamura, R. A. (Producer). (1994). *Something strong within* [Film]. Los Angeles, CA: Japanese American National Museum.

Nakanishi, D. T., & Nishida, T. Y. (Eds.). (1995). *Asian American educational experience: A sourcebook for teachers and students*. New York, NY: Routledge.

National Council of Teachers of English. (1992). The national language policy. Retrieved from ncte.org/resources/positions/123796.htm

National Indian Education Association. (2005). Preliminary report on No Child Left Behind in Indian country. Retrieved from NIEA.org

National Public Radio. (2015, July 23). From upspeak to vocal fry: Are we "policing" young women's voices? Retrieved from npr.org/2015/07/23/425608745/from-upspeak-to-vocal-fry-are-we-policing-young-womens-voices

Nebraska statewide assessment program: STARS. (n.d.). Retrieved from education.com/reference/article/Ref_Statewide_Assessment/

New FBI hate crimes confirm need for stronger federal response. Retrieved from commondreams.org/2008/10/27-6

Nguyen, A., Shin, F., & Krashen, S. (2001). Development of the first language is not a barrier to second-language acquisition: Evidence from Vietnamese immigrants to the United States. *International Journal of Bilingual Education and Bilingualism, 4*(3), 159–164.

Nicolopoulou, A., Scales, B., & Weintraub, J. (1994). Gender differences and symbolic imagination in the stories of four-year-olds. In A. H. Dyson & C. Genishi (Eds.), *The need for story: Cultural diversity in classroom and community* (pp. 102–123). Urbana, IL: National Council of Teachers of English.

Nieto, S. (1999). Critical multicultural education and students' perspectives. In S. May (Ed.), *Critical multiculturalism: Rethinking multicultural and antiracist education* (pp. 191–215). Philadelphia, PA: Falmer.

Nieto, S. (2004). Puerto Rican students in U.S. schools: A troubled past and the search for a hopeful future. In J. A. Banks & C. A. M. Banks (Eds.), *Handbook of research on multicultural education* (2nd ed., pp. 515–541). San Francisco, CA: Jossey-Bass.

Noddings, N. (1992). *The challenge to care in schools: An alternative approach to education*. New York, NY: Teachers College Press.

Noddings, N. (1996). The cared-for. In S. Gordon, P. Brenner, & N. Noddings (Eds.), *Caregiving: Readings in knowledge, practice, ethics, and politics* (pp. 21–39). Philadelphia, PA: University of Pennsylvania Press.

Norton, D. (1992). *Through the eyes of a child: An introduction to children's literature*. Columbus, OH: Merrill.

Oakes, J. (1985). *Keeping track: How schools structure inequality*. New Haven, CT: Yale University Press.

Oakes, J. (1986a, September). Keeping track, Part 1: The policy and practice of curriculum inequality. *Phi Delta Kappan, 68*, 12–17.

Oakes, J. (1986b, October). Keeping track, Part 2: Curriculum inequality and school reform. *Phi Delta Kappan, 68*, 148–153.

Obidah, J. E., Jackson-Minot, M., Monroe, C. R., & Williams, B. (2004). Crime and punishment: Moral dilemmas in the inner-city classroom. In V. Siddle-Walker & J. R. Snarey (Eds.), *Race-ing moral formation: African American perspectives on care and justice* (pp. 111–129). New York, NY: Teachers College Press.

Oh, E. (2012). Why the pretty White girl YA book cover trend needs to end. Retrieved from elloecho.blogspot.com/2012/03/why-pretty-white-girl-ya-book-cover.html

Oliva, P. F. (2009). *Developing the curriculum* (7th ed.). Boston, MA: Pearson.

Oliver, J. (2011). The story and legacy of the Foxfire cultural journalism program. Doctoral dissertation, University of Georgia, Athens, GA.

Olneck, M. R. (2004). Immigrants and education in the United States. In J. A. Banks & C. A. M. Banks (Eds.), *Handbook of research on multicultural education* (2nd ed., pp. 381–403). San Francisco, CA: Jossey-Bass.

Olson, S. L. (n.d.). Long-term academic effects of elementary school bilingual education on a national sample of Mexican American sophomores: A component analysis and the role of ancestral and cultural history. Retrieved from ncela.gwu.edu/pubs/symposia/third/olson.htm

Ormrod, J. E. (1995). *Human learning* (2nd ed.). Columbus, OH: Merrill/Prentice-Hall.

Ortiz, A. A. (2013). Why is it important to ensure instruction and interventions are culturally responsive? Retrieved from intensiveintervention.org/video-resource/why-it-important-ensure-instruction-and-interventions-are-culturally-responsive

Osajama, K. H. (1991). Breaking the silence: Race and the educational experiences of Asian-American college students. In M. Foster (Ed.), *Readings on equal education: Vol. 11. Qualitative investigations into schools and schooling* (pp. 115–134). New York, NY: AMS Press.

Otnes, C., Kim, K., & Kim, Y. C. (1994). Yes, Virginia, there is a gender difference: Analyzing children's requests to Santa Claus. *Journal of Popular Culture, 28*(1), 17–29.

Owens, L. M., & Ennis, C. D. (2007). The ethic of care in teaching: An overview of supportive literature. *Quest, 57*, 392–425.

Page, R. (1987). Teachers' perceptions of students: A link between classrooms, school climate, and the social order. *Anthropology & Education Quarterly, 18*(2), 77–99.

Pai, Y., Adler, S. A., & Shadiow, L. K. (2006). *Cultural foundations of education* (4th ed.). Upper Saddle River, NJ: Merrill/Prentice-Hall.

Palardy, J. (1969). What teachers believe—What students achieve. *Elementary School Journal, 69*(7), 370–374.

Palcy, E. (Director). (1998). *Ruby Bridges* [Film]. New York, NY: Home Box Office.

Pang, V. O., & Cheng, L–R. L. (Eds.). (1998). *Struggling to be heard: The unmet needs of Asian Pacific American children*. Albany, NY: State University of New York Press.

Pang, V. O., Kiang, P. N., & Pak, Y. K. (2004). Asian Pacific American students: Challenging a biased educational system. In J. A. Banks & C. A. M. Banks (Eds.), *Handbook of research on multicultural education* (2nd ed., pp. 542–563). San Francisco, CA: Jossey-Bass.

Pang, V. O., & Sablan, V. (1995, April). *Teacher efficacy: Do teachers believe they can be effective with African American students?* Paper presented at the annual meeting of the American Educational Research Association, San Francisco.

Papageorge, N., & Gershenson, S. (2016). Do teacher expectations matter? Retrieved from brookings.edu/blog/brown-center-chalkboard/2016/09/16/do-teacher-expectations-matter/

Paris, D. (2012). Culturally sustaining pedagogy: A needed change in stance, terminology, and practice. *Educational Researcher, 4*(3), 93–97.

Paris, D., & Alim, H. S. (2014). What are we seeking to sustain through culturally sustaining pedagogy? A loving critique forward. *Harvard Educational Review, 84*(1), 85–100.

Paris, D., & Alim, H. S. (Eds.). (2017). *Culturally sustaining pedagogies: Teaching and learning for justice in a changing world*. New York, NY: Teachers College Press.

Park, C. C. (2002). Crosscultural differences in learning styles of secondary English learners. *Bilingual Research Journal, 26*(2), 443–459.

Park, C. C., Goodwin, A. L., & Lee, S. J. (Eds.). (2003). *Asian American identities, families, and schooling*. Greenwich, CT: Information Age.

Parker, M. A., Eliot, J., & Tart, M. (2013). An exploratory study of the influence of the Advancement via Individual Determination (AVID) program on African American young men in southeastern North Carolina. *Journal of Education for Students Placed at Risk, 18*, 153–167.

Pasteur, A. B., & Toldson, I. L. (1982). *Roots of soul: The psychology of Black expressiveness*. Garden City, NY: Anchor Press/Doubleday.

Perkins, K. R. (1996). The influence of television images on Black females' self-perceptions of physical attractiveness. *Journal of Black Psychology, 22*(4), 453–469.

Perkins, M. (2009). Straight talk on race: Challenging stereotypes in kids' books. *School Library Journal, 55*(1). Retrieved from schoollibraryjournal.com/articles/CA6647713.html.

Perry, T., & Delpit, L. (Eds.). (1998). *The real Ebonics debate: Power, language, and the education of African American children*. Boston, MA: Beacon.

Perry, T., Steele, C., & Hilliard, A. G., III. (2003). *Young, gifted, and Black: Promoting high achievement among African American students*. Boston, MA: Beacon.

Peters, J., & Barone, T. (Producers). (1997). *Rosewood* [Film]. Burbank, CA: Warner Brothers.

Pewewardy, C. D. (1991). Native American mascots and imagery: The struggle of unlearning Indian stereotypes. *Journal of Navajo Education, 9*(1), 19–23.

Pewewardy, C. D. (1994). Culturally responsive pedagogy in action: An American Indian magnet school. In E. R. Hollins, J. E. King, & W. C. Hayman (Eds.), *Teaching diverse populations: Formulating a knowledge base* (pp. 77–92). Albany, NY: State University of New York Press.

Pewewardy, C. (1996/1997). The Pocahontas paradox: A cautionary tale for educators. *Journal of Navajo Education, 14*(1/2), 20–25.

Pewewardy, C. (1998). Fluff and feathers: Treatment of American Indians in the literature and the classroom. *Equity & Excellence in Education, 31*(1), 69–76.

Philips, S. U. (1983). *The invisible culture: Communication in classroom and community on the Warm Springs Indian Reservation.* Prospect Heights, IL: Waveland.

Phillips, K. W. (2014, October 1). How diversity makes us smarter. *Scientific American, 311*(4), 1–14. Retrieved from scientificamerican.com/article/how-diversity-makes-us-smarter/.

Piatek-Jimenez, K., Madison, M., & Przybyla-Kuchek, J. (2014). Equity in mathematics textbooks: A new look at an old issue. *Journal of Women and Minorities in Science and Engineering, 20*(1), 55–74.

Piestrup, A. M. (1973). *Black dialect interference and accommodation of reading instruction in first grade* (Monograph of the Language Behavior Research Laboratory). Berkeley, CA: University of California.

Plummer, D. L., & Slane, S. (1996). Patterns of coping in racially stressful situations. *Journal of Black Psychology, 22*(3), 302–315.

Porter, R. E., & Samovar, L. A. (1991). Basic principles of intercultural communication. In L. A. Samovar & R. E. Porter (Eds.), *Intercultural communication: A reader* (6th ed., pp. 5–22). Belmont, CA: Wadsworth.

Powell, R. R., & Garcia, J. (1985). The portrayal of minorities and women in selected elementary science series. *Journal of Research in Science Teaching, 22*(6), 519–533.

Prado-Olmos, P., Rios, F., & Castañeda, L. (2007). "We are multiculturalism": A self study of faculty of colour with preservice teachers of colour. *Studying Teacher Education, 3*(1), 85–102.

PreK to 12: Results matter. (n.d.). Retrieved from mheducation.com/programs/resultsMatter.shtml

Puckett, J. L. (1989). *Foxfire reconsidered: A twenty-year experiment in progressive education.* Urbana, IL: University of Illinois Press.

Pugh, P. M., & Tschannen-Moran, M. (2016). Influence of a school district's Advancement via Individual Determination (AVID) program on self-efficacy and other indicators of student achievement. *NASSP Journal, 100*(3), 141–158.

Purnell, P. G., Ali, P., Begum, N., & Carte, M. (2007). Windows, bridges and mirrors: Building culturally responsive early childhood classrooms through the integration of literacy and the arts. *Early Childhood Education Journal, 34*(6), 419–424.

Rajagopal, K. (2011). *Create success: Unlocking the potential of urban students.* Alexandria, VA: Association for Supervision and Curriculum Development.

Ramirez, J. D., Wiley, T. G., de Klerk, G., Lee, E., & Wright, W. E. (Eds.). (2005). *Ebonics: The urban education debate* (2nd ed.). Clevedon, England: Multilingual Matters.

Ramírez, M., III, & Castañeda, A. (1974). *Cultural democracy, bicognitive development and education.* New York, NY: Academic Press.

Ramírez, M., & Dowd, F. S. (1997). Another look at the portrayal of Mexican-American females in realistic picture books: A content analysis, 1990–1997. *Multicultural Review, 6*(4), 20–27, 54.

Rayford, D. D. (2014). Can you see me?: The necessity of an Afrocentric education. In F. E. Goodwyll, P. O. Ojiambo, & P. A. Bedu-Addo (Eds.), *Perspectives on empowering education* (pp. 69–89). New York, NY: Nova Science Publishers.

Reardon, S. F., Greenberg, E. H., Kalogrides, D., Shores, K. A., & Valentino, R. A. (2013). Left behind: The effect of No Child Left Behind on academic achievement gaps. Retrieved from cepa.stanford.edu/content/left-behind-effect-no-child-left-behind-academic-achievement-gaps

Reed, F. (Producer & Director). (1995). *Skin deep* [Video]. Berkeley, CA: Iris Films.

Reyhner, J. (2006, March). *Indian Education Today*, pp. 19–20.

Rickford, J. R. (2005). Using the vernacular to teach the standard. In J. D. Ramirez, T. G. Wiley, G. de Klerk, E. Lee, & W. E. Wright (Eds.), *Ebonics: The urban education debate* (2nd ed, pp. 18–40). Clevedon, England: Multilingual Matters.

Rickford, J. R., & Rickford, R. J. (2000). *Spoken soul: The story of Black English.* New York, NY: Wiley.

Rickford, J. R., Sweetland, J., & Rickford, A. E. (2004). An annotated bibliography of African American English and other vernaculars in education. *Journal of English Linguistics, 32*(3), 230–320.

Riding, R. J., & Rayner, S. G. (Eds.). (2000). *International perspectives on individual differences: Vol. I. Cognitive styles.* Stamford, CT: Ablex.

Riley, D. W. (1995). *The complete Kwanzaa: Celebrating our cultural heritage.* New York, NY: HarperCollins.

Ritts, V., Patterson, M. L., & Tubbs, M. E. (1992). Expectations, impressions, and judgments of physically attractive students: A review. *Review of Educational Research, 62*(4), 413–426.

Rocha, O. M. J., & Dowd, F. S. (1993). Are Mexican American females portrayed realistically in fiction for grades K–3? A content analysis. *Multicultural Review, 2*(4), 60–69.

Rodriguez, E. R., Bellanca, J. A., & Esparza, D. R. (2017). *What is it about me you can't teach: Culturally responsive instruction in deeper learning classrooms* (3rd ed.). Thousand Oaks, CA: Corwin.

Roehrig, G., & Moore, T. (2012, March 15). How to make STEM socially and culturally relevant. Retrieved from cehdvision2020.umn.edu/blog/make-stem-socially-culturally-relevant/

Rolstad, E., Mahoney, K., & Glass, G. V. (2005). The big picture: A meta-analysis of program effectiveness research on English language learners. *Educational Policy, 19*(4), 572–594.

Roper Organization. (1993). *America's watching: Public attitudes toward television*. New York, NY: Network Television Association.

Rosaldo, R. (1989). *Culture & truth: The remaking of social analysis*. Boston, MA: Beacon.

Rosenthal, R., & Jacobson, L. (1968). *Pygmalion in the classroom: Teacher expectations and pupils' intellectual development*. New York, NY: Holt, Rinehart & Winston.

Rosenwald, M. S. (2015, February 22). Why digital natives prefer reading in print. Yes, you read that right. *The Washington Post*. Retrieved from washingtonpost.com/local/why-digital-natives-prefer-reading-in-print-yes-you-read-that-right/2015/02/22/8596ca86-b871-11e4-9423-f3d0a1ec335c_story.html?utm_term=.ef2194b75fc7

Rothschild, A. (2015, March 8). The world of children's books is still very White. Retrieved from fivethirtyeight.com/features/the-world-of-childrens-books-is-still-very-white/

Ruggs, E., & Hebi, M. (2012). Diversity, inclusion, and cultural awareness for classroom and outreach education. In B. Bogue & E. Cady (Eds.), *Apply research practice (ARP) resources* (pp. 1–16). Retrieved from engr.psu.edu/awe/ARPAbstracts/DiversityInclusion/ARP_DiversityInclusionCulturalAwareness_Overview.pdf

Sadker, D., Sadker, M., & Zittleman, K. R. (2009). *Still failing at fairness: How gender bias cheats girls and boys in school and what we can do about it*. New York, NY: Scribner.

Sadker, M. P., & Sadker, D. M. (1982). *Sex equity handbook for schools*. New York, NY: Longman.

Saenz, B. A. (2004). I want to write an American poem III. In O. Santa Ana (Ed.), *Tongue tied: The lives of multilingual children in public education* (pp. 281–283). Lanham, MD: Rowman & Littlefield.

Samovar, L. A., Porter, R. E., McDaniel, E. R., & Roy, C. S. (2017). *Communication between cultures* (9th ed.). Boston, MA: Cengage Learning

Sampson, D., & Garrison-Wade, D. F. (2011). Cultural vibrancy: Exploring the preferences of African American children toward culturally relevant and non-culturally relevant lessons. *Urban Review, 43*(2), 279–309.

Sanchez, C. (2010, March 31). Jaime Escalante's legacy: Teaching hope. Retrieved from npr.org/templates/story/story.php?storyId=125398451

Sanchez, T. R. (2007). The depiction of Native Americans in recent (1991–2004) secondary American history textbooks. *Equity & Excellence in Education, 40*(4), 311–320.

Sapir, E. (1968). The status of linguistics as a science. In D. G. Mandelbaum (Ed.), *Selected writings of Edward Sapir in language, culture and personality* (pp. 160–166). Berkeley, CA: University of California Press.

Savage, G. C., O'Connor, K., & Brass, J. (2014). Common Core State Standards: Implications for curriculum, equality and policy. *Journal of Curriculum and Pedagogy, 11*(1), 18–20.

Saville-Troike, M. (1989). *The ethnography of communication: An introduction* (2nd ed.). New York, NY: Blackwell.

Schildkraut, D. J. (2005). *Press "one" for English: Language policy, public opinion, and American identity*. Princeton, NJ: Princeton University Press.

Schoem, D., Frankel, L., Zuniga, X., & Lewis, E. A. (Eds.). (1993). *Multicultural teaching in the university*. Westport, CT: Praeger.

Schram, T. (1994). Playing along the margin: Diversity and adaptation in a lower track classroom. In G. Spindler & L. Spindler (Eds.), *Pathways to cultural awareness: Cultural therapy with teachers and students* (pp. 61–91). Thousand Oaks, CA: Corwin.

Schrodt, K., Fain, J. G., & Hasty, M. (2015). Exploring culturally relevant texts with kindergartners and their families. *Reading Teacher, 68*(8), 589–598

Scott, E., & McCollum, H. (1993). Making it happen: Gender equitable classrooms. In S. K. Biklen & D. Pollard (Eds.), *Gender and education*, Part I (92nd Yearbook of the National Society for the Study of Education, pp. 174–190). Chicago, IL: University of Chicago Press.

Secada, W. G., Fennema, E., & Adajian, L. B. (Eds.). (1995). *New directions for equity in mathematics education*. New York, NY: Cambridge University Press.

Shade, B. J. (1994). Understanding the African American learner. In E. R. Hollins, J. E. King, & W. C. Hayman (Eds.), *Teaching diverse populations* (pp. 175–189). Albany, NY: State University of New York Press.

Shade, B. J. (Ed.). (1997). *Culture, style, and the educative process* (2nd ed.). Springfield, IL: Thomas.

Shade, B. J., Kelly, C., & Oberg, M. (1997). *Creating culturally responsive classrooms*. Washington, DC: American Psychological Association.

Shade, B. J., & New, C. A. (1993). Cultural influences on learning: Teaching implications. In J. A. Banks & C. A. M. Banks (Eds.), *Multicultural education: Issues and perspectives* (2nd ed., pp. 317–329). Boston, MA: Allyn & Bacon.

Sheets, R. H. (1995a). From remedial to gifted: Effects of culturally centered pedagogy. *Theory Into Practice, 34*(3), 186–193.

Sheets, R. H. (1995b). *Student and teacher perceptions of disciplinary conflicts in culturally pluralistic classrooms*. Unpublished doctoral dissertation, University of Washington, Seattle.

Sheets, R. H. (1996). Urban classroom conflict: Student–teacher perception: Ethnic integrity, solidarity, and resistance. *The Urban Review, 28*(2), 165–183.

Sheffield, C. M. (2014). The efficacy of students toward learning within an Afrocentric program. Dissertation, Argosy University, Atlanta, GA.

Shinn, R. (1972). *Culture and school: Socio-cultural significances*. San Francisco, CA: Intext Educational Publishers.

Shor, I. (1992). *Empowering education: Critical teaching for social change*. Chicago, IL: University of Chicago Press.

Shor, I., & Freire, P. (1987). *A pedagogy for liberation: Dialogues on transforming education*. South Hadley, MA: Bergin & Garvey.

Siddle-Walker, E. V. (1993). Interpersonal caring in the "good" segregated schooling of African-American children: Evidence from the case of Caswell County Training School. *The Urban Review, 25*(1), 63–77.

Siddle-Walker, E. V., & Snarey, J. R. (Eds.). (2004). *Race-ing moral formation: African American perspectives on care and justice*. New York, NY: Teachers College Press.

Silver, H. F., Strong, R. W., & Perini, M. J. (2000). *So each may learn: Integrating learning styles and multiple intelligences.* Alexandra, VA: Association for Supervision and Curriculum Development.

Simkins-Bullock, J. A., & Wildman, B. G. (1991). An investigation into the relationship between gender and language. *Sex Roles, 24*(3/4), 149–160.

Singleton, G. E., & Linton, C. (2005). *Courageous conversations about race: A field guide for achieving equity in schools.* Thousand Oaks, CA: Corwin.

Skelton, C., Francis, B., & Smulyan, L. (Eds.). (2006). *The Sage handbook of gender and education.* Thousand Oaks, CA: Sage.

Skerrett, A., & Hargreaves, A. (2008). Student diversity and secondary school change in the context of increasingly standardized reform. *American Educational Research Journal, 45*(4), 913–945.

Slavin, R. E. (1987). *Cooperative learning: Student teams* (2nd ed.). Washington, DC: National Education Association.

Slavin, R. E. (1992). When and why does cooperative learning increase achievement? Theoretical and empirical perspectives. In R. Hertz-Lazarowitz & N. Miller (Eds.), *Interaction in cooperative groups* (pp. 145–173). Cambridge, UK: Cambridge University Press.

Slavin, R. E. (1994). Cooperative learning and intergroup relations. In J. A. Banks & C. A. M. Banks (Eds.), *Handbook of research on multicultural education* (pp. 628–634). New York, NY: Macmillan.

Slavin, R. E. (2015). Cooperative learning in elementary schools. *International Journal of Primary, Elementary, and Early Years Education, 43*(1), 5–14.

Slavin, R. E., & Cheung, A. (2003). Effective reading programs for English language learners: A best-evidence synthesis. Retrieved from csoc.jhu.edu/crespar/reports.htm

Sleeter, C. E. (2005). *Un-standardizing curriculum: Multicultural teaching in the standards-based classroom.* New York, NY: Teachers College Press.

Sleeter, C. E. (2011). *The academic and social value of ethnic studies: A research review.* Washington, DC: National Education Association.

Sleeter, C. E., & Grant, C. A. (1991a). Mapping terrains of power: Student cultural knowledge versus classroom knowledge. In C. E. Sleeter (Ed.), *Empowerment through multicultural education* (pp. 49–67). Albany, NY: State University of New York Press.

Sleeter, C. E., & Grant, C. A. (1991b). Race, class, gender, and disability in current textbooks. In M. W. Apple & L. K. Christian-Smith (Eds.), *The politics of textbooks* (pp. 78–110). New York, NY: Routledge.

Smart-Grosvenor, V. (1982). We got a way with words. *Essence, 13*(6), 138.

Smith, B. O. (1971). On the anatomy of teaching. In R. T. Hyman (Ed.), *Contemporary thought on teaching* (pp. 20–27). Englewood Cliffs, NJ: Prentice-Hall.

Smith, G. P. (1998). *Common sense about uncommon knowledge: The knowledge bases for diversity.* Washington, DC: American Association of Colleges for Teacher Education.

Smith, K. (2009). Learning together and alone: Cooperation, competition and individualization. *North American Colleges and Teachers of Agriculture Journal, 53*(3), 71–74.

Smith, S. L., Choueiti, M., & Pieper, K. (2016). *Inclusion or invisibility? Comprehensive Annenberg report on diversity in entertainment.* Los Angeles, CA: Institute for Diversity and Empowerment Annenberg (IDEA), University of Southern California.

Smitherman, G. (1972). Black power is Black language. In G. M. Simmons, H. D. Hutchinson, & H. E. Simmons (Eds.), *Black culture: Reading and writing Black* (pp. 85–91). New York, NY: Holt, Rinehart & Winston.

Smitherman, G. (1986). *Talkin and testifyin: The language of Black America.* Detroit, MI: Wayne State University Press.

Smitherman, G. (1996). African-American English: From the hood to the amen corner. Retrieved from writing.umn.edu/docs/speakerseries

Smitherman, G. (1998). What go round come round: King in perspective. In T. Perry & L. Delpit (Eds.), *The real Ebonics debate: Power, language, and the education of African American children* (pp. 163–171). Boston, MA: Beacon.

Smitherman, G. (2000). *Talkin that talk: Language, culture and education in African America.* New York, NY: Routledge.

Smitherman, G. (2003). The historical struggle for language rights in CCCC. In G. Smitherman & V. Villanueva (Eds.), *Language diversity in the classroom: From intention to practice* (pp. 7–39). Carbondale, IL: Southern Illinois University Press.

Smitherman, G. (2005). Black language and the education of Black children: One mo once. In J. D. Ramirez, T. G. Wiley, G. de Klerk, E. Lee, & W. E. Wright (Eds.), *Ebonics: The urban education debate* (2nd ed., pp. 49–61). Clevedon, England: Multilingual Matters.

Smitherman, G. (2006). *Word from the mother: Language and African Americans.* New York, NY: Routledge.

Smitherman, G. (2007). Afterword. In H. S. Alim & J. Baugh (Eds.), *Talkin Black talk: Language, education, and social change* (pp. 153–155). New York, NY: Teachers College Press.

Smitherman, G., & Villanueva, V. (Eds.). (2003). *Language diversity in the classroom: From intention to practice.* Carbondale, IL: Southern Illinois University Press.

Songhai Empire, The. (n.d.). Philadelphia: Philadelphia Public Schools, Northwest Region. [Mimeograph]

Sonneborn, L. (2000). *Pomp: The true story of the baby on the Sacagawea dollar.* Retrieved from pompstory.home.mindspring.com/Pages/chapter6.html

Sowell, T. (1976). Patterns of Black excellence. *The Public Interest, 43,* 26–58.

Spindler, G. D. (Ed.). (1987). *Education and cultural process: Anthropological approaches* (2nd ed.). Prospect Heights, IL: Waveland.

Spindler, G., & Spindler, L. (1993). The process of culture and person: Cultural therapy and culturally diverse schools. In P. Phelan & A. L. Davidson (Eds.), *Renegotiating cultural diversity in American schools* (pp. 21–51). New York, NY: Teachers College Press.

Spindler, G., & Spindler, L. (Eds.). (1994). *Pathways to cultural awareness: Cultural therapy with teachers and students.* Thousand Oaks, CA: Corwin.

Spring, J. (1992). *Images of American life: A history of ideological management in schools, movies, radio, and television.* Albany, NY: State University of New York Press.

Spring, J. (1995). *The intersection of cultures: Multicultural education in the United States.* New York, NY: McGraw-Hill.

Springer, S. P., & Deutsch, G. (1998). *Left brain right brain: Perspectives from cognitive neuroscience* (5th ed.). New York, NY: Freeman.

Squire, J. (1995). Language arts. In G. Cawelti (Ed.), *Handbook of research on improving student achievement* (pp. 71–95). Arlington, VA: Educational Research Service.

St. John, N. (1971). Thirty-six teachers: Their characteristics and outcomes for Black and White pupils. *American Educational Research Journal, 8*(4), 635–648.

Steele, C. M. (1997). A threat in the air: How stereotypes shape intellectual identity and performance. *American Psychologist, 52*(6), 613–629.

Steele, C. M. (2010). *Whistling Vivaldi: How stereotypes affect us and what we can do.* New York, NY: W. W. Norton.

Steele, C. M., & Aronson, J. (1995). Stereotype threat and the intellectual test performance of African Americans. *Journal of Personality and Social Psychology, 69*(5), 797–811.

Sternberg, R. J. (2006). Recognizing neglected strengths. *Educational Leadership, 64*(1), 30–35.

Stevens, R. J., & Slavin, R. E. (1995). The cooperative elementary school: Effects on students' achievement, attitudes, and social relations. *American Educational Research Journal, 32*(2), 321–351.

Strauss, V. (2014, March 10). The myth of Common Core equity. *The Washington Post.* Retrieved from washingtonpost.com/newssearch/?datefilter=All%20 Since%202005&query=Burris%20%26%20Aja&sort=Relevance&utm_ term=.f51fe8bb50fd

Streitmatter, J. (1994). *Toward gender equity in the classroom: Everyday teachers' beliefs and practices.* Albany, NY: State University of New York Press.

Suárez-Orozco, C., Suárez-Orozco, M. M., & Doucet, F. (2004). The academic engagement and achievement of Latino youth. In J. A. Banks & C. A. M. Banks (Eds.), *Handbook of research on multicultural education* (2nd ed., pp. 420–437). San Francisco, CA: Jossey-Bass.

Sullivan, A. R. (1974). Cultural competence and confidence: A quest for effective teaching in a pluralistic society. In W. A. Hunter (Ed.), *Multicultural education through competency-based teacher education* (pp. 56–71). Washington, DC: American Association of Colleges of Teacher Education.

Sutton, M. (2005). The globalization of multicultural education. *Indiana Journal of Global Legal Studies, 12*(1), 97–108.

Swanson, M. C., Mehan, H., & Hubbard, L. (1995). The AVID classroom: Academic and social support for low-achieving students. In J. Oakes & H. Quartz (Eds.), *Creating new educational communities*, Part I (94th Yearbook of the National Society for the Study of Education, pp. 53–69). Chicago, IL: University of Chicago Press.

Tan, A. (1989). *The joy luck club.* New York, NY: Ivy Books.

Tan, L. (2002–2003). Implementing a social justice curriculum in an inner city school. *Teaching to Change LA's Report Card, 3*, 1–7. Retrieved from tcla. gsels.ucla.edu/reportcard/features/5–6/curriculum.html

Tannen, D. (1990). *You just don't understand: Women and men in conversation.* New York, NY: Morrow.

Tannen, D. (1994). *Gender and discourse.* New York, NY: Oxford University Press.

Tarlow, B. (1996). Caring: A negotiated process that varies. In S. Gordon, P. Brenner, & N. Noddings (Eds.), *Caregiving: Readings in knowledge, practice, ethics, and politics* (pp. 56–82). Philadelphia, PA: University of Pennsylvania Press.

Taylor, H. U. (1989). *Standard English, Black English, and bidialectalism: A controversy.* New York, NY: Peter Lang.

Taylor, M. D. (1981). *Let the circle be unbroken.* New York, NY: Dial.

Taylor, M. D. (1984). *Roll of thunder, hear my cry.* New York, NY: Bantam.

Taylor, T. (1969). *The cay.* New York, NY: Doubleday.

Teel, K. M., & Obidah, J. E. (Eds.). (2008). *Building racial and cultural competence in the classroom.* New York, NY: Teachers College Press.

Tetreault, M. K. T. (1985). Phases of thinking about women in history: A report card on the textbook. *Women's Studies Quarterly, 13*(2/3), 35–47.

Tharp, R. G., & Gallimore, R. (1988). *Rousing minds to life: Teaching, learning, and schooling in social context.* Cambridge, UK: Cambridge University Press.

Thompson, A. (2004). Caring and colortalk: Childhood innocence in White and Black. In V. Siddle-Walker & J. R. Snarey (Eds.), *Race-ing moral formation: African American perspectives on care and justice* (pp. 23–37). New York, NY: Teachers College Press.

Tiedt, P. L., & Tiedt, I. M. (2010). *Multicultural teaching: A handbook of activities, information, and resources* (8th ed.). Boston, MA: Pearson/Allyn & Bacon.

Tintiangco-Cubales, A., Kohlit, R., Sacramento, J., Henning, N., Agarwall-Rangnath, R., & Sleeter, C. E. (2015). Toward an ethnic studies pedagogy: Implications for K–12 schools from the research. *The Urban Review, 47*(1), 104–125.

Tomlinson, C. A., & Javius, E. L. (2012). Teach up for excellence: All students deserve equitable access to an engaging and rigorous curriculum. *Educational Leadership, 69*(5), 28–33.

Tong, B. R. (1978). Warriors and victims: Chinese American sensibility and learning styles. In L. Morris, G. Sather, & S. Scull (Eds.), *Extracting learning styles from social/ cultural diversity: A study of five American minorities* (pp. 70–93). Washington, DC: U.S. Office of Education, Southwest Teacher Corps Network.

Tong, F., Lara-Alecio, R., Irby, B., Mathes, P., & Kwok, O. (2008). Accelerating early academic oral English development in transitional bilingual and structured English immersion programs. *American Educational Research Journal, 45*(4), 1011–1044.

Treisman, P. U. (1985). A study of the mathematics achievement of Black students at the University of California, Berkeley. Unpublished doctoral dissertation, University of California, Berkeley.

Tuan, M. (1998). *Forever foreigners or honorary Whites? The Asian ethnic experience today.* New Brunswick, NJ: Rutgers University Press.

Tuck, K. (1985). *Verve inducement effects: The relationship of task performance to stimulus variability and preference in working class Black and White school children.* Unpublished doctoral dissertation, Howard University, Washington, DC.

Tuck, K., & Boykin, A. W. (1989). Verve effects: The relationship of test performance to stimulus preference and variability in low-income Black and

White children. In A. Harrison (Ed.), *The eleventh conference on empirical research in Black psychology* (pp. 84–95). Washington, DC: National Institute of Mental Health.

Tucker, M. S., & Codding, J. B. (1998). *Standards for our schools: How to set them, measure them, and reach them*. San Francisco, CA: Jossey-Bass.

Turkle, S. (2010). *Always on: Language in an online and mobile world*. New York, NY: Oxford University Press.

Turkle, S. (2011). *Alone together: Why we expect more from technology and less from each other*. New York, NY: Oxford University Press.

Turkle, S. (2015). *Words n screen: The fate of reading in a digital world*. New York, NY: Oxford University Press.

Turney, M. A., & Sitler, R. L. (2012). Communication challenges—Gender patterns in talking. Retrieved from womanpilot.com/?p=115.

Tyson-Bernstein, H., & Woodward, A. (1991). Nineteenth century politics for twenty-first century practice: The textbook reform dilemma. In P. G. Altbach, G. P. Kelly, H. G. Petrie, & L. Weis (Eds.), *Textbooks in American society: Politics, policy, and pedagogy* (pp. 91–104). Albany, NY: State University of New York Press.

U.S. Civil Rights Commission. (1973). *Mexican American education study: Report V. Differences in teacher interaction with Mexican American and Anglo students*. Washington, DC: U.S. Civil Rights Commission.

U.S. Department of Education. (2007, April 19). Reading First achievement data demonstrate dramatic improvements in reading for America's neediest children. Retrieved from ed.gov/news/pressreleases/2007/04192007.html

Valenzuela, A. (1999). *Subtractive schooling: U.S.-Mexican youth and the politics of caring*. Albany, NY: State University of New York Press.

Valuing diversity [Video]. (1987). San Francisco: Copeland-Griggs Productions.

Vernez, G., & Abrahamese, A. (1996). *How immigrants fare in U.S. education*. Santa Monica, CA: Rand.

Vygotsky, L. S. (1962). *Thought and language*. Cambridge, MA: MIT Press.

Wade, R. C. (1993). Content analysis of social studies textbooks: A review of ten years of research. *Theory and Research in Social Education, 21*(3), 232–256.

Wade-Gayles, G. (Ed.). (1997). *Father songs: Testimonies of African-American sons and daughters*. Boston, MA: Beacon.

Walker, A. (1985). *The color purple*. New York, NY: Pocket Books.

Walker, S. (2012, June 14). Using stories to teach: How narrative structure helps students learn. Retrieved from scilearn.com/blog/using-stories-to-teach

Walker-Dalhouse, D., & Dalhouse, A. D. (2006). Investigating White preservice teachers' beliefs about teaching in culturally diverse classrooms. *The Negro Educational Review, 57*(1–2), 69–84.

Walls, K. (2017). Fire on the mountain: The Appalachian culture. Retrieved from wander.media/fire-on-the-mountain-the-appalachian-culture

Wanless, S. B., & Crawford, P. A. (2016). Reading your way to a culturally responsive classroom. *Young Children, 71*(2), 8–16.

Ward, C. J. (1994). Explaining gender differences in Native American high school dropout rates: A case study of Northern Cheyenne schooling patterns. *Family Perspective, 27*(4), 415–444.

Ware, F. (2006). Warm demander pedagogy: Culturally responsive teaching that supports a culture of achievement for African American students. *Urban Education, 41*(4), 427–456.

Warfa, A-R. M. (2016). Using cooperative learning to teach chemistry: A meta-analytic review. *Journal of Chemistry, 93*(2), 248–255.

Warren, P. (2016). *Uptalk: The phenomenon of rising intonation.* Cambridge, UK: Cambridge University Press.

Watkins, A. F. (2002). Learning styles of African American children: Developmental considerations. *Journal of Black Psychology, 28*(1), 3–17.

Watkins, S. C. (2005). *Hip hop matters: Politics, culture, and the struggle for the soul of the movement.* Boston, MA: Beacon.

Watson, C., & Smitherman, G. (1996). *Educating African American males: Detroit's Malcolm X Academy solution.* Chicago, IL: Third World Press.

Watt, K. M., Johnston, D., Huerta, J., Mendiola, I. D., & Alkan, E. (2008). Retention of first-generation of college-going seniors in college preparatory AVID. *American Secondary Education, 37*(1), 17–40.

Watt, K. M., Powell, C. A., & Mendiola, I. D. (2004). Implications of one comprehensive school reform model for secondary school students underrepresented in higher education. *Journal of Education for Students Placed At Risk, 9*(3), 241–249.

Watt, K. M., Powell, C. A., Mendiola, I. D., & Cossio, G. (2006). Schoolwide impact and AVID: How have selected Texas high schools addressed the new accountability measures? *Journal of Education for Students Placed At Risk, 11*(1), 57–73.

Webb, J., Wilson, B., Corbett, D., & Mordecai, R. (1993). Understanding caring in context: Negotiating borders and barriers. *The Urban Review, 25*(1), 25–45.

Weber, E. (2005). *MI strategies in the classroom and beyond: Using roundtable learning.* Boston, MA: Pearson/Allyn & Bacon.

Wheeler, R. S., & Swords, R. (2006). *Code-switching: Teaching Standard English in urban classrooms.* Urbana, IL: National Council of Teachers of English.

Whorf, B. L. (1952). *Collected papers on metalinguistics.* Washington, DC: Department of State, Foreign Service Institute.

Whorf, B. L. (1956). Language, mind, and reality. In J. B. Carroll (Ed.), *Language, thought, and reality: Selected writings of Benjamin Lee Whorf* (pp. 246–270). Cambridge, MA: MIT Press.

Wigginton, E. (1985). *Sometimes a shining moment: The Foxfire experience.* Garden City, NY: Anchor Press/Doubleday.

Wigginton, E. (Ed.). (1991). *Foxfire: 25 years.* New York, NY: Doubleday.

Wiley, T. G. (2005). Ebonics: Background to the current policy debate. In J. D. Ramirez, T. G. Wiley, G. de Klerk, E. Lee, & W. E. Wright (Eds.). *Ebonics: The urban education debate* (2nd ed., pp. 3–17). Clevedon, England: Multilingual Matters.

Wilkins, R. (1982). *A man's life: An autobiography.* New York, NY: Simon & Schuster.

Williams, L. Q. (2017). How to accept and respect other cultures. Retrieved from owlcation.com/social-sciences/How-to-Accept-and-Respect-other-Cultures

Williams, R. L. (1997). The Ebonics controversy. *Journal of Black Psychology, 23*(3), 208–214.

Willig, A. C. (1985). A meta-analysis of selected studies on the effectiveness of bilingual education. *Review of Educational Research, 55*(3), 269–318.

Willingham, D. T., Hughes, E. M., & Dobolye, D. G. (2015). The scientific status of learning style theories. *Teaching of Psychology, 42*(3), 266–271.

Witherell, C., & Noddings, N. (Eds.). (1991). *Stories lives tell: Narrative and dialogue in education.* New York, NY: Teachers College Press.

Wong, M. G. (1980). Model students? Teachers' perceptions and expectations of their Asian and White students. *Sociology of Education, 53*(4), 236–247.

Wong Fillmore, L., & Meyer, L. M. (1992). The curriculum and linguistic minorities. In P. W. Jackson (Ed.), *Handbook of research on curriculum* (pp. 626–658). New York, NY: Macmillan.

Woodson, C. G. (1969). *The mis-education of the Negro.* Washington, DC: Associated Publishers. (Original work published 1933)

Wright, W. E. (2003). The success and demise of a Khmer (Cambodian) bilingual education program: A case study. In C. C. Park, A. L. Goodwin, & S. J. Lee (Eds.), *Asian American identities, families, and schooling* (pp. 225–252). Greenwich, CT: Information Age.

Wright, W. E. (2006). *Heritage language programs in the era of English Only and No Child Left Behind.* Los Angeles, CA: Center for World Languages.

Wurdeman-Thurston, K., & Kaomea, J. (2015). Fostering culturally relevant literacy instruction: Lessons from a Native Hawaiian classroom. *Language Arts, 92*(6), 424–435

You can vote however you like. (2008). [Video]. Retrieved from huffingtonpost.com/2008/10/29/vote-however-you-like-vid_n_139101.html

Zeni, J., & Krater, J. (1996). Seeing students, seeing culture, seeing ourselves. Retrieved from nwp.org/cs/public/print/resource/304

Zhou, M., & Bankston, C. L., III (1999). *Growing up American: The adaptation of Vietnamese children to American society.* New York, NY: Russell Sage Foundation.

Zirkel, S. (2008). The influence of multicultural educational practices on student outcomes and intergroup relations. *Teachers College Record, 110*(6), 1147–1181.

Zuniga, X., & Nagda, B. A. (1993). Dialogue groups: An innovative approach to multicultural learning. In D. Schoem, L. Frankel, X. Zuniga, & E. A. Lewis (Eds.), *Multicultural teaching in the university* (pp. 233–248). Westport, CT: Praeger.

Name Index

Abrahamese, A., 18–19
Abrahams, R. D., 33, 34, 119
Adajian, L. B., 187
Adam, S., 187–189
Adichie, C. N., 10, 184
Adler, S. A., 8, 29, 30, 71, 89, 209
Agarwall-Rangnath, R., 241
Albury, A., 226
Alejandro, E. A., 57–58, 59
Alemán, Enrique, Jr., xiv
Ali, P., 285–286
Alim, H. Samy, xii, 100, 239, 240
Alkan, E., 224–226
Allen, B. A., 15, 228–231
Allen, J. E., 173
Alvarez, L., xiv
Amanti, C., 17
Anderson, Lauren, xiv
Anderson, R. C., 114, 116
Andrew-Ihrke, D., 187–189
Angelou, Maya, 23–24, 100, 196
Anyon, J., 1, 145
Anzaldua, Gloria, 105–106
Apple, M. W., 144
Aragon, J., 35
Arciniega, T. A., 34
Armstrong, L. A., 9
Armstrong, T., 209
Aronson, B., 184, 241, 242, 274
Aronson, J., 19–20, 172
Asante, Molefi K., 42, 119, 237, 238
Ascher, M., 94
Ashton, P. T., 78, 79
Au, Kathryn H., xii, 12, 15, 32, 42, 120, 124, 125, 181, 212

August, D., 106–108, 111
Austin, A. M. B., 133
Axtman, K., 178
Ayers, William, 28, 61, 273

Baber, C. R., 119, 129, 216
Bailey, C. T., 205–207, 217, 220, 226, 228–229
Bailey, L., 79–80
Baird-Vogt, L., 212
Ball, A. F., 96
Banks, C. A. M., 192
Banks, James A., xi–xvii, xxx, 35, 38, 42, 192
Bankston, C. L., III, 20, 102, 110
Baratz, Joan C., xi, xii
Baratz, Stephen S., xi, xii
Barbe, W. B., 206, 209, 227
Barham, J., 221–223
Barlow, W., 175
Baron, N., 144
Barone, T., 84
Bartell, T. G., 58, 59
Baugh, J., 96, 100
Beal, G., 163–164
Bean, F. D., 19
Begum, N., 285–286
Belenky, M. F., 121
Bellanca, J. A., 204
Benally, A., 15
Bendall, R. C. A., 202
Bennett, C. I., 81, 82–83, 202, 206
Bensman, D., 62
Berman, L. M., 68
Bernardo, A., 85
Biggs, M., 84, 174
Biklen, S. K., 73
Bishop, R., 181
Bleich, E., 169
Blitch, K., 161

Bloemraad, I., 169
Bloom, Benjamin S., xi, 209
Blythe, T., 57–59
Boggs, J. W., 120
Boggs, S. T., 15, 32, 71, 90, 93, 120–122, 125, 127, 212
Bond, C., 76
Bondy, E., 67
Borker, R. A., 121
Botelho, M. J., 161
Boucher, P., 210
Bowers, C. A., 68, 81–82
Bowie, R., 76
Boyd, F. B., 161, 184
Boyd, H., 100–101
Boykin, A. Wade, xii, 1, 9, 15, 17, 31–32, 71, 105, 205–207, 217, 220, 226, 228–231
Brackett, M. A., 234
Brass, J., 154
Bravo, E., 77
Brisk, M. E., 99, 106
Brody, C. M., 217, 219–220
Brokenleg, M., 235
Brooks, Gwendolyn, 182
Brophy, J. E., 59, 73–76, 78, 81
Brown, E., 170, 171
Brown, J. C., 191
Brown, S. P., 77
Brown, Sterling, 182
Bruner, J., 2, 3, 89
Burlbaw, L. M., 144, 145
Burnett, C., 84
Butler, L., 15, 230
Byers, H., 94
Byers, P., 94
Byrne, M. M., 145

Cai, M., 161, 163

Subject Index

About the Author

Geneva Gay is professor of education at the University of Washington–Seattle. She is the recipient of the Distinguished Scholar Award, presented by the Committee on the Role and Status of Minorities in Educational Research and Development of the American Educational Research Association; the first Multicultural Educator Award, presented by the National Association of Multicultural Education; the W. E. B. Du Bois Distinguished Lecturer Award, presented by the Special Interest Group on Research Focus on Black Education of the American Educational Research Association; the Mary Anne Raywid Award for Distinguished Scholarship in the Field of Education presented by the Society of Professors of Education; and she is nationally and internationally known for her scholarship in multicultural education, particularly as it relates to curriculum design, staff development, classroom instruction, and culture and learning. Her writings include numerous articles and book chapters, co-editor of *Expressively Black: The Cultural Basis of Ethnic*, author of *At the Essence of Learning: Multicultural Education*, and editor of *Becoming Multicultural Educators: Personal Journey Toward Professional Agency*. Her professional service includes membership on several national editorial review and advisory boards. She is a frequent consultant for schools, professional organizations, and teacher education programs throughout the United States on culturally responsive teaching. International consultations on multicultural education and culturally responsive teaching have taken her to Canada, Brazil, Taiwan, Finland, Japan, England, Scotland, Australia, South Korea, Benin, and Germany.